The Age of Consent

Young People, Sexuality and Citizenship

Matthew Waites

University of Glasgow, UK

D1741652

First published in hardback 2005
This paperback edition published 2009 by
PALGRAVE MACMILLAN

Palgrave Macmillan in the UK is an imprint of Macmillan Publishers Limited,
registered in England, company number 785998, of Houndmills, Basingstoke,
Hampshire RG21 6XS.

Palgrave Macmillan in the US is a division of St Martin's Press LLC,
175 Fifth Avenue, New York, NY 10010.

Palgrave Macmillan is the global academic imprint of the above companies
and has companies and representatives throughout the world.

Palgrave® and Macmillan® are registered trademarks in the United States,
the United Kingdom, Europe and other countries.

ISBN-13: 978–1–4039–2173–4 hardback
ISBN-13: 978–0–230–23718–6 paperback

This book is printed on paper suitable for recycling and made from fully
managed and sustained forest sources. Logging, pulping and manufacturing
processes are expected to conform to the environmental regulations of the
country of origin.

A catalogue record for this book is available from the British Library.

Library of Congress Cataloging-in-Publication Data
Waites, Matthew.
    The age of consent : young people, sexuality and citizenship /
    Matthew Waites.
        p.   cm.
    Includes bibliographical references and index.
    ISBN 978–1–4039–2173–4 (cloth) 978–0–230–23718–6 (pbk)
    1. Age of consent—Great Britain.   2. Minors—Great Britain—Sexual
    behavior.   I. Title.
    KD7975.W35 2005
    346.4101′35—dc22   2005040889

10   9   8   7   6   5   4   3   2   1
18   17   16   15   14   13   12   11   10   09

Printed and bound in Great Britain by
CPI Antony Rowe, Chippenham and Eastbourne

'A subtle and original book that is bound to shake up preconceived ideas – of every kind – about the origin and nature of age of consent laws. Presenting the reader with a wealth of surprising information, the book challenges us to consider young people as sexual citizens requiring both empowerment and safety.'
– **Carole S. Vance**, *Columbia University, USA*

'...well and accessibly written, expertly researched, comprehensive, well argued and structured. This text's subject matters are of considerable current legal, political and sociological concern...An admirable piece of work in every respect.'
– **David T. Evans**, *University of Glasgow, UK*

'This book is an impressive and invaluable contribution to a controversial debate.'
– **Professor Jeffrey Weeks**, *London South Bank University, UK*

'[This] is a book of real value if you wish to understand the sexual behaviour of young people and the issues behind the law and how they have developed over the years and are still doing so.'
– *Justice of the Peace*

'This work is a very timely and informative addition to the literature on the legal regulation of childhood and lays the foundations for future scholarly inquiry and debate on this controversial topic.'
– **Dr. Raymond Arthur**, *Irish Journal of Family Law*

'Certainly the legal profession, forensic psychologists and psychiatrists may find this book of interest and it adds useful argument to current controversial debate.'
– **L. F. Lowenstein**, *The Police Journal*

'...a welcome addition to a subject area...his [Matthew Waites] investigation is original and his theoretical synthesis is invaluable.'
– **Carolyn Cocca**, *H-Net Review*

Also by Matthew Waites

SEXUALITIES AND SOCIETY: A Reader (*co-edited with Jeffrey Weeks and Janet Holland*)

Contents

Acknowledgements

There are many individuals and institutions that I wish to thank for supporting my research on age of consent laws.

The empirical research used in this book began in 1995. I would like to repeat my thanks to those who assisted in the early stages: Angela Mason and Anya Palmer at Stonewall; Peter Tatchell; Ken Plummer and Mary McIntosh. I gratefully acknowledge receipt of Economic and Social Research Council award no. R00429534343, which funded three years of research from October 1995.

The final chapters of the book draw on research for a project, *The Regulation of Sexuality: Autonomy, Protection and Consent* (1 October 2001 to 31 August 2002), funded by a grant from South Bank University's Research Development Fund which I also gratefully acknowledge. Jeffrey Weeks was my co-applicant for this grant.

I would like to express my gratitude to those who work in the various lesbian, gay, bisexual and queer organisations which publish newsletters and operate websites and e-mail lists. A constant stream of up-to-date information about campaigns for equalisation of the age of consent was invaluable in my research during the 1990s. Thanks also to Oliver Merrington and others who assisted me in using the Hall-Carpenter Archive, the UK's national lesbian and gay archive, with holdings at both the British Library of Political and Economic Science, and at the Art and Design Library, Middlesex University.

For feedback and assistance at various times which has contributed to the book's development, I wish to thank: Beverley Brown, Matthew Weait, Les Moran, Carl Stychin, Dermot Feenan, Derek McGhee, Gert Hekma and Simon Blake. Special thanks to Daniel Monk and Jenny Hugh for helpful feedback at a late stage.

I am extremely grateful to the friends who have supported me over the years. I am lucky to have a wonderful and loyal bunch of mates from my school days, especially but not only: Steven Pedersen, Anne Topping, Christine Walsh, David Horniblow, Tom Pfeiffer and Sarah Scott. Thanks also to Vernon Hewitt for his confidence in my abilities, and for love and friendship. Thanks to those who were at South Bank University with me between 1995 and 2002, including Clare Farquhar, Jane Franklin, Rajani Naidoo, Philip Gatter, Pam Alldred, Rachel Thomson, Janet Holland, Robert Bell, Sheena McGrellis, Paula Reavey, Isabel Walter, Monica Zulauf and Tampsi Tolonen. Thanks also to those who welcomed me to Sheffield Hallam University, especially Lorraine Green, Julia Hirst, Serena Bufton, Liz Lawrence, Paul Ward, Anna Coates, Rachel Abbott, Anna Weighall and Jane Morgan.

Thanks also to other friends for support, especially to Paula Kuosmanen, Fernando Serrano Amayo, Jenny Hugh and Tina McGuinness, whose love and friendship kept me going in Sheffield and made completing the book possible.

Huge thanks to Jessica Horniblow and Tim Murray for being photographed and giving informed consent to appearing on the cover; and to Steven Pedersen for providing the cover image and discussions on cover design.

Jeffrey Weeks was my PhD Director of Studies (1995–1999), and subsequently my boss while I worked as a researcher at South Bank University until 2002. Jeffrey provided great support and encouragement for my research, and I regard it as a privilege to have been able to work with him.

Brian Heaphy has seen the book develop from beginning to end, and given me enormous practical and emotional support, including comments on many draft chapters. He has contributed greatly to the development of my understanding of social theory, and I will always be grateful to him.

My grandfather, Herbert Waites, provided me with great encouragement and considerable financial support during my time as a student, for which I am very grateful. Thanks also to my brothers, Ben and Daniel Waites.

I dedicate this book to Lilian and Neville Waites, my mum and dad, who have provided me with inspiring examples of commitment to education and academic integrity, equality and social justice – and loved me too.

Copyright acknowledgements

The author and Palgrave Macmillan gratefully acknowledge permission from publishers to reprint edited extracts from the following copyright material:

Matthew Waites, 'Inventing a "Lesbian Age of Consent"? The History of the Minimum Age for Sex between Women in the UK', *Social and Legal Studies*, Vol. 11, no. 3, September 2002, pp. 323–342. Copyright Sage Publications 2002. Reprinted by permission of Sage Publications Ltd.

Matthew Waites, 'Equality at Last? Homosexuality, Heterosexuality and the Age of Consent in the United Kingdom', *Sociology*, Vol. 37, no. 4, November 2003, pp. 637–656. Copyright BSA Publications/Sage Publications Ltd 2003. Reprinted by permission of Sage Publications Ltd.

Matthew Waites, 'The Age of Consent and Sexual Consent', pp. 73–92 in Mark Cowling and Paul Reynolds (eds) (2004) *Making Sense of Sexual Consent* (Ashgate Publishing Limited, Aldershot, Hants). A 2500-word extract reprinted by permission of Ashgate Publishing Ltd.

1
Introduction

Around the world, the regulation of young people's sexual behaviour is the focus of intense conflict. Amid the culture clashes and reactionary responses produced by globalization, young people's sexuality is a subject causing deep anxiety, and has become the focus for many projects of social and moral renewal. Debates over appropriate forms of emotional and sexual expression between adolescents proceed against a backdrop of intense concern about child sexual abuse and paedophilia. For some, the involvement of children and young people in sexual behaviour amid a rising tide of sexualising imagery in the media is at the heart of social and moral breakdown. For others, the liberalisation of attitudes towards sexual behaviour and increasing openness is evidence of social progress. The meanings of childhood and youth in relation to sexuality are fiercely contested.

'Age of consent' laws – a concept I will use to refer to all laws defining a minimum legal age for young people's participation in sexual behaviour – are at the heart of these political conflicts. While the concept of an 'age of consent' is occasionally used to refer to the legal age for young people to engage in a variety of activities (for example, smoking or drinking alcohol), when *the* 'age of consent' is referred to, it is widely understood that sexual behaviour is at issue – and this in itself evidences the central place of sexuality in cultural understandings of the boundaries between childhood and adulthood. But while 'the age of consent' is commonly understood as the legal age for young people's participation in sexual behaviour, in reality most states have a multiplicity of laws regulating a range of different sexual acts, and people of different genders and sexual identities performing them. There are usually several '*ages* of consent'.

The concept 'age of consent' is itself significant as a form of representation which influences understandings of the law. The concept is often taken for granted in contemporary public and political debates that ignore even its recent history, although its meaning has shifted significantly during the past century, reflecting changing assumptions about age, gender and sexual identities. The phrase is generally absent from the law in many different states, yet is frequently invoked to describe and contest laws, and is increasingly used to compare laws between different states with contrasting legal frameworks. The concept is often invoked as though it straightforwardly describes the law, yet it is a contested concept which cannot be assumed to refer to a clearly identifiable set of statutes. Ideas about what an 'age of consent' is or should be influence the ways in which sexual life is socially patterned and regulated.

The objective of this book is to provide a systematic analysis of how we think about age of consent laws and the regulation of young people's sexuality. The book seeks to illuminate the issue by exploring international and historical evidence on how societies regulate sexual behaviour. It employs perspectives from contemporary social and political theory to analyse changing rationales for age of consent laws. Unlike so much writing about age of consent laws, which has concentrated solely upon justifying a particular political stance in favour of either a higher or a lower age of consent, a central purpose of this book is to explore and illuminate *how* we have thought, and should think, about age of consent laws – although the implications of the analysis for contemporary policy-making are also addressed in the final chapters.

Current conflicts over the regulation of young people's sexuality raise a number of questions. What is the relationship between public attitudes and understandings of the concept of an 'age of consent', and actual legal frameworks? What understandings of childhood, youth and adulthood have informed past formulations of age of consent laws? How have debates over age of consent laws historically been structured by cultural assumptions about gender, and by gendered power relations? What has been the status of same-sex sexual behaviour in relation to age of consent laws? And what is the relationship between the concept of an 'age of consent' and claims by radical social movements since the 1960s, including feminism, gay liberationism and sexual liberationism, for a more democratic, consensual sexual morality? To answer these questions requires consideration of themes including the meaning of childhood, the meaning of consent, and the meaning of sexuality in relation to citizenship.

Existing academic commentaries on age of consent laws address the issue in particular ways. Increasingly there are attempts to provide cross-national comparative surveys of age of consent laws, especially within particular regions such as Europe, but these are essentially empirical and descriptive (for example: Graupner, 2000). Sociological and historical accounts of changes in sexual life within particular states including sexual offences law provide broad outlines (for example: Weeks, 1989); and feminists have explored the origins of age of consent laws in the context of gendered power relations (for example: Walkowitz, 1992). However, sexuality has historically been a marginal area of study in the discipline of law, and in-depth, theoretically informed discussion of age of consent laws by legal scholars has been slower to develop, although critical and conceptual work is proliferating (for example: Edwards, 1981; Moran, 1996, 1997). In political science too, conflicts over age of consent laws have become a focus (Cocca, 2004). Some writers critically engage with the concept of an 'age of consent' through more philosophical analysis (Archard, 1998). But the tendency of this work is to approach the issue conceptually from first premises. An alternative approach can also be adopted to shed light on present dilemmas: to use a substantive sociological and historical study, drawing on empirical research, to explore the forms of knowledge and power relations which have structured the changing rationales for age of consent laws, past and present.

This book is intended to contribute to international research and debates concerning age of consent laws. Chapter 2 explores theoretical issues of general relevance to debates over age of consent laws worldwide. Chapter 3 then surveys international comparative research into age of consent laws in different states, and explores the role of international governmental institutions and transnational social processes and movements in the contestation and formulation of such laws. As in other matters, the conception of a state as a self-contained geographical territory with clearly defined borders is becoming increasingly inadequate. The existence of human rights conventions such as the *European Convention on Human Rights* and the *United Nations Convention on the Rights of the Child* alter the context in which citizenship is defined.

The main focus of the book, however, is the UK. Chapters 4, 5, 6, 7 and 8 comprise a detailed historical analysis of debates in the UK, although prior knowledge of UK law is not assumed and the analysis draws out theoretical themes of much wider applicability. Age of consent laws in the UK have been fiercely contested and (especially in England and Wales) fundamentally reformed in recent years. During the 1990s, equalisation of the 'gay age of consent' became a major issue in national politics, until this was achieved throughout the UK via the passage of the *Sexual Offences (Amendment) Act* 2000. A comprehensive review of sex offences and the consequent passage of the *Sexual Offences Act* 2003 have subsequently revised the entire legal framework in England and Wales. These recent developments, analysed in detail in the final chapters, make the UK a particularly illuminating example of changing approaches to the regulation of young people's sexual behaviour. For an international audience, additionally, the implementation of English law on sex offences in British colonies gives nineteenth-century conflicts in Britain, discussed in Chapter 4, and debates over the decriminalisation of male homosexuality in the 1950s and 1960s, discussed in Chapter 5, a broader relevance.

The study of age of consent laws stands at the juncture of a range of developments in social theory and the social sciences. The increasing interdisciplinarity of much social research facilitates study of the topic at the interface between law, politics, sociology, social policy, and history, as well as the interdisciplinary fields of gender, sexuality and childhood studies.

The development of increasingly sophisticated work on gender and sexuality and the emergence of a sociology of childhood bring new perspectives to bear on the issue (James, Jenks and Prout, 1998; Jackson and Scott, 2002; Weeks, Holland and Waites, 2003). The aim of the book is to provide a history of political debates and conflicts over age of consent laws in their social context, combining this with an account of changes in the law itself. My objective is to contribute to contemporary political and policy debates over the law, and also to contribute to the development of knowledge in history, law and the social sciences.

As I have already indicated, much writing about age of consent laws approaches the issue from either a protectionist or a libertarian perspective, and depends upon the dichotomy between freedom and protection for its conceptual orientation. By contrast, this book explores a number of intersecting theoretical debates. Three theoretical themes in particular are used to give structure to the historical analysis of changing rationales for age of consent laws, and hence to displace the political dichotomy between protectionism and libertarianism. The first is a critical understanding of institutionalised knowledge production in modern societies, focussing particularly upon the role of medical and psychological expertise in shaping understandings of young people's physiological and psychological development (Turner, 1995), with some attention to the changing form and role of such expertise in 'late modernity' (Giddens, 1991; Seidman, 1994). The second is the way in which prevailing understandings of gender and sexuality, and associated forms of inequality, have led to age of consent laws being formulated within a 'heteronormative' framework (that is, a framework which assumes a particular culturally dominant model of heterosexuality to represent desirable forms of gender and sexuality), which can be critically interrogated with reference to feminist, lesbian, gay and queer theoretical perspectives (Weeks, 1985; Seidman, 1996, 1997; Jackson, 1999). The third is the theme of citizenship, a concept which describes the combination of rights and obligations structuring the lives of those who are members of a particular community (Marshall, 1950; Turner, 1993; Weeks, 1998b). Age of consent laws can be understood as particular formal elements of citizenship, offering different forms and degrees of citizenship to different social groups defined by age, gender and sexuality, and are also contested through available forms of political citizenship. The theme of citizenship draws attention to the changing languages of politics, such as the emergence of rights-claims which have been used to debate age of consent laws, as well as to the less explicit conceptions of citizenship which have underpinned such debates. These theoretical issues are discussed further in Chapter 2.

My use of the phrase 'age of consent' to refer to all laws defining a legal age for young people's participation in sexual behaviour requires some immediate justification. Amid the recent expansion of critical socio-legal studies addressing sexuality, in which engagement with post-structuralism has inspired increasing attention to the language of the law and legal discourses (Smart, 1995; Moran, 1996, esp. pp. 8–10), scholars have begun to pay greater attention to the specific meanings and applications of the concept 'age of consent'. It is clear that in the late nineteenth century when the concept came increasingly into use in the English-speaking world in the context of increasing legal regulation, it was used primarily with reference to the legal age for a female to consent to sexual intercourse with a male. The concept's use to describe the law had important ideological effects; in particular, by emphasising the consent of females over the legal age it disguised an absence of full legal and social recognition of women's entitlement to such consent (see Chapter 4). There has remained a tendency to use the concept primarily with reference to the minimum age for sexual intercourse, and on occasion in the UK it has been officially withheld from application to male homosexuality (Policy Advisory Committee, 1981, pp. 3–4, 11–12: hereafter PAC). These factors have led some commentators towards the conclusion that use of the term 'age of consent' in a generalising way is now inappropriate (Moran, 1997).

However, my research suggests that the concept has in recent decades been used with a broad reference in public discourse to encompass legislation applying to a wide range of sexual acts, and also that the reference of 'age of consent' historically has been less circumscribed than others have suggested. There is limited empirical evidence on which to base a view of what most people understand by 'the age of consent', but from what is available my view is that popular usage is flexible. The phrase is typically used to refer to an age at which the law permits sexual behaviour without any straightforward assumption that this coincides with the law recognising a young person's capacity to give consent, or that the law demands that consent be positively expressed. It is widely and increasingly used in public debates, and by many legal practitioners, with reference to both male/female and same-sex contexts and a variety of different sexual acts. The dominant meanings of 'age of consent' are thus being contested and transformed. In this context it is legitimate to adopt the phrase as a convenient expression to frame discussion, while simultaneously drawing attention to and analysing the specific meanings which 'age of consent' has historically held.

Some brief comments on the scope of my studies within the UK, and on my research methods, are appropriate to clarify the book's content. The UK comprises several distinct legal jurisdictions in which age of consent laws have developed in different ways: England and Wales, governed by what is commonly referred to as English law; Scotland, governed by Scots law; and Northern Ireland – following partition from the Irish free state in 1921 – in which English law has been modified in application by, at different times, a devolved parliament and/or discretionary powers of the UK parliament in Westminster. The book describes changes in age of consent laws throughout the UK (and the nineteenth-century legislation discussed in Chapter 4 also applied in Ireland and other British colonies). However, as a consequence of selecting official reviews of English sexual offences for study in Chapters 5, 6 and 8, the main focus is on debates in England and Wales, which limits coverage of distinct legal frameworks and political formations in Scotland and, especially, Northern Ireland. More generally, it is necessarily the case that the book's analysis focusses upon selected points in history, which entails certain omissions and exclusions.

With respect to research methods, my research involved collecting and analysing a wide range of primary documentary and web sources including: government committee reports; parliamentary debates in *Hansard*; legal statutes; newspaper articles; the archives of campaigning groups (containing newsletters, minutes of meetings, posters and photographs, etc.); and interest group and political party websites, e-mail newsgroup lists, letters, press statements, newsletters, manifestos and reports. Primary data-collection also included attendance and observation at a succession of debates in the Houses of Parliament in London during 1998–1999, and at relevant public meetings. Sources used are described in the chapter summaries given at the end of this introduction, and in the introduction to each of the chapters that follow.

The analysis of various forms of qualitative data from documentary sources was informed by methodological debates over discourse analysis (Foucault, 1972; Wilkinson and Kitzinger, 1995). Attention was focussed on competing personal narratives of experience, and their relationship to the wider discourses available in politics and society which structure the meaning of youth, sexual identities, citizenship and age of consent laws. Dilemmas over representing the voices of children in relation to debates over sexual abuse and sexual consent were helpfully addressed by methodological literature which considers the social production of competing narratives representing the voices and interests of children, including the narratives available to children themselves (Alldred, 1998).

Having offered some provisional clarification of the book's objectives, scope and theoretical perspective, and of the research methods and empirical sources I employ, it is appropriate to conclude this introduction by outlining the chapters which follow.

Outline of chapters

Chapter 2 'Theorising Age of Consent Laws' introduces the theoretical themes of the book. First I discuss approaches to childhood and youth in sociology and history, and examine the problematic terminology available to describe age groups. I then discuss the theorisation of gender, sexuality, heterosexuality and homosexuality, focussing upon the 'social construction' of sexual identities, gendered power relations in heterosexuality and 'queer theory'. Next I examine the meaning of 'consent', and introduce debates over sexuality and consent. I then bring together these themes to examine debates over how children experience sexual behaviour, their competence to consent to sexual behaviour, and the meaning of 'abuse'; and offer some initial comments on the role of the law in regulating young people's sexual behaviour. The final section explores the theme of 'citizenship'. It outlines various uses of the term in public discourse and social theory, before focussing upon how T.H. Marshall's theory of citizenship has been engaged with by theorists of gender and sexuality. Following from this, I discuss the relationships between citizenship, sexual offences, and 'age of consent' law, to provide some theoretical reference points to guide the analyses developed in subsequent chapters.

Chapter 3 'Age of Consent Laws in Global Perspective' examines cross-national data on age of consent laws to develop a comparative perspective. I begin by discussing the way in which existing comparative analyses of age of consent laws have been shaped by particular political agendas and cultural understandings, and then provide a comparative discussion of age of consent laws in a variety of states worldwide, addressing different continents in turn. The diversity of forms of legal regulation and themes such as the legal legacies of colonialism are emphasised. Particular attention focusses on the diversity of regulations in states within the US, and on diversity within Europe, where the legal age is as low as 12 in some circumstances in states such as Malta. The abolition in 2002 of a non-prosecuted category of behaviour for 12–15-year olds in the Netherlands is discussed. I then examine how international sex tourism has led to extensions of national sex offences by some states to apply to their citizens travelling abroad, and analyse the increasing role of international human rights law and international governmental institutions in determining age of consent laws.

Chapter 4 'Heterosexuality and the Age of Consent' begins the book's detailed historical study of age of consent debates in the United Kingdom. The chapter commences with an outline of the emergence of minimum age restrictions on sexual behaviour in English law from 1275, and introduces the overall framework of law addressing childhood and sexual behaviour which had developed by the nineteenth century. The main body of the chapter then examines debates over age of consent laws in the late nineteenth century in their social and cultural context, particularly controversies over an increase in the age of consent to sexual intercourse for a female enacted by the *Criminal Law Amendment Act* 1885. This increase, from 13 to 16, has been identified as a key moment in the definition of gendered sexualities in the late nineteenth century (Mort, 1987, pp. 101–150; Walkowitz, 1992; Bland, 1995), and has defined the legal age for intercourse until the present day. Drawing upon evidence from parliamentary debates, the chapter outlines the gendered social context within which the law was conceived and formulated. The final section of the chapter also briefly discusses the regulation of male homosexuality in the late nineteenth century, a period which was critical in shaping understandings of gender and sexuality throughout the twentieth century.

Chapter 5 'Homosexuality and the Age of Consent' begins with a discussion of a change in the law on 'indecent assault' in 1922 which raised the minimum age for sexual behaviour other than intercourse to 16, resulting from continuing social purity campaigns in the early twentieth century. One effect of this was to increase the minimum age for sexual activity between women. In the context of little previous attention to the history of age of consent laws in relation to lesbianism, I argue via analysis of parliamentary debates that this creation of what was to become understood as a 'lesbian age of consent' in the late twentieth century was appreciated by political elites at the time. The main body of the chapter then focusses on debates over male homosexuality in the 1950s surrounding the *Wolfenden Report*, which provided the dominant rationale for the partial decriminalisation of 'homosexual acts' between men that occurred in England and Wales in 1967, creating a minimum age of 21 (Weeks, 1977, pp. 156–167; Hall, 1980; Weeks, 1989, pp. 239–244). Drawing upon analysis of parliamentary debates and the *Wolfenden Report*, I reappraise existing radical critiques of the regulation of male homosexuality during this period to develop an analysis of the form of citizenship granted to homosexual men, embodied in the legalisation of consenting behaviour within a tightly defined private sphere.

Chapter 6 'Sexual Liberationism and the Search for New Sexual Knowledge' explores the changing context of age of consent debates from the late 1960s, particularly through the emergence of movements for sexual liberation including gay liberationism and feminism which initiated transformations in sexual life. I begin by examining debates over the age of consent within these movements during the early 1970s, drawing upon primary sources including gay liberationist literature and campaigning materials held in the Hall-Carpenter Archive, the UK's national lesbian and gay archive. I argue that the radical sexual movements of the period contained, in microcosm, debates over the age of consent which have subsequently persisted and extended into mainstream politics and culture. I then proceed to examine a major official review of age of consent laws conducted by a Home Office Policy Advisory Committee between 1975 and 1981, which recommended maintaining an age of 16 for girls to consent to sexual intercourse (PAC, 1981). Drawing upon archived newspaper sources and interest group submissions to the review, as well as the committee's reports, I demonstrate how the review's conclusions were structured by a new and distinctive logic. This was influenced by the emerging agendas of new sexual movements, yet drew new social and sexual boundaries through the invocation of new forms of biomedical and psychological expertise.

Chapter 7 'Equality at Last? Age of Consent Debates in the 1990s' analyses debates and conflicts over 'equalisation' of the age of consent for sex between men, the most high-profile issue in British lesbian and gay politics for most of the 1990s. This issue moved to the heart of national political debate in the course of protracted parliamentary conflicts. Drawing upon primary sources including parliamentary debates (many attended in person during 1998–1999), newspaper reports and interest group campaigning materials, the chapter dissects arguments for and against an equal age of consent at the age of 16, including those based upon health promotion, rights to freedom and equality, child protection, legal philosophies, and medical and psychological knowledge-claims concerning the fixity or instability of sexual identities. I argue that the debates witnessed the emergence of a new hegemony in age of consent debates in favour of 'equality at 16', but demonstrate that this was premised upon assurances that heterosexual identity-formation was unthreatened, and was thus secured through strategic engagement with mainstream heteronormativity. Hence an equal age of consent does not embody belief in the equal value of heterosexuality with same-sex sexualities, or equal citizenship. The chapter also discusses developments in law during the 1990s relevant to defining the extent to which consenting activity is legal and non-consensual activity is illegal, with reference to the law on rape, consensual sado-masochism and HIV-infection. This demonstrates the persistent absence of consent as a general principle in UK sex offences law, and thus contextualises contemporary invocations of the concept 'age of consent'.

Chapter 8 'New Age of Consent Laws: Adulthood and Childhood' discusses debates over the formulation of age of consent laws during the Home Office review of sex offences between 1999 and 2002, and subsequent parliamentary debates leading to the creation of new age of consent laws in the *Sexual Offences Act* 2003. The chapter begins by developing a critique of the proposal for an offence 'Adult sexual abuse of child' applying to over-18s which emerged in the review's consultation paper *Setting the Boundaries*, focussing particularly on its employment of the concept 'abuse'. Via discussion of this proposal, and of offences including 'Sexual activity with a child' which subsequently emerged to address over-18s in its place, I develop a critical analysis of the contemporary field of policy-making in relation to young people's sexual behaviour. I argue that the offences which emerged were the consequence of problematic protectionist perspectives prevailing among leading children's organisations, allied to both conservative moralism and particular strands of feminism. In the second half of the chapter, I focus on the development of the new age of consent law addressing 'Child sex offences committed by children or young persons', applying to persons under 18 involved in sexual behaviour with under-16s. I discuss criticisms of this offence made during parliamentary debates by advocates of children and young people who sought to contest the criminalisation of under-16s. Finally I discuss wider features of the *Sexual Offences Act* 2003 including its use of different age boundaries to regulate different forms of sexual behaviour, and its regulation of non-consensual behaviour, in order to clarify the contemporary legal context in which the concept 'age of consent' is used.

In Chapter 9 'Rethinking the Age of Consent' I reflect back upon the history of age of consent debates in the UK, before considering the UK situation in the light of current evidence about young people's sexual behaviour and the international comparisons made in Chapter 3. I then return to the general themes and theoretical issues raised in Chapter 2, beginning with the theme of citizenship, considering how the new terrain structuring conflicts over age of consent laws relates to transformed formations of citizenship in relation to gender, sexuality and childhood. I reconsider the fundamental rationale for age of consent laws, developing my own perspective through critical engagement with libertarian perspectives, and by discussing how the law should be understood in relation to 'consent' and 'vulnerability'. From this discussion I draw out the implications for policy-making and sexual politics in the UK, and conclude by proposing changes to the present law.

2
Theorising Age of Consent Laws

In this chapter, I introduce a variety of conceptual themes and perspectives required for the analysis of debates over age of consent laws, drawn from sociology, socio-legal studies and social and political theory. The first section begins by exploring sociological approaches to childhood and youth. The chapter then discusses approaches to theorising gender, sexuality, hetero-sexuality and homosexuality developed in feminist theory, lesbian, gay and queer theory. The meaning of 'consent' is discussed, and considered in relation to sexual behaviour. The chapter then introduces discussions over how young people experience sexual behaviour and their 'competence' to give consent to participate, and provides an introductory discussion of the appropriate role of law in the regulation of sexual behaviour. The final section explores the concept of citizenship, examining how it has recently been conceptualised by social and political theorists in debates over 'sexual citizen-ship', and how it can be utilised in the analysis of debates over age of consent laws.

Childhood and youth

Understandings of childhood have been profoundly influenced since the 1960s by work which has argued that understandings and representations of child-hood are socially and historically extremely variable. The theorist generally credited with a leading role in initiating such work is Philippe Ariès, whose book *Centuries of Childhood* argued that the contemporary western concept of childhood began to emerge in the seventeenth century (Ariès, 1962). Ariès' thesis has subsequently been challenged, for example, by those who suggest previous eras had a different conception of childhood rather than none at all (cf. Archard, 1993, pp. 15–28). But his emphasis on how childhood is imagined and represented in society and culture had a major impact on the discipline of history, which together with anthropological research has more recently influenced work across the social sciences, and led to the birth of what is described as a 'new sociology of childhood' (Jenks, 1996; James, Jenks and Prout, 1998).

More recent work in history, sociology and anthropology now tends to accept that 'pre-modern' societies and non-western cultures had and have a multitude of understandings of childhood which should be evaluated in their broader social context. Understandings of childhood in these cultural contexts may be problematic, however, if they view childhood as being defined by some determining inner aetiology or characteristic. For example, in the west Christian religious doctrines and institutions have sometimes encouraged tendencies to view children as either 'evil' or 'innocent' (James, Jenks and Prout, 1998, pp. 10–15). Yet modern 'scientific' conceptions of childhood did not necessarily represent advances upon traditional understandings. In the twentieth century the developmental psychology advanced by theorists such as Piaget saw child development as proceeding through an inevitable process of maturation, according to a set of biologically pre-ordained stages (Archard, 1993, pp. 32–37; James, Jenks and Prout, 1998, pp. 17–19). As James, Jenks and Prout acerbically comment:

> Psychology, unlike sociology, never made the mistake of questioning its own status as a science and, in the guise of developmental psychology, firmly colonized childhood in a pact with medicine, education and government agencies. (James, Jenks and Prout, 1998, p. 17)

Subsequent 'socialisation' theories developed in the social sciences granted more significance to social processes, but continued to analyse children in relation to a teleological understanding of the requirement to accomplish 'adulthood', understood as a complete and fully rational state (James, Jenks and Prout, 1998, pp. 6, 9–10, 22–25).

By contrast, contemporary sociological theories view childhood as historically and culturally variable, emphasising a view of children as social actors with agency, while simultaneously incorporating analysis of social structures (Jenks, 1996; James, Jenks and Prout, 1998, pp. 3–34). They stress the relational character of childhood, analysing childhood and adulthood as products of dynamics of identification among adults and children as social groups (James, Jenks and Prout, 1998, pp. 4, 9, 202–203). Sociologists of childhood emphasise a range of themes: childhood as 'socially constructed'; examining children's own 'communities', social worlds and worldviews; politicised understandings of children as a group which is subject to systematic injustice and removal of power; children's standpoint epistemologies; children as citizens; children as 'subjects' in a poststructuralist sense, and so on (James, Jenks and Prout, 1998, pp. 26–34, 208–216). Such theoretical understandings increasingly underpin research on childhood (for example: Mayall, 1994; Brannen and Edwards, 1996, pp. 7–9; Economic and Social Research Council, 1997).

Such perspectives are even more influential in critical research on 'youth' and 'young people', where critiques of developmental approaches have been most forcefully advanced. Psychological literature has tended to view adolescence as a universal developmental phase, rather than as a historically specific discourse, yet many sociologists argue that the medicalisation of young people's experiences underplays social structural factors (Gillies, with Ribbens McCarthy and Holland, 1998). Concepts such as 'youth transitions' prevailing in contemporary youth policy literature subtly reproduce developmental thinking and pathologise youth by approaching it as a 'difficult phase' requiring management oriented towards the attainment of 'adulthood', understood as a stable condition and desirable goal. Forms of social behaviour by the young that are characterised as 'disruptive' by both popular culture and many forms of academic knowledge are often attributed to individual biological factors – the effects of puberty, 'raging hormones' and so on – rather than being recognised as either emotional responses to social constraints, or rational 'political' strategies to subvert local contexts. Christine Griffin, for example, has criticised the ways in which 'troubled teens' are constructed as problematic and addressed by state welfare institutions and 'treatment regimes' (Griffin, 1997).

Hence prevailing forms of knowledge are increasingly subject to challenges deriving from critical and sociologically informed understandings of childhood and youth. While sexuality tends to remain largely absent even from academic discussion of children's lives, with the exception of child sexual abuse (for example: Jenks, 1996; James, Jenks and Prout, 1998), it is clear that a sociological approach to childhood and youth has profound implications for the understanding of debates over sexuality and age of consent laws.

Sinikka Aapola has drawn upon such perspectives to challenge understandings of adolescence as a 'troublesome phase', and hence explored the interplay between ageing processes, adolescence, gender and sexual identities (Aapola, 1997). She demonstrates that the operation of gendered models of sexuality and heterosexuality, interwoven with contemporary developmental biological and psychological theories, can help explain attitudes towards adolescent sexual behaviour. Because boys are believed to 'mature' later than girls, adolescent girls are brought up with expectations that they will act as the 'responsible' partner, the partner who will 'wait' and 'resist', in contrast to boys who are expected to want sex from the moment they reach puberty.

a double standard prevails: boys are at the mercy of their 'natural' desires, whereas girls should act rationally. (Aapola, 1997, p. 63)

A particular focus of sexual differences in transitions to adulthood relates to the key symbolic signifiers that serve as 'rites of passage'. For girls, the transition from 'girl' to 'woman' is powerfully associated with *menarche*, the onset of menstruation (Matthews Lovering, 1995; Prendergast, 1995). For boys, in the absence of such a clear symbolic event determined by biology, the meaning of first heterosexual sex takes on a greater significance: 'a man gains manhood through a woman's loss of virginity' (Holland *et al.*, 1998, p. 172; cf. pp. 86, 162). These different understandings serve as examples of the gendered conceptions of 'adolescent development' which provide a crucial background to debates over age of consent laws.

Before proceeding to discuss gender and sexuality further it is useful to reflect on the important role of language in defining social groups in relation to age. The terms available, such as 'child', 'young person', 'teenager', 'adolescent', 'juvenile' or 'minor', are contested in definition, vague in scope and heavily loaded with symbolic associations. They are particularly sensitive in the context of age of consent debates because sexuality is a primary element in the drawing of boundaries between age categories.

In contemporary societies 'child' potentially spans the age group 0–18 since, for example, 18 is the boundary suggested in the *United Nations Convention on the Rights of the Child* to apply where a state does not define its own age (United Nations, 1989). Yet the western cultural concept of 'childhood' has historically been partly defined as 'pre-sexual': a meaning which is in tension with childhood's extension to 18. 'Minor' is primarily a legal term, but differs greatly in scope between legal contexts. 'Youth' is often used in social research to describe the section of the population aged 16–25, but has a widely variable reference in common usage (ESRC, 1998; Osgerby, 1998, pp. 1–2). Other mediating terms between childhood and adulthood, such as 'adolescent', 'juvenile' and 'teenager', may potentially be helpful through suggesting the exclusion of persons aged 20 or more, but tend to be problematically inflected by developmental understandings. 'Adolescence' has a particular history of being pathologised as a 'difficult' 'troublesome phase' of biological and psychological development (Aapola, 1997, p. 51).

Choice of language thus always carries assumptions and meanings. Terms such as 'young people' or 'young persons' are commonly used in place of 'children' to emphasise the competence of those referred to as 'persons'. Emphasising the status of a child as an 'individual' or 'person' carries meanings from the dominant notion of an 'individual' as rational, autonomous and fully developed. Negotiating these meanings within the limited and inflexible vocabulary available is therefore a complex task. In this study my tendency to use the term 'young people' to encompass a wide range of ages is intended to displace the traditional assumptions accompanying 'childhood', particularly views of children as non-sexual, and as subjects without any rights or degree of competence.

Gender and sexuality; heterosexuality and homosexuality

The emergence of second wave feminism and movements for sexual liberation from the late 1960s initiated an outpouring of theoretical and empirical research concerning gender and sexuality. Such work provides extensive resources for conceptualisation of the sexual behaviours and identities which are contested in debates over age of consent laws, particularly as these relate to relationships between men and women, heterosexuality and homosexuality. Theorists who have integrated insights from feminist, lesbian and gay theory and (more recently) 'queer theory' (see pp. 17–18) have developed critical perspectives on the social organisation of gender and sexuality, apparent in a web of diverse literature that now expands across the social sciences and history (for example: Weeks, Holland and Waites, 2003) and law (for example: Stychin and Herman, 2000).

Feminist theorists have produced compelling analyses of the role of patriarchal power in structuring social life. The analytical category 'gender', originally developed in contrast to biological features understood as 'sex' (though more recently extended to biology in the light of the mutability of 'sex': Butler, 1990), facilitates analysis of the ways in which men and women are socially and culturally constituted and situated (Jackson and Scott, 2002). Feminist theorists have advanced their critique of gendered power relations in a number of fields, including that of sexuality where feminists have struggled to decide the appropriate balance between liberation and regulation, pleasure and danger (Vance, 1984; Jackson and Scott, 1996). A feminist perspective is essential to understanding the historical development of age of consent laws.

The dynamics of gendered power in heterosexuality have been a particular focus. A wide range of positions in debates over the politics of heterosexual sex emerged from debates in the women's liberation movement, ranging from the radical lesbian feminist (Dworkin, 1981) to more positive feminist evaluations of sexual possibilities (Vance, 1984). More recently heterosexuality has been less susceptible to wholesale rejection, but remains the subject of critical theorisation and debate among feminists in the context of gendered power (Richardson, 1996; Holland *et al.*, 1998). Some emphasise heterosexual sex as pleasurable despite its location in gendered power relations, with a variety of possible meanings (Segal, 1994), while others continue to emphasise that heterosexuality is at the root of women's oppression (Wilkinson and Kitzinger, 1993; Jackson, 1999).

Feminist analysis has examined how heterosexuality as a form of sexual preference or 'orientation' is analytically distinct from but socially interwoven with heterosexuality as a social institution or form of social organisation, involving systematic linkages between forms of sexual behaviour, subjectivity and sexual desire, identities, the sexual division of labour (in employment, domestic labour, emotional labour), law, political citizenship and other aspects of social life. The term 'compulsory heterosexuality' was coined by Adrienne Rich to refer to the way society compelled participation within heterosexuality as a form of social organisation (Rich, 1980). Stevi Jackson's recent work provides one of the most sustained analyses of heterosexuality, drawing together past and present critiques to conceptualise heterosexuality as patterning forms of social organisation, as a form of identity and as influencing forms of desire, while seeking not to conflate these different elements (Jackson, 1999, esp. pp. 159–185). A critical perspective on hetero-sexuality is crucial to conceptualise age of consent laws, which historically have been formulated with an emphasis upon the need to protect young women from men.

Another crucial current of analysis addressing sexuality has been that emer-ging from the gay liberation movement (Abelove, Barale and Halperin, 1993; Nardi and Schneider, 1997). Work by gay and lesbian theorists has produced critiques of the institutional and cultural exclusions enforced by hetero-sexuality. This has generally complimented feminist perspectives, although sometimes challenging them, particularly where differences emerged over the extent to which sexuality requires regulation. Sometimes lesbian and gay perspectives have critiqued heterosexuality without attention to gendered power relations within heterosexuality. The best political and theoretical analyses seek to combine elements of both (see for example: Segal, 1999), and also seek to incorporate analysis of the specific forms of exclusion faced by bisexuals (Eadie, 1993, pp. 139–170; Hemmings, 1993, pp. 118–138; Dollimore, 1997).

One key debate in which theoretical work by lesbian and gay writers has been crucial, and which is significant in understanding age of consent debates, has focussed on the extent to which categories of sexual identity are products of society and culture, rather than biology. In debates over sexual identities, 'social constructionist' theories challenged those which regarded identity categories as unproblematically deriving from and representing characteris-tics of the body and/or the self understood as their aetiology, focussing instead on the production of cultural categories (Vance, 1989). Early social construc-tionists questioned the existence of shared biological or psychological characteristics within categories such as 'homosexuality' and 'heterosexuality' (McIntosh, 1968; Plummer, 1975; Weeks, 1977, 1981). Foucault's subsequent commentary on the appearance of the nineteenth-century homosexual suggested similar lines of inquiry (Foucault, 1981, pp. 42–44). The subsequent 'social constructionist/essentialist debate' raged in various directions (Vance, 1989; Stein, 1992), taking new forms in work influenced by post-structuralism (Fuss, 1989; Butler, 1990; Sedgwick, 1990; Seidman, 1993).

The case has been consistently and convincingly argued against biological theories of the causation of homosexuality, of which the latest manifestation has been the 'gay gene' (Rose, 1996; Fernbach, 1998; cf. 'No tears for passing of "gay gene" ', *The Observer*, 25 April 1999, p. 4). Some theorists who reject biological causation models, however, have turned to psychoanalysis to pro-pose that shared forms of desire and subjectivity, structured in relation to sexual difference, lie behind the strong sense of sexual identity felt by many people. Yet psychoanalytic theories also suffer from their own forms of 'essentialism', and work as narratives which constrain ways of thinking about sexual identity and subjectivity, particularly by tending to assume that sexual desires and identities are established early in childhood (cf. Plummer, 1981, pp. 53–75; Weeks, 1985, pp. 127–156). Limited attempts have been made to explore alternative possibilities, such as developing sexual script theories or symbolic interactionism to suggest a more diffuse understanding of how psychic processes and bodily sensations interact with cultural categories (Jackson, 1996b, pp. 15–22).

The view which informs this study, therefore, is that categories such as 'homosexual' and 'gay' can be understood as categories that play a profoundly constitutive role in structuring social experience. Desires are best conceived as oriented towards 'acts', 'sensations' or particular elements of 'bodies' (or perhaps better, psychic representations of these), and are only organised in relation to biological sex differences through available cultural concepts and narratives. Hence the ways in which behaviour is socially organised through sexual identity categories are more susceptible to change than is commonly accepted. Nevertheless, identity categories are meaningful constraints in the lives of individuals, associated with personal narratives concerning the degrees of 'fixity' or 'unfixity', 'determinacy' or 'choice' people experience in their sexual identity, orientation or desires. People who do not believe their sexual identity can change are thus extremely unlikely to engage in sexual practices which appear to contradict that identity, and sexual identities can be the subject of intense emotional investments linked to the constitution of self-identity, making them far from easy to transgress. Despite this, the implications of this kind of approach must be confronted and introduced into public debates, even if such perspectives are in tension with the dominant narratives of lesbian and gay people (Whisman, 1996), and their associated political strategies for claiming citizenship (Epstein, 1987, p. 243; Evans, 1995, pp. 130–137; Jackson, 1998, pp. 70–72; Waites, 2003, 2005).

The emergence of 'queer politics' and 'queer theory' since the early 1990s has in some ways reoriented these and other debates over sexuality. Both terms are highly contested (Epstein, 1996). 'Queer politics' has been used variously to describe 'lesbian, gay, bisexual and transgender' politics, to denote a renewed oppositional 'lesbian and gay' activist vigour, or to emphasise a questioning of all established sexual identity categories (cf. Warner, 1993, pp. vii–xxxi). 'Queer theory', a term coined by Teresa de Lauretis (1991), has also been used in many ways to describe diverse theoretical positions, and most of the key examples typically cited do not explicitly use the term (Butler, 1990; Sedgwick, 1990), while even those which do include a variety of work (Warner, 1993). Nevertheless, despite justified criticism of queer theory's lack of coherence (Mort, 1994), some distinctive tendencies can be discerned. Steven Seidman has argued that a discernible current identifiable as 'queer theory' has:

> sought to shift the debate somewhat away from explaining the modern homosexual to questions of the operation of the hetero/homosexual

binary, from an exclusive preoccupation with homosexuality to a focus on heterosexuality as a social and political organizing principle, and from a politics of minority interest to a politics of knowledge and difference. (Seidman, 1996, p. 9; see also Seidman, 1997)

As Epstein has commented, it is doubtful whether Seidman is right that earlier 'social constructionist' work failed to perform these tasks, at least implicitly (Epstein, 1999, p. 271). It is also clear that earlier feminist understandings of compulsory heterosexuality understood sexual and gender identities to be linked within a single structural system (Rich, 1980; Jackson, 1999). Nevertheless, queer theory has been distinguished by its explicit problematisation of 'heteronormativity', which can be defined as 'the institutions, structures of understanding and practical orientations that make heterosexuality seem not only coherent – that is organised as a sexuality – but also privileged' (Berlant and Warner, 1998, p. 548); and also by advocacy of the destabilisation of the heterosexual/homosexual binary via the promotion of other forms of sexual identification (Warner, 1993). Although 'queer' as a concept must carry some association with homosexuality, queer sexual practices have been conceived as encompassing anything which could be juxtaposed to heteronormative sex (problematically understood as oriented to reproduction via male/female vaginal intercourse), such as fetishisms, sado-masochism and so on. Thus in relation to law, queer politics and queer theory suggest the need for analysis of not only the heteronormativity of law (McGhee, 2001, pp. 1–24), but also the way in which a variety of sexual practices are regulated, without reference solely to a heterosexual–homosexual axis (Stychin, 1995).

An appreciation of gendered power, and of the ways in which heterosexuality and heteronormativity have historically structured society and shaped law, is vital for the analysis of debates over the meaning of consent in the context of sexual behaviour. These are discussed in the next section.

The meaning of consent

The meaning of 'consent' is crucial in considering debates over age of consent laws, although not all rationales advanced for legal prohibitions on young people's involvement in sexual behaviour have made reference to the capacity of young people to give meaningful consent, as will be demonstrated in subsequent chapters. There are numerous competing perspectives on the meaning of 'consent', and how it should be conceptualised in relation to childhood and sexual behaviour.

The conditions necessary for an individual to give their consent are a perennial source of debate within philosophy and social theory, but debates over consent and competence have been the subject of increasing interest and dispute in recent decades (Alderson, 1995). The boundary between consent and non-consent is contested in relation to issues such as differential power, coercion and deception with regard to relevant information (Archard, 1998, pp. 2–3).

'Consent' implies voluntary agreement, undertaken by a subject with a sufficient degree of free will and agency. To be judged valid, consent must be based upon predetermined criteria in relation to both the social context and the status of the agent (Shildrick, 1997, p. 82). The agent's capacities for 'free will' and 'reason' are therefore relevant parameters, as are contested definitions of relevant social contexts (for discussion, see Shildrick, 1997, pp. 79–90; Archard, 1998, pp. 1–18).

The capacity to 'consent' in any given circumstance can be understood as a particular kind of 'competence', which may be defined as 'the capacity or potential for adequate functioning-in-context as a socialised human' (Jenkins, 1998, p. 1). In western societies since the enlightenment, particular forms of competence associated with the intellectual capacity to 'reason' and the exercise of free will have been valued. The subject of most enlightenment thought has been associated with the attainment of capacities to reason and act autonomously as an independent, disinterested, self-complete, self-determining being (Alderson, 1990; Shildrick, 1997, pp. 86–90). Autonomy has typically been characterised as taking place in the absence of constraint, rather than being facilitated by 'positive conditions'. Moral agency within much of western ethics is characterised as 'the realisation of a capacity to choose and act, freely and rationally, within a framework of moral requirements' (Shildrick, 1997, p. 63). Such understandings have been mirrored in the assumptions of developmental psychology, as discussed above. This context implies that the characteristics attributed to certain social groups have been systematically linked to the kind of action which consent has been imagined to be.

The social distribution of rights and freedoms in western societies, including rights to consent in sexual and other activities, has historically been hierarchically structured in accordance with such perspectives. Those groups not believed to possess 'reason', such as women, non-white peoples, children, and those defined as mentally deficient, were refused rights on the grounds that they did not possess the necessary forms of competence (Alderson, 1994). Hence meaningful 'consent' has historically been associated with forms of competence facilitating 'rational' decision-making in the context of 'free will' – the preserve of adult white men. Children, like women, were historically viewed as being ruled by their bodies, and hence incapable of exercising moral agency over their bodies (Shildrick, 1997, p. 81). Consequently, where the patriarchal family has been a central institution, consent by women and children has not been deemed relevant to much sexual behaviour. This is the background to much contemporary sexual violence and abuse.

During the twentieth century, groups previously not recognised as possessing capacities for reason sufficient to justify granting of rights and autonomy were increasingly granted such recognition: not only women but also groups such as children and the mentally ill, though more recently and to a much lesser extent. This occurred through the influence of critical political perspectives, and associated philosophies and social theories. However, some have pursued change simply through a revision of beliefs about who possesses reason, and/ or through a re-conceptualisation of social contexts defining the circumstances in which decisions are made. Others have more profoundly questioned the nature of 'reason', 'rational decision-making' and the characteristic emphasis on the 'autonomous' individual in enlightenment thought.

Among the latter, critiques have emerged from a variety of theoretical streams within social and political theory and moral philosophy. Some have questioned the possibility and desirability of the self's 'detachment' from its social context. These include communitarian critiques of the characterisation of ethical decision-making as being by an 'unencumbered self', distanced from particular interests (Sandel, 1984/1992; Taylor, 1985/1992). Such perspectives suggest that the self's embedding in its social context may facilitate good ethical choices, rather than constrain them. Similar themes have been raised by feminist maternalists advocating recognition of an 'ethic of care', who have sought to re-value the role of emotions, non-rational subjectivity, the subconscious and/or the body/embodiment in decision-making and the generation of knowledge (Gilligan, 1982; see also Shildrick, 1997). Others, advocating post-structuralist and postmodernist perspectives critiquing Enlightenment thought, have more radically questioned the possibility and desirability of the subject's coherence (Foucault, 1970; Lyotard, 1984). Some have sought to bring together elements of these perspectives (Benhabib, 1992); and debates have ensued over the character of rationality in both modern and postmodern thought (Rengger, 1995, pp. 70, 77–125). These various currents collectively demand a re-conceptualisation of any rationale for granting particular rights, freedoms or forms of social status to adults but not to children.

Critiques of an emphasis upon autonomous individualism require us to approach consent within a new analytical context as a situated activity never perfectly achieved, always given with limited knowledge, cultural resources, finite degrees of competence and often in the context of unequal power. This implies understanding mental choice as a capacity which is a learned form of competence, and a socially situated understanding of the conditions for 'freedom' of action (Shildrick, 1997, pp. 86–87). Genuine rationality must be situated in the context of alternative choices, in order for discernment to become possible. The competence to 'consent' may be attained in different ways and to different degrees; the giving of 'consent' can be conceived as a situated social process.

But even if the desirability of extending 'autonomy' to social groups previously not permitted autonomy is accepted, this does not simply imply the extension of formal rights and freedoms. Margrit Shildrick has suggested that the granting of greater formal autonomy to patients in medical contexts can leave dominant conceptions of autonomy and existing structural power relations between medical professionals and patients intact (Shildrick, 1997, p. 80; cf. pp. 62–90). Recognising the extent to which competence is socially acquired does not automatically imply extending formal rights; it may imply that rights could potentially be extended, but should only be granted where appropriate forms of education or social support are available. Resources – including both learned skills and forms of competence, and material resources – are crucial.

'Consent' in the context of sexual behaviour presents particular dilemmas. These are discussed in David Archard's book *Sexual Consent*, which provides one of the most sustained treatments of the issues (Archard, 1998, pp. 19–53). Particular forms of social inequality in access to forms of competence, power and resources exist between parties involved in sexual behaviour. Judgements of who is capable to give meaningful consent to a sexual act depend upon the kinds of competence in 'consenting' which one might regard as relevant. For example (as discussed above), 'rational' capacities are deemed important by some; others value a moral sense; skills in relating to others; and/or emotional sensitivity associated with an embodied self-awareness. Competence can be enhanced by relevant knowledge, including (for example) knowledge of the likely consequences of sexual behaviour, which can be provided by sex education; however, skills and emotional assurance in handling situations are also important, and can also in some respects be taught.

Feminist analyses of both 'consensual' and 'non-consensual' sexual behaviour have collectively examined gender dimensions of what can be termed 'the social distribution of sexual consent': who is conceived as capable of consent, who is recognised as such in law, and who in practice is able to engage in consensual sexual activity. Feminists have, in particular, examined the unequal distribution of power and pleasure in the context of critical analyses of socially institutionalised heterosexuality, including the ways in which women perform emotional and sexual labour for men in contexts structured by the risk of violence or economic dependence (for example: Rich, 1980). Some feminist campaigns have exaggerated the clarity of a distinction between consent and non-consent, as with some uses of the anti-rape slogan 'yes means yes' and 'no means no'. However, other strands of feminism have conceptualised the existence of a continuum between fully 'consensual' heterosexual intercourse and rape. The notion of a continuum more adequately describes the experiences of women who may 'submit' to sex without giving a more 'active consent', implying greater agency (Holland *et al.*, 1998, pp. 131–132; Lacey and Wells, 1998, pp. 385–386). This is useful in conceptualising forms and degrees of consent in sexual behaviour involving children. It would appear that there is no absolute distinction between actions or subjective states of consciousness that could be taken to constitute consent or non-consent; yet it remains important to maintain consent as a governing principle.

What, then, are the conditions in which children should be entitled to participate in decision-making, and give their 'consent' in activities affecting them? The emergence of claims for 'children's rights' from the 1960s has steadily achieved significant social and legal transformations (Lansdown, 1994). Article 12 of the *Convention on the Rights of the Child*, adopted by the UN General Assembly in 1989, asserts:

> States parties shall assure to the child who is capable of forming his or her own views the right to express those views freely in all matters affecting the child, the views of the child being given due weight in accordance with the age and maturity of the child. [...] For this purpose, the child shall, in particular, be provided with the opportunity to be heard in any judicial and administrative procedures affecting the child. (United Nations, 1989)

In the UK the *Children Act* 1989 similarly asserts that in the legal proceedings it encompasses a court shall have regard to 'the ascertainable wishes and feelings of the child concerned' (part 1, s. 1). Such moves towards encouraging young people's participation in decision-making are echoed in a wide-range of influential contemporary policy literature (Lansdown, 1994, 1995; Schofield and Thoburn, 1996; Alderson and Montgomery, 1996a). The right to make a final decision and 'consent' is, however, generally seen as more problematic than granting rights to participate in decision-making processes with adults. Hence in many areas of policy there is currently an emphasis that children should be involved, but should not be given rights to make final decisions (Schofield and Thoburn, 1996).

Some wish to go further, however. Priscilla Alderson, who has undertaken extensive qualitative research on the subject of children and consent, has argued for the rights of children to play a prominent role in decision-making in the context of children's health care and medical treatment (Alderson, 1990, 1992a, 1994; Alderson and Montgomery, 1996a). She has also applied such perspectives, for example, in supporting guidelines for medical research on children (British Paediatric Association, 1992; Alderson, 1992b); and a proposed code of practice for children's health care rights, whereby children would be presumed competent from the age of five, unless proven otherwise (Alderson and Montgomery, 1996a). Alderson's research illustrates how a rethinking of perspectives on the meaning of consent can facilitate a re-conceptualisation of children's capacity to consent in contexts where a balance is sought between their rights to exercise autonomy and their 'protection rights' (Alderson, 1994, p. 45).

Alderson rejects the biological theories and developmental psychology which underpin many arguments for the incompetence of children (1994, pp. 50–51). She also criticises the rational autonomous subject of much enlightenment philosophy, arguing that the characterisation of 'rational autonomy' as socially de-contextualised and impervious to emotion does not reflect the situated character of ethical decision-making (Alderson, 1990). In their place she emphasises the ways in which competence is produced in particular social contexts:

> Competence is more than a skill, it is a way of relating, and can be understood more clearly when each child's inner qualities are seen within a network of relationships and cultural influences. (Alderson, 1992a, p. 123)

Hence Alderson argues that through being given sources of information and engaging in dialogue with others, children can develop forms of competence relevant to local contexts. She argues for a less exclusive redefinition of reason and self-determination, focussed less on detached objectivity.

Emphasising reference to children's own views of their capabilities to engage in decision-making, Alderson argues that the 'integrity' necessary to make decisions is contextual, and can be acquired by relatively young children (Alderson, 1994, pp. 53–54). Often children are capable of interpreting relevant knowledge with a sophistication which can match that of their parents. Hence Alderson is critical of laws which impose decisions upon children without their consent or participation. With reference to imposed medical treatments, she argues:

> These laws ignore the growing evidence of very young children's ability to reason, to understand [...] Denying children's right to physical and mental integrity, through dismissing their rational competence, means that what would be assault to an adult is legitimate discipline to a child [...]. (Alderson, 1994, p. 60)

Alderson's arguments thus make the case, gaining increasing acceptance in some areas of public policy, that children can be competent to make key decisions, if integrity is understood as a capacity acquired within particular social contexts rather than a fixed quality of certain 'rational' individuals. Whether such perspectives are valid in general in their approach to children remains hotly debated. It is interesting to note, however, that at present such arguments are advanced in many fields of policy-making, but generally not in the realm of sexual behaviour. The question this poses for the present study is whether sexual behaviour is for some reason a 'special case'; and if not, does the case of sexual behaviour reveal more general flaws in the approach of children's rights advocates or, alternatively, should sexual behaviour be a field for children's own decision-making? The next section examines whether children can meaningfully consent to sexual acts, and hence whether children should be permitted to engage in sexual behaviour.

Children, sexuality, consent and the law

How do children/young people experience sex? Can children/young people give 'consent' to sex? Do children/young people need protection from sex? And is the law an effective means to protect them? These are the questions at the heart of public debates and conflicts over age of consent laws.

To answer these questions we need to think sociologically about the narratives which define childhood sexualities (Plummer, 1990). This requires an awareness of extensive and well-documented anthropological and historical evidence that the boundaries of childhood are extremely culturally variable in relation to sexual behaviour and status. Gilbert Herdt's research is a much discussed example, demonstrating that in tribes in Papua New Guinea the ingestion of adult semen is a key symbolic moment in rites of passage from boyhood to manhood (Herdt, 1994, 1997a, pp. 64–88, 109–134). Practices which would be labelled as 'child sexual abuse' in much of the world form an integral part of community and family life.

Knowledge of children's relation to sexual behaviour and sexuality has shifted profoundly during the twentieth century. Progressive and radical social movements have challenged a Victorian legacy of attitudes which concealed sexual abuse, denied children any rights and viewed children as innocent, without sexuality (Evans, 1993, p. 212). While debate persists over what 'sexuality' is (cf. Weeks, 1985), many commentators now accept that children are 'sexual', or have 'sexuality' in ways which must be understood and accepted rather than ignored or hidden (Jackson, 1982). Victorian views of childhood purity and innocence have been steadily replaced with acceptance of children's capacities for physical sensations and excitement. As Freud helped us to see, children have their own forms of sexual pleasure; children touch themselves and enjoy their own bodies. In recognition of this, childhood masturbation and sexual play between children are no longer so deeply pathologised as 'perverse', but are regarded by many people as 'harmless' or even 'natural', though they are still institutionally regulated and discouraged (Stainton Rogers and Stainton Rogers, 1999, p. 182).

New social and political movements in the post-war period began to emphasise the importance of children's experiences in relation to sexuality. From the 1950s the politically conservative child protection movement sought to uncover and challenge forms of sexual abuse (Jenks, 1996, pp. 94–95). From the 1960s, by contrast, sexual liberationists combined arguments against abuse with claims for recognition of children's sexual desires, sexual rights and capacities to consent to sex. For some this included sex with adults (Tsang, 1981). By contrast, feminist perspectives developed in the 1970s emphasised the need for recognition of children's sexuality alongside a focus upon 'child sexual abuse' as being a widespread phenomenon linked to forms of male power (Jackson, 1982). Despite exceptional defences (Millett, 1984; Rubin, 1984), feminist analysis typically became associated with a highly critical attitude towards adult/child sexual contact (cf. Jackson and Scott, 1996, p. 19).

In recent years the issue of 'child sexual abuse' by adults has become a mainstream public concern, and has increasingly been represented and discussed in relation to the concept of 'paedophilia'. However, the use of this concept, which derives from sexology, carries particular problems. Paedophilia is defined in the *New Shorter Oxford English Dictionary* as referring to 'sexual desire directed towards children' (Brown, 1993, p. 2068); hence a 'paedophile' does not necessarily attempt or engage in sexual behaviour with children, and is not necessarily a 'sexual abuser' (on contested terminology, see Sandfort *et al.*, 1990). This is one reason why some commentators prefer to discuss 'intergenerational sex' or 'cross-generational sex' (Rubin, 1984; Weeks, 1985, p. 223), to the annoyance of others who regard them as 'euphemisms' (Jackson and Scott, 1996, p. 19). However, the current pathologisation of paedophiles by mainstream psychology and in popular culture tends to represent those involved in sexual behaviour with children as a homogenous category of 'evil monsters' who act compulsively, driven by desires and incapable of abstaining from sexual behaviour on a rational or moral basis.

Paedophiles found a space within the sexual liberationism of the early 1970s to voice their 'sexual stories' (Plummer, 1995, pp. 116–119). In a period when traditional attitudes to sexuality were cast aside, new narratives proliferated within radical social movements and the counter-culture in a context where shared criteria for legitimacy were absent. In subsequent years, paedophile organisations appeared, such as the North American Man–Boy Love Association (NAMBLA) and (in the UK) the Paedophile Information Exchange (PIE), claiming a collective identity and voicing paedophile experiences. These organisations made claims for the acceptability of 'consensual' sexual activity between adults and children, and the abolition of age of consent laws (NAMBLA, 1980; Evans, 1993, pp. 228–234; Bernard, 1997). Paedophiles drew upon new political languages of 'children's rights' to make the case for children being permitted to make decisions concerning their own lives and bodies. A variety of activists and intellectuals argued this case, including a substantial stream of gay male liberationist writers, and some prominent feminist sex radicals (Tsang, 1981; Rubin, 1984; cf. Sandfort, 1982a, p. 8; Weeks, 1985, pp. 223–231). More recently the lesbian and gay movement has struggled to distinguish itself from paedophile groups through moves such as the expulsion of the NAMBLA from the International Lesbian and Gay Association (ILGA) in its quest to achieve recognition by the United Nations (Thorstad, 1990; Gamson, 1997; Fernbach, 1998, p. 64; Graupner, 1999). But despite an increasingly hostile climate, some paedophile groups and organisations persistently question restrictions upon children's involvement in sexual behaviour (Geraci, 1997; Vereniging MARTIJN, 2001).

Paedophile claims for legitimacy emerged from the 1970s simultaneously with, and in tension with, stories of child sexual abuse. Movements of abuse survivors provided the context for shocking stories of adult cruelty to be heard, and facilitated the 'coming out' of victims. Such movements pressed for an increasing institutionalisation of listening mechanisms and processes to hear these narratives (for example, in schools). Extensive evidence emerged to demonstrate that adult/child sexual abuse is widespread (for example: Glaser and Frosh, 1993, pp. 10–13; Pilkington and Kremer, 1995).

However, movements influenced by both right-wing moral conservatism and sexually conservative forms of feminism increasingly influenced mainstream public attitudes and policy-making, applying increasingly expansive definitions of the scope of sexual abuse. These have been described as 'protectionist' by Wendy and Rex Stainton Rogers, who contrast their wide definition of 'abuse' with the more limited scope of 'abuse' understood in public 'common sense' (Stainton Rogers and Stainton Rogers, 1999, p. 182; see also Archard, 1999). While mainstream public opinion has resisted extreme protectionism, it has found influence in some organisations and areas of policy.

In considering children's and young people's experiences of sexual behaviour, both with other children and young people, and with adults, it is apparent that much existing research on how such behaviour is experienced has been methodologically flawed. Prevailing forms of psychological research concerning how sexual behaviour is subjectively experienced are embedded within problematic research paradigms which sustain expansive and reductive definitions of child sexual abuse. In particular, mainstream psychological studies (especially in the US) have produced homogenised understandings of children's experiences of sexual behaviour with adults which associate it with directly causing psychological harm. Such research has been methodologically flawed, for example, by using 'clinical' research samples, based on the experiences of persons such as those engaged in sex abuse therapy programmes – which unsurprisingly generate evidence of negative, painful experiences. This research has assumed that such experiences are representative of those who have been involved in a generalised category of behaviour involving children termed 'child sexual abuse' (commonly defined in the psychological literature as involving under-18s). Consequently, sexual behaviour with under-18s has been represented in crudely positivistic mainstream psychological literature as a direct 'cause' of psychological harm for any individual that experiences it. The category 'child sexual abuse' has been used to describe 'virtually all sexual interactions between children or adolescents and significantly older persons', and has become associated with causing intense psychological harm (Rind, Tromovitch and Bauserman, 1998, p. 22). The expansion of definitions of child sexual abuse in recent years has thus tended to characterise all adult–child sexual contact as imposed upon unwilling and resistant children.

By contrast, the limited research on non-coercive, non-incestuous sexual relationships between adults and children which exists indicates that a significant minority of children report positive experiences, with respect to both pleasures deriving from physical sexual acts, and the broader social relationships within which such acts take place. Bauserman, Rind and Tromovitch derive this conclusion from a comprehensive review of 35 relevant 'non-clinical' empirical studies published between 1956 and 1994 (Rind, Tromovitch and Bauserman, 1998, p. 46; cf. Bauserman and Rind, 1997; Rind and Tromovitch, 1997; Rind, Bauserman and Tromovitch, 1998; for a similar argument, see Jones, 1990). These non-clinical samples reveal significant numbers of positive self-reports.

Particular qualitative studies support these conclusions. A study in the Netherlands reported the experiences of 25 boys aged 10–16 who were engaged in ongoing sexual relationships with older male paedophiles (Sandfort, 1982a,b). This research, unique for its focus on children in ongoing relationships who had not experienced any legal or clinical interventions, documented predominantly positive responses with respect to both physical sexual contacts and relationships, and has been defended against methodological critics (Bauserman, 1990; cf. Finkelhor, 1990; Mrazek, 1990). An Australian study drew similar conclusions from a sample of 19 retrospective interviews with adult individuals who had previously been younger parties, aged below 16, in 'consensual' 'child/adult' relationships (Leahy, 1996). Richard Yuill has documented reports of positive experiences in male age-discrepant/intergenerational relationships in recent UK research, based on interviews with self-defined 'boylovers' and young gay males over 18 who had previously experienced age-discrepant relationships (Yuill, 2004a; see also Yuill, 2004b). There is also increasing evidence of the existence of mutually pleasurable sexual contact between male children and older women, though research focussing on gender dynamics also suggests that girls experiencing sexual contact with adult men as non-coercive, pleasurable and/or 'consensual' is rare – but it does occur (Nelson and Oliver, 1998).

Of course, distinctions between 'positive' and 'negative' experiences which are common in the psychological literature are inadequate to capture the complexity of many people's experiences, particularly where long-term relationships are involved. Furthermore, as recent work in critical and feminist social psychology influenced by post-structuralism and discourse theory suggests, feelings about sexual behaviour may change over time as people find themselves within new discourses and attempt to make sense of previous experiences (Reavey and Warner, 2002). Hence a child may experience a sexual encounter with an adult as pleasurable, but this experience might become distressing at a later date if its meaning is renegotiated in a new cultural context where it is defined as 'abuse'. Such complexities confound arguments such as those of Rind, Bauserman and Tromovich which seek to justify sexual behaviour involving a child purely on the basis that it is experienced positively by both parties at the time and has no immediately clear negative psychological consequences (cf. Bauserman and Rind, 1997; Rind and Tromovitch, 1997; Rind, Bauserman and Tromovitch, 1998).

In general, however, there is considerable evidence that a significant amount of non-coercive behaviour between children and adults is experienced as 'positive' or 'pleasurable' by children, and does not give rise to long-term negative psychological effects (for example: Leahy, 1996). Some child/adult sex, as with much sexual activity between children or young people, is pleasurable and has no directly harmful consequences. This need not necessarily imply an abandonment of attempts to define such non-coercive behaviour as 'abusive', since abuse may be defined by the existence of power relations rather than the existence of a negative psychological experience (Kelly, 1988); nor does it imply an endorsement of scepticism about the prevalence and seriousness of child sexual abuse. But it does require a rethinking of the rationale for legal prohibitions, if such are to be defended. Arguments for prohibitions must be based upon definitions of 'abuse' and the 'best interests' of children, and these definitions may run counter to children's own pleasures and choices.

What should not be lost sight of in discussing these issues, notwithstanding the need to consider relations between adults and children in their particularity, is that the vast majority of young people's sexual behaviour occurs with other young people of a similar age. Discussions over young people's capacity to give meaningful consent, and the appropriate form of age of consent laws, need to address this behaviour in a manner which enables young people to confidently negotiate the movement from childhood to adulthood, without losing focus on the issues facing most teenagers as they begin sexual activity with their peers: issues such as identity (for example, becoming a 'real man'; being labelled a 'slag'); emotions (love and friendship, fear, shame, insecurity, excitement) and sexual health (contraception, pregnancy, HIV/AIDS, etc.).

Two inter-related issues require consideration. The first is the role of a child or young person in decision-making: what kind of 'consent', if any, is relevant for a child or young person to engage in sexual acts, and can they give meaningful 'consent' accordingly? The second concerns the role of the wider society, and particularly the law, in 'protecting' a child or young person through prohibitions upon certain behaviour.

Consent and children's sexual behaviour

How might a rethinking of 'consent' in relation to childhood apply in assessing the meaningfulness of children's consent in sexual behaviour? What particular forms of 'competence', and which social contexts, are relevant to assessing the possibility of sexual consent? And what degree of consent is necessary in such an interaction? (cf. Shildrick, pp. 86–90). In thinking about these issues it is necessary to consider a range of circumstances in which there may be degrees of coercion operating, and a range of behaviour by children and young people ranging from passive acquiescence to more self-conscious and reflective behaviour which is more appropriately characterised as 'meaningful consent'.

A huge variety of social contexts influence the potential risks and likely effects of young people engaging in sexual activities. These include a range of factors which determine the status of children as 'citizens', including legal status (rights and responsibilities), political status (the extent to which children have a political voice) and social status (the extent to which children have economic and cultural resources; see discussion of citizenship, pp. 32–39). In more concrete terms, economic circumstances can influence the extent to which a child is susceptible to bribes or inducements; the age of the child and age differences from their sexual partner can create power imbalances; and various other social differences such as gender, class, and 'race' and ethnicity can have an impact.

In assessing whether it is appropriate that a young person should be able to make their own decisions about engaging in sexual behaviour, we also need to consider the extent to which an individual has learned relevant kinds of competence to make judgements in particular circumstances. Young people's competence to make decisions depends on their development of relevant knowledge and skills. Factors influencing children's ability to negotiate and make meaningful decisions include, for example, levels of sex and relationship education. Young people's competence in relation to sexual behaviour is multi-dimensional; it can be conceived as including, for example, 'intellectual competence' understood as the ability to process relevant information, and 'emotional competence' understood as the ability to express and manage emotions. Both of these develop through social interaction.

With respect to the competence of the child in the context of decisions over surgery, Alderson argues that a lesser emphasis upon rationality and knowledge and a greater emphasis upon feeling and intuition undermine the claims of adults to a distinct form of competence (Alderson, 1990, 1994). It could be argued, as some advocates of paedophile relationships implicitly have, that a similar situation exists in the context of sexual behaviour, where subjective feelings and pleasures should be the relevant issue. Children may possess forms of competence necessary to interpret their own embodied subjectivity, and possibly the desires and feelings of others. However, such arguments emphasising emotional competence underplay the importance of knowledge in such contexts, where the complex implications of behaviour require careful calculation and clear understanding not available to children.

Such arguments tend to overstate the importance of forms of individual competence which are general characteristics of a person brought to a social situation (emotional competence), rather than specifically relevant to a particular local social context (specific skills and knowledge). More emphasis is needed on the forms of competence a child develops which are directly relevant to negotiating particular social contexts, as Alderson recognises. But it is also important to retain an appreciation that social contexts form objective realities, structural constraints upon the conditions of action, imposing certain levels of risk and danger upon young people (relating, for example, to unplanned pregnancy, sexually transmitted diseases, 'abuse' or 'exploitation') irrespective of their competence. For example, a child may be educated in skills to negotiate sexual consent with older children, and given knowledge of forms of danger and risk; but certain kinds of danger and risk nevertheless impact independently upon the child. Hence some emotional consequences of an unwanted pregnancy are likely to be more serious for a younger girl because of a greater transgression of social norms. Stratified levels of risk tend to impact differentially upon younger children.

The rationale for age of consent laws

In conceptualising the rationale for age of consent laws the distinction between *risk* and *harm* is a crucial starting point. This can be demonstrated, initially, with respect to adult/child sex. Dominant paradigms of research into child sexual abuse have homogenised understandings of how child–adult sexual contact affects children. The label 'child abuse' is often used in contexts which imply that children experience all such behaviour negatively, or that it is always psychologically or physically damaging to them. Yet as research discussed above suggests, some child–adult sexual behaviour may not be experienced negatively, or have any damaging consequences for a child. Such behaviour nevertheless entails a child being placed in a situation of risk, and some patterns of risk are considerably independent of actions an individual young person may take to ameliorate them.

Arguments in favour of granting young children autonomy in sexual decision-making are therefore flawed through underestimating structural power relations. They seek to grant children formal recognition of their moral agency without challenging the unequal social contexts in which they are embedded. It might be argued that if the adult–child relationship were to be re-conceptualised not as a 'subject–object' relation, but as a relation between two self-actualising subjects, then new possibilities might be opened (cf. Shildrick, 1997, p. 80). However, this would necessitate systematic action to transform both the competences of children – to teach relevant skills and knowledge – and the social contexts that structure their conditions for action. In the absence of such challenges, the law must be formulated in the context of structural constraints.

In general, children are not capable of acquiring all the forms of competence necessary to address the risks imposed upon them by structural contexts. They have less developed competence for conceptualising complex interpersonal relationships and, for example, are less able to evaluate disruptive shifts in their own life-courses that may detach them from their peers. Though adults frequently make bad decisions about sexual partners and relationships, they have less to lose. Children are situated in a structurally disadvantaged position within the social hierarchy, particularly vulnerable in relation to many of the risks attendant on sexual behaviour. This requires that they are protected. By operating universally, even in instances where no direct harm might befall a child, age of consent laws contribute to preventing children being placed in circumstances of risk in the context of relationships with adults, where power relations are unequal.

However, this fundamental rationale provides no substantial response to the question of the age at which sexual activity should be legal, or how this should be judged in relation to other activities of young people. Priscilla Alderson has argued that children are often as able as adults to make health care decisions in the context of complex 'factual' information, judgements of relative risks, ethical dilemmas and highly emotional contexts (s. 3). She has also argued that judgements of children's legal competence should be independent of moral attitudes towards their sexual activity; and hence that competent children should have a right to receive health care relevant to their sexual behaviour, such as contraception (Alderson and Montgomery, 1996b, pp. 9–10). The *Gillick* case concerning the provision of contraception to under-16s has effectively established this principle in England and Wales, subsequently influencing the policy of providing abortion without parental knowledge or consent (*Gillick v. West Norfolk and Wisbech Area Health Authority* 1986 AC 112; Evans, 1993, pp. 224–225), and such rights have also been enacted in the *Age of Legal Capacity (Scotland) Act* 1991. This raises the question as to whether it can be consistent for young people under 16 to be deemed competent to make decisions about health which must be balanced against judgements about sexual behaviour and relationships (for example, over contraception), while not being allowed to make decisions over sexual behaviour itself. The difference in the state's role between the two scenarios (legal prohibition of sexual activity *v.* provision of sexual health services) demonstrates that different principles are being applied, and raises the question of whether these are appropriate and well-founded.

The issue of whether the law should prohibit sexual behaviour below a particular age is distinct, however, from the question of whether children have the competence to 'consent', and also from the question of whether such behaviour should be socially discouraged. One intervening consideration is that law may not be enforceable, and utilising the law entails particular costs and benefits. This implies the necessity to situate debates over age of consent laws within broader debates over law, crime and the functioning of criminal justice systems: such as, for example, the debate between legal moralists and utilitarians which was central in debates over jurisprudence in English law for much of the twentieth century (Devlin, 1959; Hart, 1963; Law Commission, 1995, pp. 245–282). Issues such as the enforceability of the law, its efficacy as a deterrent, and its cultural meanings are crucial to consider, and may have specific implications in the context of debates over the regulation of sexuality. Perspectives from criminology, as well as law, are relevant.

Specific questions arise concerning how age of consent laws are formulated to address adults, and to address children. Children below the age of criminal responsibility cannot be prosecuted, and even in relation to children above this age prohibitions upon much sexual activity are selectively enforced. Some states do not distinguish between laws applying to sexual behaviour between children and sexual behaviour between children and adults. Others distinguish between sexual acts according to the relative ages of participants with 'age-span' provisions (Cocca, 2004). The UK recently introduced different offences to apply to those over 18 and under 18 (see Chapter 8). A focus upon the issue of sex between children reveals the historical inadequacy of age of consent laws in many states in this respect.

The issues raised in this section concerning the rationale for age of consent laws are discussed throughout the book, and engaged with again in the final chapter. In order to conceptualise more clearly the relationships between sexuality, consent and law, the final section of this chapter now turns to the concept of citizenship and its relation to sexuality, and considers how age of consent laws can be conceptualised in this light.

Citizenship

The term 'citizenship' has been used to describe a wide variety of forms of political and social community, making any generalised definition problematic. However, it commonly refers to the elements in social life which determine the rights and obligations of persons, their power and social status in relation to particular communities. As T.H. Marshall argued in his classic essay *Citizenship and Social Class*:

> Citizenship is a status bestowed on those who are full members of a community. All who possess the status are equal with respect to the rights and duties with which the status is endowed. (Marshall, 1950, p. 28)

Marshall described citizenship as being differentiated between civil, political and social elements (Marshall, 1950, pp. 10–11). The 'civil' element comprised the rights necessary to individual freedom including civil rights to free speech, freedom of thought and faith, personal liberty, the right to conclude valid contracts and own property, and the right to justice. Political citizenship entailed 'the right to participate in the exercise of political power', including the democratic right to vote, to free political association and to participate in central government, institutionalised as the multi-party parliamentary political system. Social citizenship entailed the right to 'a modicum of economic welfare' compatible with full community membership, and 'the right to share to the full in the social heritage and to live the life of a civilised being according to the standards prevailing in the society' (Marshall, 1950, pp. 10–11). Marshall argued, assuming a certain model of liberal capitalism, that modern societies would progressively expand the scope of citizenship to include new social groups, granting first civil, then political and social forms of citizenship (Marshall, 1950). Though Marshall in practice emphasised 'rights', his formal definition of citizenship also encompassed responsibilities, and hence implicitly included a whole group of social practices relevant to each sphere.

More recently Bryan Turner has proposed a critical reworking of Marshall's conceptual schema and helpfully redefined citizenship:

> Citizenship may be defined as that set of practices (juridical, political, economic and cultural) which define a person as a competent member of society, and which as a consequence shape the flow of resources to persons and social groups. (Turner, 1993, p. 2)

According to Turner, a general theory of citizenship is concerned with four elements: the content of social rights and obligations; the form or type (active or passive) of such obligations and rights; the social forces that produce such practices; and the various social arrangements whereby such benefits are distributed to different sectors of society (Turner, 1993, p. 3). This redefinition emphasises that citizenship must be defined as a set of social *practices*, and is as much a matter of cultural and economic power as it is about formal rights (Turner, 1997a, pp. 6, 12; cf. Turner, 1990, 1993, 1997b; Turner and Hamilton, 1994). Turner argues that the forms of citizenship operating in any society correspond to the distribution of rights to economic, political and cultural resources, as well as forms of cultural identity, inclusion and exclusion. He rightly criticises the teleological character of Marshall's model of citizenship, and emphasises the need to view expansions of citizenship as the outcome of active contestation (Turner, 1990, p. 199). However, Turner slips between using the term to describe a single perspective or plural perspectives, and proposes its use 'to discuss all issues of social membership' while simultaneously viewing it as distinctively 'modern' and 'the dominant paradigm of Western social democracies' (Turner, 1993, pp. vii–xi, 1997a, pp. 9–10; cf. Yuval-Davis, 1997). His use of the concept, like Marshall's, already suggests particular understandings of a highly contested term with diverse histories (cf. Clarke, 1994).

'Citizenship' has very particular meanings and associations in specific social or theoretical contexts. In the UK, for example, the term is invoked in the political discourse of New Labour. It also has particular associations within academic disciplines: some political theorists using the concept, as Bryan Turner and John Solomos have commented, continue to emphasise the significance of formal political structures and rights rather than wider social forces in constituting citizenship (Turner, 1995; Solomos, 1996).

Such particular associations have made some theorists appear wary of the concept of citizenship *per se* (Pateman, 1988). But a broad understanding of citizenship as a concept with multiple theoretical histories and contested public meanings implies that such arguments can be read as critiques of particular theories of citizenship, rather than the utility of the concept as such. Hence many feminists have argued for rethinking rather than abandoning the term, recognising that its open character is precisely what makes it useful as an idea around which social theorists can muster for dialogue (Young, 1990; Mouffe, 1993; Walby, 1994; Squires, 1999). Most social and political theories can be conceived as implicitly theories of citizenship, to the extent that they provide particular perspectives on what constitutes community membership, social inclusion and exclusion, rights and obligations.

A variety of critics of Marshall have sought ways of re-conceptualising his understanding of citizenship within a less liberal progressive framework, and with a consciousness of developments such as feminism, identity politics, cultural diversification and globalization (Barbalet, 1988; Andrews, 1991; Bulmer and Rees, 1996; Werbner *et al.*, 1997; Turner, 1997a,b). Such work is almost universally critical of Marshall's teleological tendencies, his Anglo-centrism and his emphasis on formal rights, placing greater emphasis upon viewing expansions of citizenship as the outcome of active contestation (Turner, 1990, p. 199). Contemporary attempts to re-conceptualise Marshall's understanding of citizenship contest various elements of his theoretical schema: his analytical concepts (the distinction between civil, political and social elements of citizenship); his empirical claims (such as that historically, civil, political and social elements of citizenship have emerged in succession); his social theories (the broad sociological framework); and his political/ethical orientation (his belief that citizenship should expand in scope). Theorists have questioned the forms taken by citizenship, and the question of whether, or for whom, citizenship has expanded. These debates have pointed to several general conclusions.

Despite defining 'rights' in a broader sense than simply legally encoded rights, Marshall's description of citizenship in practice over-emphasised formal legal rights. It is also widely accepted that Marshall's emphasis upon the economic aspects of social citizenship underestimated the significance of a citizen's cultural identity, despite the inclusion of 'social heritage' and 'duties' in Marshall's formal definition (Marshall, 1950, p. 5; Turner, 1990, p. 192). Marshall's assumption of cultural homogenisation has been disproved by the cultural diversification in contemporary societies (Marshall, 1950, pp. 75–76; cf. Smith, 1996). Contrary to Bryan Turner's insistence, citizenship cannot be conceived only in relation to nation states, since in the context of growing global interdependence, citizenship is the complex product of a range of local, regional, national, international and global institutions and social forces, including human rights (Held, 1995; Meehan, 1995; Delanty, 2000; cf. Turner, 1993, pp. 1–2, 162–187, 1997a, p. 9).

The public, civic and political forms of citizenship which form the core of Marshall's project have been the focus of sustained debates between liberals and radicals, contesting their effectiveness as means to contesting and transforming patterns of social inequality. Liberals emphasise that formal civil and political citizenship rights historically emerged to cope with emerging social diversity and rapid social change, providing a safety valve for the new dilemmas produced in modern societies (Kymlicka, 1990). But though Marshall exaggerated the extent to which political citizenship operates to counterbalance the structures which generate social inequalities, radical criticism of these exclusionary effects has in recent years been ameliorated by an expanded and renewed conception of 'the political' (Mouffe, 1993), and more realistic recognition of the benefits of liberal democratic institutions in the context of social diversity (Squires, 1999).

Many critics concerned with gender have argued that Marshall's understanding of citizenship applied only to particular 'public' spheres of life, the 'political sphere' and/or 'civil society', but must be re-conceptualised in relation to the 'private sphere' and the family (Pateman, 1988; Okin, 1989; Turner, 1990, pp. 204–206, 209, 211; Walby, 1994, pp. 379, 383). Understandings of citizenship must be reworked in accordance with the particular concerns of feminism, the gay, lesbian and bisexual movement, and other movements for sexual liberation (for example: Pascall, 1986, pp. 8–9; Pateman, 1988; Evans, 1993; Walby, 1994; Plummer, 1995; Waites, 1996; Werbner *et al.*, 1997; Lister, 1997a; Richardson, 1998; Weeks, 1998b). These issues have been addressed in recent debates over sexuality and citizenship.

Sexual citizenship

Theorists of sexuality have utilised and contested T.H. Marshall's understanding of citizenship by coining the terms 'sexual citizenship' (Evans, 1993; Weeks, 1998b) and 'intimate citizenship' (Plummer, 1995). While the terms address related issues, each carries specific connotations, and suggests different forms of citizenship operating historically and in contemporary social life (Waites, 1996). David Evans originally employed the term 'sexual citizenship' to describe the limited forms of citizenship granted to marginalised sexual groups (Evans, 1993). Evans did not regard 'sexual citizenship' as a new sphere in Marshall's schema, but rather as a description of elements of citizenship relevant to sexuality in all areas of social life, including civil, political and social forms of citizenship. Ken Plummer subsequently proposed the idea of 'intimate citizenship' to suggest both a fourth sphere in T.H. Marshall's schema, and a description of 'a new set of claims around the body, the relationship and sexuality' (Plummer, 1995, pp. 150–151; cf. pp. 144–166).

For Plummer, intimate citizenship is a response to the trend whereby our intimate lives are increasingly politicised; yet it also contributes to this process by proposing principles of citizenship to govern the 'intimate zone'. It responds to the increasing need for people:

> to make decisions around the control (or not) over one's body, feelings, relationships; access (or not) to representations, relationships, public spaces etc; and socially grounded choices (or not) about identities, gender experiences, erotic experiences. (Plummer, 1995, p. 151)

For Plummer, intimate citizenship describes the new kinds of stories which are being formulated to articulate experiences of greater 'equality and empowerment' and the beginnings of a 'democratisation of personhood' in late modernity (Plummer, 1995, pp. 146, 152, 177). Following Giddens, Plummer sees the world moving gradually beyond emancipatory politics into an era of 'life politics' which 'brings with it the potential for new sexual stories that harbour the potential for political change' (Plummer, 1995, p. 147; cf. Giddens, 1991, pp. 209–231, 1992). Where Evans uses the concept of citizenship to describe the containment of sexually marginal groups, Plummer's usage places greater faith in the emancipatory thrust of citizenship's expansion – onward, into the 'intimate sphere'. Plummer echoes the emancipatory optimism of T.H. Marshall, updating this outlook with reference to Giddens' account of reflexive modernisation (Giddens, 1991, 1992).

One particular conceptual contrast is clear. Plummer, unlike Evans, suggests adding 'the intimate' to Marshall's original schema of civil, political and social elements of citizenship. He describes the intimate in spatial language as a 'sphere', 'zone' or 'realm', including elements of relationships, the body, sexuality, gender and the family. Plummer thus problematically slides from the theorisation of social practices under a collective theoretical label, to language suggesting that the intimate can be located in distinct physical spaces or as a distinct social sphere. Yet Plummer's conception of 'the intimate' is effectively defined by the fact that social life within it has hitherto been regarded as outside the realm in which citizenship should apply – both in social theory and in public life. This implies that the extension of citizenship into intimate life would destroy 'the intimate' as a distinctive realm of social life. Yet the various elements collectively described as 'intimate' by Plummer are too diverse to constitute a distinct social realm, or to be collectively labelled. Many aspects of relationships, sexuality, gender and the family are not experienced as 'intimate'. Hence Evans' conceptualisation of 'sexual citizenship' as cutting across other aspects of citizenship is more helpful.

Jeffrey Weeks has more recently argued that 'the sexual citizen' is a new phenomenon (Weeks, 1998b). He frames the idea thus:

> The sexual citizen exists – or, perhaps better, wants to come into being – because of the new primacy given to sexual subjectivity in the contemporary world. [...] The would-be sexual citizen, despite obvious traceable precursors

in a complex past, is a new presence because of ever accelerating transformations of everyday life, and the social and political implications that
flow from this. [...] ... this new personage is a harbinger of a new politics
of intimacy and everyday life. (Weeks, 1998b, p. 35)

The idea of the sexual citizen therefore relates to a thesis that claims to
belonging have taken new forms in relation to sexuality in 'late modernity'
or 'post-modernity', breaching previous divisions between public and private
(Weeks, 1998b, pp. 35–36). Sexual identities and behaviours, for Weeks, have
become relevant in new ways to how community rights, responsibilities and
belonging are understood. Weeks, like Plummer, thus uses citizenship to
describe a shift towards the achievement of democratic values in sexual and
intimate life. Unlike Evans, who tends to assume a somewhat static conception of what constitutes 'full citizenship', Plummer and Weeks suggest
possibilities for exploring how conflicts over sexuality may have contributed
to transformations in the dominant meanings of citizenship. However, the
latter tend to overestimate the extent to which ideals of citizenship have
been transformed.

Debate continues over the value of the concept of sexual citizenship, and
in particular over the value of claiming inclusion in particular kinds of citizenship (Richardson, 1998, 2000a; Bell and Binnie, 2000; Stychin, 2003). The
fundamental questions raised are important: how is citizenship defined in
relation to sexuality, and by whom? An issue which is not yet much explored,
however, and which I explore in this book is the relationship of children
and young people to sexual citizenship: what kinds of rights and obligations
should they have in relation to sexuality?

More specifically, how does the issue of the age of consent relate to understandings of citizenship? In a general sense, the age of consent is clearly an
issue of citizenship, and the concept of citizenship is useful to describe many
of the ways in which laws regulating sexual behaviour have been conceptualised. Definitions of age of consent laws can be conceived as articulations
of particular degrees and forms of citizenship granted to specific social
groups (defined, for example, by gender, sexuality and age) by states – or,
increasingly, by international governmental organisations via international
human rights law (see Chapter 3). The relationship between 'age of consent'
laws and citizenship has been contested from numerous competing perspectives on the appropriate balance between young people's rights to protection
and their rights to self-determination. Perspectives on age of consent laws
are structured in relation to broader debates over citizenship, concerning
issues including the appropriate role of law in relation to collective morality;
the balance between majority preferences and minority freedoms; the
balance between the equality and liberty of individuals; the definition
of 'rights' including 'human rights' (see Chapter 3) and the scope of
'privacy' (Kymlicka, 1990, pp. 247–262; see Chapter 6); and the distribution

of power between men and women, and between groups with particular sexual identities.

Importantly, age of consent laws contribute to defining the citizenship of persons both above and below a particular legal age boundary, requiring us to consider the different relationships of children and adults to citizenship. A starting point is that, rather than making the traditional assumption that it is only adults who are citizens, children also should be considered as citizens: they are persons to whom society owes some rights, such as the right to life or to free speech – a voice in decision-making processes (James, Jenks and Prout, 1998; cf. United Nations, 1989). However, a differentiated model of citizenship is appropriate, rather than a universal model: children's citizenship may take a different form to that of adults. In relation to sexual behaviour it is argued by many that young children should have a right to protection from sexual behaviour, whereas adults should have a right to self-determination. This suggests that for age of consent laws to embody appropriate forms of citizenship may involve striking a difficult balance between the protection rights of children and the rights to self-determination of adults.

How can age of consent laws be conceptualised in relation to Marshall's schema of civil, political and social forms of citizenship? (Marshall, 1950). Should they be considered as relating to civil or social forms of citizenship? Given the historical absence of sexuality from conceptions of citizenship, and (relatedly) of human rights (Petchesky, 2000), it is tempting to adopt Plummer's approach of thinking about the intimate as the latest realm in which rights and obligations are being defined. However, civil rights and human rights need to be redefined to include sexuality at their core (Petchesky, 2000); rights relating to sexual behaviour should in general be thought of as core entitlements, together with bodily autonomy. Yet if rights to protection are seen as fundamental in constituting children's citizenship, while rights to consensual participation in sexual behaviour are seen as fundamental in relation to adult citizenship, then the move to recognise both adults and children as citizens with rights may exaggerate rather than help to mediate dilemmas over the age at which age of consent laws should be fixed.

There is no straightforward relationship between age of consent laws and citizenship. It cannot be assumed that the progressive expansion of citizenship would imply the progressive lowering of age of consent laws, since the question of children's rights to protection must be taken into account. The meaning of being legally permitted to consent to sexual behaviour in any case is relative to other forms of citizenship available, since consensual sexual behaviour only becomes possible in the context of other resources, and legal regulation is only one dimension of how citizenship is linked to cultural assumptions about appropriate forms of sexuality. Furthermore, the meaning of an absence of legal prohibition in relation to citizenship may differ in different social and legal contexts: for example, an absence of legal prohibitions upon sexual behaviour may not imply respect for that activity (see Chapter 5). Debates over citizenship thus offer no theoretical panaceas or short-cuts to resolving debates over age of consent laws.

However, reflection on the ways in which particular models of citizenship, formulated in relation to gender and sexuality, have influenced past debates over age of consent laws helps facilitate historical analysis. Furthermore, analysis of contemporary debates is aided by reflection on recent shifts: the way in which sexuality has become a more explicit part of understandings of citizenship in recent years; the way in which age of consent laws have been conceptualised in relation to other, non-sexual, dimensions of young people's citizenship expressed in law and social policy; and the emergence of children's rights discourses linked to conceptions of children as citizens. The implications of changes in language for the renegotiation of the balance between autonomy and protection are not straightforward, but they are nonetheless significant. The relationship of age of consent laws to understandings of sexual citizenship is explored throughout the book.

Conclusion

This chapter has outlined a range of analytical themes which provide a conceptual framework for study. I have discussed debates over the 'social construction' of sexual identities, gendered heterosexuality, 'queer theory', and the meanings of 'consent', 'childhood', 'youth' and 'competence'. Bringing together these themes, I outlined debates over children's understandings of sexual behaviour, discussing the contested meanings of abuse and consent, and offered some provisional comments on the role of the law in protecting children. In the final section, I examined the concept of citizenship, and identified a variety of ways in which perspectives on age of consent laws are intertwined with wider debates over the form and scope of citizenship in relation to sexuality. These themes run throughout the book, and the perspectives introduced are engaged with further in subsequent chapters – most directly in the final chapter.

One important way to develop a perspective on age of consent laws is to explore their formulation in comparative cross-national perspective. To this end, in the following chapter I survey international comparative data on age of consent laws in a variety of states worldwide.

3
Age of Consent Laws in Global Perspective

This chapter examines age of consent laws in international and comparative perspective. I begin by suggesting that 'globalization' is impacting upon worldwide debates over age of consent laws, including the ways in which comparisons between states are made, and the global utilisation of the concept 'age of consent' itself. I then proceed to examine evidence from states worldwide, surveying existing comparative research and noting patterns among states. Specific states are considered in detail to illustrate how different histories and cultural attitudes have led to contrasting forms of legal regulation. Comparisons within Europe are given particular attention, and states such as the Netherlands where the legal age for some sexual behaviour has been distinctively low are discussed. I then move on to examine the extension of national sexual offences legislation from states in the 'developed' world to apply to the behaviour of citizens travelling or living abroad (including 'sex tourists'), and the increasing role of human rights and international governmental organisations, at both regional and global levels, in defining age of consent laws.

The globalization of age of consent debates

In response to global social change, research on sexuality in the social sciences is increasingly seeking to explore international and global perspectives. Issues such as the emergence of transnational feminist movements (Eschle, 2001) and lesbian and gay social movements (Castells, 1997; Adam, Duyvendak and Krouwel, 1999), the worldwide spread of HIV/AIDS (Altman, 1998, 1999a), the growth of sex tourism (O'Connell Davidson, 1998), the invocation of human rights to contest sexual practices (Petchesky and Judd, 1998; Petchesky, 2000), and the ascendance of fundamentalist religious movements endorsing repressive attitudes towards sexuality (Bhatt, 1997) have demanded that social scientists move beyond national perspectives and 'think globally' in order to analyse contemporary conflicts over the regulation of sexual behaviour.

More specifically, an appreciation of 'globalization' processes is useful to conceptualise current debates over age of consent laws. There are a multitude of understandings of globalization circulating in contemporary politics and social science, and the concept is hotly contested. However, Held, McGrew, Goldblatt and Perraton offer a provisional definition of globalization which resonates with the understandings of many social theorists, as (briefly) 'the widening, deepening and speeding up of worldwide interconnectedness' (Held *et al.*, 1999, p. 2), or (more rigorously):

> A process (or set of processes) which embodies a transformation in the spatial organisation of social relations and transactions – assessed in terms of their extensity, intensity, velocity and impact – generating trans-continental or interregional flows and networks of activity, interaction and the exercise of power. (Held *et al.*, 1999, p. 16)

Most social scientists would now accept that globalization in a sense approximating to this is occurring in a distinctive way in the contemporary world. However, debate continues over its form, scale and effects. Theorists such as Giddens, Beck and Castells view contemporary globalization as unprecedented, associating it with other forms of social transformation including the shift towards a more uncertain world, creating qualitative changes in the forms of social life, including gender, sexualities and intimate life (Giddens, 1990, pp. 63–78, 1992, 1994, 1998, 1999, 2001; Castells, 1997; Beck, 2000). However, globalization is also closely and problematically related to colonialism and neo-colonialism, global capitalist exploitation and cultural 'westernisation'.

Dennis Altman has provided the most sustained discussion of globalization in relation to sexuality, exploring its impact in relation to AIDS, gay and lesbian identities, sex tourism, the Internet and other themes, with attention to interrelated economic, political and cultural dynamics (Altman, 1998, 1999a,b, 2001). The tendency of Altman's analysis is to emphasise the ascendance of US culture and greater global cultural homogeneity, but his view is multi-dimensional and allows for countervailing tendencies. Others are also exploring the theme of globalization in relation to sexuality (for example: Povinelli and Chauncey, 1999; Weeks, 2000, pp. 238–241). It is apparent from such research that globalization processes are shaping the regulation of sexual behaviour in different states. But globalization dynamics are also shaping the ways in which comparative analysis of age of consent laws can occur and is occurring, and it is useful to reflect on this before attempting an international survey.

Increasingly attempts are being made to compare age of consent laws between different states. There is an enormous desire for comparative data in an accessible form, particularly from various kinds of political interest group, from states reviewing their own laws and, increasingly, from international governmental organisations. But attempts to draw comparisons are riddled with difficulty, and must be approached with great caution. As in other areas of policy-making and social research, the demand for quantitative data to enable comparison risks erasing vital aspects of relevant legal and social contexts.

Age of consent laws, a concept I am using to include all laws defining a legal age for young people's participation in sexual behaviour, come in a wide variety of forms which are not reducible to a single quantitative variable of 'age'. As the discussion in the previous chapter suggested, the formulation of such laws varies both between and within states depending upon, for example, the sex and/or sexual identities of the individuals involved and the kind of sexual act at issue. Other crucial differences in law between states concern the legal implications of a lack of prohibition, such as whether consent is required, and (if so) the way in which 'consent' is defined. Furthermore, the law is only one element in determining how a society regulates young people's sexuality, and the implementation of age of consent laws varies greatly between states.

It cannot even be assumed that every state has an age of consent for sexual activity *per se*. In Iran, an Islamic republic since 1979, there is no minimum age for sexual activity *per se*, since sexual activity is only legal within heterosexual marriage under Islamic *shari'a* law (Mann and Sawyer, 2003). The legality of sexual behaviour is inextricable from marriage status. Further-more, according to Helmut Graupner, a leading legal expert on age of consent laws, some states do not have a minimum age for certain kinds of sexual activity other than vaginal sexual intercourse. For example, in some former Soviet states such as Estonia there is no fixed minimum age for sexual acts other than vaginal intercourse, although such behaviour can be prosecuted if considered a 'depraving act' (Graupner, 2000, p. 421). These examples provide an indication of the problems facing comparative analysis.

Further problems derive from the social, cultural and political contexts in which comparative research takes place. National legal frameworks regulating sex offences, formulated in a variety of languages, are increasingly being drawn into comparison in legal research, and much of this is taking place in the increasingly predominant international language, English. This can be seen in the few official reports on the topic conducted for international governmental organisations and academic texts (for example: Graupner, 2000). But it is particularly notable on internet websites which have developed in the absence of official comparative literature, sometimes compiled by political activists rather than academic researchers (for example: ageofconsent, 2004; ILGA, 2004; Myers, 2004). Manuel Castells' (1997) argument that information technologies have played a crucial role in accelerating processes of globalization in the 'information age' is highly applicable to analysis of how new knowledge and vocabularies concerning age of consent laws have spread.

One consequence of the predominance of English and the power of the internet is that the concept 'age of consent' has increasingly been employed to frame comparative evidence. In tandem with the contestation of sex laws by various transnational social movements, the concept has been used to frame a multitude of tables and discussions in research detailing laws regulating sexual behaviour in diverse states (for example: ageofconsent, 2004; ILGA, 2004). This process can be described as the 'globalization' (in the sense of 'increasingly global extension') of the concept 'age of consent' itself. The term has been in usage in the English-speaking world since at least the nineteenth century (see Chapter 4), but prior to the twentieth century at least appears to have referred primarily to law regulating male/female sexual intercourse. In the west in recent years the commonly accepted meanings of the term have tended to expand to include same-sex sexual behaviour and sexual acts including anal and oral sex. Yet the fact that the concept 'age of consent' is increasingly used in global contexts implies that it changes the representation of legal frameworks in some states. The appropriation of the term 'age of consent' to serve as a universal global referent is therefore part of a process of transformation in the meanings attributed to sex laws formulated within diverse legal frameworks.

The predominance of English also has implications, for example, for the sexual identity categories used when comparisons require a 'translation' of existing cultural and legal categories, involving changes of meaning. Where tables listing age of consent laws in different states have been compiled by lesbian and gay activists campaigning for the 'equalisation' of age of consent laws applying to same-sex behaviour relative to male/female behaviour, they have sometimes framed legal surveys using identity categories such as 'heterosexual', 'lesbian' and 'gay' which disguise the cultural and legal specificities of different states, and downplay the indeterminate relationship between sexual acts and identities (for example: Tatchell, 1992, pp. 138–139). The foregrounding of particular categories inevitably means laws are represented in a particular way. In general, existing research has been shaped by particular political agendas and unequal power relationships between cultures, and hence comparative analysis should be undertaken with a critical consciousness of this.

Recognition of the profound differences between legal systems and the different ways in which age of consent laws are formulated implies severe limitations for any commentary attempting a brief overview. In the survey that follows, I use some simplifying terminology which must be understood in the context of legal complexity in order not to be misleading. For example, where I refer to 'the basic age of consent', this refers to an age applying to specific forms of sexual behaviour including male/female sexual intercourse involving vaginal penetration with a penis, plus at least some forms of same-sex behaviour. This phrasing necessarily implies a problematic prioritisation of certain kinds of sexual act ('intercourse') over others (such as 'oral sex' or 'masturbation'). The global empirical survey in this chapter should therefore be read in the light of the detailed analysis of British law in subsequent chapters, which reveals the imprecision of general statements. My objective here is to pull out some general patterns, and examples which illustrate key themes and issues.

Age of consent laws in comparative cross-national perspective

There is no unitary 'official' source of global comparative data on age of consent laws in different states provided by a national or international governmental organisation. However, the desire of international governmental organisations and interested political movements for comparative data is leading to the development of comparative research.

By far the most extensive, detailed, systematic and recent international comparative survey of age of consent laws is that undertaken by Austrian attorney Helmut Graupner. In part responding to a desire from the European Union for comparative research evidence, Graupner has conducted a research project, *Sexuality, Youth Protection & Human Rights*, to provide a detailed empirical survey of the law in different states. This was originally published in a major two-volume study, in German: volume one comprises Graupner's analysis of the compatibility of existing sex offences laws in European states with European Human Rights law (Graupner, 1997a); while volume two comprises an international empirical survey of the criminal law in European jurisdictions, including the full text of many legal provisions, plus summaries of reports on the topic by governmental expert commissions, and the most important findings of empirical studies on the issue (in English or German) (Graupner, 1997b). A summary of the legal survey, additionally covering some non-European states, has been published in English (Graupner, 2000); another article comments upon these empirical findings (Graupner, 1999). Graupner's research is drawn upon extensively in the following survey (see also: Graupner and Bullough, forthcoming 2005).

A lack of comparative academic research has also led to a proliferation of websites providing comparative data. Information concerning age of consent laws in states worldwide is catalogued on a variety of sites, of which those operated by established non-governmental organisations are the most reliable. Notable among these, the ILGA produces a *World Legal Survey*, published on its website (www.ilga.org/), which is a steadily updated survey of laws regulating sexual behaviour (ILGA, 2004). The *Age of Consent* site (http://www. ageofconsent.com/) is unique, having been developed by one individual over several years to incorporate commentaries on states from contributor's worldwide (ageofconsent, 2004). Various gay, lesbian and bisexual websites have also, at different times, compiled regional or global tables of cross-national comparisons when relevant campaigns have been in progress.

International comparisons of age of consent laws reveal an enormous diversity of legal frameworks within which age of consent laws have been formulated. Graupner identifies three main types of legal provision regulating young people's participation in sexual behaviour (Graupner, 2000, p. 418). First, 'minimum age limits', which are the most straightforward, declaring sexual contact involving persons under a certain age as criminal. Secondly, 'seduction provisions' which relate to situations in which the legality of sexual behaviour is defined by the character of an interaction and/or the older participant's motivations, as well as by age (Graupner, 2000, pp. 433–440). Thirdly 'provisions on sexual contact in relations of authority' which involve placing additional restrictions upon sexual behaviour where there is a particular institutional power inequality: for example, between a teacher and their pupil (Graupner, 2000, pp. 440–441). Most states employ more than simply minimum age limits.

Considerable variations are apparent between states where age of consent laws have been extremely low and other states where age of consent laws are extremely restrictive. States also vary greatly in how they regulate the behaviour of men and women involved in male/female sexual behaviour, and in their approach to same-sex behaviour, which is entirely illegal in some. Graupner's global survey, which included every state in Europe plus 18 others, found no state with a basic minimum age set at less than 12, an age which applies in some circumstances, for example in Malta (Graupner, 2000, p. 416). In general where the basic minimum age is low there are usually further provisions in law restricting the circumstances in which sexual activity is acceptable – for example, with reference to the age difference between the individuals involved. The highest basic age of consent identified in Graupner's global survey was 20 in Chile, applying irrespective of gender (Graupner, 2000, p. 444).

Patterns of regulation around the world tend to relate to colonial histories. Graupner notes that countries with a French or Spanish colonial inheritance tend to have lower minimum ages, reflecting the impact of an emphasis upon individual liberty in their legal frameworks historically (Graupner, 2000, p. 441). By contrast, English law in relation to sexuality has a different legacy. This is usefully illustrated with reference to the example of India, where competing conceptions of national and cultural identity shaped age of consent laws under the British Empire. Judith Whitehead has analysed debates surrounding an increase in the age of consent for girls in India from 10 to 12 in 1891, a move which emerged after pressure from social reformers (Whitehead, 1996). According to the *Bombay Guardian* the proposal inspired demonstrations which reached 200,000 at Kali Ghat in West Bengal, illustrating that controversy over age of consent laws is far from a new phenomenon (Whitehead, 1996, p. 29). Debates over the law were heavily structured by relationships to colonialism, with opposition to the amendment associated with Indian nationalist opposition to colonial intervention in the domestic sphere, regarded as 'the last remaining abode of Hindu traditions' and an idealised conception of Indian motherhood (Whitehead, 1996, pp. 29–30). British approaches to the law in India, by contrast, were heavily informed by debates over the law in the UK and the rise of social purity movements (see Chapter 4). After decolonisation following the Second World War, much of the framework of criminal law inherited by India replicated English law, including sex offences. The minimum age for a female to engage in sexual intercourse with a male in India is 16, mirroring the situation in the UK (Graupner, 2000, p. 448).

The United States is an example of the fact that many states with federal systems of government have different age of consent laws within different sub-national jurisdictions (another is Australia). Legislation relating to sexual behaviour varies widely between states within the US, as is clear from the work of Carolyn E. Cocca, the most comprehensive, reliable and up-to-date research available (Cocca, 2002a,b,c, 2004; see also Graupner, 2000, pp. 448–449; Bill Myers' *Gay Rights Info* website, including a page comparing *State Age of Sexual Consent Laws* within the US: Myers, 2004).

In the US minimum ages for sexual behaviour have historically been known as 'statutory rape laws', and this concept continues to be popularly used, although in recent reforms it has been replaced in some state laws by phrases such as 'sexual abuse of a minor', 'sexual assault', 'child molestation' and so on (Cocca, 2004, p. 164). Significantly, statutory rape laws formulated in the early twentieth century only apply to unmarried persons; hence in some states marriage represents exemption from a requirement for consent (Cocca, 2004, pp. 1, 133–136). Despite recent reforms, 'almost all states allow those under their jurisdictional age of consent to marry with judicial and/or parental approval' (Cocca, 2004, p. 9).

At the most general level, during the twentieth century the US tended to have higher minimum ages relative to western Europe, reflecting a greater tendency towards the regulation of sexual behaviour. However, any such generalisation is of little significance when considered in the light of the major differences between states within the US. Ages of consent can be as low as 12 for certain kinds of sexual behaviour excluding sexual intercourse, as in Alabama and Louisiana; this, or more commonly an age of 13, tends to be in the southern states, reflecting their sexual cultures (Graupner, 2000, pp. 448–449). However, in Cocca's authoritative survey, drawn from her reading of state statutes current in 1999, the range for the basic age of consent for male/female sexual intercourse is 14–18 (Cocca, 2004, pp. 23–24; also agreed by Graupner, 2000, p. 441). According to Cocca, only one state, Hawaii, has a basic age of consent of 14, and in only three the age is 15 (Colorado, South Carolina and Virginia). In the vast majority of states, therefore, the age for male/female intercourse is 16 or above. Somewhat surprisingly the age of consent is 18 in several states including California (Cocca, 2004, pp. 107–118; for detailed contrasting case studies of California, Georgia and New Jersey, see Cocca, 2004).

Colonial America adopted the form of statutory rape laws from English law, the history of which I describe at the beginning of the next chapter.

Cocca's research reveals that the age of consent to sexual intercourse for girls was most commonly 10 in 1885, though 12 in some states (Cocca, 2004, pp. 23–24). During the final years of the nineteenth century and the early decades of the twentieth, statutory rape laws took a new, broadly uniform shape across most states, inspired by reform in the UK and parallel purity movements (Cocca, 2004, p. 14; see Chapter 4). Profoundly gendered new laws prohibited a male of any age from having sexual intercourse with a female not his wife from a given age, 16 or 18 in almost all states by 1920 (Cocca, 2004, pp. 2, 23–24). Such restrictions did not, however, apply to sex with black female slaves or to sex with non-virgins who were deemed impure. The gendered legal framework persisted until the 1970s and 1980s, when the liberal feminist National Organisation of Women campaigned successfully for the laws to become gender-neutral (for both men and women to be potentially both 'victims' and 'perpetrators': achieved in all states by 2000), for the introduction of minimum age differences between individuals in order for prosecution of statutory rape to occur (intended to decriminalise sex between teenagers: achieved in all but seven states by 1999), and for other related reforms such as abolition of the marital exemption for rape (Cocca, 2004, pp. 16–24; see also pp. 29–92; Cocca, 2002b,c). Through a methodologically rigorous quantitative analysis, Cocca demonstrates that feminist interest groups managed to influence policies on statutory rape and achieve legal change.

More recently, since 1996, statutory rape laws have been amended in ten US states, for example to allow longer sentences for male perpetrators, and enforced with renewed vigour. This occurred in a context where the federal *Personal Responsibility and Work Opportunity Reconciliation Act* 1996 created financial incentives for states to reduce births outside marriage. Pressure for greater enforcement of statutory rape laws was led by Republican conservatives (initially allied with some feminists and liberals) seeking to target males whose under-age female partners become pregnant, as part of wider political moves against young single mothers, especially young black and Hispanic mothers, perceived as 'Welfare Queens' (Cocca, 2002a, 2004, pp. 24–27, 93–128). Cocca demonstrates that while US statutory rape laws are gender-neutral, their contemporary patterns of enforcement are disproportionately against unmarried heterosexual males rather than females, and disproportionately against gay men. She shows that they are utilised to sustain problematic cultural norms and social hierarchies with respect to not only gender and sexuality but also class, 'race' and ethnicity (for discussion of particular legal cases in the US, see also Sutherland, 2001; Levine, 2002, pp. 68–89).

Finally, with respect to the US, it should be noted that relative to western Europe, the US has been characterised by high levels of regulation with respect to homosexuality. Sodomy was universally criminalised until 1961, and same-sex behaviour and/or anal sex have remained illegal in many states into the new millennium, especially in the south (Graupner, 2000, pp. 448–453).

Whereas in western Europe different ages of consent for same-sex and male/female sexual activities have been exceptional, in the US higher ages have been common for same-sex behaviour both between men and between women.

Canada also provides an example of a state in which homosexuality has been discriminated against, and in which the age of consent for anal intercourse has been higher than that for other sexual behaviour. In Canada in 1988 the age of consent for anal intercourse was lowered to 18 (Criminal Code, s. 159(2) 1988), while the age of consent for other forms of sexual expression such as vaginal and oral intercourse has been lowered to 14 (Criminal Code, s. 150.1(1)) (Greer, Barbaree and Brown, 1997, p. 170; cited in ILGA, 2004). Additionally, according to Greer *et al.*, 'consent is a defence for non-anal sexual activity between a person who is age 12 or 13 and a person who is less than two years older or who is under 16. No such defence is available for anal intercourse at these ages' (Criminal Code, s. 1501(2)). Court decisions in Canada during the 1990s held that the denial of consent as a defence in anal intercourse prosecutions involving a person between the ages of 14 and 18 represented a violation of Section 15(1) of the Canadian Charter of Rights and Freedoms, which provides that 'every individual is equal before and under the law and [is entitled to] . . . equal protection and equal benefit of the law without discrimination and, in particular without discrimination based on race, national or ethnic origin, religion, sex, age or mental or physical disability' – because it arbitrarily disadvantaged homosexuals as a 'historically disadvantaged group' (quoted from Greer, Barbaree and Brown, 1997, p. 170; Graupner, 2000, p. 451).

Turning to Australasia, the laws in Australia and New Zealand, like Canada, show a British colonial influence. In New Zealand the basic age is 16 for both male/female and same-sex behaviour (Graupner, 2000, p. 448). In Australia, with a federal system of government, the age of consent for male/female sexual intercourse is also 16 in most states, but there have been considerable differences between states (Graupner, 2000, p. 448; for a discussion of conflict in New South Wales, see Baker, 1983). Australia, like Canada, has been influenced by English law's punitive tradition of regulation in relation to male homosexuality, and consequently in Western Australia the age of consent for sex between men remained 21 into the new millennium (Roberts and Maplestone, 2001), but was equalised at 16 in 2002. By May 2003 the age had been equalised in all states except New South Wales, and moves towards equality were afoot there (NSW Gay and Lesbian Rights Lobby, 2003).

Japan has an equal basic age of consent at 13 under criminal law, though with exceptions for sex with adults. This is clearly low by international standards, but according to Masaki Inaba 'all prefectures have their own respective laws such as "Youth Protection Law" which prohibit adults from having sex with youths who are under 17 years old' (Inaba, 1998; quoted in ILGA, 2004). Nevertheless, the age of 13 appears to reflect historical attitudes towards adolescent sexuality in Japanese culture.

In some South-East Asian states which have experienced considerable sex tourism there have been increases in regulation in recent years. Thailand increased its minimum age from 13 to 15 in 1987, and to 18 in relation to prostitution in 1996. The age of consent remains 12 in the Philippines, but since 1992 has been raised to 18 in circumstances where a minor consents to gain money or remuneration. The minimum age remains 13 in South Korea, however (Graupner, 2000, pp. 441, 448). Changes in the law in Thailand and the Philippines should also be considered in the light of increasing regulation by some western states of their citizens' sexual behaviour while travelling abroad (see discussion in pp. 53–55).

In Africa, the age of consent for male/female sexual intercourse is 14 in Ghana, for example, and 16 in South Africa, but there is little coverage of Africa in existing comparative research (Graupner, 2000, p. 448). In South America the age of consent is quite low in some states, for example 14 in Brazil, though with additional offences for 'corruption of minors' up to the age of 18 (Graupner, 2000, p. 448). In Chile, however, the legal age is 20 (Graupner, 2000, p. 448). This is suggestive of the extent to which law may be out of step with sexual cultures.

Finally I will discuss the evidence in Europe, where there has been more previous comparative research than elsewhere (Horstkotte, 1984; Tatchell, 1992, pp. 101–139). Data on the law in European Union member states was assembled at the request of the European Commission in 1993 to enable comparison of the regulation of heterosexuality with homosexuality (Waaldijk, 1993, pp. 84–88). More recently minimum age limits for both male/female and same-sex sexual relations in all European states have been summarised by Helmut Graupner, whose research has a particular European focus (Graupner, 1997a,b, 1999, 2000). Graupner represents his research as a response to the European Court of Human Rights' increasing tendency to seek comparative evidence on national age of consent laws to evaluate the legitimacy of state regulations (Graupner, 2000, pp. 416–417).

Legal ages for sexual activity have historically varied widely between states in Europe, including those within the European Union. In Graupner's survey of European states (and jurisdictions within states) the lowest basic minimum age was 12 and the highest was 17 (Graupner, 2000, p. 424). Consensual sexual relations (including sexual intercourse) involving 14-year olds were found to be legal in half (51%) of the states examined; those involving 15-year olds were legal in almost three quarters (72%), and those with 16-year olds in nearly all (98%) (Graupner, 2000, pp. 416, 424). The age of 15 appears most typical within the European Union. Most states apply a higher age limit for contacts between young people and those in a position of authority such as teachers.

With respect to the relationship between heterosexuality and homosexuality, Graupner's survey found that half of all European jurisdictions, and 26 of 41 Council of Europe states, had an equal basic age for male/female and same-sex behaviour (Graupner, 2000, pp. 427, 428–433). Most of those with unequal ages or a total prohibition on homosexual behaviour were from the former Communist Eastern bloc, although there has been some subsequent liberalisation. Within the European Union the number of states with unequal ages declined steadily through the 1990s: 4 out of 15 EU states had unequal ages in 2000 (Ireland, UK, Austria and Portugal), but all of these have now equalised their laws.

To give some indicative examples from across the spectrum in Europe: in Italy the basic age, excepting that applying to prostitution, has been 14 since the repeal of fascist legislation, with an age of 13 applying where the older partner is not more than 16 (Graupner, 2000, p. 420). In Germany the age has been 14 for all since 1994, having previously been 14 in East Germany since 1989, and 18 in West Germany (West and Green, 1997, pp. 261–262; Graupner, 2000, p. 420). In France the age has been 15 for all since 1982. In Denmark, the age has been equal for all at 15 since 1976 (von Rosen, 1994, p. 131; Graupner, 2000, p. 420). In Sweden and Greece the age of consent is equal for all at 15 (Graupner, 2000, pp. 420–421). In Belgium the age of consent has been equal at 16 since 1912 (West and Green, 1997, p. 290; Graupner, 2000, p. 420). The age of consent for sexual intercourse between men and women in the UK has been higher than in most other western European states since it was raised to 16 in 1885 (see Chapter 4).

However, it is interesting to note that sexual behaviour at comparatively low ages has been, and remains, legal in western European states. During the 1990s, Spain, Malta and the Netherlands all had legal age of 12 applying in at least some limited circumstances (Tatchell, 1992; Graupner, 2000). Yet in recent years international opinion within Europe concerned with child sexual abuse and child protection, particularly within the European Union, has contributed to pressures to reform sex offences and increase the legal age for participation in sexual behaviour in these states.

For example, until 1999 Spain operated a basic age of consent of 12 for sexual acts, including those between people of the same sex, with exceptions applying in cases of deception or abuse of a position of authority below the age of 16 (Tatchell, 1992, p. 131; Lestòn, 1998). In Spain the legal age was 12 during the nineteenth century; it was increased under General Franco's public morality laws, but then lowered again to 12 when these laws were repealed in 1978 (Tatchell, 1992, p. 131). Spain enacted a new Criminal Code in 1995 which introduced extensive anti-discrimination provisions relating to sexual orientation, and abolished the offence 'Corruption of Minors' which could cover the 'corruption' of people aged below 18 in relation to homosexuality (part of Article 452 of the old Criminal Code). The new Criminal Code affirmed an age of consent of 12 (Article 181f.) and a ban on seduction by deception until 16 (Article 183 CC) (Graupner, 1996). The age of consent was subsequently increased to 13 in 1999.

However, by contrast, Portugal provides an example of a European country in which the legal age for involvement in heterosexual sexual activity has been lowered within the past decade. In 1945, Portugal set an equal age limit of 16. According to Graupner, 'The penal code of 1982 took over this equal minimum age of consent for heterosexual acts (Articles 203 and 206) and homosexual acts (Articles 206, 207)' (Graupner, 1997c). This provided the same maximum sentence of one year in cases where no 'seduction' occurred, although the penalties laid down for the 'seduction' of 14- and 15-year-old adolescents differed: for homosexual 'seduction' ('desencaminhar') the penalty was up to three years (Article 207), whereas for 'seduction' into male/female vaginal intercourse ('tiver cópula…abusando da…inexperiência ou mediante promessa séria de casamento') the penalty was up to two years (Article 203), and for 'seduction' into all other forms of heterosexual contact it was up to one year (Article 206) (Graupner, 1997c). An extensive revision of Portugal's penal code in 1995 'lowered the heterosexual age of consent to 14 (Article 172) but kept a special offence of homosexual relations with 14- and 15-year-old adolescents (Article 175: up to 2 years jail). Heterosexual relations with 14- and 15-year-old adolescents, however, are only a criminal offence if the minor is "seduced" ("abusando da sua inexperiência") [into] vaginal (not anal, oral or other) intercourse (Article 174: up to 2 years jail)' (quoted from Graupner, 1997c; see also Graupner, 2000, p. 433).

In another southern European state, Malta, the minimum age for both male/female and same-sex behaviour has for many years been set at 12, but the age of consent in relation to both male/female and same-sex behaviour is 18 for acts which 'deprave' a minor. Sexual activity involving persons aged 12–17 is only prosecuted in cases of 'abuse of parental authority or tutorship', or where a younger person files a complaint (Tatchell, 1992, p. 121; Graupner, 1998, cited in ILGA, 2003). There are also various examples of states in which sexual behaviour other than intercourse, such as oral sex, is low. For example, the age of consent is 12 in Austria for non-penetrative sexual contact with a partner not more than four years older (Graupner, 2000, p. 445).

The Netherlands, with its international reputation for social liberalism, has often been cited by liberals as an example of a state with a progressive and pragmatic attitude towards the legal regulation of sexual behaviour, associated with better sex education and sexual health among young people (Oosterhuis, 1999). In fact, however, the widespread perception that the legal age for sexual behaviour has been distinctively low is exaggerated and not entirely accurate. The basic age of consent in the Netherlands has been 16 for many decades. However, it is the case that in certain particular circumstances sexual activity involving those aged at least 12 years was exempted from prosecution in 1990. The proposal for this emerged after a government-appointed commission, the Melai Commission (1980), recommended that sexual contact with 12–16-year olds should remain illegal only if initiated by the older partner (Graupner, 2000, p. 456). Following subsequent public controversy over government proposals, a change of the law in 1990 made sex with persons aged 12–15 subject to prosecution only in cases where an interested party – the young person, their parent/legal guardian or the Child Welfare Council – filed a complaint (Schuijer, 1990, 1993; Moerings, 1997, p. 304). But it was commented by Dutch observer Jan Schuijer in the late 1990s that this 'requirement of complaint' in the law had 'meant very little in practice' in terms of changing the practical situation for young people, given the limited ability of young people to predict and negotiate the reactions of their parents (Schuijer, 1999, p. xxiv). In 2002 the Dutch parliament abolished this exemption, despite opposition from defendants of consensual adult–child relationships such as Vereniging MARTIJN, an association founded for this purpose (Vereniging MARTIJN, 2001; updated 2002). Hence the age of consent in the Netherlands is now more straightforwardly 16, although 18 for involvement in pornography and prostitution.

A useful discussion of cultural differences in attitudes towards adolescent sexuality between the Netherlands and the US has been provided by Amy T. Schalet (2000). Schalet uses interviews with parents of 16-year olds to argue that American parents view adolescent sexuality 'as a biologically driven, individually based activity' which is disruptive, whereas Dutch parents emphasise the love relationships and social responsibility of teenagers which makes their sexuality seem 'normal'. Most Dutch parents would allow their 16-year-old son or daughter to sleep with a boy friend or girlfriend at home, whereas most American parents would not. Clearly this is suggestive of the cultural background to debates over age of consent laws in both states. But it is significant that child protectionist arguments have made advances and achieved abolition of the 'requirement of complaint' even in the previously liberal Netherlands, suggesting a diminution of national cultural specificities.

A final theme deserving attention in this European survey is the regulation of same-sex sexual behaviour. Some northern European states such as the UK have histories involving particular 'punitive traditions' of legal regulation applying to same-sex behaviour. In the UK this applied only to sexual behaviour between men, which was entirely illegal until it was partially decriminalised (1967 in England, 1980 in Scotland, 1982 in Northern Ireland) with an age of consent of 21 subsequently existing until 1994. In Denmark a tradition of liberal tolerance was established earlier: sodomy was decriminalised for men aged 21 or more in 1930 (von Rosen, 1994). However, in many western European states including Spain, France, Belgium and the Netherlands, established enlightenment traditions upholding individual freedom largely prevented the law from regulating same-sex behaviour in a manner which would reflect dominant conservative social morality and the attitudes of the Christian churches (West and Green, 1997).

The partial decriminalisation of male homosexuality in England and Wales in 1967 represented evidence of liberal attitudes, and led moves towards decriminalisation in other states, such as Canada (1969), West Germany (1969) and Austria (1975) (West and Green, 1997). States such as West Germany rapidly moved to reduce the age of consent for same-sex acts from 21 to match their age of majority. By 1993 the UK was one of only 7 out of 28 Council of Europe states, and one of only 4 out of 14 European Union states, to have an unequal age; and the legal age of 21 applying to sexual behaviour between men was the highest age of consent in Europe (Tatchell, 1992; Stonewall, 1993). By 1998, among the 15 (then) member states of the European Union only the UK, Finland and Austria had an unequal age of consent for same-sex behaviour (Stonewall, 1998). Finland equalised its age in 1998 (ILGA, 2004), the UK in 2000 (Waites, 2001; see Chapter 7), and Austria equalised its age with effect from 13 August 2002 (ILGA, 2004). However, discriminatory elements in age of consent laws remained in 2003 in several Council of Europe states: Albania, Bulgaria, Greece, Ireland and Portugal – of which some are also members of the EU (according to Nico Beger, ILGA-Europe co-delegate to the Council of Europe, quoted in Platform Against Article 209, 2003).

Sex tourism and the transnational extension of sex offences

The social forces and social movements that have influenced debates over sexuality and age of consent legislation have long been transnational; in late nineteenth-century Europe, national legal frameworks were formulated in relation to the influence of transnational knowledge formations such as sexology, and transnational social purity movements prior to subsequent export around the globe through colonialism (see for example: Phillips, 1997a). Hence recent decades are not particularly distinctive for the existence of international social movements contesting the regulation of sexuality *per se*. Nevertheless, the intensity of the activity and influence of such movements is increasing, together with the more general increase in impact of international migration, especially tourism. The increased volume of sex tourism has become a particular concern for many national governments, lobbied by interest groups seeking to prevent the exploitation and abuse of children and young people.

Questions are thus raised in debates over young people's sexuality which echo those raised in debates over globalization more broadly, including those between neoliberals and anti-capitalists concerning global economic interdependence (for discussion see for example: Giddens, 1998, 2000; Held *et al.*, 1999). Should globalization be regulated because of the inequalities of power and resources between different regions of the world? Or do benefits to the developing world, relative to alternatives available in local contexts, imply that globalization should be allowed to proceed? In relation to sexuality, for example, at what age should a Thai girl prostitute be permitted to sell sex to a white western male sex tourist? Debates between protectionist and libertarian perspectives on sex are now being played out at a global level (see for example: O'Connell Davidson, 1998; Altman, 2001).

The increasing volume of sex tourism has stimulated moves to extend legal prohibitions. Age of consent laws within any given state can be conceived as being defined by three kinds of law: laws governing behaviour by citizens within national and sub-national jurisdictions (such as Northern Ireland within the UK); laws imposed by states to regulate behaviour by their own citizens while living in other states; and international law including human rights conventions to which states are signatories. Changes in regulation have thus occurred both through the extension in territorial scope of national sexual offences legislation and through the enforcement, amendment and reinterpretation of human rights conventions internationally.

Many states in the 'developed' world have responded to international sex tourism with the export of their own national sexual offences legislation. In some cases sexual offences applying to citizens within their state of origin have been expanded in territorial scope to cover the behaviour of citizens travelling abroad, making them criminally liable for sexual acts committed with foreign citizens – for example, in states where the age of consent is lower than in their country of origin. Such legal changes have been made in response to child protection campaigns inspired by media coverage of sex tourism, paedophile activity and child prostitution abroad.

The US, for example, has introduced legislation to regulate the sexual behaviour of its citizens when travelling abroad, such that they are regulated according to sexual offences law in the US, rather than solely in the country in which a US citizen is temporarily living (Graupner, 2000, p. 454). The US Federal Criminal Code was amended in 1994 by the introduction of Section 2423 'Transportation of Minors', which states in Section (b):

> (b) Travel with Intent To Engage in Sexual Act With a Juvenile – A person who travels in interstate commerce, or conspires to do so, or a United States citizen or an alien admitted for permanent residence in the United States who travels in foreign commerce, or conspires to do so, for the purpose of engaging in any sexual act (as defined in section 2246) with a person under 18 years of age that would be in violation of chapter 109A if the sexual act occurred in the special maritime and territorial jurisdiction of the United States shall be fined under this title, imprisoned not more than ten years, or both.

Austria, Belgium, Finland, Germany, France and Norway have all passed legislation making their citizens liable to prosecution under their laws concerning minimum ages, even where such behaviour would be legal in the country where it occurred (Graupner, 2000, pp. 454–455). In the UK the *Sex Offenders Act* 1997 made sexual behaviour outside the UK involving persons under 16 subject to prosecution in the UK; however, unlike in the US this relates only to behaviour which is an offence both in the UK and in the country where it occurred. This reflects a national legal tradition more reluctant to legislate regarding behaviour beyond national borders. The *Sexual Offences Act* 2003 replaced this legislation, incorporating the same provisions in a broader revision of sex offences (see Section 72 'Offences outside the United Kingdom' and Section 140 'Repeals and Revocations').

International law and human rights

A highly distinctive feature of the contemporary era is the growing role of international governmental organisations and international law. Tendencies towards the transcendence of the nation state as the primary locus of governance are apparent. As David Held has argued, contemporary global interdependence has led to institutional developments which imply that democracy and citizenship can no longer be conceived in relation to the nation state alone (Held, 1995). Held describes tendencies including the development and growing influence of international law as contributing to the undermining of the previously existing international system of states (see also Held *et al.*, 1999).

These changes are significantly transforming the institutional focus for the contestation, formulation and enforcement of laws regulating sexuality (Petchesky, 2000; Altman, 2001, pp. 122–137). As Ros Petchesky discusses in her essay 'Sexual Rights: Inventing a Concept, Mapping an International Practice', rights relating to sexuality have never been explicitly encoded in international human rights conventions (Petchesky, 2000). 'Sexual Rights', as she puts it, 'is the newest kid on the block in international debates about the meanings and practices of human rights' (p. 81). Sexuality has been brought into human rights debates under the guise of privacy and reproduction.

The *Universal Declaration of Human Rights* 1948 asserts the rights of persons to a privacy and a family (Article 12 states that 'No one shall be subjected to arbitrary interference with his privacy, family, home or correspondence...'), but does not mention sex or sexuality. Only during the 1990s did a language of sexuality emerge in various Human Rights declarations. The *Programme of Action* which emerged from the International Conference on Population and Development (ICPD) in Cairo in 1994 addressed sexuality in positive terms such as 'sexual health' rather than solely in relation to sexual violence and abuse (Petchesky, 2000). The *Platform for Action* produced by the Fourth World Women's Conference in Beijing in 1995 went further in advancing the concept of sexual rights, producing a declaration which stated:

> The human rights of women include their right to have control over and decide freely and responsibly on matters related to their sexuality, including sexual and reproductive health, free of coercion, discrimination and violence. (para. 96, quoted from Petchesky, 2000, p. 85)

Yet proponents of concepts such as 'freedom of sexual expression' or 'freedom of sexual orientation', which are potentially more expansive in scope, have not been able to achieve their inclusion in human rights declarations (for advocacy of sexual orientation as a human right, see Heinze, 1995; Wintemute, 1995; for a critique see Morgan, 2000).

The most potentially significant development in the interpretation of international human rights conventions with respect to sexuality occurred in the *Toonen* case in Australia (Stychin, 1998, pp. 145–193; Morgan, 2000, p. 211). The case was decided by the United Nations Human Rights Committee (UNHRC) with reference to the *International Covenant on Civil and Political Rights* 1976, which includes rights to privacy and equality. The right to privacy was successfully invoked against regulations prohibiting same-sex activity between males in Tasmania. The case has potential implications for discriminatory age of consent laws in other states, but the extent to which it will have a wider impact remains unclear. An appeal to the UNHRC was only possible because the Australian government, unlike the US, had legislated to give its citizens the right to pursue such a legal challenge (Altman, 2001, p. 127).

States which are signatories to the *International Covenant on Civil and Political Rights* 1976 must submit periodical reports to the UNHRC to demonstrate how they are fulfilling their obligations. In 1998 the UNHRC found Austria's age of consent laws discriminatory: 'The Committee considers that existing legislation on the minimum age of consent for sexual relations in respect of male homosexuals is discriminatory on grounds of sex and sexual orientation. It requests that the law be revised to remove such discriminatory provisions' (concluding observations of the Human Rights Committee: Austria. 19 November 98. CCPR/C/79/Add.103; quoted and cited in Krickler and Wien, 1998; see also Graupner, 2000, p. 426). According to the International Lesbian and Gay Association, 'Article 209 was struck down by a ruling of the Austrian Constitutional Court on 24 Jun 2002. The statute implementing the repeal came into effect on 13 Aug 2002' (ILGA, 2004).

The *Convention on the Rights of the Child* 1989 (entry into force 1990) also has potential implications for age of consent laws, though how this convention might be interpreted in this respect remains an open question. The various articles in the convention, depending upon their interpretation, could have a variety of effects. Article 1 states: 'For the purposes of the present Convention, a child means every human being below the age of eighteen years unless under the law applicable to the child, majority is attained earlier' (United Nations, 1989). This definition of childhood as referring to a person aged below 18, notwithstanding the Convention's allowance for states to provide their own definition, tends to encourage extended conceptions of childhood. Article 2 states that 'Parties shall respect and ensure the rights set forth in the present Convention to each child within their jurisdiction without discrimination of any kind, irrespective of the child's or his or her parent's or legal guardian's race, colour, sex, language, religion, political or other opinion, national, ethnic or social origin, property, disability, birth or other status.' This suggests the possibility of challenging legislation which is discriminatory in relation to same-sex sexual behaviour.

As in other human rights declarations sexuality is largely absent, except with respect to 'sexual abuse', and the emphasis in relation to sexuality is very much on 'protection'. Article 19 declares that 'States Parties shall take all appropriate legislative, administrative, social and educational measures to protect the child from all forms of physical or mental violence, injury or abuse, neglect or negligent treatment, maltreatment or exploitation, including sexual abuse, while in the care of parent(s), legal guardian(s) or any other person who has the care of the child'. Article 34 declares that 'States Parties undertake to protect the child from all forms of sexual exploitation and sexual abuse. For these purposes, States Parties shall in particular take all appropriate national, bilateral and multilateral measures to prevent: (a) The inducement or coercion of a child to engage in any unlawful sexual activity; (b) The exploitative use of children in prostitution or other unlawful sexual practices; (c) The exploitative use of children in pornographic performances and materials.' In practice it appears these declarations are unlikely to impact directly upon national debates over basic age of consent laws, although they may play a greater role in relation to debates over young people's involvement in prostitution and pornography.

In the European context there are particular developments at a regional level which, although indicating possibilities for other regions, remain highly distinctive to Europe. The *European Convention on Human Rights* 1950 defines particular obligations for Council of Europe states, adjudicated by the European Court of Human Rights (an institution distinct from the European Union). The Convention enforces rights including 'respect for private life' (Article 8) and freedom from discrimination with respect to other articles in the Convention (Article 14). These have been invoked to achieve reductions in state prohibitions and increasing scope for individual autonomy with respect to various forms of sexual behaviour (Helfer, 1990; Reekie, 1997a). The European Court of Human Rights has repeatedly interpreted Article 8 of the Convention, in conjunction with Article 14, to imply that age of consent laws must be the same for same-sex sexual activity as for sex between men and women (Helfer, 1990; Graupner, 2000, pp. 425–426).

This was demonstrated for example in relation to the UK by a ruling in 1997, when the Convention was employed to contest the age of consent regulating sex between men. Article 8 of the Convention was successfully invoked in the case of Euan Sutherland to achieve a ruling that the UK's law was discriminatory by the European Commission of Human Rights – a screening body for cases to the European Court of Human Rights, subsequently abolished in 1999 (European Commission, 1997). More recently an advisory ruling against Austria by the European Court itself on 9 January 2003 condemned the former Article 209 of Austria's criminal code (already abolished in June 2002) which had defined the age of consent for sex between males as 18, in contrast to the age of 14 applying to other sexual activity (Platform against Article 209, 2003). This ruling, in which Article 14's right to non-discrimination was invoked as well as Article 8's right to respect for private life, demonstrated unequivocally that unequal age of consent laws are a violation of the Convention.

The European Union has also provided opportunities to press for lesbian, gay and bisexual equality, which have been significant in debates over age of consent laws (Tatchell, 1992). The European Parliament repeatedly voted to pass motions advocating equal age of consent laws for same-sex behaviour from the 1980s, although the Parliament does not have legislative powers to enact such change (Morgan, 2000, p. 210). In the early 1990s the European Commission published a report, *Homosexuality: A European Community Issue*, which surveyed legislation in member states and drew attention to discriminatory sex offences (Waaldijk and Clapham, 1993). More recently Article 13 of the *Treaty of Amsterdam* 1997 amended Article 6 of the *Treaty Establishing the European Community*, enabling the European Council to combat discrimination based on grounds including age and sexual orientation (ILGA-Europe, 1999), though the extent to which these provisions will be utilised remains uncertain.

According to Helmut Graupner, recent European Union policy documents from the Council of Ministers and the European Parliament declare 'sexual exploitation of children' a high priority area for cooperation, and call for some harmonisation of the domestic criminal laws (Graupner, 2003). Graupner himself has developed an analysis arguing that 'General principles found in the case law of the European Court on Human Rights suggest that the European Convention on Human Rights should be interpreted as providing comprehensive protection of the right of children and adolescents to sexual self-determination, namely both the right to effective protection from (unwanted) sex and abuse on the one hand and the right to (wanted) sexual experience on the other' (Graupner, 2003).

However, even in Europe, challenges to age of consent laws invoking international comparative evidence and human rights principles have only been successful when invoking the principle of equality between male/ female and same-sex sexual activities. There is little to suggest basic minimum ages in particular states will be challenged through international law except in this respect. Nevertheless, even these interventions can result in complex reconfigurations of existing sex offences; since it is not always clear what 'equality' entails when, for example, the law regulating male/female intercourse is framed in a particular gendered way to make only males criminally liable. Complex reconfigurations of a state's sex offences laws regulating both male/female and same-sex behaviour may be required, as occurred in the UK via the *Sexual Offences (Amendment) Act* 2000 and *Sexual Offences Act* 2003 (see Chapters 7 and 8). Legal challenges which invoke human rights in seeking to change sex offences regulating same-sex behaviour can thus have much broader implications for the form of age of consent laws.

Conclusion

This chapter has examined age of consent laws in comparative cross-national perspective and in the context of globalization. The research presented suggests that laws regulating young people's sexual behaviour are increasingly being disputed by transnational social movements, and that we are witnessing a globalization of age of consent debates. The comparative analysis of age of consent laws reveals a wide range of differences between age of consent laws in different states, not simply in the age specified but also with respect to a variety of features of the way in which laws have been formulated. Examination of the transnational extension of sex offences applying to citizens of some states, and of developing international human rights law, also shows changes in the locus and scope of legal regulation.

The remainder of the book focusses specifically upon the development of age of consent laws in one state, the UK. The chapters which follow provide a historical analysis of changing debates over age of consent laws in the UK, beginning in Chapter 4 with an outline of the origins of age of consent laws in the thirteenth century, and then commencing detailed analysis in the late nineteenth century. The analysis of the UK can be seen as a 'case study' which demonstrates the irreducible specificity of law and culture in particular national contexts, but which nevertheless illuminates a variety of conceptual themes and issues applicable to thinking about age of consent laws in states worldwide. I return to reflect on global comparisons and general conceptual issues in the final chapter.

4
Heterosexuality and the Age of Consent

This chapter begins my study of the development of age of consent laws in the UK. It first describes the origins of age of consent laws in English law from the thirteenth century, and then focusses on debates surrounding changes in the legal regulation of sexuality in the late nineteenth century, particularly those enacted by the *Criminal Law Amendment Act* 1885. I begin by outlining the historical development of the law in relation to childhood and sexual behaviour prior to and during the nineteenth century, and indicate how the consenting subject of legal discourse can be conceptualised with reference to existing legal scholarship. The chapter then focusses on the late nineteenth century, drawing upon parliamentary debates to explore the contestation of an increase in the age of consent for a female to engage in sexual intercourse from 13 to 16, and hence analysing the gendered basis upon which contemporary age of consent law was conceived within a heterosexual framework. The chapter also briefly discusses the regulation of male homo-sexuality through the new offence of 'gross indecency'. It thus examines the social attitudes and forms of citizenship structuring age of consent legislation in a period which profoundly shaped the regulation of sexuality in the UK throughout the twentieth century.

The origins of law on sex and childhood in the UK

It is appropriate to begin with an introduction to the historical emergence of age of consent laws, but this needs to be conceptualised in the context of broader shifts in the law (differing between Scottish and English law).[1] Criminal law and its sub-field known as 'offences against the person' from the nine-teenth century are the areas of law that regulate sexual behaviour (Stone, 1999), and other areas of the law concerning children are also relevant to contextualise children's legal status. This section sketches relevant areas of the law as they had developed by the late nineteenth century.

A useful place to begin is with the general legal status of childhood. Historically there was no certain distinction between the treatment of adults and that of children in the law. However, in common law the rebuttal presumption of *doli incapax* involved the presumption that a child under 14 was 'not capable of crime' in the absence of clear and positive evidence from the prosecution that a child understood the wrongfulness of an action (*doli incapax* was abolished by the *Crime and Disorder Act* 1998, s. 34; Card and Ward, 1998, pp. 295–297; Bandalli, 2000). From the seventeenth century an age of criminal responsibility of 7 emerged in English law which entailed a conclusive presumption that no child under the age of 7 could be guilty of any offence (Bandalli, 2000, p. 83). In 1933 the *Children and Young Persons Act* (s. 50) raised the age of criminal responsibility to 8; it also defined a 'child' as a person aged below 14 years, and a 'young person' as aged 14–17, and these measures were repeated in Scotland by the *Children and Young Persons (Scotland) Act* 1937. In England, Wales and Northern Ireland the age of criminal responsibility was later raised to 10 by the *Children and Young Persons Act* 1963 (s. 16.1), but remained unchanged at 8 in Scotland (Card and Ward, 1998, pp. 295–298; Bandalli, 2000, pp. 82–83).

Children in the past were regarded, in legal terms, as the property of their parents rather than as having individual entitlements to protection or rights. Their legal status was thus largely defined by family law (on which see Cretney, Masson and Bailey-Harris, 2002). Child law seeking to challenge this developed during the nineteenth century in a highly incoherent fashion in different areas of law. Legal restrictions upon child labour, for example, began to emerge, such as the *Factories Act* 1833 which prohibited employment in factories for children under the age of 9. There has historically been remarkably little consistency between laws regulating the age at which various acts become legal for young people (for an excellent chronological survey see Bell and Jones, 2000, 2004). The law regulating young people's involvement in sexual activity therefore developed largely independently of law regulating their other activities, tending to be governed by specific attitudes towards gender and sexuality.

Offences against the person regulating sexual behaviour became referred to as sexual offences in the twentieth century. However, it is noteworthy that not all law regulating sexual behaviour is clearly designated within sexual offences statutes, since consensual sado-masochism has recently been regulated through interpretation of other offences (see Chapter 7). Sexual offences is a field which has only become a major area of interest in the study of law in recent decades, outlined in a variety of academic commentaries (Honoré, 1978; Edwards, 1981; Crane, 1982; Weeks, 1989; Smart, 1995; Moran, 1996; West and Wöelke, 1997; Stychin and Herman, 2000; Stychin, 2003).

Fundamental to understanding the historical development of the regulation of sexual behaviour, and the history of age of consent laws, is an appreciation of the historical absence of any presumption of a right to sexual consent in English law. Laws defining a minimum age for sexual activity did not come into existence in a context where all non-consensual sexual activity was illegal or socially unacceptable. Rather, age of consent sex laws were fundamentally patriarchal in their conception, embodying male power and control over women and children, embedded in patriarchal heterosexuality understood as a system of social and legal property relationships and sexual relationships.

This is apparent from consideration of the historical limits of legal prohibitions against non-consensual behaviour. Legislation regulating non-consensual sexual acts in England, Wales and Ireland was consolidated by the *Offences Against the Person Act* 1861 which prohibited the offences of 'rape' (s. 48), 'indecent assault on a woman' (s. 52) and 'indecent assault on a male' (s. 62); all of these tended to be interpreted as being possible only for a man to commit during the nineteenth century (Edwards, 1981, pp. 40–45). A distinct framework applied in Scotland, also criminalising 'rape', but with the offence of 'shameless indecency' governing non-penetrative acts (as defined in Baron Hume's *Commentaries on the Laws of Scotland Respecting Crimes*: Dempsey, 1998; Chalmers, 2003). However, such laws did not encompass the behaviour between a husband and wife, since marriage was assumed to indicate an exemption from any requirement for consent in sexual activity. Prior to the twentieth century the law assumed a woman was the property of her father until marriage, and then of her husband, without independent legal rights. Until a court ruling in 1954, which found a husband guilty of 'indecent assault', a married woman had no right to refuse consent to any sexual acts with her husband, and rape did not become a crime within marriage until 1991 (Honoré, 1978, p. 22; Temkin, 2002, p. 75).

Furthermore, historically the crime of rape was defined as existing only when accompanied by the use or threat of force or violence, in addition to absence of consent. Only in 1845 did case law develop such that rape could take place in the absence of the use of force, and interpretation of the law remained contested during the twentieth century, with some court rulings until the 1970s requiring a woman to physically 'resist' in addition to an absence of consent (for full discussion see Temkin, 2002, pp. 90–91). Consent was thus not fundamental or sufficient in defining the legality of sexual behaviour. To the extent that the phrase 'age of consent' has been used in ways which assume the existence of a legal requirement for consent in all sexual activity, therefore, it has been misleading, and has contributed to rendering women's inability to enforce consent in heterosexual contexts invisible.

Prohibitions upon non-coercive sexual activity involving minimum age requirements for a female to engage in sexual intercourse emerged in the same patriarchal context, reflecting understandings of female children as the property of their father, and of female children's virginity as requiring preservation. A minimum age was first introduced for sexual intercourse in English law in the Statute of Westminster, 1275: 'The King prohibeteth that none do ravish . . . any Maiden within age.' Significantly this law was part of a single offence also outlawing rape, described in the same terms (Temkin,

2002, p. 137). 'Within age' has been assumed by recent legal scholars to refer to the age of 12, since this was the age of marital capacity at the time (Temkin, 2002, p. 137). Intercourse with an under-age female was made a capital offence in 1285 (Statute of Westminster I, 3 Edw., c. 13, 1275; Statute of Westminster II, 13 Edw., c. 34, 1285; cited in Cocca, 2004, p. 10). Minimum age legislation at such an early date was highly exceptional among European countries, in most of which a fixed minimum age did not exist until the eighteenth century (Graupner, 2000, p. 419). A law passed in 1576 subsequently stated that 'carnal knowledge' of a girl under 10 was a felony, but sexual behaviour below the age of 12 also remained prohibited (18 Eliz., c. 7 ss. 4, 1576; Temkin, 2002, p. 137).

Legislation in 1828 confirmed 'carnal knowledge' of a girl under 10 as a crime punishable by death, and with a girl under 12 as a misdemeanour punishable by imprisonment, though penalties were reduced in 1841 and 1861 (Temkin, 2002, p. 137). This legal age of 12 was restated by the *Offences Against the Person Act* 1861, which enacted a major re-codification of the law applying in England, Wales and Ireland. Separate offences applied to 'Carnally knowing a Girl under Ten Years of Age' (s. 50) (maximum sentence: penal servitude for life or two-years imprisonment with or without hard labour); and 'Carnally knowing a Girl between the Ages of Ten and Twelve' (s. 51), defined as follows: 'Whoever shall unlawfully and carnally know and abuse any Girl being above the Age of Ten Years and under the Age of Twelve Years shall be guilty of a misdemeanour' (maximum sentence: three years penal servitude or two years imprisonment with or without hard labour). The age of 12 was also stated for another offence of 'indecent assault on a female': 'Whoever shall be convicted of any indecent assault upon any Female, or of any Attempt to have carnal Knowledge of any Girl under Twelve Years of Age, shall be liable at the Discretion of the Court to be imprisoned for any Term not exceeding Two Years, with or without Hard Labour' (s. 52). This held the potential to encompass acts other than sexual intercourse, such as masturbation of another person, oral sex or penetration with objects; however, 'indecent assault' was conceived and interpreted as a public order offence, restricting its scope of application. 'Indecency' tended to be defined as applying only to public rather than private behaviour; and 'assault' was interpreted as restricting the offence to behaviour involving the use of force.

The age 12 also remained the legal age for marriage throughout the nineteenth century, until it was raised to 16 by the *Age of Marriage Act* 1929. However, as the nineteenth century progressed, attitudes towards the state's role in regulating sexual behaviour began to change. The minimum age for a female to have sexual intercourse was raised to 13 in England, Wales and Ireland by the *Offences Against the Person Act* 1875 (s. 4), and this act also raised the maximum sentence for intercourse with a girl under 12 to penal servitude for life (s. 3); although the age for intercourse was not raised to

13 in Scotland (s. 6). The subsequent *Criminal Law Amendment Act* 1880, applying only in England and Wales, stated in its sole substantive clause 2 that:

> It shall be no defence to a charge or indictment for an indecent assault on a young person under the age of thirteen to prove that he or she consented to the act of indecency.

This removal of 'consent' as a defence to the offences of 'indecent assault' on a male or on a female under 13 extended the scope of regulation.

In relation to sexual intercourse, understood as vaginal penetration with a penis, a fundamentally different situation applied to males and females. Due to the overwhelming impact of prevailing understandings of masculinity, boys were not regarded as requiring legal protection, so no minimum age for boys to engage in intercourse existed in law. From the early nineteenth century, however, boys under 14 were legally presumed to be incapable of sexual acts involving penetration with the penis, and hence incapable of offences such as 'unlawful sexual intercourse', 'rape' and 'buggery' (this presumption was abolished by the *Sexual Offences Act* 1993); although boys of any age could be charged with 'indecent assault'. But with respect to over-14s the law applied its prohibitions upon men engaging in sexual acts without making distinctions concerning criminal liability or the seriousness of an offence according to the age of male participants. It is apparent that the law tended to develop without clear or consistent distinctions between children and adults, with the consequence that sexual behaviour between older children was not regulated in a systematically differently way from sex between children and adults.

This outline of the development of the law regulating heterosexual sexual behaviour, however, needs to be understood in the context of a broader understanding of the law regulating sexual behaviour regarded as deviant, and of how the legal relevance of consent was defined for different groups. No general requirement for 'consent' existed in sex offences law, only a series of prohibitions against specific forms of sexual activity; and even offences covering non-consensual acts, such as rape, applied only outside marriage. Certain kinds of sexual activity involving particular kinds of person were prohibited irrespective of 'consent'; and even where consent became a criterion of legality, recognition of competence to give consent, and the existence of consent itself, was defined by legal processes according to different criteria in different contexts.

Same-sex sexual activity was subject to particular approaches to regulation. Sexual activity between males was subject to a particular punitive tradition, in which buggery (sodomy in Scotland) was outlawed, and during the nineteenth century 'attempted buggery' was employed to prohibit a range of behaviour (Moran, 1996; Cocks, 1998; Dempsey, 1998). In contrast, however, legislation regulating consensual sexual acts between women was largely absent from UK law prior to the twentieth century, reflecting a male view of sexual activity between females as unthreatening in a context where women were overwhelmingly subject to patriarchal control (Edwards, 1981; Oram and Turnbull, 2001; Waites, 2002a; see discussion later in this chapter).

Prohibitions against sexual activity also applied on grounds of mental illness, with some individuals excluded after psychiatric intervention via institutionalisation. However, it was not until the law was reformed in the early twentieth century by the *Mental Deficiency Act* 1913 that various forms of sexual activity with those diagnosed as mentally ill became prohibited. The *Sexual Offences Act* 1956, which re-codified these earlier laws, prohibited any form of sexual contact with males or females categorised as 'defective' (ss. 7–9, 14, 15, 45) (for relevant discussion of competence, consent and the legal regulation of sexual behaviour, see McCarthy and Thompson, 2004).

But while blanket exclusions from legal sexual activity applied to some types of person and behaviour, even where consent was deemed relevant, and individuals were regarded as competent to give consent, the conditions necessary for an individual to be legally recognised to have given their 'consent' varied greatly between areas of the law. Within the law regulating sexual behaviour, as in other areas of criminal law, separate 'regimes for consent' operated with respect to different sexual acts (Law Commission, 1995, p. 3). There was no single positively defined standard of consent. And even where consent was one condition of legality, it was in some instances not sufficient. For example, consent was not a straightforward defence against assault; the circumstances in which it applied were circumscribed in relation to different offences.

Critical legal theorists have suggested that 'the woman of legal discourse' and 'the homosexual of law' represent complex, contradictory, gendered and sexualised 'subject-positions' located within legal institutions and processes (Smart, 1992a, 1995; Moran, 1995, 1996). Similarly, as existing legal scholarship on gender, sexuality and consent implies (see also Jamieson, 1996; Lacey, 1997), 'the consenting sexual subject of law' can be conceived as a subject-position made available by legal discourses to particular kinds of persons in particular circumstances; and the historical development of 'age of consent' laws can be approached in this light (cf. Moran, 1996, pp. 191–196, 1997). Legal processes define who is recognised as giving consent in a particular instance with reference to legal statutes, together with sources of 'professional' or 'scientific' expertise, and sometimes also to popular common sense. In certain instances the law operates to define 'consent' as present or absent in ways which circumvent the understandings and experiences of participants in sexual behaviour (Lacey and Wells, 1998, pp. 385–390). Legal statutes, terminology and institutional processes are value-laden, and play a role in defining and situating the persons, actions and interpretative contexts on which they are brought to bear. The emotional and intellectual character of participants, their knowledge, identity and purposes, biological and mental health, become part of a definitional framework which determines whether an act of 'consent' is legally recognised to exist.

One profound implication of this approach for analysing the development of age of consent legislation within a heteronormative legal framework is that it reveals the extent to which women's claims concerning the absence of their consent in sexual activity with men have historically been rejected during legal processes. Patriarchal legal institutions have defined the presence or absence of a woman's consent with reference to a range of criteria other than a woman's own account, notably women's sexual biographies, which have been used to stigmatise and discredit. Hence even outside marriage where the crime of rape could historically be charged, the law's interpretation by a male-dominated judiciary meant that the criteria used to define consent systematically undermined the enforcement of consent as a principle (Temkin, 2002).

Furthermore, prevailing conceptions of male and female subjectivity have interacted with central categories in legal discourse, with problematic effects. Traditional legal theory in English criminal law has presented the law as embodying 'general principles of criminal liability', including two main elements: 'actus reus', the 'external'/'conduct' element; and 'mens rea', the 'mental'/'internal' element (Lacey and Wells, 1998, p. 32). Criminal liability, according to this presentation, generally consists in a person performing or causing the 'actus reus' of an offence with the requisite 'mens rea' in the absence of any relevant defence; that is, doing something prohibited while also having the required mental competence. The ways in which 'actus rea' and 'mens rea' have been defined in relation to each other has worked in particular ways in the definition of sexual offences, with particular negative implications for legal recognition of women's capacity to consent (Temkin, 2002). The requirement for 'mens rea' has tended to assume a legal subject who is a rational agent with capacities for cognition, self-control and agency (Lacey and Wells, 1998, p. 32), the interpretation of which has resulted in gendered effects such as women's claims to know their own minds when refusing consent in sexual encounters being discredited in rape trials (see Reynolds, 2002/2003). Full exploration of these issues is beyond the scope of this book, but an awareness of them is important to contextualise the account of changes in the broad contours of the law, and of political debates over age of consent law, that follow.

To summarise, the criminal law as it developed over many centuries, and as it became consolidated in the nineteenth century, addressed sexual behaviour within a framework founded upon patriarchal assumptions about the legitimacy of male authority over women and children within the family. This heteronormative framework extended to the regulation of gender relations in society as a whole, with respect to property, marriage, and civil and political rights as these emerged.

With respect to sexual behaviour, the law assumed the legitimacy of all sexual behaviour within marriage irrespective of consent, while regulating some other sexual activity outside marriage via a series of prohibitions (rape, unlawful sexual intercourse, buggery, etc.). Consent was not a general requirement for legal sexual behaviour, nor consistently defined in offences regulating sex. The development of 'age of consent' laws, described in this and subsequent chapters, emerged from this context.

Having outlined the historical development of the law relating to childhood, sexuality and consent until the nineteenth century, I will now turn to a more detailed social and political analysis of developments in the late nineteenth century which led to an increase in the age of consent.

Social purity and the age of consent in the late nineteenth century

The state's conservative ethos during much of the nineteenth century implied a view of sexual behaviour as a matter largely beyond the appropriate realm of state intervention. Early Victorian political ideologies, both conservative and liberal, preserved a 'private' sphere for men as heads of households and autonomous actors in civil society (Kymlicka, 1990, pp. 247–262). In practice this preserved the power of men to ensure sexual access to women, both within families where women and children were regarded as their property, and in their employment of prostitutes (for discussion, see Mort, 1987, pp. 11–99; Weeks, 1989, pp. 19–95).

During the late nineteenth century, however, Victorian sexual moralism – a product not only of Christian beliefs but also of utilitarianism and secularist science (Mason, 1994) – increasingly favoured state regulation of sexuality outside the family. Feminist arguments contributed to this shift, whereby male behaviour became the subject of greater public scrutiny, particularly in relation to prostitution (DuBois and Gordon, 1984). The social purity movement, in which middle-class feminists allied with male moralist campaigners, emerged to assert collective morality and regulate sexual activity, increasingly using the criminal law to contain sexual behaviour within the 'private' realm of the patriarchal family, central in the emergent bourgeois imaginary (Mort, 1987, pp. 103–150). Emergent moral and sexological discourses of sexuality viewed non-procreative sex as acceptable within a heterosexual marital context, but condemned illicit practices such as prostitution and homosexuality (Walkowitz, 1992, pp. 136, 207–208). The social purity movement had evolved from earlier campaigns against repressive forms of state regulation of prostitution through the *Contagious Diseases Acts*, but moved steadily towards favouring repressive legislation during the 1880s (Walkowitz, 1980). Purity movements simultaneously brought discussion of sexuality into the public realm, while seeking to prohibit sexual behaviour beyond the sanctified realm of the family. This process of moral regulation imposed an ethic of collective social responsibility, without a concurrent collective respect for sexual rights or freedoms.

The social purity movement emerged in response to public anxieties over shifting gender and sexual identities in the context of urbanisation and rapid social change. Fears of the transgression of class and sexual boundaries by middle-class men surfaced in the fiction of the period, such as Robert Louis Stevenson's (1886) *The Strange Case of Dr. Jekyll and Mr. Hyde*, which employed metaphors of duality, double-life and the closet (Showalter, 1992, pp. 106–107). Late nineteenth-century society was increasingly preoccupied by the advance of the 'New Woman' and changing ideas about female sexuality (Smith-Rosenberg, 1989); sexually transmitted diseases such as syphilis; and the corrupting influence of decadent homosexuals. As Elaine Showalter has argued, these social transformations generated a climate of fin de siècle 'sexual anarchy' and a search for new moral certainties (Showalter, 1992).

It was in this context that purity movements pressed for greater regulation of sexuality, including increases in the minimum age for a girl to participate in sexual intercourse. An initial increase in the legal age for sexual intercourse from 12 to 13 occurred in England, Wales and Ireland via the *Offences Against the Person Act* 1875, a brief piece of legislation that did not cover Scotland. This act stated that: 'Whoever shall unlawfully and carnally know and abuse any girl being above the age of twelve years and under the age of thirteen years, whether with or without her consent shall be guilty of a misdemeanour...' (s. 4). The maximum sentence specified was two years, also applying to the same activity with a girl under 12 prohibited by a separate offence (s. 5).

The 1885 *Criminal Law Amendment Act*, applying in English law (including Ireland at this time) and Scottish law, subsequently created the 'age of consent' for a young woman to engage in sexual intercourse with a male which remained on the statute book in England, Wales and Scotland throughout the twentieth century. Section 5 of the act (later recodified in the *Sexual Offences Act* 1956, part 1, s. 6) raised the age below which 'unlawful sexual intercourse' with a girl was prohibited to 16, although the minimum age for other sexual activity such as oral sex or masturbation remained 12:

5. Any person who –
(1) Unlawfully and carnally knows or attempts to have unlawful carnal knowledge of any girl being of or above the age of thirteen years and under the age of sixteen years; or
(2) [...]
shall be guilty of a misdemeanour, and being convicted thereof shall be liable at the discretion of the court to be imprisoned for any term not exceeding two years, with or without hard labour.

An exception was permitted by the same section in instances where the person charged had 'reasonable cause to believe that the girl was of or above the age of sixteen years', and prosecutions were not allowed more than three months after the claimed offence (s. 5); these provisions were subsequently often used by men to evade prosecution, and hence were fiercely contested in continuing purity campaigns (Jeffreys, 1985, pp. 74–76). 'Defilement of a girl under thirteen years of age' became punishable by an increased maximum sentence of life imprisonment (s. 4).

The law was thus highly gendered. A female under 16 having sexual intercourse with a male committed no offence. Yet all males deemed capable of intercourse, those aged over 14 according to common law, were liable for the offence (Honoré, 1978, p. 60). The legislation therefore encoded a 'double standard of sexual morality' (Jackson, 1982, p. 4). The legal framework assumed the 'innocence' of females below the minimum age, while creating no 'age of consent' for males. It was premised upon a view of sexual activity between men and women in which the female is passive, while the male takes the sexual initiative and must obtain her consent (McIntosh, 1997, pp. 206–207; see also Smart, 1989, pp. 51–53). As Stevi Jackson commented while this law still existed (prior to change in 2003):

> The age of consent is a gendered concept – it applies only to heterosexual women. [...] In other words, the law encodes a model of heterosexual acts as something men do and women merely consent to (or not). (Jackson, 1998, p. 75)

This captures the conceptual basis of the legal framework created in 1885.

The *Criminal Law Amendment Act* 1885 was to a considerable extent conceived through a concern with the suppression of prostitution, and needs to be understood in this context. Aside from raising the age of consent, the act also introduced a variety of other new prohibitions, including measures regulating 'procuring' (ss. 2, 3), and giving police new powers to prosecute streetwalkers and brothel-keepers (ss. 6, 12, 13). The act was passed as the result of campaigns by the social purity movement.

The immediate context was a public outcry over prostitution among young girls, generated by a four-part series of articles in the *Pall Mall Gazette*, written by its editor W.T. Stead, collectively entitled 'The Maiden Tribute of Modern Babylon' (Walkowitz, 1992, pp. 81–134). These articles, beginning on 4 July 1885, claimed to expose a hidden traffic in young virgins, being sold into 'white slavery', though subsequent historical investigation has suggested that the extent of child prostitution may have been exaggerated by social purity campaigners including Stead (Walkowitz, 1992, p. 83). The Maiden Tribute articles represented the first instance of an arresting and populist 'new journalism', often focussing upon 'sex crimes' which had previously been deemed improper subject matter for discussion in the press (Walkowitz, 1992).

Versions of the *Criminal Law Amendment Act* had previously been introduced yet defeated in parliament during 1883, 1884 and 1885, despite the recommendation of a House of Lords committee for an increase of the minimum age for sexual intercourse to 16 in 1882 (Hansard, HL 28 April 1885, col. 943). But the Maiden Tribute articles generated such public outrage that the legislation was now accepted by parliament. The strength of feeling which impelled the legislation is conveyed in a parliamentary speech by the Home Secretary, Sir R. Assheton Cross:

> This is a question which has stirred England from one end to the other. [...] there is nothing more sacred to the English people, and there is nothing which they are so determined to maintain, as the purity of their own households. The feeling has gone abroad that the purity of their households and the honour of their daughters has been and is liable to be violated, and they have made up their minds that this shall no longer be the case. (Hansord, HC 30 July 1885, col. 582)

The scope of support for an increase in the age of consent was evident in subsequent public campaigns demanding the new laws be strictly implemented, including a demonstration of 250,000 people in Hyde Park (Walkowitz, 1992, p. 82).

The context surrounding debates over the age of consent requires conceptualisation in relation to prevailing understandings of biological differences between the sexes. Male sexuality was widely assumed to be selfish, egoistic and lustful, a view condoned by prevailing medical practice which often legitimated male adultery (Bland, 1992, pp. 60–61). By contrast, despite some developments in medical opinion from the 1880s onwards, female sexuality was conceived as naturally chaste and largely passive. Female sexual pleasure was regarded as the perverse province of prostitutes, or at best only incited through a response to male agency (Bland, 1995, p. 61). Established religious and traditional views were challenged first by Darwinism and later sexology, and belief in eternal natural differences between the sexes was superseded by belief in evolved differences (Bland, 1995, p. 72). However, the structure of male/female sexual relations maintained its basic form, dominated by male agency and female passivity. This can be interpreted as an obstinately consistent heterosexual pattern (though the concept 'heterosexuality' was only invented in sexological discourse in the 1890s: Katz, 1995, pp. 19–112).

The age of consent legislation in the *Criminal Law Amendment Act* 1885 was therefore founded on a polarised view of male and female sexuality whereby the 'beast' of male lust required legal containment to preserve the virtue of a passive, innocent female sexuality (Bland, 1995). The question of an age of consent for men did not arise, due to the overwhelming assumption that women did not initiate sexual activity. Prevailing views of gender saw men as having greater intellectual capacities for reason, yet also as more potentially lustful, hence requiring the moral guidance of women to manage their desires and ensure restraint. Women were divided neatly between the virtuous virgins and mothers who embodied the ideals of social purity, and the whores who became demonised figures in popular iconography. The morality of women was reconciled with their less rational status through the common understanding that women were governed by emotions linked to their essential womanly nature (Bland, 1995, esp. pp. 48–91).

The regulation of sexuality in late Victorian society has been documented and interpreted from a variety of perspectives situated within contemporary sexual politics (Mort, 1987, p. 118; Bland, 1995, pp. xviii–xix: cf. Walkowitz, 1980, 1992; Jeffreys, 1985; Mort, 1987, pp. 103–106, 126–136; Weeks, 1989, pp. 81–95; Bland, 1992, 1995). Historians have placed different interpretations upon Purity feminism and the Maiden Tribute controversy. Where some have tended to be critical of prohibitive uses of the criminal law (Weeks, 1989, pp. 81–95), others have been more sympathetic to purity feminism and more sympathetic towards prohibitive legislation (Jeffreys, 1985). The implications of these different perspectives for interpreting the change in age of consent law are explored in the following section which examines how young women were conceptualised during debates over the regulation of sexual intercourse.

Gender, class, competence and citizenship

Age of consent legislation can be more clearly understood through investigating its relationship to dominant understandings of citizenship in the late nineteenth century, particularly the political languages which were used to argue for a change in the law. Hence it is possible to assess how the age of consent contributed to defining the citizenship of young people.

A crucial starting point is a broad appreciation of women's citizenship status in the late nineteenth century. In 1885, women in Britain lacked many aspects of civil and political citizenship as defined by T.H. Marshall (Marshall, 1950; Walby, 1990, 1994; see Chapter 3). Women did not have the vote, which was granted to property-owning and married women aged over 30 after the First World War in 1918, and to all adult women in 1928. Obtaining a divorce was extremely difficult; access to many forms of employment was prohibited; 'liberty of the person' was limited by restrictions upon contraception and the illegality of abortion; and married women did not have the right to own property or conclude valid contracts (Walby, 1990, pp. 160–171, 1994, pp. 380–381). Female children were regarded as the property of their fathers, and when married women became viewed as, in many respects, the property of their husbands, while unmarried women were socially stigmatised as failures (Lewis, 1984, p. 3). Hence women lacked most of the forms of citizenship status possessed by men.

Such formal exclusions did not, however, imply that women were universally deemed to lack competence in all matters. The confinement of bourgeois women to domestic life led to the development of theories which attributed women important forms of moral competence, and a status as the moral conscience of the family and nation, deriving largely from their maternal emotions (Banks, 1981, pp. 85–102). However, such capacities were only believed to develop in adult life. In any case, belief in such capacities did little to contradict views of women as requiring protection. Women were regarded as profoundly lacking in the forms of rational competence necessary to make decisions as autonomous subjects, as described by Olive Banks:

> Frequently, however, the view was expressed that women were weaker than men, not only physically but also mentally and morally, so that their protection from evil was absolutely essential if they were to remain pure and good. Thus their lack of reasoning power, their lack of self-control, their failure to calculate consequences, were all put forward to explain women's special need for dependence. (Banks, 1981, p. 87)

Such attitudes towards sexual difference thus contributed to an emphasis upon the necessity of paternalistic protection for girls, which was accentuated by class dynamics in the arguments of middle-class moralists and feminists:

> The desire to protect young girls entailed imposing on them a social code that stressed female adolescent dependence. This code was more in keeping with middle-class notions of girlhood than with the lived reality of the exposed and unsupervised daughters of the labouring poor who were on the streets. (Walkowitz, 1992, p. 133)

Class played an important role, since debate over the age of consent was largely structured in relation to the government of sexual behaviour among working-class prostitutes. The age of consent was an issue of less direct concern in relation to respectable middle-class girls, who were assumed to remain virgins prior to marriage, though the more distant possibility that they might 'fall' was nevertheless a source of great anxiety (Bland, 1992, p. 48).

The lack of decision-making competence attributed to working-class girls was not only generated by the projection of middle-class cultural assumptions. It was also generated through class hierachies in other ways. During the 1880s, according to Walkowitz, evolutionary and biologising theories began to replace an emphasis upon the individual moral responsibility of the poor, by accounting for poverty as a product of determining environmental and bio-logical factors. These scientific theories, together with popular journalism also dominated by middle-class men, increasingly denied the agency of the poor:

> Whereas earlier Victorian writings had emphasized pauperism as a failure of the moral will, these new writings relocated the locus of poverty, putting it within the homes and bodies of the poor themselves. (Walkowitz, 1992, p. 30)

Such theories contributed to the removal of agency from young working-class girls, whose competence was thought to be weakened by the impact of social deprivation upon their bodies. These new scientific claims weaved together with middle-class understandings of girlhood as a delicate and innocent stage of life to create a view of young working-class girls as passive innocents requiring protection.

Furthermore, the exaggerated emphasis upon girlhood innocence contributed to producing harsh responses to those who failed to assume socially acceptable roles. As Lucy Bland has argued, purity feminist responses to working-class girl prostitutes became structured by strict distinctions between the natural status of young girls as pure, innocent and barely sexual, in contrast to those who had 'fallen' and lost their modesty (Bland, 1992, p. 48). The exaggerated frailty and innocence attributed to young girls was also juxtaposed against pervasive forms of medical knowledge viewing adult women's bodies as dominated by their menstrual cycles and reproductive capacities, and particularly by contrast with the sinfulness and immorality of prostitutes (Smart, 1992b, pp. 11–15).

Such perspectives were accentuated by the exaggerated emphasis upon imagery of virginal innocence in Victorian culture. Walkowitz has argued that the narrative of the Maiden Tribute articles in which a young girl was sold to a man mirrored sadistic scenarios of Victorian pornography, generating a fantasy of childhood sexual innocence in opposition to images of adult seduction in a manner which erased the real experiences of working-class girl prostitutes (Walkowitz, 1992, pp. 99–100). The increase in the age of consent can be seen as reflecting an expanded and fetishised understanding of childhood as a realm of innocence, a product in part of transgressive male fantasies.

However, to evaluate the age of consent's formation and effects in 1885 involves examining the reality behind representations. W.T. Stead's portrayal of innocent young girl prostitutes as sexually innocent passive victims of individual evil men created the image of girls being forcibly compelled into prostitution. Such imagery did not reflect young working-class women's sexual attitudes and knowledge, and ignored the opportunities offered to them by prostitution to combat poverty and dismal employment prospects, with the consequence that social purity's moral campaigns ignored the need for structural social reforms (Weeks, 1989, p. 88; Walkowitz, 1992).

Nevertheless, given that 'consent' is only meaningful when informed by relevant knowledge, it is important to appreciate the conditions which structured the ability of young people to understand their actions. There was much confusion in popular beliefs about sexuality, no sex education in schools, and girls were given minimal information about sex to protect their 'innocence'. Even when the *British Medical Journal* responded to the Maiden Tribute of Modern Babylon exposé by calling for commencement of sex education in schools, it remained ambivalent about such education being extended to girls, for fear of undermining their purity (Bland, 1995, p. 59). Many girls having sex above the so-called age of consent would therefore not have known what they were consenting *to*, including the risks of pregnancy and sexually transmitted diseases. These factors placed very real constraints on the extent to which girls could make meaningful choices.

Parliamentary debates

The dominant axis of debate over the *Criminal Law Amendment Act* 1885 was the opposition between male libertarians who sought to protect their sexual prerogatives and the forces of social purity who favoured regulation. However, a strong emphasis upon the need for protection did not necessarily always imply a straightforward disregard for adult autonomy. Both sides contained those who linked their proposals to greater sexual autonomy for adults, although women's lack of legal rights to sexual consent within marriage remained unquestioned.

In general the ideology of social purity involved a strong scepticism towards sexual freedoms, reflected in support for legal prohibitions (Weeks, 1989, pp. 81–83). But some women allied to the social purity movement were already beginning to place greater emphasis on women's sexual agency, despite also seeking to protect young girls. Such differing emphases within social purity were evident in debates over prostitution, where a minority of feminists led by Josephine Butler argued for women being legally permitted to choose for themselves, despite believing prostitution to be evil. Bland notes the positive effect which these elements of social purity campaigns had in enabling women to speak of sex for the first time, foreshadowing more 'sex-positive' forms of feminism in the early twentieth century (Bland, 1995). A reduction in ignorance about sexuality, and the beginnings of a more public negotiation of appropriate sexual behaviour between men and women, initiated a process of constituting women as having needs, desires and rights. However, the thrust of much of social purity was to repress debate. Social purity was on the whole disempowering with regard to both young people's sexuality and women's sexuality (Bland, 1995, p. xvii).

Most of those men who opposed the social purity movement's demand to raise the age of consent, including MPs, did so in a manner which sought to defend male access to and power over women, rather than conceptualising this in relation to support for individuals being able to consent to sexual behaviour. But there were a few, such as Charles Hopwood, MP for Stockport, who did so on the basis of a more pragmatic view of the law's limited efficacy, despite supporting the social purity view of prostitution. During parliamentary debates, Hopwood questioned the effectiveness of prohibitive legislation, emphasising instead the need for education and employment for young working-class women (HC 9.7.1885, col. 199–202; cf. Weeks, 1989, p. 89).

Thus, on both sides of the 1885 debate, the beginnings can be found of arguments emphasising the rights of the individual citizens to have their sexuality respected, both through protection against exploitation and abuse and through respect for the abilities of competent individuals to make choices. These can be seen as representing early attempts to apply emerging ideals of citizenship to the realm of intimacy and sexual relations, to grant minimal forms of 'sexual citizenship' through a framework of state regulation (cf. Evans, 1993; Plummer, 1995, pp. 144–166; Weeks, 1998b, see chapter 1). Emerging liberal political languages did increasingly emphasise the state's role in translating collective responsibilities into law to promote respect for the individual, and parliamentary debates show these ideas beginning to filter into discussion of sexual behaviour. But even those favouring improvements in the resources available to young women to facilitate a greater degree of agency in their negotiations of sexual relations with men did not question women's lack of rights to sexual consent within marriage. Conceptions of age of consent law were more concerned with prohibition than consent.

The concept of an 'age of consent' was widely used in the debates over the 1880s, but it is clear that although the capacities of girls to give consent was certainly an issue in the determination of legislation, the concept was utilised with an elastic understanding of 'consent'. 'Age of consent' could be used to argue for a range of potential ages from 13 to 21 because many saw consent as achieved in degrees along a scale of competence, and viewed the level of competence necessary for a girl to meaningfully consent as much less than might be required for the responsibilities of adult males (reflected in the age of majority, 21). A degree of emphasis on girls as decision-makers is evident, for example, where the issue was framed in terms of 'individual responsibility' by figures such as the Archbishop of Canterbury. The Archbishop believed, according to Hansard, that '...without any exception, 16 was the earliest age at which the law recognized the right of girls to exercise independent responsibility' (HL 28 April 1885, col. 946). However, the use of concepts such as 'rights', 'responsibility' and 'consent' in the debate did not carry clear associations. Only a limited degree of competence was considered necessary for legal intercourse.

Prevailing attitudes to the gendered legal framework are illuminated by a series of exchanges during the third reading of the *Criminal Law Amendment Bill* (HC 6 August 1885, cols 1391–1397). There was disquiet among some MPs that the bill's increase in the minimum age for sexual intercourse to 16 would only apply punishments to boys, leaving girls unpunished. Mr Staveley Hill MP thus proposed an amendment which would impose a punishment, though less severe, upon girls:

Upon the conviction of any prisoner under sub-section one of section five, the judge shall inquire of the jury whether they find that the act of which the prisoner has been convicted was done with the consent of the girl, and, if the jury shall find that she did so consent, the judge shall order her to be sent to a reformatory school for a period not exceeding two years. (HC 6 August 1885, col. 1391)

Mr Stavely Hill MP argued strongly in favour of his amendment:

what was it the House was doing? They were saying, as the Bill stood at the present, that where a girl was in this condition, and induced a boy or a young man to commit an offence, the boy was to be punished and the girl was to go scot free, not only with regard to punishment for her share in the offence, but in regard, also, to any education she might obtain in a reformatory to which she might be sent for the purpose of improving her mind and teaching her better habits. Now he asked the House, was that fair? (HC 6 August 1885, cols 1391–1392)

The proposed amendment recognised girls as being capable of giving 'consent', and hence responsible for their own actions. Hence Mr Staveley Hill MP challenged the Bill's implied assumptions about girls' lack of responsibility and sought to moderate gendered understandings to achieve 'justice between the two sexes'. However, his references to girls being 'led astray' demonstrate that this attribution of decision-making competence remained limited (HC 6 August 1885, cols 1391–1392).

The new proposals were also inspired by a desire to prevent cases being 'trumped up' and 'used as a means to extortion' in circumstances where a girl under the age of 16 had 'tempted a boy to the commission of an offence'; hence Staveley Hill's attribution of agency and responsibility to girls carried ambivalent implications for women (HC 6 August 1885, col. 1392). These attitudes were also reflected in a supporting speech by Charles Hopwood, who argued that:

cases [...] constantly occurred in which girls under 16 were a hundred times more culpable than the youths whom, in reality, they seduced – cases where the girls were more advanced and matured, both in body and mind. (HC 6 August 1885, col. 1394)

In the context of the parliamentary debate this argument implied a punitive response to sexually active girls.

The clause was opposed by the government and defeated by MPs on the basis that the proposed legislation did not make the girl guilty of any crime, and hence she could not legitimately be sent to a criminal institution (HC 6 August 1885, col. 1393). The amendment also appears to have been defeated partly due to the technical difficulty of a court establishing whether a girl had 'consented'. This suggests that had an alternative formulation of the age of consent law been developed at an earlier stage, parliament might have been willing to impose punishments upon girls. Hence assumptions of female innocence were not all-pervasive.

Nevertheless, arguments against the amendment show that a highly gendered, protectionist logic was operating. Opponents of the amendment, such as Sir William Harcourt, argued that 'the assumption of the Bill was that a girl under 16 could never be a consenting party', and hence they could not legitimately be held criminally responsible (HC 6 August 1885, col. 1394). Others such as Mr Gregory MP, who attributed sufficient agency to girls to acknowledge that 'they might have yielded to temptation', nevertheless argued that they needed 'every protection', while also noting the extreme stigmatisation which would apply to girls if they were criminalised, more than to boys (HC 6 August 1885, col. 1395). The final argument made in relation to the clause asserted that it would prevent parents coming forward in circumstances where their daughters might be punished (HC 6 August 1885, col. 1397). A desire to legally enforce some recognition of girls' responsibility was thus confounded by the overwhelming structure of existing gender relations.

The age of protection

The previous discussion illustrates that though the legislation introduced in 1885 was debated as an 'age of consent', the law was conceived largely as a prohibition upon behaviour below a minimum age, under which the state was responsible for protecting young women. It was not conceived with an emphasis upon applying the principle of consent above the legal age boundary. This is apparent in the fact that it did not create any clear *right to consent* above the 'age of consent'; in particular, women still had no legal recourse against non-consensual behaviour within marriage. The capacity of young women to make important decisions was not the central theme of the debate; the central issue was the need for protection. In this sense the law created in 1885 is better described as a paternalistic 'age of protection', a legal prohibition placing limits upon men's sexual access. As the language of 'defilement' and 'carnal knowledge' in the statute reveals, women were cast in the role of victims.

The precise age at which the age of consent was set provides some insight into the logic which lay behind the legislation. According to Walkowitz, scientific theories of biological or psychological development were not a key factor:

> For reformers, 'girlhood' was a stage in life marked by dependency, but not by any specific psychosexual development. Accordingly, debates over the age of consent rarely included reference to the actual sexual development of the girls to be protected. The age of consent was arbitrary; indeed many reformers wanted to raise it to eighteen, some to twenty-one. (Walkowitz, 1992, p. 284)

Though parliamentary debates do include references to 'puberty' being reached at 12 or 13, puberty was not regarded as indicating readiness for sexual activity (for example, Mr Staveley Hill MP: HC 6 August 1885, col. 1391). The protection of post-pubescent girls was deemed necessary due to the risks they faced, and the dominant moral framework. Only later, in the early twentieth century, did arguments for further increases in the age of consent to 18 become linked to new medicalised conceptions of adolescence as an unstable time when boys and girls were unfit to make important decisions (Hooper, 1992, p. 62).

However, contrary to Walkowitz's argument, the age of 16 was not arbitrary. Walkowitz and Bland provide only brief discussions of the rationale for the age of 16, both concentrating on a broader assessment of the social context in which reform occurred (Walkowitz, 1992, pp. 82, 284; Bland, 1995, pp. xiv–xvi, 58–59). Yet the particular arguments invoked in favour of this age reveal more clearly how it was understood to relate to the competence and citizenship status of young people.

According to Lord Norton, during a parliamentary debate in 1885, the age of 16 was recommended to parliament by many purity campaigners and a House of Lords committee which reported in 1882 (HL 28 April 1885, cols 943–944). This was partly because it matched existing legislation on 'abduction of a girl', in the *Offences Against the Person Act* 1861 s. 55. It also mirrored a variety of legal regulations concerning child custody, the responsibilities of child guardians, and the ability of persons to join friendly societies and trade unions. Lord Norton was therefore able to claim that it was:

> according to the general principle of our law that the discretion of a girl under 16 should not be thought sufficient to permit her the un-protected disposal of herself. (HL 28 April 1885, cols 943–944)

Hence there was some suggestion of consistent boundaries being drawn between age groups in law. The Archbishop of Canterbury, among others, echoed this argument, also noting that a girl under 16 could not marry without parental consent (HL 28 April 1885, col. 946). Such examples suggest that the minimum age for intercourse was not conceived in entirely prohibitive terms, but was also seen as indicating the beginning of a period of greater individual agency.

Feminist commentaries provide a number of suggestive indications of how the logic structuring age of consent law was conceived through gendered ideologies which sustained unequal and apparently contradictory attributions of sexual blame and responsibility. Carol-Ann Hooper (1992) has argued with reference to the age of consent that:

> Below it girls were perceived as without responsibility, justifying (sometimes) protection. But above it they bore responsibility not only for

themselves but also for men, as illustrated by the prosecution of women for soliciting. (Hooper, 1992, p. 62)

Hooper's comment on the prosecution of prostitutes illustrates a double-standard, whereby young women were held accountable for criminal behaviour, without being granted most forms of citizenship status.

Girls below the age of consent were also subject to double-standards. Carol Smart has argued that the *Criminal Law Amendment Act* 1885 embodied a legal approach to adult/child sexual abuse which:

> combines a recognition that children need to be protected with an ambivalence towards the victims of abuse. Its aim was to maintain the ideals of purity and innocence in childhood, yet the defiled and 'knowing' child became an anathema and an embarrassment. (Smart, 1989, p. 51)

In this sense the legislation embodied the dichotomy between virgins and 'fallen' young women. Significantly, as Smart has noted, while the law did not criminalise young women, it extended the scope of institutionalised moral vigilance, such that girls could be forcibly incarcerated in industrial schools or reformatories. Hence 'protection' had its disadvantages (Smart, 1989, p. 51). Girls who repeatedly transgressed sexual regulations remained subject to discipline and blame, although on the other hand age of consent legislation was conceived as part of a tendency to define women in relation to their bodies, and hence deny them responsibilities (Smart, 1992b, pp. 26, 30–32).

The increase in the age of consent from 13 to 16 can be seen as a shift to a new situation in which a growing emphasis was placed upon the innocence of childhood, and the needs of girls for protection. This shift occurred with little increase in emphasis upon the capacities of women above the minimum age for competent autonomous decision-making. Yet it must also be recognised that the terms within which the law was conceived included some emphasis upon women's rights to both protection and consent, which should not be altogether overlooked. Some of the arguments used made reference to the capacities to make decisions and exercise autonomy, and also to their status as individuals deserving state protection beyond that afforded by their families.

While capacities to 'consent' were not at the centre of the debate over the law, they were nevertheless one part of the formation of ideas circulating. While not regarding women as capable of the most important forms of decision-making available to male citizens with full rational capacities, MPs regarded a limited degree of understanding of sexual behaviour, and hence a degree of meaningful and informed consent, as a necessary condition for the absence of state regulation. The age of consent created in 1885 cannot, therefore, be conceptualised as the product of understandings of young women as wholly lacking in citizenship status. The debates show that the dominant framework of citizenship attributed limited forms of entitlements to young women, both as individuals with a right to state protection and as individuals with a degree of decision-making competence demanding recognition. The law was largely determined as a compromise between mythical images of childhood purity and innocence and the continuing demands of men to sexual access. But it was also influenced by emerging understandings of women's sexual rights as individuals.

Both Judith Walkowitz and Lucy Bland have vividly described the conflicting political impulses of feminists and progressives in relation to social purity movements and prohibitive law reform strategies. Yet both remain somewhat opaque in relation to the question of whether a higher age of consent served the interests of young women within the context of late Victorian society (Walkowitz, 1992, pp. 82, 284; Bland, 1995, pp. xiv–xvi, 58–59). Walkowitz, for example, suggests that social purity exaggerated the extent of child prostitution, but is not clear whether this implied that the increase in the minimum age for sexual intercourse was undesirable, though she is critical of the state's orientation towards regulating rather than empowering young women. This stance reflects a analytical strategy of addressing the profoundly different 'problematic' operating in nineteenth-century debates by contrast with contemporary circumstances. Questioning whether a change in the law from 13 to 16 was 'a good thing' if all 'other factors remained equal' is not very helpful when one is arguing from a perspective which assumes a desire to profoundly transform the social context by empowering young women.

By contemporary standards the age of 16 was conceived with a highly prohibitive logic. But in its context it also represented a compromise by the state between two contradictory aspects of women's emerging claims as individual citizens: claims for protection of girls, and claims for adult women's capacity to make decisions as autonomous individuals.

The major part of this chapter has analysed the regulation of sexual behaviour between men and women by the *Criminal Law Amendment Act* 1885. However, this legislation also introduced new forms of regulation applying to sex between men. The final section of the chapter discusses this, demonstrating further dimensions of the ideological relationship between familial and extra-familial forms of sexuality which produced the legal framework in the late nineteenth century. This discussion also introduces the social and legal context relevant to the more extended discussion of homosexuality in the following chapter.

The regulation of male homosexuality

Legislation regulating 'consensual' sexual acts between women has historically been almost entirely absent from UK law. Legislation governing sexual acts between men, however, developed in the context of a 'punitive tradition' particular to the UK (West and Wöelke, 1997, p. 197; for detailed discussion, see Moran, 1996). A key element of such legislation was the offence of 'buggery' which in England, Wales and Northern Ireland involved anal intercourse by a man with either a man, a woman or an animal (Moran, 1996, pp. 21–88); while in Scotland the offence of 'sodomy' applied only to anal intercourse between two men (Crane, 1982, p. 24; Dempsey, 1998, p. 156). The *Offences Against the Person Act* 1861 abolished the death penalty for 'buggery' in England, Wales and Ireland, while preserving the offence together with 'attempted buggery' (s.61), which as Cocks (1998) has shown could be interpreted flexibly by the courts to prohibit various sexual contact between males. The death penalty for sodomy was not abolished in Scotland until 1887 (*Criminal Procedure (Scotland) Act* 1887, s.56).

A new offence of 'gross indecency' was introduced throughout the UK in the *Criminal Law Amendment Act* 1885 through the notorious 'Labouchère amendment' which became commonly known by the name of its author Henry Labouchère MP, a 'demagogic radical' (Weeks, 1977, p. 15). Section 11 of the Act, headed 'Outrages on public decency', stated:

> 11. Any male person who, in public or private, commits, or is a party to the commission of, or procures or attempts to procure the commission by any male person of any act of gross indecency with another male person, shall be guilty of a misdemeanour, and being convicted thereof shall be liable at the discretion of the court to be imprisoned for any term not exceeding two years, with or without hard labour.

This legislation quickly became known as the 'Blackmailer's Charter'. Although previous buggery laws remained on the statute, it became the legal basis for the vast majority of legal proceedings against men having sex with men. 'Gross indecency' involved a more explicit criminalisation of all sexual activity between men than 'attempted buggery', including sexual acts not involving physical contact. The scope of prohibition remained broadly consistent with that defined by the previous legal framework, although in practice the new law was enforced more vigorously (Cocks, 1998). In Scotland the common law offence of 'shameless indecency' was also commonly used to regulate male same-sex behaviour (Dempsey, 1998, p. 156).

The amendment was passed in the final stages of parliamentary debates over the *Criminal Law Amendment Act*, during its third reading in the House of Commons. Only three MPs rose to comment on the new clause, contributing to exchanges which occupy less than two columns in *Hansard* (HC 6 August 1885, cols 1397–1398). However, Weeks has argued that the amendment's acceptance by the government and Speaker was indicative of a wider political context, a climate of opinion favouring regulation (Weeks, 1977, pp. 14–22, Weeks, 1990). The amendment was located in a bill intended to legislate against dangerous male desire, which social purity campaigners believed required legal containment to protect the social institution of the family.

However, the report in Hansard of Henry Labouchère's speech proposing the amendment conveys considerable confusion over the existing legal framework and the amendment's potential effects:

> That was his amendment, and the meaning of it was that at present any person on whom an assault of the kind here dealt with was committed must be under the age of 13, and the object with which he had brought forward this clause was to make the law applicable to any person, whether under the age of 13 or over that age. (HC 6 August 1885, col. 1397)

A comment by Charles Hopwood MP echoed this understanding that the existing age of consent for same-sex behaviour between males was 13; neither Hopwood nor Labouchère was challenged by other MPs or the government. The exchanges, though opaque, support the view that the 1885 legislation was passed in the context of a widespread belief in the need to tighten existing legal regulation (Weeks, 1977). However, they also suggest that Henry Labouchère, even following conversations with government members who had conveyed their support for his amendment, believed he was addressing an existing legal framework which was relatively relaxed.

The context in which the Labouchère amendment was passed was dominated by the Maiden Tribute furoré. There had been little concern over male same-sex behaviour expressed in social purity campaigns. While the contestation of appropriate age limits for sexual behaviour between men and women took place, the possibility of parallel legislation applying to same-sex behaviour was not publicly contemplated. Interestingly, Walkowitz suggests that W.T. Stead employed dramatic devices selectively in his Maiden Tribute newspaper articles in order to preserve a clear narrative dichotomy between young girls as passive 'innocent victims' and the dominance and agency of male sexuality. When employing Ovid's myth of the Minotaur, Stead omitted to mention the Minotaur's male victims, despite knowing of London establishments where acts of male prostitution and flogging occurred (Walkowitz, 1992, pp. 98, 118, 278).

Walkowitz also argues, concurring with Weeks (1977, pp. 18–20), in relation to the Labouchère amendment that:

> An anti-aristocratic bias may have prompted its inclusion in the bill (reformers accepted its inclusion but did not themselves propose it), as homosexuality was associated with the corruption of working-class youth by the same upper-class profligates, who, on other occasions, were thought to buy the services of young girls. (Walkowitz, 1992, p. 278)

Hence a similar class dynamic operated in relation to the prohibition of male homosexuality as that operating in debates over male/female sexual behaviour.

Considering the broad historical context, there has been extensive debate over the periodisation of the shift from the 'sodomite' to the 'homosexual', and the role of sexology and sexual subcultures in this shift. Much of this debate has focussed upon Foucault's argument that the 'perverse implantation' produced the category of 'the homosexual' during the nineteenth century (Foucault, 1981, pp. 42–44, 101). Mary McIntosh and subsequently Randolph Trumbach have placed greater emphasis upon the emergence of effeminate male subcultures and a distinguishable 'homosexual role' in the early eighteenth century (McIntosh, 1968; Trumbach, 1997, pp. 88–89). It appears increasingly clear that sexology applied its labels to pre-existing subcultures where collective identities were already established, and hence accounts which exaggerate the formative role of sexology are unhelpful (Vicinus, 1989b, pp. 185–186; Chauncey, 1995; Weeks, 1998a, pp. 139–140). In the late nineteenth century, new forms of sexology remained in their early stages, and achieved limited acceptance.

Hence the Labouchère amendment was passed in the context of growing public awareness of long-established effeminate male subcultures, and changing social attitudes towards the emerging category of the male 'homosexual' (Weeks, 1977, 1981; cf. Weeks, 1989, 1990, 1993, pp. 124–126). The amendment did not encode 'homosexuality' as such into law, making its relationship to concerns with either the sodomite or the homosexual ambiguous (cf. Moran, 1996, 1998). But it is clear from the subsequent Wilde trial that public attitudes towards the regulation of sexual behaviour between men hardened significantly in the late nineteenth century.

In assessing the social and legal significance of the Labouchère amendment, an important issue to consider is the extent to which its legal interpretation and application differed from the previous law. That the scope of 'attempted buggery' was potentially comprehensive in relation to male same-sex behaviour, including both public and private behaviour, has been widely recognised by commentators (Weeks, 1980, pp. 199–200, 1989, pp. 91, 99; Bartlett, 1997, p. 556; Moran, 1998, p. 20). However, the interpretation of the scope of buggery laws and the practice of their enforcement prior to 1885 are contested. In his early work, Jeffrey Weeks placed an excessive emphasis on the Labouchère amendment, arguing that previously there was not 'any comprehensive law relating to male homosexuality', and stressing that gross indecency applied 'whether in public or private' which 'in effect made all male homosexual acts and all homosexual "procuring" illegal' (Weeks, 1980, p. 199). His later work maintains an emphasis on the amendment's facilitation of easier enforcement, though without claiming the law was only previously applied in public (Weeks, 1989, pp. 91, 99). By contrast, Leslie J. Moran has sought to downplay the amendment:

it is far from clear that the introduction of the Labouchère amendment in general or its application in the instance of the Wilde trial was a new departure or an escalation of law's concern with male-to-male genital relations. To suggest that this amendment criminalized acts in private which had not been previously criminal is incorrect. (Moran, 1998, p. 20)

In support, Moran cites Peter Bartlett's recent research which argues that in the eighteenth century attempted buggery 'was a flexible offence, not well-defined, embracing a wide variety of activity between men'. However, though Bartlett identifies cases in which it is unclear that a literal attempt at buggery was taking place, he provides no examples of strictly private behaviour being prosecuted (Bartlett, 1997, pp. 556–557).

The recent work of Harry Cocks suggests that committals for sodomy and related offences were extremely variable prior to 1840, but then steadily declined from a peak, and remained largely constant from the 1850s to the 1880s (Cocks, 1998). Given that existing legislation was being used in a diminishing number of cases, it becomes more difficult to interpret the Labouchère amendment as a response to a sustained increase in public anxieties during the 1860s and 1870s. However, it is clear that public attitudes became increasingly hostile to male same-sex behaviour in the final decades of the nineteenth century, and that the new legislation facilitated more repressive regulation – whether directly by demanding a lesser standard of proof, or more indirectly by expressing the subject of regulation, 'gross indecency', in a new form (Weeks, 1980, pp. 199–200, 1989, pp. 91–108).

The Labouchère amendment held significance in the wider context of social purity and the increasing social delineation of male same-sex activities and identities in the late nineteenth century. The moral climate became increasingly hostile to all extra-familial sexual activity. Given the rise of social purity and changing Victorian attitudes to the role of state regulation, it seems highly likely that if new legislation had not been created by a hurried amendment in 1885, more stringent enforcement of existing buggery laws or alternative new legislation would have subsequently emerged. The Labouchère amendment does therefore represent the legislative expression of increasing social differentiation and stigmatisation of male same-sex behaviour during the late nineteenth and early twentieth century.

The Labouchère amendment did not, however, regulate sexual behaviour between women. Nor did the subject of sex between women arise during parliamentary debates over the *Criminal Law Amendment Act* (cf. Weeks, 1977, pp. 87–111). Widespread belief in essential sexual differences between active male sexuality and passive female sexuality rendered same-sex contact between women invisible or unthreatening, and limited the availability of languages for self-definition (Bland, 1995, pp. 54–55). While sexological discourses began to label 'deviant' sexual desires between women from the mid-1880s (Vicinus, 1989a, p. 227), only four medical cases of female homosexuality had been reported in Europe and America by 1884, all transvestites, although sexual relationships between women were represented in some art and literature (Showalter, 1992, p. 23). Although the founding of girls' boarding schools, for example, had begun to generate middle-class anxieties over romantic attachments between girls and women teachers, romantic friendships remained largely unthreatening (Vicinus, 1989a, p. 227). While various definitions of women's same-sex attraction were available during the nineteenth century, these tended to remain sufficiently de-sexualised and lacking in the potential to cross boundaries of class or age to remain unregulated (Vicinus, 1989b). Hence to the extent that homosexuality was a matter of political concern, it was as an example of unrestrained male sexuality.

Finally a brief comment on the trials of Oscar Wilde in 1895 is appropriate, since this reveals attitudes towards homosexuality in relation to youth which have persisted and underpinned subsequent debates over the age of consent in relation to same-sex behaviour. Though the passage of the Labouchère amendment was largely overshadowed by public debates over the sexual exploitation of young girls, it has been widely argued by historians that the trials of Oscar Wilde in 1895 marked an explosion of public consciousness concerning sexual behaviour between men. Earlier scandals, such as the Cleveland Street male brothel scandal of 1889–1890, had already generated public alarm subsequent to the Labouchère amendment (Kaplan, 1999); hence an excessive emphasis upon the Wilde trials, encouraged by Wilde's contemporary iconic status, is to be avoided. Nevertheless, the Wilde trials brought repressive new legislation to bear upon a celebrated public figure, whose name subsequently became a byword for the legal regulation of homosexuality (Moran, 1998). They came to symbolise the beginning of a new period of strict law enforcement and repressive public attitudes.

The tragic downfall of Oscar Wilde has been well-documented (Ellmann, 1987; cf. Bartlett, 1988; for a brief account, see David, 1997, pp. 3–27). Wilde was accused by the Marquess of Queensbury, father of his young lover Lord Alfred Douglas, of 'posing as a somdomite' [*sic*]. Wilde sued for libel, but the trial collapsed, and he was eventually prosecuted. The highly publicised court cases involved detailed questioning of numerous adolescent boy prostitutes. Press coverage of the Wilde trials, despite not specifying the sexual acts of which Wilde was accused, was vital in generating public consciousness, debate and moral panic over sexual behaviour between men (Cohen, 1993). Controversy over Wilde fixed an equation between effeminacy and same-sex sexual behaviour between men in the public mind, which pro-foundly structured understandings of homosexuality during the subsequent century (Sinfield, 1994).

The limited debates surrounding same-sex desire in relation to the Labouchère amendment (1885), together with evidence from the Cleveland Street scandal (1889–1890) and the Wilde Trial (1895) all point to public anxieties focussing on the transgression of age boundaries, together with those of class. Hence the apparent isolation of the Labouchère amendment in an act concerned with female prostitution and male/female behaviour should not disguise a common structure influencing public debate and regulation in relation to both same-sex and male/female behaviour. Moralist opinion became preoccupied with limiting the excessive transgressions of privileged powerful men beyond the family, especially across acceptable boundaries of sexual identity, class and age.

In the Cleveland Street scandal the corruption of working-class telegraph delivery boys aged 15–19, who were being paid for sex by middle- and upper-class men, was seen as a key threat to public morality (Kaplan, 1999). Similarly in the Wilde trial the age of the young male prostitutes involved caused much public consternation. While the social climate was shifting against same-sex behaviour, and new legislation enforced a blanket prohibition, a specific focus of public concern was upon sexual behaviour between older and younger males. As already noted, Labouchère himself in his parliamentary speech drew attention to the low age of consent he believed to exist for sexual acts between men, suggesting that a particular motive may have been to prohibit sexual behaviour with young men (HC 6 August 1885, col. 1397). An association between homosexuality and the seduction of young boys by older men loomed large in late nineteenth-century debates, and influenced attitudes towards age of consent laws for same-sex behaviour throughout the twentieth century.

Conclusion

This chapter began by outlining the historical origins of age of consent laws, before analysing debates over an increase in the age of consent to sexual intercourse in 1885, examining how the meaning of the law was conceived in relation to gendered definitions of citizenship. The analysis demonstrated that the rationale for the new legislation which emerged was protectionist; the age of consent was conceptualised with reference to only a very limited level of competence, not of a degree or form comparable to that required, for example, by men acting as citizens in the public realm above the age of majority. The chapter then proceeded to explore the regulation of male homosexuality, linked to a tightening of social boundaries and definitions of deviance. Concerns over sexual relationships between older and younger men became a key focus of public anxiety.

During the early twentieth century, continuing attempts were made to increase the age of consent to sexual intercourse by social purity movements, yet these proved unsuccessful. Attempts to raise the age for sexual intercourse continued through the early decades of the twentieth century until the 1930s, but failed despite, for example, the recommendation of a Departmental Committee on Sexual Offences against Young Persons in 1925 that it should be raised to 17 (Weeks, 1989, pp. 88, 94–95). The age of 16 has remained the legal age for sexual intercourse until the present. However, the age of consent to sexual intercourse created by the *Criminal Law Amendment Act* 1885 was supplemented in the 1920s by regulation prohibiting other forms of sexual behaviour below the age of 16 as 'indecent assault'. This had important implications in relation to same-sex behaviour between women that are discussed in the next chapter, which examines early and mid-twentieth-century debates over age of consent laws with respect to homosexuality.

5
Homosexuality and the Age of Consent

This chapter explores how the UK's heteronormative legal framework was amended in relation to same-sex sexual behaviour during the twentieth century, up to the late 1960s. It begins by discussing a change in the minimum age applying to sexual acts other than intercourse in the 1920s, which had effects including the creation of a minimum age for sexual behaviour between women. Since the history of age of consent laws in relation to lesbianism has been subject to little previous attention, I analyse this development in the context of a growth of public concern about female homosexuality after the First World War. The main body of the chapter then focusses on the 1950s and 1960s, discussing the *Wolfenden Report* 1957, and the subsequent partial decriminalisation of male homosexual acts in England and Wales via the *Sexual Offences Act* 1967 to which it led. I examine the rationale for the creation of a minimum age for sexual behaviour between men at the age of 21. After an overview of events, I analyse the *Wolfenden Report*'s conclusions, examining the understandings of citizenship for male homosexuals which informed its arguments. Through engagement with existing analyses, I argue that the *Wolfenden Report*'s assertion of a universal right to privacy entailed a complex strategy, seeking to contain male homosexuality while also granting limited forms of citizenship. Drawing upon this argument, I then explore the rationale behind the creation of a minimum legal age of 21 for male 'homosexual acts', analysing the interplay between theories of the causes of homosexuality, legal philosophies and wider social attitudes.

Lesbianism and the age of consent in the inter-war years

In relation to consensual acts other than sexual intercourse, such as masturbation of another person, oral sex, and penetration with objects, the legal age in England, Wales and Ireland was set at 12 by the *Offences Against the Person Act* 1861 (s. 52). This age was not raised to 13 alongside that for sexual intercourse in 1875, but was raised to 13 by the *Criminal Law*

Amendment Act 1880, a piece of legislation applying only in England and Wales which is often overlooked in histories of sex offences. The sole substantive clause of the 1880 act, clause 2, stated:

> It shall be no defence to a charge or indictment for an indecent assault on a young person under the age of thirteen to prove that he or she consented to the act of indecency.

This measure removed 'consent' as a defence to the offences of 'indecent assault' established in the *Offences Against the Person Act* 1861, applying separate offences to indecent assaults on a female, with a maximum sentence of 2 years (s. 52) and on a male, with a maximum sentence of 10 years (s. 62). However, the legal age in such instances was not raised alongside that for sexual intercourse to 16 by the *Criminal Law Amendment Act* 1885. Hence acts such as oral sex, masturbation of another person, kissing and other forms of behaviour considered sexual remained subject to less prohibitive forms of regulation. Only after the First World War did the *Criminal Law Amendment Act* 1922 raise this minimum age for consent to be a valid defence to 16 (significantly the age of marriage was also subsequently raised from 12 to 16 by the *Age of Marriage Act* 1929). This legislative history encompasses important changes in the law potentially applicable to sexual behaviour between women, and since this history has not been subject to detailed examination in previous research, I make it the focus of my discussion here.

Prior to the twentieth century, legislation regulating consensual sexual acts between women was almost entirely absent from UK law. Although research has suggested that sodomy laws were occasionally invoked to regulate sex between women in Europe from mediaeval times, such research appears to have uncovered no British examples (Crompton, 1980; discussed in Faraday, 1985, 1988). Lilian Faderman noted only a dozen court cases where women were accused of lesbianism in court prior to the twentieth century, though the high-profile defamation case of *Miss Pirie* and *Miss Woods v. Lady Gordon* in 1810, relating to sexual behaviour involving teachers in a Scottish school, illustrates some potential for controversy (Faderman, 1985; Oram and Turnbull, 2001, pp. 156–161). Reasons for the historical lack of legal regulation emerging with the reform and extension of criminal law in the nineteenth century include widespread beliefs in essential sex differences and the passivity of female sexuality, which rendered same-sex contact between women invisible or unthreatening (Edwards, 1981; Faderman, 1981).

In the 1885 case of *R v. Armstrong*, Justice Lopes ruled that a woman could be found guilty of indecent assault on another woman, if an assault were accompanied by indecent circumstances (Justice of the Peace 49, 1885, at 745, cited in Edwards, 1981, p. 43). However, this ruling appears to have assumed a non-consensual context. Edwards has commented that in any case Lopes 'may have stood alone in this matter' (1981, p. 43). Her analysis situates this apparently isolated ruling in the context of an overwhelming belief in female sexual passivity in the nineteenth century, which became embodied in statutes and legal judgements assuming that women could not commit rape, indecent assault or homosexual acts (Edwards, 1981, p. 37). Hence it appears that it was not until the 1920s and an increase in the minimum age that the interpretation of the law began to shift. Changing social attitudes produced legislative attempts to criminalise sex between women.

The 1920s was a period of growing public concern with female homosexuality and its regulation (Weeks, 1977, pp. 87–100; Faraday, 1985; Weeks, 1989, pp. 115–117; Doan, 1997, 2001). As Martha Vicinus has argued, in some ways lesbianism posed less of a threat to the social order than male homosexuality because it had less potential to cross boundaries of age and class (Vicinus, 1989a). Yet the association of lesbianism with the changing social status of women rendered it profoundly threatening. Women's entry into the workforce during the First World War, and their achievement of limited suffrage in 1918, had challenged previous gender roles.

Annabel Faraday's detailed study of lesbianism in the inter-war years has described how discussions about lesbians began to proliferate, accompanied by a desire to control an apparent increase in lesbianism (Faraday, 1985). She notes that sexological theories of sexual 'need' played a role in generating concern over lesbian sexual agency (Faraday, 1985, p. 39). Faraday explores how the perceived threat of lesbianism was linked to an increase in the population of 'spinsters' or 'bachelor women', a population of increasingly independent and self-sufficient 'surplus' single women (Faraday, 1985, pp. 38–82; see also Jeffreys, 1985). The period encompassed a number of libel and obscenity trials, most notoriously the prosecution relating to Radclyffe Hall's *The Well of Loneliness* in 1928 (Faraday, 1985, pp. 200–244; Doan, 2001; Oram and Turnbull, 2001, pp. 181–200).

The involvement of girls and young women in lesbianism was a particular anxiety. The founding of girls' boarding schools in the early twentieth century began to generate middle-class anxieties over romantic attachments between girls and women teachers (Vicinus, 1989b, p. 227). Faraday discusses how anti-lesbianism provided a significant motivation for co-educationalist movements (Faraday, 1985, pp. 131–199). From this social context emerged a desire for regulation.

The most prominent event in the history of twentieth-century conflicts over the legal regulation of sex between women occurred in 1921. An unsuccessful attempt was made to prohibit all sexual acts between women through an extension of the offence of 'gross indecency', applying between men under Section 11 of the *Criminal Law Amendment Act* 1885, via an amendment to the *Criminal Law Amendment Bill* (HC 4.8.1921, cols 1799–1807). This new offence was initially approved by the House of Commons but then rejected by the House of Lords. The Lords' rejection derived largely from a concern that prohibition would be counter-productive in publicising sex between women. In many discussions of the regulation of homosexuality in the UK this failed attempt at prohibition is the major focus with respect to lesbianism, and the parliamentary debates over this proposal have received considerable analysis (Edwards, 1981, p. 44; Faraday, 1985, 1988, pp. 12–15; Jeffreys, 1985; Weeks, 1989, pp. 105–106; Doan, 1997; Oram and Turnbull, 2001, pp. 166–169). Laura Doan's recent research has suggested that the motivation for the proposed law derived from antagonism towards women entering the police service (Doan, 1997).

The creation of the present minimum age applying to sex between women has received far less attention, despite being achieved via an act developed from the same *Criminal Law Amendment Bill* which had been the subject of attempts to extend 'gross indecency'. It goes entirely unmentioned in most feminist and critical commentaries on sex offences and homosexuality in the UK (Warner, 1983; Weeks, 1989; Ainley, 1995, pp. 14–29; Edwards, 1996, pp. 60–61; Doan, 1997; Oram and Turnbull, 2001, pp. 155–158). The *Criminal Law Amendment Act* 1922, applying only in England and Wales, stated (s. 1):

> 1. It shall be no defence to a charge or indictment for an indecent assault on a child or young person under the age of sixteen to prove that he or she consented to the act of indecency.

This removed 'consent' as a defence to the offence of 'indecent assault' against a person under 16. The clause did not define the sex of the offender, and hence potentially applied to female offenders.

Section 4 of the same act addressed Scotland. This stated (in Sub-section 1):

> Any person who uses towards a girl of or above the age of twelve years and under the age of sixteen years any lewd, indecent or libidinous practice or behaviour which, if used towards a girl under the age of twelve years, would have constituted an offence at common law, shall, whether the girl consented to such practice or behaviour or not, be guilty of an offence against this Act, and shall be liable on conviction on indictment to imprisonment with or without hard labour for a period not exceeding two years, or on summary conviction to imprisonment for a period not exceeding three months.

This formulation was also phrased in a way potentially covering sexual behaviour between females. But the Scottish law encompassed sexual behaviour not involving physical contact, whereas this remained unregulated in England and Wales until the *Indecency with Children Act* 1960, which encompassed any person 'who commits an act of gross indecency with or towards a child under the age of fourteen, or who incites a child under that age to such an act with him or another' (s. 1.1).

The term 'age of consent' was used to describe the new legislation: for example, the measure in Section 1 was described by the Secretary of State for the Home Department, Mr Shortt, as dealing with 'the age of consent for indecent assault' (HC 5.7.1922, col. 403). However, the concept of a 'lesbian age of consent' is a problematic way in which to describe the legal framework, since the law made no reference to the identity 'lesbian', and regulated all sexual behaviour between women irrespective of sexual identity.

Existing scholarship gives the impression that the age of consent for sex between women originates in legislation never intended to encompass such behaviour, and that the law's application to sex between females has been the consequence of appropriation in more recent times. For example, Edwards has commented that 'no legislation was passed that directly prohibited indecency between females during the early decades of the twentieth century' (Edwards, 1981, p. 44). Yet there has previously been no systematic discussion of whether the law was originally conceived as applying to sex between women. In part this is because of the generally limited attention paid by historians to inter-war debates over child protection and sexuality, as noted by Carol Smart (Smart, 1999, pp. 398–403, 2000, p. 60).

The *Criminal Law Amendment Act* 1922 developed from a long series of attempts to tighten sex offences following the First World War. Legislative agendas on these issues were increasingly influenced by women, including the first women MPs (Law, 1997). The predominant concern was to regulate men having sex with young women and girls. Parliamentary debates were pre-occupied first and foremost with a defence available for men accused of having 'carnal knowledge' of an under-age girl, that they had 'reasonable cause to believe' that a female was over 16 (created by the *Criminal Law Amendment Act* 1885). However, the debates did not assume female passivity, purity or lack of desire to the same degree as those in the late nineteenth century. Female sexual agency, particularly the agency of older women prostitutes, was frequently referred to. For example, Frederick Macquisten MP referred to young boys of 12 or 13 being 'led astray' and 'initiated into vice by an older woman' (HC 20.7.1922, col. 99), while Sir G. Hamilton MP commented that 'we should go for the old rogues of both sexes' (HC 5.7.1922, col. 424). Many opponents of the Purity campaigners stridently advocated equality of treatment for both sexes by the law.

In order to appreciate how proposals for the law on indecent assault developed, it is necessary to understand the sequence of parliamentary debates. A *Criminal Law Amendment Bill* seeking to tighten the law on sex offences was first introduced by the Bishop of London in 1914, but abandoned due to the war. In 1917 the Home Secretary Sir George Cave introduced a *Criminal Law Amendment Bill* which led to the creation of a Joint Select Committee on Offences Against Young People in 1918, but this was dissolved before publishing conclusions. Three new bills were introduced into the House of Lords in 1920: the *Criminal Law Amendment Bill*, the *Criminal Law Amendment*

(No. 2) Bill (a government bill), and the *Sexual Offences Bill* (House of Lords Papers, 1920, Vol. III, Bills 8, 16; Vol. VII, no. 31). These were referred to a reformed Joint Select Committee of the Lords and Commons which eventually reported (Joint Select Committee, 1920). The committee's proposals, which included keeping the age of consent to sexual intercourse at 16, were originally introduced into the Lords in 1921 via the *Criminal Law Amendment Bill*, a Private Members Bill. The bill was defeated following controversy over a late Commons amendment seeking to prohibit all sexual behaviour between women as gross indecency (see above). The *Criminal Law Amendment Bill* 1922 was subsequently introduced by the government in the House of Commons to salvage a set of popular reforms, and eventually passed.

The formulation of the clause dealing with consent to acts of indecency changed significantly during the bill's development. The 1917 bill proposed the following in clause 1:

> 1. (1) Any male person of the age of sixteen years or over who commits an act of indecency with a girl under the age of sixteen years shall be liable on conviction on indictment to imprisonment [. . .]; and it shall be no defence to a charge under this section to prove that the girl consented to the act of indecency. (Public Bills 1917–1918, Bill no. 7)

This formulation assumed a male offender and a female 'victim'. However, clause 1 was revised by Standing Committee to read:

> 1. (1) It shall be no defence to a charge or indictment for an indecent assault on a young person under the age of sixteen to prove that he or she consented to the act of indecency. (Public Bills 1917–1918, Bill no. 25)

The clause was thus revised into a form which potentially allowed for both the offender and the subject of an 'indecent assault' to be either male or female. The three bills subsequently introduced into the House of Lords in 1920, and subsequent versions in 1921 and 1922, contained similar formulations that also did not specify the sex of the offender or 'victim'. According to the government's spokesman, the Earl of Onslow, speaking in 1921, the Joint Select Committee of 1920 had carefully considered the clause, and decided to leave it in a gender-neutral form, in preference to the proposal of Sir George Cave's 1917 bill (HL 9.3.1921, cols 426–427). The clause's gender-neutral formulation was then largely undisputed during the parliamentary debates of 1921 and 1922.

Was this age of consent law envisaged as covering sex between females? In understanding the context in which this law was created, it is important to recognise that clause 1 was the subject of repeated attempts between 1920 and 1922 to criminalise sex between women by extending 'gross indecency'. Hence debates over a universal minimum age for sexual behaviour therefore took place directly alongside debates over sex between females.

It is also clear that attempts to criminalise sexual behaviour between females were particularly motivated by concern over sexual activity involving young women and girls. The issue of 'gross indecency between women' was first raised in the Joint Select Committee of 1920 (Doan, 1997). The committee's report records exchanges with an expert witness, Mr Cecil Maurice Chapman, Metropolitan Police Magistrate for Westminster (Joint Select Committee, 1920, paras 1479–1501). Chapman expressed approval of the (gender-neutral) form of clause 1 in the existing government bill, commenting that: 'Consent ought not to be a defence to a charge of indecent assault on anybody up to the age of 16. I think that is a reasonable provision' (paras 1466–1468). He then advanced a proposal for the extension of 'gross indecency' to criminalise sex between women via clause 1, commenting:

Mr. Chapman: [...] I have had very serious cases in my experience in which women have been in the habit of getting girls to their flats and houses in London, and I remember a case that took place in Bournemouth, where girls were practically being treated as if they were prostitutes. It is an offence which people speak of as if it was almost unknown to the public, but it is very well known to the police, and it is very well known to many people who are students of criminology that women as well as men corrupt girls. There is no question about it that in regard to all these acts there ought to be absolute equality between the sexes as far as is humanly possible. There cannot be a doubt about it if there is an act of gross indecency between a woman and a girl. I may tell you that I know of a Home which was started for the reformation of girls where the police had to interfere because of the girls being corrupted by the woman controller of the Home. (Joint Select Committee, 1920, para. 1479)

Similar evidence of a particular concern about young women is evident in debates over gross indecency in the Commons and the Lords. For example, Frederick A. Macquisten MP, the lawyer responsible for introducing the 'gross indecency' amendment, stated in a moment of dramatic exaggeration: 'I proposed this Clause in good faith, [...] knowing there is as much victimisation of young women by their own sex' (HC 17.8.1921, col. 1606).

Sex between women remained a topic of continuing discussion and concern after the failed attempt to extend 'gross indecency' in 1921. Macquisten attempted unsuccessfully to re-introduce his amendment at the bill's second reading (HC 5.7.1922, cols 452–458), in Standing Committee (HC 20.7.1922, col. 107), and at the Report Stage (HC 25.7.1922, col. 365). The issue must therefore have remained in the minds of MPs during the passage of age of consent legislation in 1922.

Furthermore, debates during the bill's committee stage in 1922 provide explicit evidence showing key figures recognised that clause 1 could apply to sex between females. The Home Secretary, the Rt. Hon. E. Shortt MP, was responsible for the bill's introduction and passage. In the process of criticising an amendment proposing to make consenting 15-year olds criminally responsible (eventually rejected), he commented:

> Take the case of an older man or woman who has got hold of a girl, who has polluted her mind and committed an indecent assault upon her. If that girl is going to be prosecuted, she will never give any information against that man, nor will a boy give any information against the woman. Hon. members talk about equality of the sexes. I see nothing in this which distinguishes one sex from another. So far as the provisions go, they treat both sexes exactly alike. An accusation could be brought under this clause against a woman as well as against a man. (HC Standing Committees, May–July 1922, 12.7.1922, col. 9)

The first sentence of this quotation clearly acknowledges the possibility of an older woman committing an indecent assault on a girl which could be prosecuted under clause 1. The passage is somewhat ambiguous since the following sentence assumes a heterosexual context. Nevertheless, subsequent sentences emphasise that the provisions 'treat both sexes exactly alike' and that women are liable to prosecution. These comments, though the only example of speech explicitly referring to a same-sex context detectable from a systematic reading of the parliamentary debates of 1920–1922, are nonetheless significant. When seen in the broader context already outlined, they suggest that for at least some key politicians the 1922 age of consent legislation was formulated and passed with the deliberate intention of encompassing sexual activity between females.

The creation of the age of consent for sex between women can thus be interpreted in a new light. Following the frustration of attempts to criminalise all sexual behaviour between women as 'gross indecency', political elites appear to have recognised 'indecent assault' as a means to achieve regulation of consensual sexual behaviour between females. This offence offered the potential to enable prosecutions of consensual behaviour in the same terms as non-consensual behaviour, without the law itself or the decisions of parliament drawing public attention to the existence of lesbianism. The age of consent for sex between women was thus conceived within the prevailing rationale of silence and concealment.

The subsequent interpretation and implementation of the law in relation to sex between women is presented differently in existing commentaries. Edwards observed in 1981:

> it has generally been the rule that woman [*sic*] cannot commit a rape, and indecent assault or a homosexual act. This remained the case until the 1930s when the statute relating to indecent assault was interpreted in a significantly new way. (Edwards, 1981, p. 37)

She argues that the case of *R v. Hare* (1934) marked a turning point, since Justice Avory ruled that a woman could commit indecent assault on a male (I KBD at 354; 24 Crim. App. Rep. at 108, cited in Edwards, 1981, p. 41). Nevertheless, in Edwards' account, it was not until the *Sexual Offences Act* 1956, which recodified existing sex offences, that an age of consent for sex between females was fixed:

> It was not until 1956 that sexual activity between women was recognized in law and made a criminal offence in the *Sexual Offences Act*, ss.14 and 15. From thereon a woman could be prosecuted for the indecent assault of another female, although no such case appears to have been brought before the courts. (Edwards, 1981, p. 45)

However, Faraday (1985, 1988) presents a somewhat different interpretation, arguing that the applicability of the law to sex between women suggested by the 1885 *R v. Armstrong* ruling was confirmed in a judge's comments in a 1933 case, unmentioned by Edwards. Faraday's discussions of lesbian sex and the law note that a legal ruling by Justice Avory in 1933, after the 1922 reform, confirmed this interpretation of the law on indecent assault being applicable to sex between women (Faraday, 1985, pp. 240–241, 1988, p. 15). In ruling that a woman could commit indecent assault on a 12-year-old boy, Justice Avory also remarked that as the law was phrased:

> There can be no reason for saying that a woman cannot be guilty of indecent assault on another female. (*Times Law Reports*, 22 December 1933, col. 104; quoted in Faraday, 1988, p. 15)

Hence Faraday's discussion of this case suggests that the 1922 law's potential applicability to cases of assenting or consenting sex between females may have been understood by judges during the inter-war years. Nevertheless, prosecutions remained extremely rare even after the Second World War, despite sex between women being increasingly legally recognised in divorce cases and libel actions (cf. Edwards, 1981, pp. 44–45). A quite different situation applied in relation to male homosexuality.

The *Wolfenden Report* and the decriminalisation of male homosexuality

The *Wolfenden Report*, published in 1957, represented a crucial statement of reformist principles concerning the role of law in the UK, providing the conceptual basis for a wide range of subsequent legislation including the partial decriminalisation of male homosexuality in England and Wales in 1967, and subsequently in Scotland in 1980, and in Northern Ireland in 1982 (Committee on Homosexual Offences and Prostitution, 1957; cited hereafter as CHOP, 1957).[1] Its principles were also influential in shaping subsequent UK legislation concerning issues including abortion, pornography and divorce. As Stuart Hall has argued, the *Wolfenden Report* is a vital document in understanding UK state 'reformism' from the 1950s to the early 1970s:

> It set out to articulate the field of moral ideology and practice which defines the dominant tendency in the 'legislation of consent'. (Hall, 1980, p. 9)

The report also influenced subsequent debates over the legal regulation of homosexuality in numerous states including Australia, Canada, the US, Ireland and New Zealand (Moran, 1996, pp. 14–15).

The report and the subsequent decriminalisation of male homosexuality have been the subject of extensive critical commentary and analysis (Weeks, 1977, pp. 156–182, 1989, pp. 239–272; Bland, McCabe and Mort, 1979, pp. 100–111; Hall, 1980; Mort, 1980; Jeffery-Poulter, 1991, pp. 1–89; Grey, 1992, 1997; Newburn, 1992, pp. 49–70; Evans, 1993, pp. 53–54, 65–88; Moran, 1995, 1996, pp. 21–32, 91–117; Higgins, 1996; David, 1997, pp. 177–196). Hence this chapter provides only a brief account of the report in its historical context, before proceeding to analyse the report's understanding of the role of 'age of consent' legislation in defining non-heterosexual citizenship, and the legal framework that emerged.

On 24 August 1954 a Conservative government appointed a joint departmental committee, answerable to both the Home Office and the Scottish Home Department, to investigate what the government and general public perceived as two increasing social problems: homosexuality and prostitution. The Committee on Homosexual Offences and Prostitution subsequently became known as the Wolfenden Committee, after its chair Sir John Wolfenden. The committee's terms of reference asked its members to consider the law and the practice of law throughout the UK in relation to homosexual offences and offences connected to prostitution, and to report any changes in the law it deemed desirable (CHOP, 1957, p. 7, #1). The association between homosexuality and prostitution, previously evident in debates over the *Criminal Law Amendment Act* 1885, reflected the assumption that both were forms of deviance threatening the 'basic unit of society', the family.

The Wolfenden Committee was not created with a 'permissive' intent, but was a product of increasing social anxieties concerning the increasing incidence and public visibility of homosexuality and prostitution. The committee was formed to find ways of efficiently managing and controlling what were perceived as two growing social problems. As Stuart Hall has argued, the immediate circumstances surrounding the Wolfenden Committee's creation can legitimately be described as a 'moral panic' (Hall, 1980, p. 8; cf. Cohen, 1972), generated by a series of high-profile spy scandals and trials (Weeks, 1977, pp. 156–167; Jeffery-Poulter, 1991, pp. 8–27; Newburn, 1992, pp. 49–51).

Nevertheless, significant sections of public opinion were moving in favour of decriminalisation prior to the committee's creation. An editorial from the *Sunday Times*, published following the paper's proposal to the government for a public enquiry, but prior to the committee's creation, illustrates this clearly:

> Homosexuality is rich pasture for the blackmailer; for the social stigma and the legal penalty of disclosure are alike terrifying to the wretched invert who, perhaps by a single reckless deed, has given way in secret to his warped desires... One may well ask whether, in regard to consenting acts between adult males, the truth is not that the real offence is to be found out... Notorious inverts occupy eminent places... In all this matter our society is riddled with hypocrisy. The law it would seem is not in accord with a large mass of public opinion... The case for a reform of the law as to acts committed in private between adults is very strong. (Editorial: 'Law and Hypocrisy', *Sunday Times*, 28.3.1954)

Hence more tolerant attitudes, favourable to investigating the possibility of decriminalisation, played a role in the committee's formation (Weeks, 1977, p. 164, 1989, p. 241). Evidence from committee records shows that most committee members expected decriminalisation as the outcome of their enquiries soon after the committee began its sittings (Higgins, 1996, p. 63).

The review was not only the product of short-term controversy over homosexuality, but must be interpreted in the context of long-term social trends. The social upheavals of the Second World War appear to have contributed to high levels of same-sex activity, as suggested by the first Kinsey Report on sexual behaviour (Kinsey, Pomeroy and Martin, 1948). Partly in reaction to such disruptions, the 1950s witnessed a strengthening of the ideology underpinning the nuclear family, with carefully segregated gender roles and minimal space for deviation (Weeks, 1977, pp. 157–159). This in turn appears to have encouraged greater policing zeal. Indictable 'homosexual' offences known to the police in England and Wales had increased at an accelerating speed since the 1930s, from 622 in 1931 to 2000 in 1945, 4416 in 1950 and 6357 in 1954 (CHOP, 1957, Appendix I, table I). Increasing press coverage of homosexuality led to growing public and political concern.

The committee investigated theories of the 'causes' of homosexuality (CHOP, 1957, pp. 11–17, #17–36); examined evidence of its incidence (CHOP, 1957, pp. 17–20, 37–47); and sought to define the relationship between existing sexual offences and the concept of 'homosexuality' intro-duced by its terms of reference (CHOP, 1957, p. 7, #1; Moran, 1995, 1996, esp. pp. 21–32, 91–117). Among those who provided evidence to the committee were three self-declared homosexuals, Peter Wildeblood, Patrick Trevor-Roper and Carl Winter. Trevor-Roper and Winter, both respected as professionals, used evidence of blackmail and suicide resulting from the prohibition to argue confidently in favour of decriminalisation (Higgins, 1996, pp. 39–45).

In 1957 the committee published its report, recommending the partial decriminalisation of consensual homosexual acts in private between men aged over 21 (CHOP, 1957, p. 115, #355), while also proposing the tightening of the law concerning street prostitution, though leaving the act of prostitution itself legal (CHOP, 1957, pp. 116–117). However, the report was very clear in refuting any intention to fully legitimise homosexuality, and emphasised that its argument for decriminalisation was 'not to be taken as saying that society should condone or approve male homosexual behaviour' (CHOP, 1957, p. 22):

> It is important that the limited modification of the law which we propose should not be interpreted as an indication that the law can be indifferent to other forms of homosexual behaviour, or as a general licence to adult homosexuals to behave as they please. (CHOP, 1957, p. 44, #124)

The limits of official tolerance were clear.

The report gave careful consideration to the question of the minimum age (CHOP, 1957, pp. 25–28, #65–74). Its considerations placed emphasis upon the evidence of medical witnesses:

> Our medical witnesses were unanimously of the view that the main sexual pattern is laid down in the early years of life, and the majority of them held that it was usually fixed, in the main outline, by the age of sixteen. (CHOP, 1957, p. 26, #68)

However, despite this the report argued that a boy could only make decisions about his actions after the age of 21:

> a boy is incapable at the age of sixteen of forming a mature judgement about actions of a kind which might have the effect of setting him apart from the rest of society. (CHOP, 1957, p. 25, #71)

Hence the report premised its recommendations upon a disjunction between the formation of sexual aetiology and the attainment of the decision-making competence associated with mature judgements, which could legitimise the right to exercise choice.

The committee's investigations concerning female homosexuality were extremely brief, though its terms of reference had potentially included all 'homosexual offences'. The committee considered the sole offence relating to sexual acts between women, 'indecent assault' on a female, for which 'consent' had been removed as a defence for girls aged under 16 by the *Criminal Law Amendment Act* 1922, s. 1 (re-codified in the *Sexual Offences Act*

1956, s. 14.1). This offence was included in the committee's list of homosexual offences (CHOP, 1957, pp. 36–38, #95–103; Moran, 1996, pp. 97–98, 100). However, the committee were unable to find a single instance of an act with another female 'which exhibits the libidinous features that characterise sexual acts between males', and concluded that all recorded convictions referred to the aiding and abetting of sexual assaults by males (CHOP, 1957, p. 38, #103). Hence the existence of 'indecent assault' did little to destabilise the committee's assumption of women's lack of sexual agency, and its attentions appear not to have focussed on lesbianism, as is evidenced by committee correspondence showing that 'homosexual offences' were in general assumed to be male (Moran, 1996, pp. 97–101). The implication of the *Wolfenden Report*'s comments is that lesbians were not regarded as likely to engage in improper behaviour with young women and girls, and hence no necessity was seen for reforming existing age of consent legislation. However, the fact that a rationale of 'difference' rather than 'equality' was applied in relation to male homosexuality was probably also influenced by the rationale which had operated in the inter-war period, that explicitly pro-hibitive legal regulation might be counter-productive in spreading knowledge about lesbianism.

The report's conclusions concerning male homosexuality received a 'mixed, but by no means entirely hostile reception', being endorsed by the Church Assembly,[2] as well as *The Times* and the *Daily Mirror*. However, decriminal-isation was dismissed as 'nonsense' by the *Daily Express*, and the *Daily Mail* claimed decriminalisation would lead to an increase in perversion, though the *Daily Telegraph* remained more ambivalent.[3] Hence while the government enacted the report's recommendations concerning the effective regulation of prostitution almost immediately, through the *Street Offences Act* 1959, the proposals concerning homosexuality were shelved (cf. CHOP, 1957, pp. 116–117).

The report's publication was followed by a 10-year period of lobbying for decriminalisation, particularly by the Homosexual Law Reform Society as documented by its former secretary, Antony Grey (Grey, 1992; see also Grey, 1997). A series of attempts were made to implement the report's proposals in parliament, though reform proposals were strategically limited in application to England and Wales (Dempsey, 1998, p. 157). The bill which, in amended form, eventually became the *Sexual Offences Act* 1967 was first introduced into the House of Commons in June 1960 by Kenneth Robinson MP, but was defeated by a majority of more than 2:1. It was first successfully introduced into the House of Lords by Lord Arran in May 1965. During its passage through the Lords, senior peers amended the Wolfenden proposals with a strict new privacy clause, applying a stricter standard of privacy to homosexuality than existed for male/female behaviour. This specified that a homosexual act would not be considered 'private' if 'more than two persons take part or are present', or if occurring in a public lavatory (*Sexual Offences Act* 1967, s. 1(2)).

The Bill passed through the Lords in July 1965, and was first introduced into the Commons as a Private Members Bill by Conservative MP Humphrey Berkeley, known to be homosexual by many in parliament though not the public.[4] After a general election and Labour victory in 1966, Berkeley lost his seat and was replaced as the bill's sponsor by Labour MP Leo Abse. With backing from the new Home Secretary Roy Jenkins, and despite the misgivings of Harold Wilson and the vehement opposition of Foreign Secretary George Brown, parliamentary time was set aside by the government. The *Sexual Offences Act* was eventually passed by the Commons at 5.44 a.m. on the 3rd of July 1967, after an all-night debate (HC 23.6.1967, cols 2115–2200; 3.7.1967, cols 1403–1526; for a first-hand account, see Grey, 1992; see also Jeffery-Poulter, 1991, pp. 28–89; Newburn, 1992, pp. 55–62; Higgins, 1996, pp. 123–148).[5]

The new law stated:

> Notwithstanding any statutory or common law provisions, but subject to the provisions of the next following section, a homosexual act in private shall not be an offence provided that the parties consent thereto and have attained the age of twenty-one years. (*Sexual Offences Act* 1967, s. 1.1)

A 'homosexual act', a concept introduced by the legislation, was defined as follows:

> For the purposes of this section a man shall be treated as doing a homosexual act if, and only if, he commits buggery with another man or commits an act of gross indecency with another man or is party to the commission by a man of such an act. (*Sexual Offences Act* 1967, s. 1.7)

Hence much of the commissioning of homosexual acts, in addition to sexual activity itself, remained within the scope of prohibition. Decriminalisation in the same form, with a minimum age of 21, was not extended to Scotland until 1980, by Section 80(7) of the *Criminal Justice (Scotland) Act* 1980 (amending Scottish sexual offences which had been recodified in the *Sexual Offences (Scotland) Act* 1976), or to Northern Ireland until 1982 by the *Homosexual Offences (Northern Ireland) Order* 1982 (see Jeffery-Poulter, 1991, pp. 142–154; Reekie, 1997a, pp. 180–181; Dempsey, 1998).

Decriminalisation was informed by a growing degree of tolerance among political elites. The fact that John Wolfenden's own son was openly homosexual within his social circle and to his father is indicative of establishment dilemmas (Faulks, 1996, pp. 209–309). Evidence continues to emerge that homosexuals such as prospective Conservative Prime Minister Lord Robert Boothby were peppered throughout parliament and the establishment, and hence that their political colleagues had every interest in decriminalising their activities.[6] The *Wolfenden Report* and decriminalisation did not represent the state's concession to public attitudes, but rather political elites moving ahead of public opinion, although public opinion was certainly shifting by the time decriminalisation eventually occurred.

The political climate which facilitated the eventual passage of the *Sexual Offences Act* 1967 was significantly less conservative than that which structured the conclusions of the *Wolfenden Report*. By 1967 after such a long process of debate, '...the heat had largely been dissipated from the question' (Weeks, 1977, p. 156; cf. pp. 168–182). Nevertheless, those arguing for decriminalisation employed many of the same arguments advanced by the *Wolfenden Report*. They emphasised that homosexuality was the 'condition' of a particular group, possibly treatable but largely fixed. Leo Abse, the bill's sponsor, argued that homosexuality was a psychological problem requiring prevention and understanding: arguments which he has subsequently declared that he knew were 'absolute crap'.[7] Abse and others emphasised the threat of blackmail under existing law as a pragmatic reason for decriminalisation, particularly to protect national security in the light of the Burgess and Maclean spy scandals. These were strategic claims, more assertive than the *Wolfenden Report*, yet still largely within the same framework.

The establishment of a minimum age of 21 for male 'homosexual acts' needs to be conceptualised in the context of the surrounding legal framework. Decriminalisation had the effect of nullifying existing legislation which outlawed acts of buggery and gross indecency between men within a tightly delimited private sphere. However, partial decriminalisation did not remove the offences of 'buggery' or 'gross indecency' from the statute, and many consensual acts remained subject to prosecution. Decriminalisation applied only with no more than two men present, due to the House of Lords amendment imposing a specific, strict definition of privacy (*Sexual Offences Act* 1967, s. 2). The merchant navy and armed forces were also exempted (*Sexual Offences Act* 1967, s. 5). Soliciting (cruising or propositioning men) and procuring (inviting, encouraging and facilitating homosexual acts) remained completely illegal. Additionally, a legal judgement in 1972 by the House of Lords subsequently decided that the 1967 Act exempted homosexuals over 21 from criminal penalties without making their actions 'lawful in the full sense' (Weeks, 1989, p. 275).

Furthermore, in accordance with the *Wolfenden Report*'s recommendations, the law imposed new regulations upon public behaviour at the same time as it enacted limited decriminalisation in private. New strict sentences for buggery were introduced for offences with people aged below 21. The law was tightened with regard to importuning, and with regard to behaviour involving young people below the new minimum age (Moran, 1996).

Different rationales underpinning laws applying to 'heterosexual' and 'homosexual' behaviour made utilisation of the term 'age of consent' to describe the age of 21 applying to sex between men problematic for policymakers. The *Wolfenden Report* chose not to employ the phrase 'age of consent' in its recommendations, preferring to describe the minimum age as an 'age of "adulthood"' (CHOP, 1957, p. 115); and the subsequent *Sexual Offences Act* 1967 did not utilise 'age of consent' either. The Wolfenden committee's choice of language reflected their belief that a young man aged 16, like a young woman, did have the psychological competence to consent to sexual activity, but was not 'sufficiently adult to take decisions about his private conduct and to carry the responsibility for their consequences' (CHOP, 1957, p. 26, #69) – 'age of adulthood' was used to emphasise the conception of the legal age as signifying 'adulthood'. However, 'age of consent' appears to have been used in debates over decriminalisation to some extent by both supporters and opponents. The Policy Advisory Committee on Sexual Offences which subsequently reviewed the law in the late 1970s also rejected 'age of consent' and used 'minimum age' in relation to the post-1967 legislative framework, on the grounds that it would be unrealistic to imply that the law assumed males under 21 were incapable of granting consent, particularly in a context where they were nonetheless held criminally responsible for partici- pation in illegal sexual behaviour (PAC, 1979, p. 14, 1981, p. 11; for full discussion, see Chapter 6).

It can be argued, and was often argued during post-1967 campaigns for 'equalisation', that the concept 'age of consent' was inappropriate to apply to the post-decriminalisation legislative framework. This has been argued for various reasons: because of the law's conception in relation to 'adult- hood' rather than psychological capacities to consent; because it did not correspond to the gendered notion of the age of consent originating in nineteenth-century social purity movements which informed conceptions of the law operating in a heterosexual context; and/or because the law did not apply a clear general principle of respect for legal entitlement of males aged over 21 to make choices concerning consenting sexual behaviour. As I argued in Chapter 1, the term 'age of consent' does not currently carry a highly determinate meaning, and is an acceptable way to frame discussion of various forms of minimum age legislation, so long as a particular model of what an 'age of consent' would imply is not assumed. Nevertheless, atten- tion to the 1967 legal framework reveals how subsequent uses of the concept 'age of consent' with respect to male homosexuality in mainstream public debate risked rendering invisible continuing forms of legal persecution, and how contestation of the concept's applicability became an appropriate strategy post-1967 for gay campaigners such as the Campaign for Homosexual Equality to draw attention to the law's discriminatory form (see Chapter 6). However, interestingly assertions by the Policy Advisory Committee (1979, 1981) and some activist and academic commentators that the concept 'age of consent' was inappropriate to describe the 1967 law have tended to assume that the minimum age for sexual intercourse with a female represented an authentic age of consent conceived in relation to female competence to consent (for discussion, see Moran, 1997); whereas analysis of debates over the Criminal Law Amendment Act 1885 suggests only a limited emphasis on female competence in decision-making informed the creation of this law, which tended to be conceived as an 'age of protection' (see Chapter 4); and feminist scholarship on rape suggests that sexual offences operating in a heterosexual context could not be conceptualised as granting females any 'right to consent' above the age of 16 (Temkin, 2002; see Chapter 4).

Having described the *Wolfenden Report*'s proposals and subsequent legal reforms in their social and political context, and having problematised the concept 'age of consent' in relation to the 1967 law, I will now develop my analysis of the *Wolfenden Report*'s approach to the decriminalisation of 'homosexual acts'. To explore the meaning of the new minimum age for sexual behaviour in strict privacy, the following section focusses on how the Wolfenden committee and supporters of its report conceptualised the 'public' and 'private' lives of homosexuals in relation to citizenship. Via engagement with existing critiques of Wolfenden, I develop my own perspective on the rationale for decriminalisation. This analysis underpins and contextualises the discussion in the chapter's final section, which considers the precise rationale for fixing the legal age for 'homosexual acts' at 21.

Rethinking the *Wolfenden Report*'s rationale for decriminalisation

The critical aspect of the *Wolfenden Report*'s conceptual framework was its distinction between *public* acts, regarded as being within the legitimate realm of state intervention to preserve public order and decency, and *private* morality. The report stated that the function of the law:

> is to preserve public order and decency, to protect the citizen from what is offensive and injurious, and to provide sufficient safeguards against exploitation and corruption of others... (CHOP, 1957, p. 9, #13)

Hence:

> It is not, in our view, the function of the law to intervene in the private lives of citizens, or to seek to enforce any particular pattern of behaviour, further than is necessary to carry out the purposes we have outlined. (CHOP, 1957, p. 10, #14)

The sphere of privacy was to be carefully delimited, tightly patrolled at the boundaries where public order and decency were threatened. The public/private divide became the crucial axis upon which the Wolfenden Committee built its case for decriminalisation (CHOP, 1957, p. 12, #12; p. 20, #49–52); and hence is of central importance in conceptualising the significance of the minimum age for consensual behaviour.

The *Wolfenden Report*'s advocacy of decriminalisation and its distinction between public and private behaviour were the product of a number of overlapping tendencies producing change in the principles structuring social life. It derived from a complex interplay of knowledge and beliefs generated by different social institutions: ethical perspectives, legal philosophies, medical knowledge, and social attitudes towards homosexuality. A broad tendency away from ethical collectivism towards the individualisation of moral decision-making among adults, growing steadily since the nineteenth century, was one significant factor. This growing belief that society should respect the choices and feelings of individuals was linked to a growing sense of autonomy and potential self-determination generated in capitalist societies characterised by the movements of people, rising levels of education, formal democratisation and extension of the franchise. A steady movement towards secularisation and acceptance of religious diversity simultaneously reinforced this shift, inducing doubt over the authority of traditional institutions, and placing responsibility for ethical decisions increasingly upon the individual.

A more specific, but related, shift in understandings of the role of the state and law occurred during the 1950s from what can be described as 'legal moralism' to 'legal utilitarianism'. The *Wolfenden Report*'s distinction between public and private spheres was framed squarely in relation to debates between utilitarian liberals and conservative paternalists. It represented a revival of nineteenth-century liberal utilitarianism espoused by Bentham and Mill, asserting a clear distinction between the appropriate scope of law and the dictates of morality (Mill, 1962, 1974). The principles at stake were most clearly articulated in the debate between Lord Devlin and H.L. Hart which occurred in response to the report's publication (Devlin, 1959; Hart, 1963). Lord Devlin used his Maccabean lectures of 1959 to argue that the criminal law should embody key elements of a nation's morality, preserving and fostering these values; Hart responded by supporting the Wolfenden committee's distinction between sin and crime, and rejecting the law as an effective medium for the transmission of social values.[8]

Christie Davies has subsequently described the shift in the role of law represented by Wolfenden in slightly different terms, as a shift from 'moralism' to 'causalism', a distinction which focusses more upon the practical effectiveness of prohibitive laws and less upon the ethics of legal intervention, thus distinguishing changing conceptions of law from the wider social shift towards ethical individualism already described (Davies, 1975, 1980). Davies' work makes clear that though legal utilitarianism was clearly aligned with a movement towards ethical individualism, this depended upon a particular conjuncture of attitudes towards homosexuality and the possibilities for its prevention and regulation.

Changes in ethical and legal perspectives only contributed to the case for decriminalisation in the context of changing understandings of 'homosexuality'. The Wolfenden committee's investigations occurred in the context of two simultaneous tendencies in the cultural definition and social positioning of 'the homosexual': increasing social visibility and increasing delineation. 'Homosexuality' became increasingly visible due to the agency of 'homosexuals', as the growth of urban subcultures developed and identities hardened, and also due to increasing investigations by modern institutions seeking to define and control the 'problem of homosexuality', including the media, the law and the medical science. Simultaneously, and through the same dynamics, there was a movement towards the increasing delineation of homosexuality from heterosexuality. Proposals for decriminalisation were therefore intertwined with the production of new authoritative conceptions of scientifically defined homosexual subjects. The Wolfenden inquiry was situated at the juncture of these contradictory tendencies, which are embodied in its conception, its investigations and its conclusions. A limited progressive movement occurred within a wider framework of social forces in which mechanisms for homosexual containment were also embedded. The committee's proposal for partial decriminalisation offered both a measure of tolerance and the promise of effective regulation.

The committee premised its conclusions upon the view that homosexuality was the unfortunate 'condition' of a distinct group of individuals, and hence, despite being unconvinced by existing theories of homosexuality as a sickness or by existing treatments, recommended the pursuit of further medical research into psychiatric and hormone 'treatments' (CHOP, 1957, p. 11, #18; p. 116, #xvi–xviii).[9] By articulating homosexuality as a 'condition' characterising a distinct group of people, and claiming that adult sexual identity was fixed by the age of 16, the report was able to draw a distinction between strategies for addressing under-16s, and for addressing older homosexuals. The *Wolfenden Report* thus entailed a shift away from theories emphasising the flexibility of an individual's sexuality, towards an emphasis upon its fixity in adulthood; from a deviant choice to a 'condition'. Dominant forms of sexology advanced arguments that, as Moran puts it, 'If homosexuality is fundamental to the sense of self and is innate, it cannot be regarded as punishable by rational persons who respect the laws of nature' (Moran, 1996, p. 3). According to Higgins, evidence to the committee confirms that many of the strongest advocates of law reform were those who believed most strongly in the definition of homosexuality as a medical condition (Higgins, 1996, p. 51).

The rationale for decriminalisation thus implied managing the deviant desires of an inherently perverse group in society who could never aspire to join the dominant moral community, but would remain socially marginal. Decriminalisation would not, according to its advocates, promote the quantity of homosexual activity. The narratives of homosexual identity, subjectivity and behaviour invoked in the process of making these arguments, particularly medical theories stressing the early fixity of the homosexual 'condition', involved a sharpening of the definition of the homosexual/heterosexual binary (cf. Sedgwick, 1990; Bech, 1997).

Hence the *Wolfenden Report*'s advocacy of decriminalisation of homosexuality within a narrowly defined private sphere must be conceptualised as occurring at a complex conjuncture, the product of a variety of simultaneous shifts in culture and prevailing forms of knowledge: a tendency towards the individualisation of moral decision-making; an associated, though more specific, shift towards utilitarian and causalist legal philosophies; a hardening of the homosexual/heterosexual distinction; an apparent failure to find ways to effectively prevent homosexuality; and a limited growth in social tolerance towards homosexuality. Only the coincidence of these tendencies facilitated the removal of legal regulation. This context must be understood in order to grasp the meanings of the public and private spheres defined by Wolfenden.

An analysis of the public and the private spheres can be developed through engagement with existing critiques. It has been widely argued that the *Wolfenden Report* represented a legal strategy of control and an attempt to eradicate the problem of male homosexuality from public view, rather than pure 'permissiveness', 'liberalisation' or a straightforward step towards equality (Weeks, 1977, 1989; Bland, McCabe and Mort, 1979; Greenwood and Young, 1980; Hall, 1980; Mort, 1980; Moran, 1996). Jeffrey Weeks has expressed this by arguing that Wolfenden was motivated by a desire to control, not liberate homosexuality (Weeks, 1989, p. 242). Greenwood and Young have characterised the *Wolfenden Report* as promoting a combination of 'normalisation' (in the sense of 'liberalisation' and equalisation), 'medicalisation' and 'criminalisation' (Greenwood and Young, 1980). Stuart Hall has described the report as representing 'a shift in the disposition of moral regulation', emphasising:

> Wolfenden's 'double taxonomy': towards stricter penalty and control, towards greater freedom and leniency, together the 'two elements . . . in a single strategy'. (Hall, 1980, p. 14)

In more recent commentary, Moran has described the report as pursuing 'strategies of eradication' in relation to homosexuality (Moran, 1995, pp. 21–22, 1996, pp. 102–117, esp. p. 115; see discussion below).

These critical theorists, interpreting the *Wolfenden Report*'s definition of homosexual citizenship from post-gay liberation perspectives, have drawn upon different strains of radical thought, including deviancy theory, Marxist theory, feminist theory and Foucauldian theory, challenging assumptions that the rationale for decriminalisation was ever straightforwardly 'liberal' or 'progressive' in intent. Such work[10] has convincingly challenged the appropriation of the *Wolfenden Report* and decriminalisation into teleological liberal progressivist narratives of modernisation, civilisation, development and expanding citizenship (cf. Marshall, 1950).[11] It has convincingly made the case for a critical reading of the *Wolfenden Report*'s rationale for decriminalisation, which sought both public and private forms of containment to address homosexuality. Weeks, Mort, Hall, Greenwood and Young, and subsequently Moran, have advanced broadly similar accounts, emphasising a strengthening of 'public' regulation, while simultaneously drawing attention to new forms of medical and moral regulation applying to homosexuals in their 'private' lives, replacing legal prohibition. Nevertheless, there are differences between these theorists which merit attention.

Weeks has emphasised the increasing vigilance of the law in relation to the extensive scope of regulation applying to 'public' acts beyond the 'private' sphere: '... the logic of their position was that penalties for public displays of sexuality should be strengthened' (Weeks, 1977, p. 165; cf. Weeks, 1989, p. 243).

> What was proposed was that the offences which were difficult to discover and troublesome (and politically embarrassing) to prosecute should be removed from the statute book, the better to preserve public decency. (Weeks, 1977, p. 166)

In relation to private behaviour, Weeks has commented that 'the key point is that privatisation did not necessarily involve a diminution of control', but that the report accepted the psychologisation of homosexuality, while endorsing a continued search for 'treatments' and 'cures'.

> In part at least, the Committee was proposing no more than a shift of emphasis away from the law towards the social services as foci for social regulation (Weeks, 1989, p. 244).

Greenwood and Young similarly emphasised the committee's hope that decriminalisation of adult relations in private might discourage public proselytisation in favour of homosexuality, and sexual activities with minors. They note that Wolfenden advocated the more effective criminalisation of public homosexuality, coupled with medicalisation of prisoners to quiesce (rather than cure) their desires (Greenwood and Young, 1980, pp. 164–166).

A somewhat greater emphasis is placed upon the continuing effects of regulation in the 'private' sphere in the work of Hall (1980) and especially Mort (1980; see also Bland, McCabe and Mort, 1979, pp. 100–111). Both strain to escape the strictures of 1970s Marxist and feminist approaches which would seek to analyse the report as a straightforward expression of ideology working functionally in the maintenance of capitalism and patriarchy. Both invoke the work of Foucault as a means to theorise the continuing regulation of homosexuals in the private sphere, in the absence of direct state intervention (Foucault, 1981; cf. Bland, McCabe and Mort, 1979, pp. 109–111; Hall, 1980, pp. 11–14; Mort, 1980, pp. 41–44).

Hall, like Weeks, notes the strengthening of public regulation, but places more emphasis on the limits of 'private' freedoms: in place of prohibition came not equal respect, but the welfare-statisation and medicalisation of deviant groups, who continued to be seen as 'social problems' needing treatment (Hall, 1980, pp. 9–11). Hall refers briefly to Foucault's concept of a 'micro-physics of power' to explain how the private arena of decriminalisation nevertheless remained a sphere of moral regulation:

> Wolfenden clearly staked out a new relation between the two modes of moral regulation – the modalities of legal compulsion and of self-regulation. (Hall, 1980, pp. 11–12)

But the nature of 'self-regulation' is little explored. Hall's account also somewhat overplays moral reformism as a 'signifying strategy' which 'declared and represented what its practice was aimed at accomplishing' by 'giving a message' advocating self-restraint by homosexuals after decriminalisation (Hall, 1980, p. 20). This suggestion that the report was a significant vehicle for transmitting moral values somewhat overstates the extent to which the committee expected their arguments to be accepted by homosexuals. The language of the report was in part designed to legitimate the proposals it contained.

Frank Mort also invokes Foucault in seeking to explore forms of regulation operating in the private sphere (Mort, 1980, pp. 41–44; see also Bland, McCabe and Mort, 1979, pp. 109–111; cf. Foucault, 1981). Mort argues that the *Wolfenden Report* 'does not envisage the total abandonment of strategies of regulation' in the private sphere:

> Power is no longer to be exercised through the direct operation of the law, but rather through the mobilisation of a variety of non-legal practices. Henceforward, medicine, 'therapy', psychology, and forms of applied sociology are all envisaged as forming new principles of regulation. (Mort, 1980, pp. 43–44)

Subsequent work by Moran (1995, 1996) can be interpreted, in part, as proceeding with the investigation of the possibilities suggested by Hall and Mort for a Foucauldian exploration of new forms of regulation operating in both public and private realms, including 'self-regulation' (Hall, 1980, pp. 11–14; Mort, 1980, pp. 41–44). Moran explores the new legal category of 'the homosexual' as, in Foucault's terms, a set of technologies, 'a whole machinery for speechifying, analysing and investigating' (Foucault, 1981, p. 32; cited in Moran, 1996, p. 16). Moran stresses that the installation of the term 'homosexual' in law itself implied the installation of a new set of regulatory technologies of medical and psychological examination, various forms of treatment and policing (Moran, 1995, p. 21). He identifies two 'strategies of eradication' through which the committee addressed homosexuality (Moran, 1995, pp. 21–22, 1996, pp. 102–117, esp. p. 115). First, 'juridical eradication' – the hope that homosexual acts might disappear into a decriminalised 'space beyond the law'; and secondly, the hope that homosexuals would seek treatment for their condition, leading to heterosexuality or abstinence. The Wolfenden committee also proposed more research into homosexuality, to enable the possibility of future eradication (Moran, 1995, pp. 21–22, 1996, pp. 102–117, esp. p. 115). Moran also argues that the committee's reformulation of sexual offences was important in conveying and sustaining certain cultural conceptions of homosexuality, particularly through conjoining 'buggery' and 'homosexual offences' (Moran, 1996, pp. 21–32). The proposed new legal framework encoded cultural understandings of homosexuality which entailed regulative effects, spanning both 'public' and 'private' worlds.

These various critiques of Wolfenden have convincingly challenged liberal interpretations of Wolfenden by demonstrating the extent of new forms of public regulation and the persistence of forms of regulation in the private sphere. However, a significant feature of these various critiques of Wolfenden is that they have tended to derive from radical sociology, history and cultural studies rather than political theory, utilising theoretical resources deriving from Foucault and Marxist understandings of ideology. Reappraisals of liberalism in post-Marxist and feminist political theory since the 1980s (Mouffe, 1993; Squires, 1999), where the value of individual rights and citizenship have been granted greater value than in earlier Marxist/left and feminist formulations, suggest the potential to develop a more nuanced interpretation of Wolfenden. Existing radical critiques of Wolfenden, it can be argued, do not give sufficient attention to the liberal conceptions of citizenship which inform the report, and tend to underestimate the significance of these in some respects.

Radical critiques of Wolfenden have tended to lack an explicit articulation of the ways in which proposals for the decriminalisation of homosexuality entailed new forms of recognition of homosexuals as citizens, particularly in relation to the differentiated and stratified realms of citizenship identified in much political theory. Existing critiques have not adequately conceptualised the meaning or significance of homosexual life within the restricted private realm, since this cannot be reduced to the effects of medicalisation or self-regulation. Political theory suggests some useful theoretical tools to develop analysis of non-heterosexual citizenship in this context.

It is certainly true that the extent to which the *Wolfenden Report* offered homosexuals forms of 'citizenship' in the broad sense of status as full members of a society was quite minimal. The report's view of homosexuality as a medical condition and the acceptance of the desirability of its eradication through medical or psychological treatments (subsequently including hormone treatment and electric-shock therapy) illustrate a lack of respect for the right of homosexuals to exist. In relation to T.H. Marshall's citizen-ship schema, the *Wolfenden Report* offered no clear articulation of homosexuals as deserving of most civil or political forms of citizenship, and certainly made no case for social citizenship in forms such as social welfare rights (cf. Marshall, 1950). As critics have argued, homosexual lives were subject to the intensified enforcement of legal prohibitions against 'public' sexual behav-iour, and sexual behaviour with people below the minimum legal age of 21. Other forms of containment by various agencies of the welfare state were also encouraged, together with homogenising understandings of homosexuality.

However, attitudes towards homosexuality were more complex than the emphasis upon containment and regulation in some existing accounts allows. The *Wolfenden Report* drew upon contradictory impulses. The report sought ways to eliminate homosexuality if this were feasible; yet simultaneously, in a context of the apparent absence of effective treatments, the report advanced a strategy of granting some minimal citizenship rights to homosexuals. These can be identified as taking two particular forms which I shall explore: a right to engage in consensual sexual behaviour within the narrowly defined private sphere; and a right to limited forms of political citizenship. Though each was granted in forms unequal to those available to heterosexuals, each also opened possibilities for homosexual advancement.

In general the presence of the concepts of 'citizenship', 'rights', 'freedom of choice' and 'privacy' in the language of the *Wolfenden Report* has more positive significance than previous radical critiques have recognised. For example, the report discusses how far the law 'properly applies to the sexual behaviour of the individual citizen', implicitly including homosexuals (CHOP, 1957, p. 20, #52). The committee cites one argument as 'decisive' in its decision to advocate decriminalisation:

> the importance which society and the law ought to give to individual freedom of choice and action in matters of private morality. […] to empha-sise the personal and private nature of moral or immoral conduct is to emphasise the personal and private responsibility of the individual for his own actions. (CHOP, 1957, p. 24, #61)

Hence homosexuals were addressed in the language of 'individual freedom of choice' within a liberal humanist schema of universal citizenship. While such language is clearly fundamentally at odds with the equally apparent desire of the Wolfenden committee to eradicate homosexuality through medical treatment, it is important to acknowledge this Janus-faced, contradictory and ambivalent character of the report, rather than representing the impulse to eradicate as predominant or more fundamental.

The concept of privacy was employed with contrary intentions applying to homosexuals and heterosexuals. While privacy for heterosexual sexual behaviour was seen to contribute to the flourishing of the family, society and good citizenship, privacy for homosexual sexual behaviour was intended to manage and contain irrevocably deviant individuals. For the Wolfenden committee, homosexual acts were inherently incompatible with the dominant values of society. However, it is important to understand arguments for privacy with an appreciation of the ideological frameworks of those who advanced them. For many liberals and utilitarians, freedom of choice in the private realm was (and is) not simply a limit upon state interference; the act of choice and the processes of deliberation and education they entail are understood as a means to the improvement of both the individual and the wider society (cf. Mill, 1974). Hence for liberal advocates these arguments implied the attribution to homosexuals of important decision-making responsibilities, which were in turn key elements in the constitution of the liberal understanding of citizenship. The Wolfenden framework was not straightforwardly 'liberal', but did draw extensively on liberal utilitarian arguments.

The *Wolfenden Report*'s tentative invocation of a citizen's right to 'privacy' drew upon forms of liberal political philosophy in which 'liberty', 'rights' and 'privacy' represented the most basic and fundamental aspects of citizenship, universally applicable to all individuals. For example, 'privacy' had been encoded within post-war international conventions including the *European Convention on Human Rights* 1950 (Article 8). This status of 'privacy' in much liberal political theory and in the philosophy of human rights derived from a dubious patriarchal history, since 'privacy' had historically been the prerogative of male heads of households. Nevertheless, such definitions of citizenship implied a degree of valuation of homosexuals. They also created the potential for further positive developments, apparent in recent decades as claims for 'privacy' have become a major vehicle for the contestation of homophobic laws. For example, the right to privacy encoded in the *European Convention on Human Rights* was successfully invoked by Euan Sutherland in support of a lower and equal age of consent for sexual behaviour between men.[12]

The *Wolfenden Report*'s understanding of the public/private divide was thus situated within a long-term transformation in the political meanings of 'privacy' and wider political ideologies, overlapping with simultaneous changes in the social status of homosexuals. Its articulation of 'privacy' as a basic universal right applying to all citizens therefore entailed complex effects, both progressive and regulatory. As many critics have noted, the realm of privacy was conceptualised in association with the tighter regulation of public acts, in addition to forms of regulation within the 'private' realm which it was hoped would ensure homosexuality did not transgress its boundaries. Public regulation and medicalisation conspired in an attempt to ensure the privatisation and containment of homosexuality. Yet this cannot be understood as the whole story. Through its association with understandings of universal citizenship, 'privacy' also had a more positive implication and expansive potential.

Alongside this argument for recognition of Wolfenden's 'privacy' as embodying a certain positive form of citizenship, though contextually circumscribed, it can also be argued that Wolfenden's public sphere was not exclusively characterised by regulation, as radical critiques have tended to imply. The decision to decriminalise private sexual behaviour was also associated with some significant, though minimal and informal, recognition of other aspects of the civil and political citizenship of homosexuals, relating to the public sphere. The Wolfenden committee's review involved homosexuals in a process of consultation and deliberation, in which they were treated with basic respect. These consultations represented very limited engagements in political dialogue, since the committee meetings were held away from public view, and only three homosexuals gave evidence in person (Higgins, 1996, pp. 39–45). Nevertheless, the polite exchanges which occurred, in which Wolfenden referred to homosexuals as a 'community' (Higgins, 1996, p. 44), embodied a minimal level of recognition that homosexuals deserved a political voice. The subsequent formation of the Homosexual Law Reform Society illustrates that the report contributed to a shift in the political climate, producing greater recognition of homosexual 'rights' including free speech, and freedom of political organisation. While the change in the law proposed by the committee referred only to the legalisation of sexual acts, and continued to deny homosexuals the ability to communicate in some ways, such as via contact advertisements, it nonetheless signalled an acceptance that homosexuals could legitimately meet and have relationships.

Expanded understandings of 'the political' have been endorsed in recent political theory by theorists who conceptualise political citizenship as existing beyond traditional political institutions, throughout social life, wherever political dialogue, political identity-formation and political contestation are possible (Honig, 1992; Mouffe, 1993). Such a perspective implies the need to recognise that Wolfenden's proposals for decriminalisation held implications not only for 'sexual behaviour', conceived as pre-political, but also for homosexual lives and relationships more broadly, and hence for political citizenship. Wolfenden began a process of legitimating a minimal level of political participation by homosexuals in the public sphere.

This section has argued that the Wolfenden rationale for partial decriminalisation entailed recognition of limited forms of citizenship for homosexuals, both in the form of a right to privacy and in the form of political citizenship – each defined narrowly and contextually circumscribed, yet each nonetheless significant. This has significance for how we interpret the meaning of consensual sexual behaviour in the private sphere as conceptualised by the Wolfenden committee, and hence for our understanding of the age of consent for male homosexuals in its social and political context. Though the motives for advocating decriminalisation were contradictory, advocacy of the freedom to engage in sexual behaviour in private embodied a degree of social respect, notwithstanding hopes for the eradication of homosexuality. The following section argues that the attribution of these limited forms of citizenship to homosexuals has implications for conceptualising the specific rationale informing the *Wolfenden Report*'s proposal for a minimum age of 21 for sexual behaviour between men.

The male homosexual age of consent

The Wolfenden committee's recommendations raise a compelling question concerning the age of consent for sexual behaviour between men: why, given that its medical witnesses were near-unanimous in their belief that 'the main sexual pattern is [...] fixed, in the main outline by the age of sixteen' (CHOP, 1957, p. 26, #68), did the report persist in advocating a minimum age of 21, and hence enforce a disjunction between the fixity of desires and the attainment of sexual autonomy?

The committee's deliberations over the age of consent occurred within a logic of containment, premised first and foremost upon a desire to ensure the prevention of any increase in the prevalence of homosexuality. Hence the evidence of medical witnesses concerning the age at which sexual desires are fixed represented the primary parameter dictating the minimum conceivable age which could be accepted. Only once sexual orientation was established as a *fait accompli* were other factors, including adult citizenship rights, considered. This emphasis upon the fixity of sexual desires by the age of 16 was to remain crucial in subsequent age of consent debates, as I demonstrate in the following chapters.

Beyond this primary constraint, however, the committee were faced with a range of potential ages. The age 21 was effectively the highest option, given that it marked the highest age at which the actions of young people were significantly constrained in UK law. The age 21 was the age of majority, the minimum age to vote and to form valid legal contracts, and also to marry without parental consent. It therefore represented a secondary parameter in determining the minimum age.

The evidence received by the committee provided it with considerable room for manoeuvre. A variety of recommendations concerning the minimum age were received, including the highly influential evidence of the Church of England Moral Welfare Council, which called for a minimum age of 17 (cited in Newburn, 1992, p. 54). Yet despite such proposals, the committee ultimately advocated the age of 21, the most conservative option available short of retaining a complete prohibition. It justified this case with the argument that

> a boy is incapable at the age of sixteen of forming a mature judgement about actions of a kind which might have the effect of setting him apart from the rest of society. (CHOP, 1957, p. 25, #71)

This implied a significant disjunction between the fixity of desires and the removal of protection, which demands careful investigation.

In relation to the debate over the age of consent within the Wolfenden committee, Patrick Higgins' research has led him to argue that:

> The existence of National Service during the 1950s shaped a major recommendation of the Wolfenden Committee, the decision to set the age of consent at twenty-one. (Higgins, 1996, p. 63)

A critical factor, according to Higgins' research, was the fear of homosexual activity among the armed forces, sparked by several trials involving soldiers and sailors during the 1950s, prior to the end of national service in 1960 (Higgins, 1996, pp. 63–80). Wolfenden himself attended one such trial, in which drummer boys aged 16–18 were revealed to have received presents and money in exchange for sex with a group of men in Windsor. Together with a minority on the committee, Wolfenden subsequently argued that young soldiers, sailors and airmen, in receipt of low levels of pay, were especially susceptible to the advances of predatory older homosexuals. Lord Chief Justice Goddard's evidence to the committee argued in favour of a minimum age of 21 on this basis, and his arguments appear to have influenced Wolfenden (Higgins, 1996, p. 73).

Such anxieties concerning the immoral behaviour of young men engaged in national service corresponded to wider social concerns over young men's delinquency. While the school-leaving age was 15, national service between the ages of 18–20 was the norm. An 'awkward and troublesome hiatus' existed, a period in which young men were unable to settle into training for long-term employment, which became the subject of public anxiety during the 1950s (Osgerby, 1998, p. 20; cf. pp. 19–21). The prospect of young men aged below 18 being permitted to engage in homosexual behaviour would have been particularly unthinkable to the Wolfenden committee, given the implication that such young men would then have to be subjected to renewed prohibitions upon entering national service.

However, while Wolfenden's own firm support for the age of 21 may have derived from particular concerns over the armed forces, the committee's acceptance of his view appears to have been more of a consequence of their pragmatic assessment of public attitudes and the possibilities for achieving decriminalisation. According to Higgins the committee record shows that in a poll of thirteen committee members after a year of sittings, seven supported 18 as the age of consent, one supported 17, and four supported 21, while one member, James Adair, was vehemently opposed to decriminalisation and refused to express a preference (Higgins, 1996, p. 65; cf. pp. 63–73). One supporter of 21 also argued that the age for heterosexual sex be raised to 21. But Wolfenden himself, following the view of the Lord Chief Justice Goddard, insisted on 21. He invoked public opinion to back his case, expressing the fear that a lower age would jeopardise decriminalisation's acceptance altogether (Higgins, 1996, pp. 65, 73). After 1967, Wolfenden himself stated quite publicly that he had insisted on 21 on grounds of 'expediency'.[13] Higgins is scathing in his assessment of Wolfenden's motives for this decision, arguing that the chair was motivated by careerism, seeking to preserve his own reputation within the establishment, and was also bowing to pressure from the Home Office which had signalled its desire for a cautious report (Higgins, 1996, p. 65). However, this judgement focusses upon blaming an individual, rather than understanding the wider social and political context which shaped possibilities.

The committee recognised that the symbolic importance of the age of majority as an age for ethical decision-making by adults would be powerful in convincing MPs of the case for decriminalisation. But for most of the committee the abstract principle of linking the age of consent to the age of majority was less of a priority than practical issues, including minimisation of the dangers of seduction into homosexuality, but particularly focussed upon achieving decriminalisation (Higgins, 1996, pp. 63–73). This political pragmatism mirrored the committee's utilitarian pragmatism in relation to the role of law.

The *Wolfenden Report*'s formulation thus did not represent evidence of consent in relation to sexuality being increasingly linked by principle to the adult capacities for competence and reason associated with the age of majority. The committee showed little sign of believing that the minimum legal age for sexual activity should be linked to an age at which intellectual competence to make key decisions was socially recognised. The possibility of such a conceptual linkage was undermined by dominant cultural under-standings of homosexuality. Male homosexuals were regarded as driven by deep desires and compromised by weak-willed, effeminate minds, as suggested by typologies of homosexuality in research from the period (Hauser, 1962). They tended to be regarded as lacking capacities for rational, responsible, strong-willed, ethical decision-making and for self-restraint, being compro-mised by uncontrollable deviant sexual desires requiring judicious legal constraint outside a narrow private sphere. One element of the rationale for decriminalisation was that homosexuals could not control themselves, and therefore that the law would not work as a deterrent.

The committee's advocacy of the age of 21, though led by Wolfenden, represented a collective response to public anxieties, based upon a pragmatic assessment of the possibilities for achieving decriminalisation. The committee played to doubts among MPs and the wider public about the fixity of desires, and to strong fears of seduction by older homosexuals, though it also utilised the symbolic importance of the age of majority to convince MPs of the case. The high age of consent reflected public belief in the need for the protection of young men, and the depth of prejudice against homosexuality.

Nevertheless, the age of consent must be conceptualised in the context of new forms of citizenship being attributed to adult homosexuals, as discussed in the previous section. Despite the strong protectionist impulse applying to young men until the age of 21, and the continuing forms of regulation operating in the private realm, the age of consent was nevertheless determined in the context of a double-movement, at a point of tension between impulses towards regulation and claims for specific forms of citizenship applying to adults. As argued above, particular limited forms of citizenship rights to 'privacy' and political citizenship, specific to homosexuals, were embodied in the new legal framework.

Conclusion

The ideological formations evident in the *Wolfenden Report* can be contrasted with the logic structuring arguments over the age of consent to sexual inter-course in 1885. The imagined sexual innocence and passivity of women aged below 16 was an assumption paralleled by wider assumptions about the lack of female desire. The rationale for the minimum age applying to sex between men, by contrast, involved a balance between protecting young men, with a presumed potential for heterosexual desires, and creating a private legal outlet for the uncontrollable desires of adult homosexuals. The discrepancy between the ages of 21 and 16 reflected the contrasting relationships of heterosexual women and homosexual men to 'hegemonic' forms of mascu-linity (Connell, 1995). These relationships involved strong homophobia and fears of seduction among heterosexual men in relation to male homosexuality, in contrast to feelings of desire and the reluctant denial of male access to young women. Both laws, however, represented prohibitions upon activity below the age of consent, without full endorsement of any clear principle of a 'right to consent' and/or equal sexual citizenship for those above.

I began this chapter by outlining the origins of legislation regulating sexual behaviour between women in the UK, focussing on a change in the law in 1922 that increased the minimum age for a range of non-penetrative sexual behaviour to 16. The main body of the chapter then analysed the *Wolfenden Report*'s advocacy of a partial decriminalisation of male homosexual acts, and argued that while decriminalisation was not undertaken as a step towards granting homosexuals equal citizenship, it did involve granting some minimal forms of citizenship to homosexuals in both public and private spheres. I argued that the *Wolfenden Report*'s advocacy of a minimum age of 21, and the creation of a private realm for consenting behaviour, must be conceptualised in the context of the contradictory impulses at work in the Wolfenden rationale. Crucially, decriminalisation was underpinned by the firm belief that an individual's sexual condition is determined prior to the age of 16.

Decriminalisation represented an amendment to a framework of sexual offences law which remained highly gendered and overwhelmingly hetero-normative in its constitution. The following chapter explores how the emergence of movements for sexual liberation, and other challenges to dominant forms of social knowledge during the 1960s, began to transform the dominant conceptual framework for debates concerning the regulation of young people's sexual behaviour.

6
Sexual Liberationism and the Search for New Sexual Knowledge

This chapter examines the emergence of radical sexual movements from the late 1960s, and consequent changes in debates over the regulation of young people's sexual behaviour which became apparent in a major official review of age of consent laws in the late 1970s. I begin by outlining the emergence of second wave feminism, gay liberationism and sexual libertarian movements, and discuss how they can be conceptualised in the context of wider 'epistemological transformations' during the 1960s and 1970s. I examine the meaning of claims for equality and liberation which were advanced in relation to age of consent laws among those instigating a new sexual politics, with particular attention to debates within the UK Gay Liberation Front (GLF). Drawing on sources from the Hall-Carpenter archive, the national lesbian and gay archive, I argue that these debates over equality, liberty and gendered power can be interpreted as a microcosm of later conflicts over the regulation of young people's sexuality which subsequently emerged in mainstream culture. The second half of the chapter then focusses on a major government review of age of consent laws in the late 1970s, conducted by the Home Office Policy Advisory Committee of Sexual Offences. This was the first government review of age of consent laws since the 1920s; it remains the most recent UK review to have considered changing the age of 16 for sexual intercourse, and provided a new validation for this age. I draw upon press coverage from the Hall-Carpenter Archive to analyse shifting political debates over age of consent laws prior to and during the review. I then describe how the review conceptualised the rationale for the law in relation to men and women, heterosexuality and homosexuality; and hence develop a critical analysis focussing upon the Policy Advisory Committee's problematic utilisation of biomedical and psychological knowledge-claims to justify its conclusions.

New social movements and epistemological transformations

In the late 1960s and early 1970s, new kinds of social movement emerged to challenge existing forms of sexual knowledge and culture. Second wave feminism became a cauldron of debate over sexuality as it emerged in western states from the late 1960s, and particularly after taking more radical forms in the Women's Liberation Movement of the 1970s. The gay liberation movement, deeply influenced by 'anti-sexism' and the feminist critique of gender, sought to transform attitudes to same-sex relationships. Other forms of sexual libertarianism also emerged during the 1960s, advancing 'free love' and opposition to existing forms of regulation; paedophile groups, for example, seeking to legitimise child/adult sexual relationships and abolish age of consent laws. Debate between these perspectives exploded within the radical counterculture.

These shifts must be understood in the context of profound shifts in the basis of knowledge about human beings and society both within the social sciences and the academy, and in society more generally. A combination of factors affecting developed societies in the 1960s, including the expansion of higher education, rising living standards and greater individualisation, led to the growth of a 'sociological imagination' which steadily influenced both academic and popular knowledge (Mills, 1959). Within the social sciences, crude forms of positivism and empiricism, naive claims for 'value-freedom' and objectivity, and structural-functionalist 'grand theory' became subject to increasing criticism (Gouldner, 1970). During the same period a variety of social movements emerged to make claims 'from below' on behalf of systematically excluded social groups. The Women's Liberation Movement, the Black civil-rights movement and the New Left challenged established social hierarchies and exclusionary forms of knowledge. These transformations condensed to provoke the political upheavals of 1968, which marked a critical symbolic moment in a longer-term process of critique of socially institutionalised forms of knowledge production. Demands surfaced for more reflexive forms of social science which incorporated analysis of social conflict and structural inequalities of power (Gouldner, 1970; Giddens, 1971).

Social movements thus contributed to shifts in dominant knowledge-paradigms, expanding the scope of existing thought by posing new questions. A particular tendency of new forms of social theory, notably structuralism and post-structuralism, was to question ideas of human subjectivity as fixed or pre-given in favour of emphasis upon the social character of the human self (Althusser, 1971; Foucault, 1972). The theoretical innovations of the period thus opened possibilities for human 'self-invention', and the living of lives in the absence of pre-ordained traditions in a manner which has subsequently been taken to characterise 'late modernity' (Giddens, 1990, 1991, 1992).

Thus social movements and new critical perspectives generated shifts in a variety of paradigms of knowledge, stretching across the human sciences (Seidman, 1994). Public debates and social scientific research subsequently confirmed the validity of many of the challenges posed by new social movements and radical theoretical perspectives. For example, radical criminology, feminism, critiques of the disempowerment of youth and critiques of positivistic psychology began to become established as positions in the academic mainstream. However, while challenges to established paradigms of knowledge led to a shift to a new field of contestation, they remained highly contested. The social sciences became characterised by epistemological pluralism and political conflict. A continuing interplay between academic and popular knowledge, the claims of science and those made by social movements became the ongoing, unresolved legacy of the radical era.

These shifts in the dominant structure of knowledge influenced several debates relevant to knowledge-claims concerning age of consent laws. Significant fields of contestation emerged concerning gender relations, the role of law, medical science, and adult/child relations. These can be briefly commented on in turn.

Second wave feminism's critique of gendered forms of power generated a variety of new ideas with implications for the conceptualisation of age of consent laws (Radicalesbians, 1970; Firestone, 1971; Greer, 1971; Millett, 1971). Feminist perspectives questioned the gendered structure of heterosexuality, including gendered legislation regulating the legal age for heterosexual sexual behaviour. Hence feminists debated whether a gender-neutral legal framework was desirable, or whether it might become desirable following a transformation of relations between men and women. 'Heterosexual' age of consent legislation became situated within wider feminist debates over the role of sexuality in sustaining women's unequal social position, including debates over 'equality' versus 'difference'.

New perspectives on law and crime in radical criminology and 'deviancy theory' examined the role of law and the criminal justice system in systematically reproducing categories of crime and deviancy (Cohen, 1971, 1972; Hall, 1974). Such perspectives tended to share utilitarian scepticism concerning the efficacy of prohibitive legislation, but also tended to more radically question the assumed moral and socio-political objectives of law enforcement. Thus prohibitive age of consent legislation was increasingly evaluated in the context of arguments concerning not only the difficulties of effective law enforcement and the inefficacy of the law as a deterrent to sexual behaviour, but also the detrimental effects of criminalising young people.

New approaches to medical knowledge challenged hierarchies privileging the knowledge of medical authorities over those of patients. Radical perspectives on medicine and psychiatry profoundly questioned the scientific status of 'expert' knowledge (Foucault, 1967; Goffman, 1968). Medical sociology became more well-established, introducing sociological reflection upon issues of power and epistemology in relation to concepts of health and illness (Turner, 1995, p. 6). This produced resistance to the institutional power of medical authorities, scepticism of medical expertise, interest in 'lay' and dissident definitions of health and illness, critiques of positivistic research, and critiques of medicalisation of personal experiences. Feminist work of this kind led to critiques of the characterisation of women's bodies as particularly vulnerable and unstable by the male-dominated medical profession, which had influenced nineteenth-century conceptions of female sexuality (see Chapter 4). The assumption of homosexuality as a biological or psychological 'condition' with a distinctive cause, which had informed the *Wolfenden Report*, was challenged by gay liberationists (Committee on Homosexual Offences and Prostitution, 1957; Weeks, 1977).

The social status of children and young people was challenged by appeals for the integrity of the needs and experiences of youth, expressed in the emergence of claims for 'children's rights' (National Council for Civil Liberties, 1971). Thus age of consent laws were questioned in the context of new claims for children's autonomy and their capacities to make decisions. The prominence of youth in the counterculture, particularly the role of students in the 1968 uprisings, gave emphasis to the political concerns of young people.

The emergence of the gay liberation movement from the 1969 Stonewall Riots onwards marked the beginning of public and collective claims for equality which were to have a major impact on debates over age of consent laws over subsequent decades. However, debates within the gay liberation movement also problematised heterosexuality as an assumed norm, hence problematising the standard for 'equality', and explored a variety of perspectives on age of consent laws. Gay liberationism was influenced by sexually libertarian strands of the 1960s counterculture, and was also heavily influenced by and drew explicitly upon feminist analysis (apparent in its shared terminology of 'anti-sexism'), though beginning prior to the development of the Women's Liberation Movement. The gay liberation movement, together with overlapping radical sections of the feminist movement, was the site for the generation of critical perspectives on heterosexuality as a system of gendered power relationships. Because gay liberationism occurred at this unique juncture in sexual politics, and also because it was a movement involving men and women and people of a variety of ages, the debates that took place within the movement over the age of consent and the regulation of young people's sexuality more broadly can now be seen as a microcosm of the debates that subsequently spread into the public sphere. Hence in the following section, I focus on the UK Gay Liberation Front, using material from the Hall-Carpenter Archive, as a rich source of primary data on a variety of competing perspectives emerging in debates over age of consent laws, including sexual libertarian and feminist arguments concerning the law in relation to sex between men and women as well as in relation to same-sex activity. The discussion of gay liberationist conceptions of sexual identity also introduces debates over the problematic relationship between claims for equality and citizenship, and theories concerning the nature of sexual identity, which are the central theme of the following chapter.

Gay liberation: Liberty, equality and the age of consent

The international gay liberation movement, born in 1969 from the Stonewall riots in New York, emerged as a radical challenge to existing social institutions, transforming political debates over the relationship between homosexuality and heterosexuality with its distinctive demand for equality (Altman, 1971/ 1993; Weeks, 1977, pp. 183–230; see also Altman, 1980; Watney, 1980; Adam, 1987, pp. 75–101; Cant and Hemmings, 1988; Jeffery-Poulter, 1991, pp. 98–108; Cruikshank, 1992, pp. 69–72; Plummer, 1995, pp. 81–96; Power, 1995; David, 1997, pp. 220–240). The GLF flourished in the early 1970s, fuelled by the post-1968 climate of radical political activism; its ideals and political objectives were carried around the globe by influential statements of principle (Radicalesbians, 1970; Shelley, 1970; Wittman, 1970; Altman, 1971, 1993). Dennis Altman's classic *Homosexual: Oppression and Liberation*, for example, articulates a radical critique of 'liberal tolerance' (p. 55), incorporates an understanding of deviance as a political definition (p. 62) and offers a critique of dominant psychological or biologically determinist theories of homosexuality, viewing homosexuality as 'entirely a product of social pressures' (Altman, 1971, p. 39).

In the UK the Gay Liberation Front (GLF) began meeting on 13 October 1970 at the London School of Economics.[1] The organisation survived only three years, and ended its brief life in 1973 due to a variety of divisions (Power, 1995, pp. 247–282). GLF's initial 'Demands' in 1970 included 'that the age of consent for gay males be reduced to the same as for straight', and also called for an end to discrimination; same-sex feelings being recognised as normal; non-heterosexual sex education; that psychiatrists cease treating homosexuality as a problem or sickness; freedom of communication (through contact ads or on the streets) and freedom from police harassment; and freedom to hold hands and kiss in public (see leaflet 'The Gay Liberation Front Demands...' in HCA GLF file 1; cf. Power, 1995, pp. 23–24). Subsequently a statement of the 'Principles of GLF', published in its newspaper *Come Together* (no. 2), emphasised resistance to discrimination and oppression of gays; the need for a profound critique of social structures including the Judaeo-Christian tradition and the nuclear family; and the need to situate Gay Liberation within a critique of other forms of social oppression (HCA GLF file 3; Power, 1995, pp. 35–37). The *GLF Manifesto* made a series of claims for the rights and needs of gay people, an end to 'oppression' and a 'liberated life-style' (Gay Liberation Front, 1971; reprinted in Power, 1995, pp. 316–330). It repeated the claim for an equal age of consent, and condemned a range of institutionalised sources of gay oppression: the family, schools, the church, the media, language, employment practices, the law, physical violence and psychiatry (Power, 1995, pp. 316–321). The manifesto called not only for reform, tolerance and legal equality – the civil rights which are the basis of a liberal democratic society – but also for revolutionary transformation of the attitude that homosexuality is an inferior way of life, rooted in the patriarchal family. A strong 'social' critique of the idea of sexual differences being 'inborn' was made, together with arguments for the abolition of the family and the 'gender-role system' (pp. 321–330).

In *Coming Out*, Jeffrey Weeks describes gay liberation as a movement which stressed 'openness, defiance, pride, identity and above all, self-activity' (Weeks, 1977, p. 185). The three basic concepts of the GLF are defined as: 'coming out' as an individual; 'coming together' to challenge oppression; and identifying the roots of oppression in 'sexism' (Weeks, 1977, pp. 191–192). The construction of gay identity was expressed most clearly in the process of 'coming out' which 'brought together the positive self-affirmation of our sexuality as individuals and as a political act on which could be built the whole edifice of the movement' (Birch, 1988, p. 54). According to Simon Watney:

> The use of the word 'gay' – our own word for ourselves – marked a decisive break with the institutions and discourses of heresy and disease within which all homosexuals were, by definition, previously confined. For the first time it became possible to make a positive homosexual self-identification in terms other than those of the dominant heterosexual culture. (Watney, 1980, p. 64)

Non-pathologising histories of homosexuality and descriptions of the contemporary gay world were circulated. The social critique of existing biological and psychological models of homosexuality, which had already begun to emerge in British and American sociology prior to the advent of gay liberation, was publicised and further explored (Gagnon and Simon, 1967, 1970; McIntosh, 1968). Dennis Altman, for example, cited McIntosh in his text (Altman, 1971, p. 10).

In the UK, GLF was deeply embroiled in debates over various new strains of political thinking. It saw itself as inspired by and closely allied to the early Women's Liberation Movement in a common battle against sexism (Power, 1995, pp. 117–136). Its Youth Group provided a site for the generation of new knowledge based upon the experiences of young gays, lesbians and bisexuals, challenging the parameters of childhood and adulthood, and claiming autonomy for young people (*Come Together*, no. 8; Power, 1995, pp. 109–116). Gay liberationists debated libertarian stances on the law in relation to issues such as sado-masochism and paedophilia, and contributed to critiques of established forms of psychology (Gay Liberation Front, 1973, available in HCA GLF file 4).

To participants, and subsequently to sympathetic historians and social theorists, gay liberation represented an upsurge of suppressed grassroots knowledge 'from below', challenging knowledge imposed from above by a variety of hierarchical institutions, both traditional and modern (Weeks, 1977; Power, 1995). Yet while the movement made claims to represent the authentic lived experiences of people with same-sex desires, it simultaneously questioned the basis of sexual subjectivity and identities. It offered the prospect of a new form of 'standpoint' knowledge (cf. Altman, 1971, p. 11), while simultaneously generating theoretical perspectives to dissect such standpoints and transform their conditions of existence (cf. Altman, 1971, pp. 229–239). Gay liberationism's understanding of 'gay' contained a tension between these contradictory impulses, a tension which operated within individual understandings and which was also sustained in subsequent theoretical work. This was a tension between the exploration of diversity, challenging to the boundaries of sexual categories, and the assertion of gay identity, associated with community building.

In order to conceptualise gay liberationism's employment of claims for equality, and hence the application of these claims in relation to age of consent laws, it is important to consider how the movement's equality claims related to its understandings of sexual subjectivity and identity. Gay liberationism was not simply making claims for a pre-existing social identity, but was producing new narratives of social and sexual identity. Gay liberationism marked the origin of a public and collective articulation of a claim for equality with heterosexuality, but simultaneously – and together with feminism – involved the redefinition of both heterosexuality and homosexuality, and re-drew boundaries between them.

The extent to which those at the heart of the gay liberation movement were interested in asserting sexual identities as opposed to challenging them is contested. Some of those who were central participants in the movement, and subsequently became its historians and leading social theorists of sexuality, have emphasised that gay liberationism did not advance from foundational, taken-for-granted assumptions about the existence of a shared gay identity. Gay liberationist historians who developed their 'social constructionist' perspectives on sexual identity within the movement have attributed gay liberationism distinctive significance for its understandings of sexual subjectivity and identity as socially formed. A sustained stream of thought has sought to validate the understanding of 'gay' which emerged from gay liberation by articulating a view of gay identity as distinctive for its self-conscious invention (Altman, 1971/1993; Weeks, 1977; Watney, 1980; Plummer, 1995).

However, other commentaries suggest that these writers have tended to over-emphasise the extent to which 'gay' was a self-consciously produced narrative for participants in the movement. David Fernbach, a leading former member in GLF, has argued that gay liberationism, despite its critique of aetiological theories, shared with homophile movements a belief in 'gayness as a psychological characteristic [. . .] rooted deep in the personality': 'To be gay' was 'to experience same-sex attraction' (Fernbach, 1998, pp. 63–64).

This suggests that despite the movement's interest in questioning the origins of desires, there was nonetheless widespread acceptance that subjectivity was constituted in particular forms defined by same-sex desire.

On balance it appears that much of GLF's understanding of the links between political and personal identities, together with its political demands and assertive style, had the effect of producing and asserting a gay identity in contrast to heterosexuality. The liberationist agenda of 'coming out' and demanding equality; the emphasis upon a movement with gay leadership; a degree of neglect towards bisexuals and people whose sexual experiences did not fit a clear straight/gay dichotomy; a belief in the subjective element of gayness as a psychological characteristic shared by gay people; and a focus on asserting and sustaining gay identity; all these entailed the generation of a new 'gay' narrative which inevitably excluded those who did not feel 'gay enough'. The movement produced a new 'gay' cultural and political project which defined appropriate relationships between subjectivity, personal identity and community allegiances.

The significant point in the present context is that notions of sexual identities as discreet and fixed subsequently came to predominate within lesbian and gay movements and communities as these grew and expanded from the late 1970s, notwithstanding the impact of some strands of lesbian feminism which challenged such beliefs among women (Rich, 1980). In particular, essentialist conceptions of sexual identity were utilised by gay movements in political campaigns oriented to win support from liberal hetero- sexuals. A particular gay standpoint emerged from gay liberation, advocating a politics of asserting gay identity rather than destabilising the heterosexual/ homosexual binary.

Queer theory, its ambiguous definition notwithstanding (Epstein, 1996), has more recently challenged established lesbian and gay standpoint perspectives and coming out narratives (Smyth, 1992; Warner, 1993; Bravmann, 1996; Seidman, 1996, 1997; see Chapter 2). The consequences of such perspectives have also been criticised from a range of perspectives by those arguing that various social groups (ethnic minorities, disabled people, transgender people, bisexual people, people with HIV, etc.) have lower access to or political interest in a gay grand narrative of 'coming out' which overstates linkages between personal identity, community participation and political radicalisation. Whatever our verdict on these debates about past and present political projects and strategies, the significant point for historical analysis is that gay liberation's inauguration of claims for equality occurred simultaneously with, and was entwined with, the production of new narratives of identity and difference, of 'gay' and 'lesbian' and 'heterosexual' as different categories. Hence claims for an equal age of consent were expressed in relation to new conceptions of the sexual subjects to which this equality would apply. A public claim for equality and a critique of heterosexuality were accompanied by the emergence of ideas in some ways problematising the heterosexuality/homosexuality dichotomy, but in other ways reproducing it in a new form. With this in mind, it is possible to analyse the debates within gay liberationism and the radical counter-culture over the age of consent, in which discussions over gender and the relationship between heterosexuality and gay and lesbian identities intersected with those over the merits of 'liberation', often understood in terms of a removal of legal prohibitions.

The GLF made equalisation of the age of consent a central issue, instigating a range of actions to publicise the injustice of the age of consent law, including the first major GLF march and rally in Trafalgar Square on 28 August 1971 (Power, 1995, pp. 113–115). However, within gay liberationism the age of consent was caught in wider debates over political priorities. The age of consent tended to be a key issue for those who focussed on the law reform strategies advocated by the liberal reformist Campaign for Homosexual Equality,[2] whereas some liberationists considered claims for an equal age of consent to be insufficiently radical, part of a 'civil rights politics' (Power, 1995, p. 191). But on the whole, equalisation of the age of consent was regarded as a simple step which could be swiftly accomplished. A feature article from *Gay News* in 1973 entitled 'Looking Ahead', painfully optimistic with hindsight, began:

> The first priority must be to penetrate the political barriers of hostility and inertia and to set on foot further reforms of law on homosexuality. The most important and the most obvious, because the present state of affairs is so patently ridiculous, is to bring the age of consent for men down to 16. (*Gay News*, no. 14, New Year 1973, p. 8)

Little did the writer suspect that equality would take a further quarter century to achieve.

Previous claims for an equal age of consent in the political mainstream, made during the debates within the Wolfenden Committee from 1954 to 1957, had focussed on the supposed fixity of gay desires by the age of 16, and the negative effects of criminalising young men. These arguments had worked within a logic which appealed to the political centre-ground. Equality was not a primary principle of such arguments, but a secondary consequence which did not reflect any wider principle of equal citizenship for heterosexuals and homosexuals. Within gay liberationism, however, equality became a key foundational principle. Yet gay liberationists did not simply apply an abstract principle of equality to heterosexuality and homosexuality. Claims for an equal age of consent were linked to a complex and thoroughgoing critique of numerous socially institutionalised forms of knowledge production which made equality unthinkable, relating to the family, gender, psychology and psychoanalysis, the law, the church, the media, and dominant political formations. In some respects these new perspectives did not necessarily imply clear support for equal treatment before the law.

The inauguration of radical new forms of feminist analysis opened the possibility for a critical understanding of the inequalities between men and women in relation to sexual behaviour (Radicalesbians, 1970; Firestone, 1971; Greer, 1971; Millett, 1971). The ensuing debates over the meaning of consent in heterosexual relationships redefined the subject to which gay liberationists compared themselves when claiming an equal age of consent. New feminist debates opened the question of what a male homosexual age of consent could be equal to, and explored the gendered structures of hetero-sexuality. The gendered basis of the UK's 'heterosexual' age of consent law was questioned, alongside whether the lesbian age of consent should be the same as the gay male, or whether gay forms of sexuality were in themselves problematically gendered in ways which might preclude a right to an equal age of consent.

However, the advent of gay liberationism preceded the growth of radical feminism, with its greater focus upon rape and sexual violence and prob-lematisation of the meaning of consent in heterosexual sex. The Women's Liberation Movement had yet to include a woman's right to define her own sexuality among its demands; feminist activism in relation to lesbianism was limited. In early GLF, with its tendency towards libertarianism, feminists had no objection to campaigning for an equal age of consent, though they were sometimes faced with male attitudes which over-emphasised the significance of the issue. Ted Walker Brown, a member of GLF's Youth Group, recalls:

> I remember there was a certain amount of unfair resentment towards the few young lesbians in the group because lesbian sexuality wasn't illegal and a lot of the men's attitude was, we're more oppressed than you ... (quoted in Power, 1995, p. 112)

While the GLF's demand for an equal age of consent was formulated early in the movement's lifespan, within GLF debates increasingly focussed on whether any age of consent law regulating 'consensual' behaviour was justified. Attitudes within the radical counterculture tended to view law as oppressive, and the criminal justice system as institutionalised repressive state control. Questions were raised about whether the law was practical, about who had access to it, and most of all about its effects on the young people it was supposed to protect. Though abolition of the age of consent was only a concern for a minority libertarian tendency within the movement, it was demanded by the GLF Youth Group[3] and widely debated – for example, at the 'Homosexual Oppression? Freedom?' conference at the London School of Economics in the autumn of 1971 (Power, 1995, p. 97).

Such discussions were influenced by new attitudes to youth. Demands surfaced among radicals that the social status of children and young people should be higher, and that the needs and experiences of youth should be respected. From the political formations of the late 1960s which saw youth as an 'oppressed group' emerged new languages of 'children's rights'. This movement to empower youth was most shocking in its claims for young people's sexual autonomy, and the acceptability of paedophilia. Key intellectual influences included Frankfurt School Freudian Marxist Herbert Marcuse, especially his book *Eros and Civilisation*, which argued that paedophilia, along with other 'perversions', had revolutionary potential to disrupt capitalist-inspired sexual repression (Marcuse, 1955; Geoghegan, 1981, pp. 38–63; Weeks, 1985, pp. 165–170).

The GLF played a part in the general social movement to empower youth, providing young gay people who had previously been denied a voice with a space to share and collectively articulate their experiences. GLF's manifesto included a critique of 'The Youth Cult', the market-driven obsession with denial of ageing, and concomitant objectification of young people, particularly among gay men (Gay Liberation Front, 1971; reprinted in Power, 1995, p. 326). The GLF Counter-Psychiatry Group recognised and discussed the sexuality of children and young people in its 1973 pamphlet 'Psychiatry and the Homosexual', drawing on critiques of Victorian assumptions of childhood sexual innocence (Gay Liberation Front, 1973; copy held in HCA GLF file 4).

The GLF's Youth Group for people aged under 21 was 'one of the more together and visible elements of GLF' (Power, 1995, p. 109). The group leafleted gay pubs, sent speakers to London schools and organised the first major GLF march on 28 August 1971, marking the anniversary of Stonewall, which ended with a rally calling for an equal age of consent (*Homosexuals Come Out*, GLF Youth Group flyer, 28 August 1971, in HCA GLF file 13; Power, 1995, pp. 109–116). Its basic demands included: 'the reduction and eventual abolition of the age of homosexual consent' ('GLF Youth Group', flyer, HCA GLF file 3).

The Youth Group produced issue 8 of the GLF magazine *Come Together* in August 1971. A front page article titled 'Age of Consent' questioned why consent should be restricted at any age, noting that 'while an 18-year old can drive a car, buy a house, vote for a government, he cannot choose who he can fuck' (p. 1). Further articles stressed the age of consent as a basic civil rights issue, and questioned the absence of rights available to children for privacy, freedom and self-respect, including 'freedom to explore their growing and developing sexuality without the oppressive prejudices of their parents distorting and conditioning it' (p. 2). Age of consent legislation was dismissed as 'ludicrous nonsense', based on the assumption that children are the possessions of their parents, rather than 'independent thinking, feeling human beings' (p. 2). The objective of 'abolishing age limits for sexuality altogether' was stated (p. 7), and a customary call to arms issued:

Young people all over the world are beginning to realise this situation, and if these basic human rights are not granted soon, there will be enough of them to take them for themselves. There may even be enough of them to impose their ideas...of love, of instinctive respect for others, of disregard of frontiers of any sort, of compassion...on their parents. (*Come Together*, no. 8, August 1971, p. 2; in HCA file 253)

The radicalism of the Youth Group's language and the demand for abolition of the age of consent were contentious even by GLF standards, possibly due to the emphasis placed by the group's driving force, Tony Reynolds, upon sexual libertarianism, and possibly due to the lack of women's involvement due to the Youth Group's focus on the age of consent issue (Power, 1995, pp. 110–112).

The GLF more broadly provided a site for new debates on paedophilia. These subsequently surfaced in the newspaper which emerged from the movement, *Gay News*.[4] Within GLF paedophiles were permitted a voice, which contributed to the emergence of paedophile organisations during the 1970s, including the Paedophile Information Exchange (1974–1984) (Evans, 1993, pp. 228–239; see also Grey, 1992, pp. 207–215). Meanwhile GLF's Youth Group generated shared knowledge based upon negative experiences of dealing with older gays. According to one member, Alaric Sumner, the Youth Group 'was partly set up to be protective of us against the chicken hunters...[...] The Youth Group did quite a lot about the way that even in the general meetings we were being harassed' (quoted in Power, 1995, p. 112). Another member, Ted Walker Brown, recalls: 'There was a lot of nervousness about some of the older men who used to hang out around us and be rather predatory' (quoted in Power, 1995, p. 112).

It appears that proposals to abolish the age of consent altogether were always controversial. There was much disagreement over the analysis of youth and sexuality, particularly between feminists and male libertarians in relation to paedophilia. Calls for abolition of the age of consent epitomised a libertarian strand of thought which became increasingly unacceptable to many women. Divisions also surfaced within the movement, for example, over various Freudian understandings of children's sexuality. There was agreement that sex education should be improved. But debates emerged over whether the purpose of political challenges was 'liberationist', to facilitate sex among younger people, or pragmatic, to avoid criminalisation, while promoting education and informed decision-making.

Seen in historical perspective, it is apparent that these debates over the age of consent within the gay liberation movement, and within sexual politics and the radical counter-culture more broadly, represented new forms of exploration of the social conditions necessary for young people's participation in sexual behaviour. Age of consent laws were no longer to be legitimised by tradition or patriarchy. Henceforth they were to be critically appraised in relation to an analysis of the oppression of gay people and the structure of gendered heterosexuality, the patriarchal family and the power of men; a greater understanding of the negative effects of criminalisation of youth and the role of law; and the social structures which disempowered young people. Though wide differences emerged among sexual radicals, the new movements addressing sexuality brought new critical attention to the age of consent, and profoundly reoriented the frameworks structuring future debates.

This section has analysed gay liberationism as a microcosm of emerging debates, situated at the interface between competing perspectives upon the role of law, gender inequalities and the status of children and young people. I have argued that the GLF's assertive claims for gay equality marked an important moment in the development of debates over homosexuality, heterosexuality and the age of consent. Yet I have also shown that more diverse strands of thought existed, including radical sexual libertarianism, more cautious reformism and feminist perspectives sceptical of male libertarianism. While the gay liberation movement advocated an equal age of consent as an immediate legal reform, participants also envisaged such reforms contributing to a society structured by new sexual attitudes and gender roles. A simplistic understanding of 'liberation' led some sex radicals to believe that removal of legal prohibitions would in itself move society towards a liberation of desire and sexuality, rendering problems of unequal power and exploitation in sexual relationships obsolete. As the 1970s progressed, these various ideas began to filter into mainstream public debate.

From the margins to the mainstream: Emerging challenges

From the early 1970s, claims for a reduction in the age of consent for sexual behaviour between men became increasingly assertive. A key development was the publication of the Latey committee report in July 1967 (Committee on the Age of Majority, 1967). The Latey report, covering only England and Wales, advocated that young people be treated as adults from the age of 18, rather than 21, in almost every respect except the male homosexual age of consent, including: the legal age of majority; the legal age for marriage without parental consent; the maximum age for being made a 'ward of court'; the minimum age for making contracts or wills; and the minimum age for acting as a trustee, executor or administrator, or for owning property. Ironically the report appeared within days of the final House of Commons vote securing the creation of a new male homosexual age of consent at the age of 21. Its recommendations were rapidly enacted: the *Children and Young Persons Act* 1969 redefined 'young person' to refer to persons below the age of 18; the age of majority was subsequently reduced to 18 by the *Family Law Reform Act* 1969; the voting age was reduced to 18 by the *Representation of the People Act* 1969; the legal age for making valid contracts by the *Finance Act* 1969; and the minimum age for jury service was reduced to 18 by the *Criminal Justice Act* 1972.[5]

Following GLF's dissolution after 1973, the age of consent remained a contentious issue within the organised gay movement. Conflicts over both strategy and ultimate objectives generated incidents such as the dismissal of the Vice-Chairman of the Campaign for Homosexual Equality (CHE) (in England), Michael De-la-Noy, in 1974, following his criticism of internal proposals to endorse an age of 12 in circumstances where a defendant could prove consent.[6] However, after an internal review of the law initiated in 1973,[7] it became the CHE's policy from 1974 to campaign for equality at 16.[8] The organisation lobbied MPs and party leaders on the issue during the 1974 election campaign.[9] In July 1975 the CHE, together with the Scottish Minorities Group and the Union for Sexual Freedoms in Ireland, launched a new joint campaign in favour of a draft *Sexual Offences Bill* designed to achieve comprehensive equality in relation to all sexual behaviour (Sturgess, 1975).[10] Approximately 200 males aged 16–20 were being prosecuted each year for 'homosexual offences' (buggery, attempted buggery or gross indecency).[11]

Calls for a lower age of consent in relation to heterosexuality had also begun to find wider support. In April 1972 a conference of Quakers, the Society of Friends Social Responsibility Council, passed a resolution in favour of an equal age of consent at 14.[12] Dr John Robinson, Dean of Trinity College, Cambridge and chair of the Sexual Law Reform Society, argued the case for equality at 14 in the Beckley Lecture to the Methodist Conference of July 1972, provoking re-consideration among the legal establishment.[13] Meanwhile the official Speijer Committee in the Netherlands had recommended equality at 16 in 1969, following a lengthy investigation into homosexuality (discussed in Grey, 1992, pp. 196–206).

In September 1974 the Sexual Law Reform Society, which had evolved from the former Homosexual Law Reform Society, published the report of a working party which had reviewed the law on sexual behaviour (Sexual Law Reform Society, 1974). This argued in favour of abolishing existing 'age of consent' laws and replacing them with what it described as an 'age of protection'. The society regarded the term 'age of consent' as representing a 'legal fiction' by implying that 'consent' is only possible above the existing legal age, and hence ignoring the actual existence of consent by persons below that age (Grey, 1997, p. 45). People aged below the 'age of protection', which the society argued should be set at the legal age of majority (18), would be subject to a context in which the onus of proof that valid consent existed would lie with the older partner. This would be enforced through an expanded non-criminal framework of protection orders and injunctions, deriving from care and control proceedings under the provisions of the *Children and Young Persons Act* 1969 which applied to persons aged below 17. This would 'not involve criminal penalties that treat consent as irrelevant' (Grey, 1997, pp. 45–46). Alternatively, if abolition of 'age of consent' laws could not be accepted, the society argued for an equal minimum age at 14, in combination with the 'age of protection' (Grey, 1997, p. 49; cf. pp. 43–50, 165–183).[14]

Hence by the mid-1970s the case for a lower minimum age for all was finding wider support, with questions being posed concerning the merits of lowering the legal age for male/female sexual behaviour – not only within grassroots sexual movements, but also within religious organisations and liberal intellectual circles. This liberalisation of public attitudes allowed government to review legal prohibitions.

The Policy Advisory Committee on Sexual Offences

It was Roy Jenkins, the liberal-minded first Home Secretary of the 1974–1979 Wilson/Callaghan Labour government, who instigated a thoroughgoing review of sexual offences law.[15] Having previously overseen the partial decriminalisation of male homosexuality, Jenkins sought to continue what he regarded as a process of progressive modernisation, a view encapsulated in his well-known remark that 'the permissive society is the civilised society'.[16] He received little endorsement of his sexual liberalism from Prime Ministers Harold Wilson (1974–1976) and James Callaghan (1976–1979), or from other Labour cabinet members. Yet the review's initiation nevertheless marked a significant achievement for sexual progressives.[17] Despite its important influence upon subsequent age of consent debates, however, the review has until recently been the subject of little sustained academic commentary or analysis, aside from brief references (Hindley, 1986; Weeks, 1989, pp. 273, 288; Moran, 1996, p. 192; McGhee, 2001).

The Home Secretary ordered the Criminal Law Revision Committee, a standing committee comprised of 17 senior judges and lawyers, to comprehensively review the law relating to sexual offences. This they were asked to do in conjunction with a new Policy Advisory Committee on Sexual Offences, set up in December 1975 specifically to examine law on the age of consent (PAC, 1979, p. iii). Both committees' investigations were limited to England and Wales (PAC, 1979, p. 1, #2). The Home Office conducted new research on the sentencing of sex offenders to assist the two committees (Walmsley and White, 1979, 1980; PAC, 1981, Annex V).

The Criminal Law Revision Committee's composition reflected the conservatism of the legal establishment. The Policy Advisory Committee, by contrast, was appointed by the Home Secretary with the intention of bringing more specialised expertise and a wider range of opinions to bear on the age of consent, and hence to balance the composition of the Criminal Law Revision Committee. In contrast to the narrower legal issues which were the focus for the CLRC, the Policy Advisory Committee's function was 'to look into the medical, sociological and other wider issues which arise on [*sic*] a review of sexual offences and to provide an assessment of lay opinion' (PAC, 1981, p. 1). Though it included five members of the Criminal Law Revision Committee, these were balanced by others including a psychiatrist, a journalist, two senior probation officers, a headmistress, a social worker and a senior sociologist – Mary McIntosh, the founding theorist of 'the homosexual role' and 'social constructionist' perspectives on sexual identities, as well as a leading activist in the gay liberation and women's liberation movements (cf. McIntosh, 1968; Weeks, Plummer and McIntosh, 1981; Weeks, 1998a).[18] Eight of the fifteen members were women, by contrast with the Criminal Law Revision Committee which had only two female members.

Both committees consulted widely with interested parties, including unions, professional associations, youth organisations and individual members of the public (PAC, 1979, p. 1). A variety of organisations ranging across the spectrum of sexual politics, from the Christian National Festival of Light (NFL) to the Sexual Law Reform Society (SLRS), consulted their members and published written submissions to the committee.[19]

Morally conservative organisations forcefully opposed reform. The Responsible Society argued that age of consent laws relating to both sexual intercourse between a male and a female, and to male 'homosexual acts', should remain unchanged (HC 11 March 1976, col. 615). The Josephine Butler Society argued against a reduction in the age of consent for girls, on the basis that this would 'reduce the existing legal protection against traffickers and procurers and still further encourage irresponsible sexual behaviour'.[20] The Police Superintendents Association of England and Wales argued for the age of 16 for sexual intercourse to remain unchanged for girls, though with a higher maximum penalty, while conveying a profoundly reactionary attitude towards homosexuality:

> Again we must register our strong opposition to any relaxation in the law on sexual offences of a non-heterosexual nature particularly with regard to buggery with another human being or an animal. The very nature of this type of offence is so abhorrent to all Police officers that we cannot conceive any right-minded, caring body recommending any alteration to the existing law.[21]

Though less extreme, the medical profession's attitudes were also conservative. The British Medical Association's (BMA) submission in June 1976 argued in favour of the minimum age remaining 16 for sexual intercourse.[22] However, in relation to homosexuality it argued:

> We acknowledge that a lowering to 18 of the age of consent for men to homosexual acts in private would be reasonable. This would correspond to the legal age of majority. The age of consent to sexual acts would still vary 2 years as between men and women, but the age of 18 for men would reflect, in general, their slower rate of biological development. (quoted in British Medical Association, 1994, p. 2)

By contrast, the Royal College of Psychiatrists (RCP) was more liberal, supporting a universal age of 16 and singling out non-heterosexual offences as an area deserving particular attention:

Only in this area of the term [*sic*] of reference did we encounter any strong feelings and these were in the direction of making the age of consent for male homosexuals the same as for girls [....] ... on the whole we agree that it is now appropriate to make no distinction in the age of consent between heterosexual and homosexual practices. (Royal College of Psychiatrists, 1976, s. 4)

Similarly, in May 1976, the annual conference of the National Association of Probation Officers voted in favour of the age for male homosexual acts being reduced to 16.[23]

The CHE also put the case for equality at 16, in a submission which was taken to represent mainstream homosexual opinion, based upon its earlier draft Bill (CHE, 1976, Appendix D; cf. Sturgess, 1975). The detailed proposals advocated new offences to mirror existing 'heterosexual' legislation, such as a more serious penalty for sexual acts with a boy aged under 13, and a new 'reasonable belief' defence for sex between males where one party mistook the age of another. By contrast with supporters of equality among professional organisations, however, the CHE placed less emphasis upon the pragmatic benefits of equality at 16 for health and social policy, and more upon the principle of equality. Hence the CHE argued that parity of treatment 'will encourage greater support from society as a whole for relationships between homosexuals' and emphasised 'the principle that individual homosexuals should enjoy the same basic human rights as individual heterosexuals' (CHE, 1976, pp. 5, 9).

Others held more radical views. The Sexual Law Reform Society's working party submitted its working party's proposals to the committee, advocating equality at 14 if not outright abolition of definitive prohibitions (Sexual Law Reform Society, 1974; Grey, 1997, pp. 43–50, 165–183; see p. 132). Similarly, in March 1976 the National Council for Civil Liberties generated extensive newspaper coverage when it published its submission to the Criminal Law Revision Committee, calling for equality at 14 (National Council for Civil Liberties, 1976).[24] The report proposed a range of controversial measures including abolition of the crime of incest, and more liberal court attitudes to paedophiles. It presented the retention of a prohibition upon sex below the age of 14 as a compromise with public attitudes:

Although it is both logical, and consistent with modern knowledge about child development, to suggest that the age of consent should be abolished, we fear that, given the present state of public attitudes on this topic, it will not be politically possible to abolish the age of consent. (NCCL, 1976, p. 6)

The report also proposed a minimum age of 10 in circumstances where both partners were over 10 but below 14. Where only one partner was in this age bracket, real proof of consent would be required; and an overlap of two years on either side of 14 was proposed to achieve legal flexibility, such that 12–16-year olds could legally have sex (NCCL, 1976, p. 6).[25] The proposals were subsequently dubbed a 'Lolitas Charter' by *The Sun* newspaper.[26]

As is clear from this discussion of written submissions, the Policy Advisory Committee was faced with a remarkably broad spectrum of conflicting views, ranging between moral conservatism and radical libertarianism. This represented a strikingly different context to that which the Wolfenden Committee had addressed 20 years previously, evidencing a dissipation of moral orthodoxy and the emergence of radical pluralism. Twenty years previously, the Wolfenden Committee had received oral evidence from only three self-declared homosexuals; by contrast, the Policy Advisory Committee was faced with lengthy submissions from numerous lesbian and gay groups (including, for example, the Joint Council for Gay Teenagers, Gay Switchboard, Gay Humanists, and gay sociologist Dr Kenneth Plummer), and from sexual libertarians (including Paedophile Information Exchange), many of which incorporated lengthy and detailed arguments for law reform (cf. PAC, 1981, Annex II). More significantly, many mainstream religious and liberal organisations and individuals were advocating liberal reforms.

Following consideration of the diverse recommendations it received, the Policy Advisory Committee published a working paper setting out its provisional views in June 1979 (PAC, 1979). The working paper produced two provisional unanimous conclusions for public comment: first, the age of consent for sexual intercourse between a man and a woman should remain 16; and second, the minimum age for homosexual relations should be lowered to 18 (PAC, 1979, p. 3).[27] However, an additional minority report by five committee members argued in favour of 16 as a minimum age for male homosexual acts (PAC, 1979, Appendix A). Though the working paper was a prelude to further consultation, both its conclusions and the dissenting minority report were to remain largely unchanged in the final version.

A few months after the working paper's publication came a controversy over another government-sponsored report. In September 1979, following a detailed four-year investigation incorporating a survey of 443 secondary schools, a joint working party of the National Council for One-Parent Families and the Community Development Trust called for abolition of the age of consent law regulating sexual intercourse (Joint Working Party on Pregnant Schoolgirls and Schoolgirl Mothers, 1979). Its report argued that the existing law failed to protect girls or act as a deterrent to men against repeating their offences, while unjustly criminalising boys and inhibiting girls from seeking contraception, abortion or ante-natal care. The working party emphasised the need for improved sex education, and focussed upon the fact that 1 in 8 girls had sexual intercourse below the age of 16, and 1 in 500 girls under 16 became pregnant each year, while in 1975 there had only been 700 prosecutions.[28] The measure would in fact have left some prohibitions in place via 'indecent assault', for which consent was no defence below the age of 16 (rarely implemented in relation to consensual behaviour at this time; on its origins see Chapter 5, pp. 88–96), and the provisions of the *Indecency with Children Act* 1960 (s. 1) concerning 'gross indecency' with a child, which applied below the age of 14.[29] However, the proposal generated outrage and was widely reported in press coverage as if it would have abolished regulations upon consensual behaviour altogether. This press coverage illustrated the primacy attributed to regulation concerning the specific act of sexual intercourse.[30] The newly elected Conservative Prime Minister Margaret Thatcher wrote to 'morality' campaigner Mary Whitehouse, with assurances that she was 'entirely unconvinced' by such arguments, and that the government had no plans to lower the age of consent[31] – comments which accurately foretold subsequent policy during her three terms in office.

The Policy Advisory Committee published its final conclusions in April 1981, upholding its provisional views and hence recommending no change in the age of consent to sexual intercourse, and a reduction in the minimum age for male homosexual acts to 18 (PAC, 1981, p. 3). The latter proposal met with vocal opposition from the Police Federation,[32] as well as the tabloid press.[33] Even the left-wing *Guardian* praised the committee's 'stately centrism' rather than criticising its advocacy of continuing inequality.[34] Such responses contrasted with moves towards equality elsewhere in Europe.[35]

Two proposed forms of 'special provision' in law were considered but rejected by the Policy Advisory Committee. Modifying the law in relation to young men only a few years above the minimum age, engaging in sexual acts with those below the legal age, was felt to be unjustified. Introducing a higher legal age in relation to adults in a position of advantage or authority over a young person, as existed in Canada and the Netherlands, was rejected on grounds of clarity and because of the difficulty of drafting and enforcing such laws in relation to the existing legal framework, following advice from the Criminal Law Revision Committee (PAC, 1981, pp. 8–10, 17–19).

The Criminal Law Revision Committee had meanwhile produced a working paper addressing sexual offences in October 1980 (CLRC, 1980),[36] and subsequently published its final recommendations in 1984 (CLRC, 1984).[37] Both these reports accepted and reiterated the recommendations of the Policy Advisory Committee concerning the age of consent laws, without challenge. After the 1984 report's publication, therefore, the CHE described its verdict on the 'homosexual' age of consent as 'profoundly disappointing [. . .] a halfway measure for which there is no basis in fact or logic'.[38]

The Criminal Law Revision Committee's reports did however make a variety of other recommendations which would, if implemented, alter the legal framework within which age of consent laws operated. Most of these were initially outlined in the working paper (CLRC, 1980, pp. 58–63). The committee's final report included proposals for the decriminalisation of incest between brother and sister aged over 21; the preservation of the two existing offences of unlawful sexual intercourse with a girl aged under 13 and with a girl aged under 16; decriminalisation of buggery between men and women aged over 16; the creation of a separate offence of buggery with a girl or boy under 13; an increase in the age range covered by the gender-neutral offence 'gross indecency with a child' from 14 to 16, together with the abolition of 'indecent assault' on a boy or girl under 16 in cases where consent existed; creation of a new offence of 'gross indecency with a child under 13'; abolition of the assumption that a boy aged under 14 is incapable of sexual intercourse; and the criminalisation of marital rape, though only where the partners were living separately (CLRC, 1984, pp. 93–99). The replacement of 'indecent assault' by 'gross indecency with a child' in relation to children aged under 16 where consent existed was proposed to end the 'fiction of assault', the implication of the existing law that it did not recognise the actually existing consent of children aged under 16 (CLRC, 1984, p. 57). These proposals illustrate significant general shifts in attitudes including moves towards gender-neutrality; although many of these proposals were left unheeded by Conservative governments until 1997, and were super-seded by another Home Office review of sex offences initiated in 1999 (see Chapters 8 and 9).

Notwithstanding the Criminal Law Revision Committee's proposals concerning the surrounding legal framework of sex offences, it was the investigations of the Policy Advisory Committee which largely determined the review's conclusions concerning age of consent legislation. Significantly, the committee's outlook remained a peculiarly British one, making little effort to investigate the rationale for lower ages of consent elsewhere in Europe, despite noting comparative data in appendices (PAC, 1979, Annex VI, 1981, Annex VI). In particular, the committee's report did not discuss the findings of the Dutch Speijer Committee which had produced a detailed study recom-mending an equal age of 16 in 1969 (discussed in Grey, 1992, pp. 196–206).

The most significant general feature of the committee's review was its structuring by a definitive heterosexual/homosexual binary which embodied the committee's heteronormative theoretical framework. The committee divided its investigations between consideration of 'heterosexual' and 'homosexual' age of consent laws: the titles of the two parts of the 1979 working paper were 'the heterosexual age of consent' and 'the minimum age for homosexual relations between men' (PAC, 1979, p. iv); while sexual behaviour between women remained largely outside the committee's scope, an approach justified with reference to the existing law. Yet the category 'heterosexual' was not used in law itself, and the category 'homosexual' had only been introduced by the *Sex Offences Act* 1967 (Moran, 1996); hence the structure of the inves-tigation and the committee's analysis reflected prevailing conceptions of social and sexual identity rather than the existing law. As had occurred with the Wolfenden committee (cf. Moran, 1996), investigations of the law proceeded from categories not present in the law, and sought to interpret the law with reference to these. Although part one of the final report referred to 'the age of consent to sexual intercourse' rather than 'the heterosexual age of consent' employed in the 1979 working paper, perhaps following a late realisation of the indeterminate relationship between sexual identity and sexual behaviour, this belated shift did not occur early enough to induce problematisation of prevailing conceptualisations of heterosexuality and homosexuality as homogenous and discreet. The following sections explore the Policy Advisory Committee's arguments concerning age of consent laws in relation to heterosexuality and homosexuality.

Heterosexuality and the age of consent to sexual intercourse

To contextualise the committee's discussion of the 'age of consent' it is first important to consider developments in the law in relation to non-consensual behaviour, and hence to clarify the extent to which the law contributed to enforcing principles of consent. By the late 1970s, in response to the challenges of second wave feminism, changes were beginning to occur to the framework of sex offences law inherited from the nineteenth century (see Chapter 4), and in the practices of the criminal justice system in relation to rape and indecent assault. However, non-consensual sexual intercourse (vaginal penetration with a penis) between a husband and wife remained exempt from prosecution as rape (until 1991: see Lacey and Wells, 1998, pp. 380–385), although from 1954 it had become possible to prosecute accompanying acts of 'indecent assault' (Temkin, 2002, pp. 75, 72–89).

The *Sexual Offences (Amendment) Act* 1976 was introduced to reform rape law, defining rape explicitly as unlawful sexual intercourse with a woman without her consent (unlawful in this context meaning outside marriage). This removed previous ambiguity in the definition of rape which had led some judges to require some use of force and/or resistance in addition to non-consent (Temkin, 2002, pp. 90–91). Nevertheless, rape law continued to be contentious in its scope. Because absence of consent was a criteria for the offence which prosecutions were required to establish (unlike 'indecent assault' in some instances), together with the *mens rea* element of a man 'knowingly' or 'recklessly' committing the act, prosecutions for rape focussed on the subjective intentions of the (purported) victim (Lacey and Wells, 1998, pp. 385–386). Rape was therefore an offence unlike some other offences against the person (Molan, 1996, pp. 95–96), and this definition of rape has remained subject to criticism from some feminists and ongoing debate (Temkin, pp. 90–107).

Despite making absence of consent a clear and central requirement for sexual intercourse with a woman, other than a wife, to constitute rape, the *Sexual Offences Amendment Act* (1976) offered no definition of 'consent'. Hence sex offences law continued to lack a consistent definition of 'consent', defining its presence or absence in particular ways in different circumstances, with gendered consequences (Temkin, 2002, pp. 91–93). Furthermore, the *Sexual Offences (Amendment) Act* 1976 Section 1(2) stated:

> It is hereby declared that if at a trial for a rape offence the jury has to consider whether a man believed that a woman was consenting to sexual intercourse, the presence or absence of reasonable grounds for such a belief is a matter to which the jury is to have regard, in conjunction with any other relevant matters, in considering whether he is so believed.

Although introduced to qualify men's ability to assert belief that consent had occurred, this legislation continued to define the conditions for 'consent' to be recognised with an emphasis on the beliefs of the accused (for discussion, see Lacey and Wells, 1998, pp. 390–393). According to Lynn Jamieson, in Scottish law this legislation was subsequently interpreted to mean that:

> a man cannot be guilty of rape if he honestly, genuinely, believed that the woman consented, even if the man had no reasonable basis for his belief. (Jamieson, 1996, p. 55)

A jury could decide that a man believed a woman was consenting without reference to whether such a belief was based on 'reasonable grounds'. Only if they have to *consider* what the man believed need the jury have regard to 'reasonable grounds' (Jamieson, 1996, pp. 55–73). Hence the legal scope of 'consent' continued to be determined within a framework which evaded women's definitions of their experiences (see also Smart, 1995, pp. 110–114; Edwards, 1996; Lacey, 1997; Temkin, 2002).

Alongside rape, the offences of 'indecent assault on a male' and 'indecent assault on a female' regulating other forms of sexual behaviour had historically developed with no integral requirement for non-consent to be established. 'Assault' was simply required to be accompanied by circumstances of 'indecency'. 'Consent' emerged as a possible defence but was not necessarily adequate in all circumstances, and non-consent to assault was not sufficient to constitute the offence unless 'indecency' could be established (Law Commission, 1995; Hall, 1996). The existence of 'indecency' was historically contingent upon the social context of the offence, especially whether it occurred in public or private; hence the scope of 'indecent assault' also remained ambiguous.

In sum, no general governing principle of consent or universal prohibition of non-consensual acts emerged in reforms of the regulation of sexual behaviour during the 1970s. Hence debates over 'age of consent' laws continued to take place in a context where not all non-consensual behaviour was prohibited, and where consent was defined in particular ways by the law within a framework of understandings heavily influenced by gendered power relations. In short, despite amendments the law retained its fundamental patriarchal and heteronormative foundations, oriented towards prohibiting public and extra-familial 'indecency' while accepting non-consensual behaviour in private within heterosexual marriage.

Turning back to the Policy Advisory Committee, this gendered perspective was also evident in the committee's consideration of minimum age legislation to regulate male/female behaviour. The most striking aspect of the consideration given to male/female behaviour in both the working paper (PAC, 1979) and the final report (PAC, 1981) was the singular focus upon the age of consent to 'sexual intercourse'. The act of penetrative vaginal intercourse is examined almost to the exclusion of all other heterosexual sexual behaviour.

The Policy Advisory Committee initially noted that the offence of 'indecent assault' on a girl aged under 16, to which consent was no defence (*Sexual Offences Act* 1956, s. 14), was 'closely associated' with the offence of unlawful sexual intercourse (*Sexual Offences Act* 1956, s. 6; PAC, 1979, p. 4, #11). However, it proceeded on the basis that 'indecent assault' upon a girl under 16 who consents would be 'more conveniently' dealt with by the Criminal Law Revision Committee (PAC, 1979, p. 4, #11). Though the Policy Advisory Committee was subsequently consulted by the Criminal Law Revision Committee on this issue, this decision itself reflected a particular understanding of 'heterosexual sex', and restricted the parameters of the inquiry to the extent that the working paper's section on 'the heterosexual age of consent' was re-titled 'the age of consent to sexual intercourse' in the final report, which almost entirely omits discussion of indecent assault (PAC, 1979, p. 4; cf. PAC, 1981, p. 3). It is clear that the Policy Advisory Committee's decision on sexual intercourse strongly influenced the Criminal Law Revision Committee's subsequent conclusion that 16 would be the appropriate minimum age for all sexual behaviour other than that between men (CLRC, 1984, p. 57, #7.5), and the Policy Advisory Committee would probably have reached the same conclusion. The Criminal Law Revision Committee argued that a different age would 'undermine the protection afforded by the law against unlawful sexual intercourse' (CLRC, 1984, p. 57, #7.5). It did however propose replacing existing legislation on 'indecent assault' with a new gender-neutral offence of 'gross indecency' applying within the same age range (CLRC, 1980, pp. 30–34, 60–61, 1984, pp. 56–62, 96). This new offence would remove the legal fiction of 'assault' in such cases, the necessity of proving active agency by an adult, and also remove the possibility of questioning the 'indecency' of an act (cf. Hall, 1996).

The Policy Advisory Committee's focus on sexual intercourse echoed wider public attitudes (apparent in press responses to the report of the Joint Working Party on Pregnant Schoolgirls and Schoolgirl Mothers, discussed above), which viewed vaginal penetration as *the* ultimate sexual act, *the* definitive heterosexual act, and hence tended to view the legal age for vaginal sexual intercourse as *the* 'age of consent'. The committee thus reproduced the dominant taken-for-granted structure of heterosexuality, in which it tends to be assumed that 'proper sex' entails 'penetrative vaginal intercourse' and 'a notion of sex that privileges male needs and desires in a sexual division of labour in which he is the sexual actor while she is acted upon' (Holland *et al.*, 1998, p. 6). Such attitudes were reflected in the fact that the PAC's reports did not even question the correctness of the term 'age of consent' for heterosexuals, despite the prohibitive, protectionist logic which had structured the legislation when created in 1885 (see Chapter 4) and the fact that rape was not a crime within marriage; and despite rejecting the term in relation to homosexuality (see discussion in p. 145–155).

The committee's consideration of the appropriate age for male/female sexual intercourse revealed a considerable mainstream social consensus. Submissions on this issue reflected 'no movement to raise the age' and a clear majority in favour of retaining the age of 16, with only a minority arguing for 15 or 14 (PAC, 1979, p. 4, #12). The committee considered the Sexual Law Reform Society's proposal to abolish age of consent laws, but concluded that the law had an important protective role to play. Protection could not be ensured by the limited provisions of the *Children and Young Persons Act* 1969 as the Sexual Law Reform Society advocated; such a strategy held the prospect of penalising girls through care orders, while allowing their older male partners to go unpunished (PAC, 1979, p. 5, #14, 15, 1981, pp. 5–6, #9, 12–13). The committee settled upon the age of 16 as a balance between the disincentives posed by criminalisation to boys seeking contraceptive and medical advice (PAC, 1979, pp. 5–6, #16; p. 9, #27), and the medical and psychological risks associated with early sexual behaviour for girls, including increased risks of cervical cancer, complications in pregnancy and the ill-effects of abortion (PAC, 1979, pp. 6–11, 1981, pp. 6–8, #15–19). The committee rejected proposals to introduce exemptions for males close in age to their female partners, and proposals to extend prohibitions in the context of 'special relationships' with teachers, employers and others in a position of trust (PAC, 1981, pp. 8–10, #20–23).

The understandings of gender and male/female 'heterosexual' sex which had generated the legal framework created in 1885 were sustained in key respects by the committee. Both reports emphasised that 'most girls are not eager to have sexual intercourse before the age of 16' (PAC, 1981, p. 7, #18; cf. PAC, 1979, p. 8, #24). Desire was thus represented as a male prerogative. This perspective corresponded to a lack of specific concern for the position of young boys. Sexual activity between boys and older women was not discussed in either report. While such sexual activity involving boys aged under 16 was already prohibited as 'indecent assault', the committee made no reference to this whatsoever when referring this offence to the Criminal Law Revision Committee (PAC, 1979, p. 4, #9, 11). Nor did the Policy Advisory Committee's reports even discuss the possibility of creating a specific offence for boys under 16 engaging in sexual intercourse with adult women.

The structure and presentation of arguments within both the working paper and the committee's final report suggest that the existing law on the age for sexual intercourse set the agenda, and little consideration was given to a fundamental revision in terms of gender neutrality. The age of consent to sexual intercourse was evaluated at some remove from the consideration of claims for 'equality' for homosexuals (Part II of both reports), and hence the conceptual incompatibility of the claim for 'equality' with the existing gendered law was not permitted to destabilise the heterosexual legal framework. Nor do claims for 'equality' appear to have impeded the committee's willingness to consider lowering the age for sexual intercourse, although this option was rejected.

The Policy Advisory Committee advanced several arguments in favour of its proposal that the age of consent to sexual intercourse should remain at 16. First, it emphasised the 'physical harm which may arise from premature sexual experience and the undesirability of pregnancy at too early an age' (PAC, 1981, p. 6). Increased risks of cervical cancer were cited, together with risks of complications in pregnancy and the adverse effects of abortion upon the future fertility of girls under 16 (pp. 6–8). The committee's presentation of these issues thus drew upon problematically medicalised understandings of adolescence and sexual health. These arguments, invoking biological factors in opposition to a lowering of the age of consent, asserted physiological constraints upon the possibilities for young women's choice and agency, rather than exploring the possibility of promoting the social conditions and availability of resources for young women to make informed choices (for example, via sex education and sexual health promotion). The body was represented as placing absolute material constraints upon possibilities for agency. In accordance with sociological and feminist critiques of the medicalisation of female adolescence (Aapola, 1997; Griffin, 1997) the committee's arguments can be critiqued for underestimating social mediations of the assumed direct relationship between bodily vulnerability and a requirement for legal protection.

Secondly, the committee emphasised the 'emotional and social harm which a girl may suffer when she has sexual relations at an age when she is not mature enough to cope with the consequences of a sexual relationship' (PAC, 1981, p. 6). The committee's tendency to equate the legal age with 'the ability to make a deliberate and reasoned choice to consent' (PAC, 1979, p. 8, #22) emphasised the idea of cognitive capacities and competence attained at a certain age, although the reports blurred this cognitive understanding of maturity with a more vague understanding of maturity associated with an end to both 'emotional' (psychological) and other forms of social harm resulting from sexual behaviour. The repeated utilisation of the concept 'maturity' by the committee suggests the subtle influence of developmental models of adolescence, which have been widely critiqued in sociological research on youth and childhood (James, Jenks and Prout, 1998, pp. 1–25).

The influence of developmental thinking was not straightforward, since the committee downplayed a direct link between psychological maturity and physiological development, noting that: 'although there had been a gradual fall in the average age at which the menarche occurred in girls [...] there had been no significant increase in recent times in the level of psychological maturity of girls under 16' (PAC, 1981, p. 7). Nevertheless, the committee did clearly articulate the age of 16 as an age of psychological maturity with reference to medical and psychological expertise. While the degree of maturity required was discussed in the committee's reports with reference to social and cultural contexts, the rationale for the age of 16 was not directly theorised or justified in relation to these, but rather was asserted alongside invocation of evidence from the BMA and RCP (PAC, 1981, p. 7). Medicine thus provided the review with a form of expertise which could define a particular age of psychological maturity as the age of 16, but without any systematic exposition of how this would relate to determination of the law in its social context. The average age of psychological maturity acquired through developmental processes was assumed to be the correct age for the removal of legal prohibitions.

The committee's arguments made considerable reference to evidence submitted by the BMA, which argued that 'emotional and psychological development do not significantly outstrip physical growth' (quoted in PAC, 1981, p. 16). The BMA's evidence claimed that 'the age of 18 for men would reflect, in general, their slower rate of biological development' because boys achieved puberty two years later than girls (cited in BMA, 1994, p. 2; cf. PAC, 1981, pp. 16–17). The committee's advocacy of an age of consent of 18 for sex between men on the grounds of their later maturity, alongside the age of 16 for men having sex with women, can be convincingly argued to be confused and inconsistent (Hindley, 1986), but illustrates that developmentalist conceptions of adolescence were at play, albeit selectively and inconsistently employed.

It would be wrong to overstate the influence of developmental psychology, particularly since the British Psychological Society did not submit evidence. It is also important to note the distinct role played by psychiatry: the Royal College of Psychiatrists supported a universal age of 16, but without assuming the reductive links between biological development, psychological competence and the law operating in the understandings of the BMA (RCP, 1976; for discussion of the conflicting evidence, see Hindley, 1986). Developmental understandings came to the fore primarily in the context of the committee's quest for a scientific rationale to legitimise a distinct age of consent for sex between males. Nevertheless, the evidence of the BMA and the RCP was invoked to argue that 16 represented an age of psychological competence and 'maturity' which could be verified by medical science, and could in turn be used to determine the appropriate legal age for sexual intercourse.

The review can thus be interpreted as marking a significant shift from the previous epistemological frameworks which had underpinned the age of consent. In contrast to the prevailing rationale of the late nineteenth century, when the age of 16 had been conceived as an age of protection marking the end of a gendered conception of female childhood innocence, the Policy Advisory Committee placed considerably greater emphasis on the idea that the age of 16 represented an age of psychological maturity marking the attainment of decision-making competence. This emphasis upon a direct link between an age of psychological maturity for decision-making and the law reflected the fact that the review did not draw upon sustained sociological and criminological research into young people's experiences in relation to the law, which might have suggested factors mediating this relationship. I will comment further on the emphasis on medical and psychological knowledge-claims in the conclusion of this chapter.

Homosexuality

As I have shown above, the committee's heteronormative approach accepted the deeply gendered structure of the law regulating male/female sexual inter-course in accordance with prevailing cultural conceptions of heterosexuality. Only from this foundation followed consideration of same-sex behaviour including claims for equality; these were not permitted to destabilise hetero-sexual premises. The committee utilised a dichotomy between heterosexual and homosexual age of consent laws, a theoretical framework which conflated behaviour with subjectivity and identity.

This was facilitated by a failure to contemplate bisexuality as a significant or widespread phenomenon. The committee's final report makes reference to bisexuality on a few occasions, but always in the context of legitimating a higher minimum age for same-sex acts between men. For example:

> Even though his basic heterosexual pattern may remain unaffected, an immature young man could be disturbed by a homosexual relationship. This may apply, too, to bisexual young men, who may find it less easy to encourage the heterosexual part of their sexual make up. (PAC, 1981, p. 17, #44)

The needs and experiences of bisexuals were only invoked to justify continuing inequality of treatment for same-sex sexual acts (PAC, 1981, p. 16, #41).

The committee's discussions of same-sex behaviour between women were also extremely brief (Waites, 2002a). The 1979 working paper, after remind-ing readers who it presumed might have forgotten that 'Lesbian sexual rela-tions are...also homosexual relations', briefly noted that Section 14 of the *Sexual Offences Act* 1956, 'indecent assault on a woman', effectively provided a minimum age for consensual sexual acts between women (PAC, 1979,

p. 15, #40; see Chapter 4). It commented that '. . . no particular social need has ever arisen or arises today for creating new criminal offences to penalise this kind of sexual activity' (PAC, 1979, p. 15, #40). The Policy Advisory Committee omitted all mention of same-sex sexual activity between women from its final report (PAC, 1981).

The offences of 'indecent assault', including 'indecent assault on a female', were left for the Criminal Law Revision Committee to address, with the consequence of a less in-depth discussion. This division of labour demonstrates that sex between women was debated outside mainstream discussion of 'age of consent laws'. Advice from the Policy Advisory Committee was accepted:

> They have told us that the considerations which led them provisionally to recommend a minimum age of 18 for male homosexual conduct do not have the same force in the case of females. They say that homosexual relationships tend to arise later in life among women than among men, and that there is no comparable group of 16 to 18 year old girls whose sexual orientation has not yet become fixed and who are consequently in need of special protection. We are told too that adolescent girls do not seem especially attractive to older women in search of a partner of the same sex and that there is not the same emphasis as in male homosexual culture on this age group. [. . .] Accordingly we can see no ground for treating homosexual relationships between women any differently from relationships between men and women . . . (Criminal Law Revision Committee, 1980, p. 53)

The Criminal Law Revision Committee's final report repeated this view, expressing some doubts but still recommending no change in the law (CLRC, 1984, pp. 86–87; Waites, 2002a). The lack of support for increasing the age in line with that applying to sex between men was in part the product of a review focussed upon addressing perceived social problems. The Home Office's research had found that in a sample year, 1973, only six women had been convicted of indecent assault. However, researchers had not analysed the contexts of the offences, the sexual identities or ages of the women involved, the degree of coercion used or the length or type of their sentences, in contrast to their analysis of men guilty of the same offence (Walmsley and White, 1979, pp. 31–33). In the light of this lack of evidence of a 'problem', maintaining the existing law was acceptable because lesbianism did not have sufficient visibility in the criminal justice system or in mainstream political discourse to require legal reform.

In the case of campaigning groups there appears to have been a desire to avoid the introduction of new and more explicit prohibitions upon consensual behaviour between women. For example, the National Council for Civil Liberties submission to the Policy Advisory Committee carefully stated:

We are particularly concerned that the present review of the law should not introduce new restrictions where none exist at present. The ages of consent would therefore continue to apply only to girls participating in heterosexual acts, and to boys participating in homosexual acts. (NCCL, 1976, p. 6)

This strategy of not rocking the boat was no doubt conceived through wariness that the committee might recommend that the lesbian age of consent should be raised to equal that for sexual activity between males. The committee's subsequent decision to recommend leaving the minimum age for sexual activity between women at 16 reflected the lack of a perceived threat from seducing older lesbians among moral conservatives, combined with a low-profile strategy among lesbian, gay, feminist and radical groups.

In relation to male homosexuality, by contrast, the Policy Advisory Committee engaged in a lengthy analysis. The committee sought to clarify the phrase 'age of consent', which appeared in their remit from the Home Secretary, but did not appear in the law. They proposed that the term 'minimum age' was more appropriate, since there was no general principle of consent in operation for individuals aged over 21, and male homosexuals below the legal age were criminalised, whereas women who were subject to 'unlawful sexual intercourse' or indecent assault were not (PAC, 1979, p. 14, #35). The final report of 1981 is careful to use this terminology throughout, despite it being criticised by the CHE, who argued that employing a distinct concept was stigmatising (PAC, 1981, pp. 11–12, #27). The committee's use of terminology reflected the specific legal status of male homosexuality embodied and sustained in its proposals.

Both the committee's reports emphasised that lowering the minimum age to 18 would not change the legal framework enacted by the *Sexual Offences Act* 1967, which upheld the criminality of acts not conducted in strict privacy, male homosexual soliciting and prostitution (see Chapter 5). The committee did not seek to challenge the fundamental disequilibrium between the scope of homosexual and heterosexual consensual acts defined in law (PAC, 1979, p. 3, 1981, p. 21, #53). Its recommendation for a male homosexual minimum age of 18 was framed in terms of three issues which can be examined in turn: the age of majority; public attitudes to homosexuality; and the needs of young men for protection.

In relation to the age of majority, the committee argued that there no longer existed any other offence where the age of 21 was relevant to individual liability. In accordance with the recommendations of the Latey report, published in 1967 (Committee on the Age of Majority, 1967), the age of majority had been reduced from 21 to 18 by the *Family Law Reform Act* 1969; the voting age reduced to 18 by the *Representation of the People Act* 1969; and the minimum age for jury service reduced to 18 by the *Criminal Justice Act*

1972 (PAC, 1981, pp. 13–15, #33–37). The Policy Advisory Committee deemed that it was

> in accordance with the spirit of the *Wolfenden Report* today that the minimum age should be 18 and that the age of majority was a most important factor to be taken into account in deciding what the minimum age for homosexual relations should be. We think that a person deemed by society to be adult for many important social purposes should be able to take responsibility for dealing with pressures from homosexuals. [...] The time must come when a person should be expected to be able to stand on his own two feet. (PAC, 1981, p. 15, #37)

By contrast the committee's discussion of male/female sexual behaviour had made no reference to the age of majority.

In relation to public attitudes, the committee showed awareness of greater understanding and openness in relation to homosexuality throughout society, which would make a reduction in the minimum age to 18 acceptable (PAC, 1981, p. 15, #39). Nevertheless,

> most of us believe that a recommendation that the minimum age should be reduced to 16 would prove to be wholly unacceptable to public opinion. These members consider that public opinion would support the proposition that the minimum age for homosexual relations should be higher than the age of consent for sexual intercourse: the law would then be regarded as a factor in encouraging those young men who need protection and assistance to avoid homosexual relations while they are immature. (PAC, 1981, p. 16, #39)

'Protection' was critical for the committee, discussed in relation to two issues: the age at which a young man's sexual pattern becomes fixed; and the possibility that young men would not be 'sufficiently mature to cope with the consequences of their actions' (PAC, 1981, pp. 16–17, #40–44). In both respects the committee made heavy reference to dominant forms of medical knowledge, and particularly the evidence of the BMA.

In relation to the fixity of a young man's 'sexual pattern', the Policy Advisory Committee departed from the Wolfenden committee's conclusions. The majority of the Policy Advisory Committee insisted that their medical witnesses, unlike Wolfenden's, were not unanimous in believing the orientation of desires to be fixed by the age of 16:

> A minority of commentators, however, are of opinion [sic] that there is a significant number of young men, including bisexuals (who are attracted to both men and women), whose sexual pattern is not fixed by that age. [...] Most of us [...] take the view that a reduction in the minimum

age to 16 could only be justified if there were stronger evidence than at present exists to the effect that such a reduction would not have harmful consequences for 16- and 17-year-olds and are strongly influenced by the lack of unanimity in the medical evidence on the subject. We all accept, however, that the sexual pattern of the overwhelming majority of young men is fixed by the age of 18. (PAC, 1981, p. 16, #41)

Hence the committee's majority expressed, in extremely strong and clear terms, the importance they attributed to the fixity of young men's 'sexual pattern' as a factor in determining appropriate legislation (on the few sources of medical expertise which challenged the consensus that sexual patterns are fixed by the age of 16, see Hindley, 1986, discussed below).

The committee also invoked medical expertise to justify a higher age of consent on the grounds of a more general male immaturity, arguing that young men mature later than young women, and thus require greater protection from seducing older homosexuals (PAC, 1981, p. 17, #44). They cited evidence from the BMA concerning the 'slower rate of biological development' of males (quoted in BMA, 1994, p. 2) which was claimed to be 'in general two years behind that of females', and also echoed the BMA's assumption that 'emotional and psychological development do not significantly out-strip physical growth' (PAC, 1981, p. 16, #42). The committee argued that differences between the sexes implied that the principle of 'equality' with heterosexuals was invalid.

It is our experience that between the ages of 16 and 18 girls are on the whole more mature than boys in their approach to sexual relationships and that, insofar as it is possible to generalise, boys have caught up with girls in the process of maturing by the age of 18. (PAC, 1981, pp. 16–17, #42)

Yet the committee managed to evade the obvious argument that this would imply an age of consent of 18 for heterosexual males:

we feel that it is far easier for them [boys under 18] to cope with the usual complexities of youthful heterosexual relationships, which are accepted by parents, friends and society, than the greater complexity of homosexual relationships with all the difficulties and pressures involved. (PAC, 1981, p. 17, #43)

Its argument thus rested upon a contradictory stance, simultaneously invoking biological development and social attitudes.

The conflicting medical evidence received by the committee has been carefully explored by J. Clifford Hindley, focussing upon the key issue of whether sexual orientation is determined before the age of 16 (Hindley, 1986, pp. 598–603).[39] Hindley notes the brevity of submissions concerning homosexuality from medical institutions and associations, among which that provided by the RCP, supporting equality at 16, was the longest (though only one page), and gave the only detailed discussion of sexual maturation. The Royal College accepted somewhat later male biological development, but rejected the idea that seduction into homosexuality could occur after 16 (RCP, 1976; Hindley, 1986, p. 599). By contrast, the Medical Women's Federation recommended 21 without reference to a change in the legal age of majority in 1969, while the Association for the Psychiatric Study of Adolescents made no argument for its conclusion in favour of 18 (Hindley, 1986, p. 599). The BMA argued for the age of 18, emphasising that 'the physical development of males is in general about two years behind that of females', and arguing, though it is unclear why, that 'emotional and psychological development do not significantly outstrip physical growth' (PAC, 1981, p. 16, #42).[40] The perfunctory reports of the BMA's evidence given both by the Policy Advisory Committee, and subsequently in a later BMA report, strongly suggest that the BMA provided no clear rationale for these arguments (nor did it in a later report: BMA, 1994, p. 2, see Chapter 7). As Hindley concluded, while the majority of medical institutions submitting evidence favoured 18, the organisation with the most relevant expertise and sophisticated analysis, the RCP, made a strong case for 16; and the Policy Advisory Committee gave no account of evidence to counter this (Hindley, 1986, pp. 599–601). This suggests that the committee lacked rigour in its employment of evidence to support a position favouring 18, and/or was deliberately selective.

The Policy Advisory Committee, in both its working paper and its final report, included significant appendices entitled 'Views of the Minority on the Minimum Age' (PAC, 1979, Appendix A, pp. 25–26; PAC, 1981, Annex III). The consistent collective view of five of the committee's members, expressed in hardly altered form in both reports, was that the minimum age for male homosexual acts should be lowered to 16. These five were all women, five of the eight women on a committee of fifteen members; among them was Mary McIntosh, then Senior Lecturer in Sociology at the University of Essex (CLRC, 1984, Appendix A).

The persistent dissent of the minority is particularly significant when it is considered that two further committee members would have given 16 their support if 'special provisions' could have been devised to regulate the behaviour of those in a position of authority, such as teachers and employers (PAC, 1979, pp. 22–23, #63, 64; PAC, 1981, pp. 17–18, #45, 48). Though such provisions existed in many countries, including the Netherlands and Canada, the committee were advised by the Criminal Law Revision Committee that such restrictions would not be practicable within the existing legal framework in England and Wales. However, the doubts of wavering committee members illustrate clearly that 'on the general principle of allowing male homosexual acts between consenting adults in private, the majority in favour of an age of consent set at 18 rather than at 16 was only eight to seven' (Hindley, 1986, p. 596).

The minority made their arguments in pragmatic, rather than radical terms. Their statement accepted the Wolfenden view that the law should protect those who cannot protect themselves; challenging the actual effects of the law in *criminalising* young men aged below 16 would have involved challenging the larger legal framework. However, the minority did make use of the Home Office's research to demonstrate the tiny number of convictions for consensual sexual relations in private, and hence argue along utilitarian lines that a law which is little used cannot have a great deterrent effect (PAC, 1981, Annex III). The practical effects of the law were emphasised: young men needed to be warned of the medical risks of homosexual activity; and the need to encourage counselling was invoked, alongside public 'tolerance'. The minority's statement was couched in terms of the needs of the young for advice and support, avoiding any reference to the benefits of sex, but did invoke the principle that 'the individual should be free to make his own decisions on these matters' (PAC, 1981, Annex III).

Crucial to the difference in arguments was a different interpretation of the medical evidence in relation to the fixity of sexual orientation. The minority emphasised the lack of evidence for discrepancies between the sexes, and cited the conclusions of the Wolfenden Committee, the Dutch Speijer Committee and the RCP, that a person's primary sexual orientation is fixed before the age of 16. The minority view emphasised that even if homosexual behaviour increased as a consequence of reducing the minimum age, it would not 'increase the number of those permanently converted to a homosexual way of life' (PAC, 1981, Annex III).

The Policy Advisory Committee's conclusion in favour of a minimum age of 18 was thus highly contested and almost defeated. Nevertheless, it reflected continuing profound differences in attitudes towards the regulation of male homosexuality relative to heterosexuality. The committee's rationale for the 'minimum age' applying to male 'homosexual acts' can be analysed in the context of changing conceptual frameworks and underlying social forces.

In presenting their conclusions, the Policy Advisory Committee drew heavily upon the distinction between law and morality articulated in the *Wolfenden Report*, which represented the most significant precedent as a review of sexual offences law and had formed the basis of a wide range of legislation including the *Sexual Offences Act* 1967 (Committee on Homosexual Offences and Prostitution, 1957; PAC, 1979, p. 2; see Chapter 5). The conclusions of the Policy Advisory Committee (and those of the Criminal Law Revision Committee) were presented as an expansion of the scope of Wolfenden's 'liberal' principles. The introduction to the Policy Advisory Committee's working paper quoted at length from the *Wolfenden Report*, stressing the principle that the function of the law is to preserve public order and decency, and to protect the vulnerable, but not to intervene in the private lives of citizens on moral grounds (PAC, 1979, p. 2; cf. CLRC, 1984, p. 2, #1.5). Jeffrey Weeks has echoed the committee's account of its own rationale, describing its recommendation that the minimum age for homosexual acts should be reduced to 18, the new age of majority, as 'a logical continuation of Wolfenden' (Weeks, 1989, p. 288).

However, the Policy Advisory Committee's recommendations concerning the legal age for sexual behaviour between men cannot be entirely understood as an extension of the same conceptual logic which structured the *Wolfenden Report* more than two decades previously. The new rationale must be understood in a new social context. The Policy Advisory Committee's reports suggest that some of the epistemological transformations of the 1960s and 1970s, discussed at the beginning of this chapter, had influenced the committee's conceptual framework. The committee appeared to endorse a less homogenising understanding of homosexual lives and behaviour than the *Wolfenden Report*'s view of the homosexual 'condition', despite arguing that 'there is usually a congenital factor in the cause of homosexuality' (PAC, 1981, p. 13, #30). The volume and sophistication of the evidence received by the committee from lesbian and gay groups illustrates that the committee's conclusions were formed in a new political context, shaped by assertions of gay pride and visibility within mainstream society. A new formulation of homosexual citizenship was sought, which could accommodate changing social attitudes to a degree, yet simultaneously reassert the preferential status of heterosexuality.

The Policy Advisory Committee sought a diminution in the stigma applying to male homosexuals, while simultaneously seeking to prevent the existence of homosexuality where possible. This approach is conveyed by a passage in the committee's working paper, which illustrates both a sense of progressive reform and a view that some discrimination is 'necessary':

> We believe that the law has a part to play in bringing about acceptance of homosexuals by not discriminating unnecessarily against homosexuality. However, most of us think that the law should, as regards protecting young people, advance cautiously and while being compassionate towards the difficulties of those with homosexual leanings, should not attempt to take an exaggerated lead in seeking to change public attitudes towards homosexual acts. (PAC, 1979, p. 20, #56)

As homosexuality and heterosexuality became regarded as closer in social status, and less distinct in character, the legitimacy of prohibitions based upon conceptions of profound difference diminished. New forms of legitimate boundaries were therefore required to sustain new hierarchical definitions of difference. A diminution of emphasis upon the deeply problematic and socially marginal nature of homosexuality, particularly once desires were fixed, necessitated a more precise articulation of boundaries. The new approach sought to ensure that a decrease in the segregation of homosexual subcultures did not increase the prevalence of homosexuality, or undermine heterosexuality's dominant status. The quest to articulate new cultural boundaries and legal boundaries, to define the form and scope of heterosexual and homosexual citizenship, was undertaken through a turn to medical knowledge concerning psychological development.

As described above, the Policy Advisory Committee's majority support for a minimum age of 18 in relation to male 'homosexual acts' derived from two key arguments. First, young men's 'sexual patterns' may not be settled prior to the age of 18 (PAC, 1981, p. 16, #41). Secondly, according to the BMA, young men in general mature later than young women (PAC, 1981, p. 16, #42). The unequal application of the second argument to 'homosexual' and 'heterosexual' males, however, was in turn argued through reference to 'the greater complexity of homosexual relationships with all the difficulties and pressures involved' (PAC, 1981, p. 17, #43). These arguments implied a shift to a new theoretical basis upon which age of consent laws could be founded, which can be conceptualised as a change in dominant understandings of the appropriate relation between the age of consent, and three other ages: (i) the legal 'age of adulthood', associated with the attainment of forms of competence and social status not closely related to biological development (age of majority, age of marriage without consent, age to make valid contracts, etc.); (ii) an age of psychological maturity representing competence necessary to make decisions concerning sexual behaviour, defined by medical/psychological expertise in relation to biological development; and (iii) the age by which an individual's 'sexual pattern' (sexual orientation) is determined, also defined by medical/psychological expertise.

Psychological maturity achieved through biological development had not been a primary issue in previous age of consent debates, whether concerning heterosexuality or homosexuality. The age of consent to sexual intercourse created in 1885 had been conceived without an emphasis upon the necessity for competence equivalent to that associated with full adult status or citizenship rights; it was primarily generated through an emphasis upon the necessity of protecting girls below the age of 16 (see Chapter 4). The Wolfenden Committee had equated the male homosexual age of consent with the prevailing legal age of adulthood, 21, yet this had reflected a pragmatic response to public fears, rather than the committee's considered view (see Chapter 5). Competence to make adult decisions had been invoked as a specific requirement to engage in homosexual behaviour because of the particular risk that it might set a young man 'apart from society', but this was not seen as linked to biological or psycho-sexual development (Committee on Homosexual Offences and Prostitution, 1957, p. 25, #71).

However, the Policy Advisory Committee's investigations witnessed an increasing emphasis being placed upon the claims of developmental psychology in relation to all sexual behaviour. In relation to male homosexual behaviour the committee's emphasis upon psychological maturity was stronger than in the heterosexual context, despite conflicting evidence from the BMA and the RCP (discussed above). The committee accepted the evidence of the BMA that boys' psychological maturity was attained at the age of 18 (PAC, 1981, p. 16, #42). Its advocacy of a minimum age of 18 rather than 16 for male homosexual acts was rationalised with an emphasis on this male age of maturity defined by developmental psychology.

A difference with the age applying to boys involved in 'heterosexual' sexual behaviour (16 via 'indecent assault') was legitimated through brief reference to a vague 'fall-back' argument concerning 'the greater complexity of homosexual relationships' (PAC, 1981, p. 17, #43). This represented evidence of some continuing reliance upon the *Wolfenden Report*'s arguments concerning homosexuals being 'set apart from society', and also a gendered understanding of heterosexual behaviour in which boys' participation was not viewed as demanding a high level of psychological competence, due in part to the absence of pregnancy as a potential consequence. The committee's rationalisation of different ages applying to male behaviour with females and with other males was clearly theoretically incoherent. However, it is apparent that 'the greater complexity of homosexual relationships' was invoked to fill the gap created by the committee's adherence to 'scientific' understandings of psychological maturity.

A new reliance upon medical and psychological expertise to provide a rationale for an unequal and higher homosexual age of consent was also evident in the committee's consideration of the age at which a young man's sexual pattern becomes fixed. Where the Wolfenden Committee had accepted the unanimous verdict of its medical witnesses that the main 'sexual pattern' is fixed by the age of 16, the Policy Advisory Committee's majority emphasised the evidence of a minority among medical witnesses that sexual patterns might vary until the age of 18. Hence by selecting the age of 18 the committee were able to assure the public that there would not be an 'increase in the number of homosexuals in our society' (PAC, 1981, p. 20, #49–50). Dissident medical knowledge claiming that the sexual pattern might not be fixed prior to the age of 18 had in fact barely increased in volume or sophistication since the *Wolfenden Report*'s investigations, and remained unconvincing even within the terms of dominant medical and psychological paradigms for theorising sexual identities as Hindley (1986) has shown.

In a new social context, medical and psychological expertise was thus appropriated in the service of a new form of legitimation for inequality. The committee drew upon 'scientific' expertise to endorse an unequal age on grounds which focussed upon male psychological competence, and on prevention of the homosexual condition. The strategic appropriation of medical and psychological expertise in the service of discrimination explains the stronger reference to psychological competence in relation to male homosexuality compared to heterosexuality (and female homosexuality) within the report.

A change in the logic of argument applying to the male homosexual age of consent had therefore occurred since the *Wolfenden Report*. The decline in social stigma towards homosexuality and growing public visibility of the homosexual subculture had resulted in a shift whereby it could no longer be argued that an enforced 'waiting period' should be imposed due to the enormity of deciding to join a highly marginalised and segregated community. The rationale for the age of consent was therefore realigned, to equivalence with the minimum age necessary to prevent homosexual seduction, and also with an age of maturity and competence in decision-making defined by the medical profession via crude invocations of developmental psychology. Though this also implied equivalence with the new age of majority, this was only one aspect of the rationale.

The Policy Advisory Committee's conclusions represented an uneasy compromise, in the context of a significant social realignment between homosexuality and heterosexuality. The committee's invocation of selected medical and psychological expertise answered the necessity for new forms of knowledge-claim with credibility in the public realm to define and legitimate unequal forms of sexual citizenship. These knowledge-claims sustained faith in the containment of homosexuality, though they could also be reconciled with limited liberal respect and tolerance. The rationale for the age of consent thus shifted in order to police the boundaries of heterosexuality in a post-gay liberation context.

Conclusion

This chapter began by discussing epistemological transformations initiated during the 1960s, and proceeded to analyse developments in debates over the age of consent during the 1970s. The first half of the chapter showed how a dissipation of a previous moral consensus led to the emergence of a new radically pluralist field of political contestation structuring age of consent debates. A shift from Victorian beliefs in childhood sexual innocence to an acceptance of children as sexual beings led to new conflicts over the regulation of sexual behaviour among progressives and radicals engaged in a new sexual politics. These perspectives steadily began to influence mainstream political debates.

In the second half of the chapter, I analysed the rationales advanced by the Policy Advisory Committee for age of consent legislation in relation to both male/female and same-sex sexual behaviour. I demonstrated that an assumed model of gendered heterosexuality dominated the review, and that the age of consent for sexual intercourse was revalidated with reference to new forms of medical and psychological knowledge-claim. A similar tendency was evident in the rationale provided for the 'male homosexual age of consent'.

A central feature of the Policy Advisory Committee's review which I have emphasised was its employment of forms of medical and psychological expertise to construct new rationales for age of consent laws, paralleling broader tendencies towards the influence of the psychological sciences in post-war governance identified by social theorists such as Nikolas Rose (1999). In relation to heterosexuality and the age of consent to sexual inter-course this occurred primarily via knowledge-claims concerning the potential negative effects of sexual activity upon female bodies and mental health, linked to claims that the law was required as an instrument of protection in relation to these. To a lesser extent, more particular forms of psychological knowledge-claim concerning the acquisition of psychological competence were also made with reference to developmental psychology. In relation to male homosexuality, invocations of developmental psychology were more to the fore, together with knowledge-claims concerning the acquisition of a fixed sexual 'pattern' ('orientation').

With respect to both heterosexuality and homosexuality I have demon-strated that such knowledge-claims were made selectively, and often in crude ways, sometimes inconsistent with one another and frequently lacking well-argued validation from the medical and psychological authorities invoked. Nevertheless, seen in a broad social and historical context, it is apparent that the Policy Advisory Committee's review witnessed a general tendency to turn to science, medicine and psychology to provide authoritative expertise in determining appropriate age of consent laws.

This turn to medicine and psychology can be interpreted in the light of contemporary debates in social theory. Theorists such as Rose have emphasised the rise to prominence of the 'psy-sciences' in the late twentieth century, their influence on forms of governance (Rose, 1999). But the debate can also be seen in the light of perspectives which have emphasised that epistemo-logical challenges and uncertainties associated in part with postmodernity or late modernity led to a requirement for new answers (Giddens, 1991; Seidman, 1998). The government's review of age of consent laws can be seen as representing a quest for new sources of expertise and forms of social knowledge to define age of consent laws in the context of epistemological uncertainty, following the demise of traditional assumptions about childhood sexual innocence, the biological basis of gender differences, the legitimacy of patriarchy and the privileged status of heterosexuality (which can be understood with reference to what Giddens calls 'detraditionalisation'; Giddens, 1990). In the face of sexual pluralism and assertive claims for equality, the Policy Advisory Committee devised new rationales for age of consent laws which embodied a reassertion of gender differences and heterosexuality's superior normative status, alongside an attitude of liberal tolerance towards homosexuality.

As suggested at the beginning of this chapter, institutionalised constella-tions of medical and psychological knowledge were increasingly subject to critique by the late 1970s, deriving from both external challenges from radical social movements and from tendencies towards a greater degree of 'institutional reflexivity' (Giddens, 1991) within medical institutions and greater reflexivity in medical research (such as the decline of crude forms of positivism) (Turner, 1995). Consequently, as I have shown, the claims advanced by the medical profession and psychological sciences concerning the age of consent were unsophisticated, heterogeneous and relatively cautious. The emphasis placed upon medical and psychological evidence by the Policy Advisory Committee can therefore be interpreted in part as a pragmatic political strategy, an attribution of authority in order to rationalise and lend support to the committee's conclusions. Thus the review suggests not a straightforward assertion of medical and psychological authorities, but a more mediated appropriation of these authorities. Medical and psychological expertise-claims provided forms of apparently 'scientific' expertise which fitted the requirements of policy-makers.

The new rationale produced by the Policy Advisory Committee for the age of consent to sexual intercourse effectively ended mainstream political debate over the issue during the following decade, and has remained influential until the present, underpinning the age of 16. However, the age of 18 applying in relation to same-sex behaviour between men remained contested by the lesbian and gay movement. The Conservative governments of the 1980s, led by Prime Minister Margaret Thatcher, stalled change, but in the 1990s campaigns for 'equality' emerged with renewed vigour. The following chapter focusses on the protracted debates that ensued, which dominated political discussion of age of consent laws during the 1990s, and hence contributed to stalling debate over the legal age for male/female sexual activity. The influence of medical and psychological knowledge-claims remained apparent.

7
Equality at Last? Age of Consent Debates in the 1990s

For most of the 1990s, the so-called 'gay age of consent' was the highest-profile issue in British lesbian and gay politics, with intense campaigning activity and media coverage surrounding the reduction of the legal age for sex between men from 21 to 18 in 1994, and subsequent attempts to achieve an age of 16 (17 in Northern Ireland) from 1998 onwards. An 'equal' age of consent was finally attained with the passage of the *Sexual Offences (Amendment) Act* (2000) on 30 November 2000. In this chapter, I analyse these debates to reveal emerging social and political relationships between heterosexuality and homosexuality, arguing that age of consent debates witnessed the ascendance of a new 'hegemony' supporting 'equality at 16', constituted through the interweaving of knowledge-claims generated within the mainstream epistemologies of biomedicine, law, criminology and child welfare. I draw upon extensive research on age of consent debates since 1993, analysing primary sources of qualitative data including observations of numerous parliamentary debates during 1998–1999 from the public galleries of the House of Commons and House of Lords, press coverage and interest group campaigning materials (cf. Waites, 1995, 1999a). Beginning with a brief overview of events and campaigning activity, the chapter presents a critical analysis of the forms of knowledge which were invoked to attain 'equality at 16'. Particular attention focusses on how biomedical knowledge-claims concerning the age at which the 'fixity' of sexual identities is established circulated in political debates. I argue that the debate's structure enabled 'equality at 16' to be endorsed alongside the persistent operation of rationales of containment in the political mainstream, and hence that equalisation of the age of consent did not embody recognition of the equal value of hetero-sexuality and same-sex sexualities.

The primary analytical focus in this chapter is thus upon this relationship between heterosexuality and homosexuality. In the following chapter the focus shifts as I explore debates emergent from the late 1990s over other aspects of the form of age of consent laws, particularly the appropriate age boundaries between groups to address adults, children and young people of different ages.

Age of consent debates 1993–2000: An overview

During the 1980s the lesbian, gay and bisexual movement's assertive public claims for equality grew in strength. The demands of earlier homosexual law reform movements and gay liberationism developed into a sustained critique of discrimination and inequalities, pursued by new campaigning organisations and endorsed by increasingly visible and confident lesbian, gay and bisexual people, working for change throughout society. However, the Conservative government led by Prime Minister Margaret Thatcher between 1979 and 1990 resisted all pressures for changes in the age of consent applying to sex between men. The recommendations of the Policy Advisory Committee and the Criminal Law Revision Committee for a reduction in the minimum age for 'homosexuals acts' to 18 in England and Wales were ignored (see Chapter 6). The partial decriminalisation of male homosexual acts, largely in accordance with the framework applying in England and Wales, was achieved for Scotland in 1980 and for Northern Ireland in 1982, creating a minimum age of 21 in each (for discussion, see Jeffery-Poulter, 1991; Dempsey, 1998). Yet the 1980s witnessed a resurgence of right-wing sexual moralism which forestalled even moderate proposals to reduce the 'homosexual' age of consent below 21 in any part of the UK. Government legislation to forbid local authority funding of the 'promotion' of homosexuality as a 'pretended family relationship', enacted by Section 28 of the *Local Government Act* 1988, was indicative of a profound shift in the political climate with respect to debates over young people's sexuality, and particularly homosexuality (Weeks, 1989, pp. 273–304; Durham, 1991; Jeffery-Poulter, 1991, pp. 199–267; Stacey, 1991; Abbott and Wallace, 1992; Thomson, 1993, 1994; Cooper, 1994; Reinhold, 1994; Smith, 1994; Evans, 1995; Epstein and Johnson, 1998, pp. 44–72; Rayside, 1998, pp. 19–43). While gay, lesbian and bisexual teenagers increasingly found a collective identity and public voice (Trenchard and Warren, 1984; Warren, 1984), their claims for recognition remained unacknowledged by the government.

The slow and contested progress of claims for an equal age of consent, even as public debates over the gay age of consent began to intensify in the early 1990s, needs to be understood in the context of continuing inconsistency in the law relating to young people. Despite shifts in child law, childhood and youth remained subject to fragmentary forms of regulation. An important reform in British child law occurred with the introduction of a general definition of childhood as below 18 by the *Children Act* 1989 and the *Children (Scotland) Act* 1995, which emphasised a fundamental principle that in decision-making processes the interests of the child should be the primary issue. However, these applied only in certain areas of policy. Meanwhile the age of criminal responsibility remained 10 in England and Wales, and 8 in Scotland. There also remained extremely little consistency or coherence in the way in which the law addressed children and young people in different areas of policy (see Cretney and Masson, 1997, pp. 575–607; Fortin, 1998). For example, in contemporary law the age varies between 18 as the age of majority, and for marriage without parental consent, 18 for tattooing or buying alcohol; 17 for driving; 16 for legal capacity in Scotland (for example, to choose a home), 16 for marriage with parental consent and entering the armed forces, or to buy cigarettes; and below 16 a variety of other ages apply to less significant activities such as buying pets (Fortin, 1998, p. 82; Bell and Jones, 2000, 2004). This legal context formed the backdrop to emerging debates.

Following the ascendance of John Major as the new Conservative Prime Minister in 1990, government attitudes towards lesbian and gay issues began to change, evidencing 'a significant shift in the balance of forces' from those which generated Section 28 (Rayside, 1998, p. 45). A new phase of campaigning on the age of consent was initiated in 1993 by a legal case taken to the European Court of Human Rights by three young gay men, Will Parry, Hugo Greenhalgh and Ralph Wilde, with the support of lesbian and gay lobbying group Stonewall, invoking Articles 8 (privacy) and 14 (freedom from discrimination with respect to the convention) of the *European Convention on Human Rights* (McGhee, 2001, pp. 145–147).[1] A free vote on the issue in parliament was subsequently announced in December.[2] The subsequent campaign by lesbian, gay and bisexual groups provoked extensive media coverage, often overlapping with public debates in the aftermath of John Major's 'Back to Basics' campaign, which provoked reassessment of traditional attitudes to sexual morality (Durham, 1994; Smith, 1995).

The lesbian and gay lobbying group Stonewall played a leading role as an organisational focus for parliamentary lobbying, and articulated a sophisticated and clearly defined framework of arguments for equality (Stonewall, 1993).[3] Opposition to equality, by contrast, was fragmented and disorganised (cf. Rayside, 1998, pp. 67–68). The Conservative Family Campaign provided the most visible organised resistance, though it became discredited when Director Stephen Green referred to equality campaigners as the 'forces of Satan'.[4] Otherwise, public opposition tended to derive from religious leaders including Cardinal Basil Hume, the Chief Rabbi, the Archbishop of York and the Church of Scotland's Board of Social Responsibility, and particularly Catholic newspaper columnists (Piers Paul Reid, William Oddie, Paul Johnson, Ferdinand Mount); hence Dr David Starkey noted the revived voice of 'authoritarian Christianity, boldly pleading in the political sphere'.[5]

Parliamentary debate focussed upon a proposed amendment (clause 3) to the *Criminal Justice and Public Order Bill* 1994, tabled by Conservative Edwina Currie MP, proposing a minimum age of 16; and a rival amendment tabled by Conservative Sir Anthony Durant MP (clause 5) proposing an age of 18.[6] Retention of an age of 21 also remained an option, but rapidly lost support as a credible alternative. Aside from consideration of the pending European Court case, the age of 21 no longer applied to any other significant legal definition of maturity in the UK; it represented the highest age of consent in the European Union and the Council of Europe for any sexual behaviour (Stonewall, 1993); and it had been rejected by the Policy Advisory Committee and the Criminal Law Revision Committee a decade previously (PAC, 1981; CLRC, 1984).

On 21 February 1994, following extensive public debate and media coverage, Members of Parliament voted in favour of a reduction from 21 to 18 by 427 votes to 162, but against equality at 16 by 307 to 280 (HC 21 February 1994, cols 74–123). This measure was subsequently approved by the House of Lords (HL 20 June 1994, cols 10–67, 74–108). Section 148 of the *Criminal Justice and Public Order Act* also explicitly removed 'shameless indecency' from application to the scope of decriminalised behaviour in Scotland (Dempsey, 1998, pp. 156, 165). Despite the failure to achieve equality, the campaign witnessed significant shifts in attitudes among both MPs and the general public (for discussion, see Waites, 1995; Moran, 1996, pp. 191–196; Epstein and Johnson, 1998, pp. 51–53; Rayside, 1998, pp. 48–52; McGhee, 2001, pp. 135–147).[7]

Other significant changes to sex offences also occurred via the *Criminal Justice and Public Order Act* 1994. In 1991 the House of Lords had ruled that rape of a woman by her husband was a criminal offence (Palmer, 1997), and this extension in the definition of rape was formalised by the act (Lacey and Wells, 1998, pp. 380–385). The definition of rape was also extended to encompass acts including non-consensual anal intercourse, involving penetration of a male or female by a penis (ss. 142–143). The legislation also decriminalised 'buggery' in private between persons with a minimum age of 18, with the effect of decriminalising male/female anal intercourse for the first time. Hence there was movement in these respects towards a principle that non-consensual acts should be unlawful and consensual acts between adults should be lawful, changing the context in which the concept of an 'age of consent' was utilised, although in other respects the law continued to evade consent as a consistent principle of legality (see next section, in pp. 162–166).

The election of a Labour government on 1 May 1997 was widely seen as the beginning of a new phase for lesbian, gay and bisexual politics in Britain, though the Labour Party's 1997 manifesto made no explicit mention of lesbian and gay rights or the age of consent issue, committing the Labour government only to 'end unjustifiable discrimination wherever it exists' (Labour Party, 1997, p. 35). However, Labour leaders had given public assurances to lesbian, gay and bisexual groups during the previous parliament that they would facilitate a free vote on the age of consent and repeal Section 28 during their first term of government. The manifesto commitment to incorporate the *European Convention on Human Rights* into UK law also carried clear positive implications.

Soon after Labour's victory in 1997, the European Commission of Human Rights (a screening body for the European Court of Human Rights, since abolished) concluded in relation to the Euan Sutherland case that the UK was in violation of the *European Convention on Human Rights* (European Commission of Human Rights, 1997). A protracted series of parliamentary debates ensued surrounding attempts to amend legislation, with the ages of 18 and 16 for sex between men emerging as two polarised positions attracting conflicting political allegiances. An amendment to the *Crime and Disorder Bill* (1998) in favour of 16, tabled by Labour backbench MP Ann Keen, was first agreed by the House of Commons on 22 June 1998 by 336 votes to 129 (this and subsequent proposals implied an equal age of 17 in Northern Ireland). However, Baroness Young, a former Conservative leader of the House of Lords, organised a campaign of resistance, and the Lords defeated the amendment by 290 to 122 on 22 July (Epstein, Johnson and Steinberg, 2000).

The government subsequently introduced a new *Sexual Offences (Amendment) Bill* (1998) in the following parliamentary session to reduce the age for sex between men to 16. This bill, in response to previous attempted amendments from backbench Labour MP Joe Ashton, incorporated new provisions prohibiting sexual activity between under-18s and persons in an institutional 'position of trust', such as teachers and youth group leaders (although significantly not family members, indicating a persistent emphasis upon sexual abuse as a problem outside rather than inside families). While many equality campaigners objected to the perceived implication that 'abuse of trust' was a problem only in relation to sexual behaviour between men, the effect of proposed abuse of trust provisions was to criminalise some male/female and female/female behaviour for the first time.

The Commons passed the *Sexual Offences (Amendment) Bill* in March 1999, but in the Lords on 13 April Baroness Young invoked a rarely used form of amendment to wreck the bill. The government stated that it would invoke the *Parliament Act* (1911) to force the legislation through, but this could only occur after an obligatory delay of one year. The *Sexual Offences (Amendment) Bill* was reintroduced in the Commons, and then returned to the House of Lords where Baroness Young introduced a series of amendments in committee, further delaying the bill. On 30 November 2000, the final day of the parliamentary session, the *Parliament Act* was invoked and the bill received Royal Assent (for more detailed chronological accounts of the parliamentary debates, see Waites, 1999a, 2001).

Legal developments: Childhood and consent

Before proceeding to analyse the 'equalisation' of the age of consent, it is first appropriate to consider the broader legal context, including other reforms to child law and sex offences during the 1990s. This enables a critique of prevailing assumptions that age of consent laws reflected legal recognition of an age of competence to consent, reflection on the limited scope of consent as a principle in the law regulating sexual behaviour, and hence clarification of the implications of utilisations of the concept 'age of consent'.

It would be wrong to assume that a more enlightened approach to the status of children in law was developing systematically. An enduring common law presumption had asserted that a boy under the age of 14 was incapable of sexual intercourse, and hence could not be liable for rape or unlawful sexual intercourse with girls aged less than 16 (for background, see Honoré, 1978, p. 60). This presumption was abolished by the *Sexual Offences Act* 1993 (s. 1). Furthermore, *doli incapax*, the common law rebuttal presumption that a child under 14 is 'not capable of crime' in the absence of clear and positive evidence from the prosecution that a child understood the wrongfulness of an action, was subsequently abolished by the *Crime and Disorder Act* 1998 (s. 34) (Card and Ward, 1998, pp. 295–297; Bandalli, 2000). This made all children above the age of criminal responsibility automatically responsible for prohibited acts. This liability contrasted with the continuing exclusion of children from consensual sexual behaviour below 'age(s) of consent'. This situation created such absurdities as making 10-year-old boys criminally liable for unlawful intercourse with girls aged 15 who were not subject to prosecution. Despite the opposition of some children's welfare organisations (Hodgkin, 1998; Bandalli, 2000), children under 14 increasingly became criminally responsible for sexual behaviour with others of similar age.

'Indecent assault', for which consent was not a defence for under-16s (see Chapter 5), was increasingly invoked by the police and prosecuting authorities to serve as a de facto 'age of consent' for sexual behaviour other than intercourse. It was increasingly used to cover sexual activity involving boys under 16 – a response to changes in cultural attitudes towards boys, increasingly seen as requiring protection from women as well as men. Yet the increasing use of 'indecent assault' also had implications for girls. Stonewall reported the existence of at least two prosecutions utilising indecent assault in relation to sexual activity between females involving girls under 16 during the 1990s, contributing to increasing references in public debates to the existence of a 'lesbian age of consent' (Stonewall, 1997b; Waites, 2002a). Reinterpretation and increasing enforcement of indecent assault also tended to extend the liability of under-16s as offenders, however, while simultaneously extending the extent to which they could be positioned as victims of crime. While some child advocates argued that this was a contradictory stance, for government and the criminal justice system it appeared there was no contradiction between the discourse of child protection used to justify enforcing age of consent laws and extensions of criminal responsibility to children. Yet if children over the age of criminal responsibility could be viewed as competent to know the meaning of right and wrong and hence be responsible for crime, how could age of consent laws reflect an age of decision-making competence? What is clear is that prevailing assumptions that the age of consent corresponded to an age at which young people achieved cognitive capacities or moral responsibility for their decisions over sexual behaviour were inconsistent with parallel discourses concerning the punishment of child sex offenders.

A second conceptual issue which is useful to reflect upon to clarify the implications of utilisations of the concept 'age of consent' is the continuing absence of consent as a consistent or universal principle in the regulation of sexual behaviour. This first became apparent in the early 1990s in relation to sado-masochism and has more recently been evident in court cases concerning HIV-infection. Legislation prohibiting 'offences against the person' in fact involves a basic principle that 'the consent of the injured person does not normally provide a defence to charges of assault occasioning actual bodily harm or more serious injury' (Law Commission, 1995, p. 4, s. 11). However:

> Onto this basic principle the common law has grafted a number of exceptions to legitimise the infliction of such injury in the course of properly conducted sports and games, lawful correction, surgery, rough and undisciplined horseplay, dangerous exhibitions, male circumcision, religious flagellation, tattooing and ear piercing. (Law Commission, 1995, p. 4, s. 1.11)

Yet, although 'the concept of consenting to the intentional infliction of injury is well-established in UK law' (Law Commission, 1995, p. 7, s. 1.16), the circumstances in which consent is recognised have been decided incrementally, without attention to consistent principles. A variety of acts which might or might not be considered 'sexual' by participants have historically been permitted.

The legal status of sado-masochistic behaviour was transformed by the case of *R* v. *Brown* (1993, 2 All ER 75, HL) which ruled acts of consensual sado-masochism with the potential to inflict serious injury to be illegal, despite their infliction of comparable levels of injury to other legal activities (for discussion, see Thompson, 1994; Smart, 1995, pp. 114–120; Stychin, 1995, pp. 117–126; Molan, 1996, pp. 68–71; Moran, 1996, pp. 129, 180–191; Weait, 1996; Lacey and Wells, 1998, pp. 410–418). A 3:2 majority in the House of Lords ruled that:

> public policy required that society be protected by criminal sanctions against a cult of violence which contained the danger of the proselytisation and corruption of young men and the potential for the infliction of serious injury. Accordingly, a person could be convicted of unlawful wounding and assault occasioning actual bodily harm, contrary to ss.20 and 47 of

the 1861 [*Offences Against the Person*] Act for committing sado-masochistic acts which inflicted injuries which were neither transient nor trifling, notwithstanding that the acts were committed in private, the person on whom the injuries were inflicted consented to the acts and no permanent injury was sustained by the victim. (*R v. Brown* [1993] 2 All ER 75, HL)

The significance of *Brown* is that the scope of the law in relation to sexual behaviour remained a matter of shifting interpretation, and that 'consent' was not regarded as sufficient to constitute legality. Interestingly the Law Commission subsequently proposed that while in general the validity of consent from persons of capacity should be recognised, a distinctive 'age of consent' of 18 for consensual S/M should be created (Law Commission, 1995, p. 148, s. 10.55).

The contested scope of consent can also, and in related ways, be seen in changing interpretations of the law with respect to transmission of disease, disputed in relation to HIV-infection. During the early 1990s the existing *Offences Against the Person Act* 1861 was interpreted by many as not prohibiting any sexual acts leading to disease transmission, including those legally provable to be 'intentional', in contrast to other non-violent 'intentional' acts that cause harm, such as poisoning (Terrence Higgins Trust, 1998). However, the interpretation of the existing law and the appropriate scope of new legislation have been contested. The Law Commission in 1995 proposed that reformed offences against the person should criminalise both 'reckless' and 'intentional' transmission (Law Commission, 1995; for critical responses, see Bronitt, 1994; Terrence Higgins Trust, 1997; Moran, R., 1998; Gatter, 1999, pp. 150–156). A subsequent green paper, *Violence: Reform of the Offences Against the Person Act 1861*, 1998, and a white paper including a draft *Offences Against the Person Bill* 1998 proposed to criminalise only persons who 'it can be proved beyond reasonable doubt have deliberately transmitted a disease intending to cause a serious illness' ('Violence', para. 3.18; for discussion, see Dine and Watt, 1998; Gatter, 1999, pp. 144–157). However, the government has not introduced legislation to clarify the law.

Meanwhile the scope of existing law remained contested. Most legal commentators suggested that 'intentional' transmission via sexual behaviour was encompassed by existing prohibitions, although there were no successful prosecutions on these grounds. However, Dine and Watt (1998) have noted a successful prosecution for the transmission of the HIV virus in the context of medical surgery as 'public nuisance' under common law, and argue that this could be utilised to cover some types of sexual transmission. In 2001, Stephen Kelly was convicted in Scotland for transmission of HIV to his girlfriend, on the grounds of 'reckless' conduct (Corteen, 2004, p. 171). In 2004, in England, Black African asylum seeker Mohammed Dica was convicted of inflicting grievous bodily harm under Section 20 of the *Offences Against the Person Act* 1861, on the basis that he had 'recklessly' transmitted HIV due to non-disclosure of his HIV positive status (Spencer, 2004; Weait, 2004). In this ruling the court drew upon the *Brown* ruling, to argue that consent was not a valid defence to deliberate infliction of bodily harm where sexual gratification was at issue. Although this ruling was overruled by the court of appeal, the case is currently subject to retrial (*R v. Dica* 2004 EWCA Crim 1103, discussed in Spencer, 2004; Weait, 2004). The contested legality of reckless transmission demonstrates tendencies towards a differential distribution of legal responsibility for safe sex between sexual partners, delimiting the scope of legal consensual behaviour for People Living with HIV and AIDS ('PWA') who have tested positive (see Weait, 2001). This illustrates the ambiguous (and racialized) status of the concept of an 'age of consent' for people with sexually transmissible diseases.

These developments in the law in relation to sado-masochism and disease transmission, demonstrate the persistent absence of consent as a sufficient condition for the legality of sexual behaviour. This has clear implications for interpreting the phrase 'age of consent' invoked throughout the public and political debates of the 1990s. It is apparent that laws referred to as age of consent laws did not and do not signal a minimum age above which 'consent' operates as a universal principle determining the legality of sexual behaviour. Rather 'consent' is a sufficient condition for such legality only for selected subjects. The scope of legality and the significance of consent are circumscribed in legal discourse by reference to the bodies and subjectivity of those involved in sexual activity, and the types of behaviour involved.

Having demonstrated the limited scope of consent as a regulatory principle during the 1990s, and hence having contextualised uses of the concept 'age of consent' and revealed them to be problematic, I will return to analysis of the reduction in the legal age for consensual sexual behaviour between men from 18 to 16. My analysis focusses on demonstrating that the prevailing rationale for an equal age of consent did not embody a view of heterosexuality and homosexuality as having equal value.

The emergence of a new hegemony in age of consent debates

Political conflicts over the age of consent for sex between men during the 1990s were structured by familiar oppositions between moralist and progressive forces. Sexual conservatives, disproportionately associated with the political right (Waites, 2000), defended the age of 18, emphasising the role of the law in upholding traditional sexual values. Campaigning organisations such as the Conservative Family Campaign (in 1994) and the Christian Institute (post-1997) played a leading role (Christian Institute, 1999). Religious leaders including the Archbishop of Canterbury George Carey and the Chief Rabbi Lord Jacobovitz were also vocal in their opposition.

Sexual progressives, by contrast, argued for 16 and were disproportionately associated with the centre and left of the political spectrum, as is revealed by

MPs' voting behaviour (Read *et al.*, 1994; Rayside, 1998; Waites, 1999b, 2001). The lesbian and gay lobbying group Stonewall played a central organisational role, and contributed to structuring the terms of public debate through its articulation of arguments in favour of equality at 16 (Stonewall, 1993, 1998). A reduction of the age of consent to 16 was also supported by a wide range of organisations concerned with the promotion of children's and young people's welfare, many of which endorsed Stonewall's position: Barnardo's, Save the Children, the National Society for the Prevention of Cruelty to Children, National Children's Bureau, National Children's Homes Action for Children, the British Association of Social Workers, the National Association of Probation Officers, the Family Welfare Association and the National Youth Agency. Authoritative medical opinion, represented in particular by the British Medical Association (1994), was also invoked. The British Medical Association and several child welfare organisations were cited, for example, in Stonewall's advertisement in *The Times* titled 'Age of Consent for Young Gay Men: Whose Side are You On?' (*The Times*, 13 April 1999, p. 14; cf. Stonewall, 1998).

A large swathe of opinion was won to the case for equality at 16. While moralists and lesbian and gay radicals remained broadly consistent in their views, it was in the political centre-ground that significant shifts took place. In 1994 an NOP poll found that 44 per cent of those asked favoured 21, 35 per cent favoured 18, and only 13 per cent favoured 16 (*The Sunday Times*, 20 February 1994, p. 1). However, by February 1999 an NOP poll demonstrated that 66 per cent believed 'the age of consent should be equal for everyone', and that of these 54 per cent favoured the age of 16 (36 per cent favoured 18, 2 per cent less than 16) (NOP Solutions, 1999).

Debates over the age of consent were dominated by support for and opposition to 'equality', and hence the process through which the concept of equality was defined and contested held important consequences for the forms of knowledge and political discourse which predominated. The status quo, with an age of 18 for sex between men and an age of 16 for other sexual behaviour, was pitted against an alternative position best described as supporting 'equality at 16'. Other positions, such as advocacy of equality at 18, or the proposals for equality at 14 made by gay activist Peter Tatchell (Tatchell, 1996a) and Queer direct action group Outrage (between 1996 and 1998: Lucas, 1998, pp. 214–215), were marginalised. The dichotomous structure of the debate which emerged, particularly after 1994, impelled participants to ally themselves with one of the two opposing positions. Liberal, progressive and radical political forces in favour of a *lower* age of consent (liberty) and/or in favour of an *equal* age of consent (equality) became aligned with the case for *equality at 16*, the available option which most closely matched their objectives. Hence diverse constituencies were harnessed to the case for equality at 16, ranging across the political spectrum. The alliance forged encompassed not only liberals and left-wing radicals but also

Conservative social liberals (for example, Edwina Currie MP, who tabled the 1994 amendment in favour of 16) and some New Labour modernisers influenced by communitarianism (for example, senior minister Jack Straw MP) – despite the tendency of communitarian politicians to endorse conservative agendas on gender and the family (for example, David Blunkett, who voted against equality as Labour's Shadow Education Minister in 1994).

The flexible concept of equality both facilitated and disguised this diversity of perspectives among supporters of equality at 16. Descriptions of the position as being in favour of 'equality' concealed differences of view, for example, as to whether equality at 16 signalled only formal equality before the law or, alternatively, social and/or state recognition of the equal normative status of homosexuality and heterosexuality. Attempts to maintain such distinctions between 'formal' and 'substantive' equality were erased by the dichotomous structure of the public debate. Both equality campaigners and their moralist opponents broadly shared terms of debate which represented an equal age of consent at 16 as embodying recognition of the equal normative status of homosexuality and heterosexuality. As a matter of strategy, Stonewall and pro-16 politicians sought to systematically identify their position with 'equalisation' rather than 'lowering' of the age of consent, as 'an issue not of age but of equality' (Tony Blair, *Hansard* HC 21 February 1994, col. 98; cf. Stonewall, 1998). The debate presented the opportunity to self-consciously employ and circulate the concept of equality, transcending the discursive conditions which had structured earlier debates. Yet such political rhetoric also tended to obfuscate underlying attitudes.

Laws or institutional arrangements which are formally 'equal' in their application to different groups may conceal persistent social inequalities. In feminist political theory extensive debates have developed, particularly over 'equality' and 'difference' (Squires, 1999, pp. 115–139), and such themes have been addressed in theoretical work on lesbian and gay politics (Wilson, 1993; Herman, 1994; Weeks, 1995, pp. 101–123; Jackson, 1998; Rahman, 2000, 149–201; Richardson, 2000a,b). Such scholarship demonstrates that radical social movements are subject to systematic pressures to formulate their demands in terms of equality in relation to unquestioned norms. This raises questions concerning whether achieving substantive 'equality' implies claiming equality in terms of 'sameness' or 'difference' in relation to heterosexual norms (Richardson, 2000a, pp. 260–263), and what formal equalities may conceal.

However, political and theoretical analyses during the age of consent debates, whether by activists or academics, tended to allow slippages in the meaning of equality. Dissident lesbian and gay activists, such as Peter Tatchell and the Queer direct action organisation Outrage, Chris Morris (editor of *Outcast* magazine), and the Labour Campaign for Lesbian and Gay Rights, sought to identify a variety of distinctive radical agendas in age of consent debates. Interventions included criticism of new abuse of trust laws, proposals for a lower age of consent at 14, and questioning the Labour government's commitment to achieving equality (cf. Tatchell, 1996a; *Outcast* and LCLGR newsletter *Left Out* 1997–2000). Yet even these dissident voices tended to express their arguments in ways which implied that attainment of an equal age of consent would embody a social recognition of the equal value of homosexuality and heterosexuality. Some academic commentators, such as David Rayside who examined campaigning activity surrounding the 1994 debate, also tended to reproduce this equation (Rayside, 1998, pp. 45–75). However, other analyses have suggested the need to question such assumptions (Epstein, Johnson and Steinberg, 2000; McGhee, 2001, pp. 155–161). Critical perspectives allow the debates to be analysed in a different way, with attention to how they evaded challenges to the assumed normality and preferential status of heterosexuality.

'Equality at 16' can be described as having become 'hegemonic' within age of consent debates. In the work of Marxist Antonio Gramsci (1971), 'hegemony' refers to a position of ideological leadership within culture, a stabilised and durable ideological formation formulated through contestation and compromise between social groups – what Connell has described as 'the cultural dynamic by which a group claims and sustains a leading position in social life' (Connell, 1995, p. 77; cf. Laclau and Mouffe, 1985). According to Turner: 'The idea of hegemony [...] argues that in order for cultural leadership to be achieved, the dominant group has to engage in negotiations with opposing groups, classes and values – and that these negotiations must result in some accommodation' (Turner, 1996, p. 195). Hegemony is therefore a usefully suggestive way to describe the current dominance of 'equality at 16' in British age of consent debates – and it is particularly fitting that hegemony is often defined as 'the organisation of consent' (Barrett, 1991, p. 54). 'Equality at 16' was a position used by an alliance of political forces to claim and sustain a defining position in the terrain of ideological conflicts over childhood and adulthood, gender and sexuality, finding its clearest articulation in Stonewall's influential leaflet *The Case for Equality* (Stonewall, 1998). Describing equality at 16 as hegemonic captures the historical distinctiveness and the durability of the formation, which can be contrasted with previous more conceptually and politically precarious formulations of rationales for age of consent laws (PAC, 1981; see Chapter 6).

A focus on the hegemony of 'equality at 16', rather than the lowering of the age for sex between men to 16, helps to keep in mind a critical perspective on heterosexuality. The age of consent debates of the 1990s were not simply about bringing sex between men into line with an established heterosexual norm; rather they involved the production of rationales supporting an age of consent of 16 for male/female and female/female, as well as for male/male sex. This was reflected not only in political discourse but also in moves towards reform of the framework of age of consent laws. Invocations of equality corresponded to momentum towards legal reform to create a universal gender-neutral framework of age of consent laws. This became more apparent after the Home Office review of sex offences was initiated in 1999 (Home Office, 2000a); reform subsequently occurred via the *Sexual Offences Act* 2003 (see Chapter 8).

The case for equality at 16 achieved wide support from diverse political constituencies, but support was also entrenched in the prevailing frameworks of knowledge and social practices operating within a wide range of social institutions: medicine, the criminal justice system, child welfare expertise, social policy and political institutions. The varieties of arguments employed were intricately interwoven into an apparently seamless assemblage to promote equality at 16. The strategic employment of professional knowledge-claims by campaigners created the appearance that respected sources of expertise provided a sound rationale for endorsing equality at the specific age of 16. The remarkable alignment of forms of knowledge emanating from different sources was naturalised. Assisting in the formulation of amendments to existing legislation, Stonewall contributed to setting the terms of debate, presenting MPs and the public with a claim for equality with an unquestioned heterosexual norm of 16 within the existing framework of sexual offences (Stonewall, 1993, 1998). Other arguments, such as those of Peter Tatchell (post-1998) for 'special provisions' to regulate small age differences between partners, were sidelined.

Yet the very coherence of the ascendant hegemony disguised the conditions of its formulation, and its political limitations. An equal age of consent at 16 was not a straightforward step towards full equality, since it was secured through compromise with dominant forms of knowledge operating in politics, law, criminology, biomedicine, social policy and child welfare, and hence via strategic engagement with heterosexuality.

Political discourses

The principle of equality was at the heart of campaigns during the 1990s, a fact illustrated by Stonewall's leaflet *The Case for Equality* which argued that 'the equality of all citizens before the law is a fundamental principle of democracy' (Stonewall, 1998, p. 1), as well as by Stonewall's wider *Equality 2000* campaign (Stonewall, 1997a). Ann Keen MP opened the first post-1997 debate with the words: 'This debate is about equality' (HC 22 June 1998, col. 756). Tony Blair's influential speech as Shadow Home Secretary in 1994 argued:

> the issue . . . is not at what age we wish young people to have sex. It is whether the criminal law should discriminate between heterosexual and homosexual sex. It is therefore an issue not of age, but of equality. (HC 21 February 1994, col. 98)

Other key concepts in the liberal democratic political lexicon were also invoked to construct the hegemony of equality at 16. Appeals to human rights were important, particularly in the context of the case invoking the European Convention's rights to privacy (Article 8) and freedom from discrimination (Article 14). Stonewall invoked the *Universal Declaration of Human Rights'* assertion that 'all human beings are born free and equal in dignity and rights' (Article 1) as the central argument in its petition to Baroness Young in early 1999 (Ellis and Kitzinger, 2002). 'Privacy' was claimed with reference to the *Wolfenden Report*'s assertion of a private realm (Committee on Homosexual Offences and Prostitution, 1957), and also via invocations of the European Convention, since the crucial ruling of the European Commission depended upon the right to a private life defined in Article 8 (European Commission of Human Rights, 1997). Citizenship was increasingly a buzzword, but not used extensively. Libertarianism, associated with 1970s radicalism and the 1980s New Right, had become unfashionable in relation to children, and hence appeals to 'liberty', 'freedom' and 'rights' were displaced by emphasis on the effective promotion of children's welfare.

As suggested above, the structure of mainstream political discourse created systematic pressures for the lesbian, gay and bisexual movement to formulate claims in terms of equality with an existing heterosexual norm. Some theorists have interrogated campaigners' claims for an 'equal' age of consent from a feminist perspective, arguing that such claims disregarded distinctive forms of gendered inequality which operate in heterosexual social and sexual relations, which were reflected in the gendered age of consent law regulating sexual inter-course (McIntosh, 1997; Jackson, 1998). However, these commentaries have tended to exaggerate the systematic inequalities operating in heterosexual sexual contexts, while underplaying the gendered inequalities operating within same-sex relationships, and – as Weeks (1995, pp. 116–123) suggests – the extent to which equality claims in political rhetoric can be transformative and redefine citizenship. They have also understated the extent to which equality campaigners endorsed a feminist critique of heterosexual behaviour: Edwina Currie MP memorably remarked that 'No-one seems equally bothered about rapacious, middle-aged heterosexuals chasing young girls' (HC 21 February 1994, col. 80). The feminist critiques of McIntosh (1997) and Jackson (1998, 1999) also underplayed the existence of the law on 'indecent assault', increas-ingly utilised during the 1990s, which provided a minimum age of 16 for all sexual behaviour involving physical contact (see Chapter 5 on the origins of this). Hence Jackson (1998, 1999), in particular, criticised gay campaigners for claiming equality in the context of a gendered legal framework, without recognising momentum already apparent during the 1990s in government and mainstream policy discourse, and in law enforcement practices utilising 'indecent assault', towards the creation of a gender-neutral legal framework.

However, while adoption of the political claim to equality was justifiable and beneficial, the new predominance of 'equality' in political discourse nonetheless created a new set of problems by disguising persistent underlying inequalities and power relations operating in gendered heterosexuality, including heterosexual sex (Holland *et al.*, 1998; Thomson, 2000, 2004) and between homosexuality and heterosexuality. With respect to heterosexuality and homosexuality the scope of application of equality, privacy, human rights, citizenship and liberty was selectively defined, as they were mobilised overwhelmingly in relation to over-16s. The general problem was the way in which these principles were articulated in relation to wider frameworks of knowledge and institutional practices which delimited their scope.

Legal discourses

Opponents of lowering the age to 16 often advanced the argument that the law transmitted important moral messages to young people, reflecting an enduring strain of 'legal moralism' (Law Commission, 1995, pp. 245–282). Such arguments were increasingly rejected by leading legal opinion, which emphasised in a more utilitarian spirit that 'the law has become increasingly flouted and hence unworkable' (New Law Journal, 1994, p. 257). Yet a more moderate strain of legal moralism continued to inform the legal philosophies and criminological approaches influencing criminal justice policy and New Labour's New Youth Justice (Goldson, 2000a).

Labour ministers, including Home Secretary Jack Straw, espoused a renewal of faith in the criminal law as an effective instrument of social policy for the regulation of youth and childhood as in other areas – widely critiqued in sociological work on youth and crime (Brownlee, 1998; Goldson, 2000a). The *Crime and Disorder Act* (1998), to which an amendment to reduce the age of consent was first introduced, contained new measures including child curfews, custodial sentences for 10–11-year olds and the abolition of *doli incapax* – the presumption that a child under 14 was not capable of crime. Such measures were opposed by some children's organisations, while the age of criminal responsibility, the lowest in Europe at 10 in England and Wales and 8 in Scotland, remained unchanged (Hodgkin, 1998).

The reformulation of age of consent laws was shaped in various ways by this renewal of faith in the power of law as a deterrent. The government's introduction of 'abuse of trust' legislation in the *Sexual Offences (Amendment) Bill* (1998) criminalised individuals in institutional positions of trust engaging in sexual behaviour with 16–17-year olds, and the government supported a Conservative proposal to increase the maximum sentence to 5 years (HC 1 March 1999, cols 776–785). This extension of the criminal law was opposed by teaching unions such as the National Union of Teachers, who argued that existing disciplinary regulations were sufficient.

A reversal of government policy occurred during the debates, in concession to pro-gay equality campaigners, such that an initial intention to criminalise all males involved in illegal activity including under-16s was rejected in favour of the decriminalisation of males under 16 when involved in sexual activity with over-16s (paralleling the legal situation of females under 16 in relation to sexual intercourse) (*Sexual Offences (Amendment) Act* 2000, s. 2). Yet despite this, Home Office minister Paul Boateng continued to defend the government's willingness for under-16s to remain criminally responsible in their sexual relations with other under-16s (HC 1 March 1999, col. 755). Most importantly, the age boundary of 16 was itself reaffirmed, with stress placed upon its effective enforcement by government ministers and suggestions that equalisation represented a step towards a lower universal age strongly repudiated. In a context of persistent discrimination by the police in the implementation of the law, this held particular implications for lesbian, gay and bisexual people.

Social policy, health and young people's welfare

Opponents of an equal age of consent typically argued that a reduction in the legal age would damage health and increase the spread of AIDS. In contrast, equality campaigners argued the necessity for decriminalising young men's sexual activity to facilitate effective sex education and health promotion via the provision of information, advice and counselling, particularly to assist the fight against HIV/AIDS:

> We know that personal health depends on good self-esteem, accurate health information, access to advice and support. (Ann Keen MP, HC 22 June 1998, col. 759)

Leading health policy interest groups, including the BMA, the Family Planning Association, the Royal College of Nursing and the Terrence Higgins Trust, advocated lowering the age to 16 to facilitate effective health promotion (BMA, 1994; Stonewall, 1998). Teaching unions and child welfare organisations emphasised the benefits of decriminalisation for facilitating effective social policy interventions such as the provision of sex education, relationship counselling and safe sex literature. Such organisations typically also offered underlying support for the age of 16 as an age of consent offering the best balance between intervention and legal protection.

These interventions can be critically examined, however, with reference to critical perspectives from sociological work on health, education and youth, questioning the ways in which biomedical knowledge and child welfare are invoked to legitimate interventions in young people's lives by welfare agencies, educationalists and health professionals. Such critiques, for example, in relation to sex education (Monk, 1998a,b), suggest that social policy interventions providing information, skills and moral guidance via health, education and other services can operate in discriminatory ways, and do not necessarily embody equal respect for homosexuality and heterosexuality.

Reducing the age of consent to 16 was supported as a means to facilitate easier interventions in the lives of over-16s and, also to a certain extent, under-16s; but while the change in the law was supported by many professionals working with young people as a means to empower and support lesbian, gay and bisexual youth, it was also in part motivated by the representation of their lifestyles and behaviour as problematic. The BMA's concern about sexual health, for example, can be seen in this light (BMA, 1994). These dynamics imply persistent inequalities, particularly in the lives of under-16s. An equal age of consent did not embody belief in the equal value of hetero-sexuality and lesbian, gay and bisexual sexualities.

Biomedical knowledge of sexual identity and psychological development

A critique of the role of biomedical sciences (Foucault, 1980, 1981; Turner, 1995) can be employed to critically analyse knowledge-claims concerning psycho-sexual development which circulated. Social constructionist and queer theory perspectives on sexual identity have radically questioned the coherence of sexual categories including homosexuality and heterosexuality which are commonly assumed to derive from biological or psychological characteristics (McIntosh, 1968; Plummer, 1975; Weeks, 1977; Foucault, 1981; Butler, 1990; Stein, 1992; Warner, 1993; see Chapter 1). Claims concerning the progressive psychological development of decision-making competence can also be challenged with reference to critiques of developmental psychology and its models of adolescence, widely espoused in the sociology of childhood (James, Jenks and Prout, 1998, pp. 1–25; Gillies, 2000).

The risk of seduction into homosexuality, and the relevant medical evidence were central issues throughout the age of consent debates of the 1990s (cf. Epstein *et al.*, 2000, pp. 14–18). Opponents of equality emphasised the threat from predatory seducing older homosexuals, and the gay com-munity's desire to convert young men. In 1994 Home Secretary Michael Howard maintained that 'there are likely to be, not all, but a number of young men between the ages of 16 and 18 who do not have a settled sexual orientation' (HC 21 February 1994, cols 93–94; Waites, 1995). As Derek McGhee has argued, the threat of seduction and 'homosexual spread' (McGhee, 2000, 2001, pp. 116–161) remained central to opposition in the late 1990s:

> The homosexual community, by its nature, is sterile, and it can survive and grow only by proselytising. There is an agenda to make it easier for that community to grow. (Desmond Swayne MP, HC 1 March 1999, col. 797)

Yet such arguments were steadily eradicated in the face of an apparently definitive medical consensus emphasised by equality campaigners that sexual identity-formation occurs before the age of 16. The Wolfenden committee's conclusion that 'the main sexual pattern is [...] usually fixed in the main outline by the age of sixteen' (Committee on Homosexual Offences and Prostitution, 1957; see Chapter 5) was invoked by Stonewall, which argued that 'all medical opinion' now corroborated this view, while omitting to address social constructionist arguments (Stonewall, 1998).

Stonewall also emphasised the evidence of the British Medical Association (BMA), which had voted overwhelmingly in favour of a reduction to 16 prior to the 1994 debate (Stonewall, 1998). The association's report stated that 'the "causes" of homosexuality remain poorly understood and are almost certainly multifactorial', noting theories emphasising 'neuroanatomic variations' ('gay brain' theories), 'genetic linkage' ('gay gene' theories) and 'psychological influences during childhood [...] in particular the nature of the mother–child relationship' (BMA, 1994). It concluded that 'A common feature of these factors is that they operate at a much earlier age than 16' (p. 5). Hence despite the highly dubious and contested basis of these theories, the BMA claimed the authority to assert that homosexuality is determined well before the age of 16. Its stance evidenced a desire to assure that fears of seduction were misplaced.

An emphasis upon the 'natural' status of homosexuality, implying a view of homosexuality as a distinct, homogenous and stable condition, was particularly evident in the discourse of many heterosexuals positioned in the centre-ground of the debate, seeking a rationale to support equality. Arguments such as that of Tony Blair suggested an emphasis upon the fixity of sexual orientation in early life, and the extent to which gayness is deeply embedded:

> It is not against the nature of gay people to be gay; it is in fact their nature. It is what they are ... (HC 21 February 1994, col. 98)

Neil Kinnock MP, a crucial voice in winning support from Labour tradition-alists, was influenced in this way (HC 21 February 1994, cols 82–86), as was John Bercow MP, a Conservative who declared in a memorable speech that he had changed sides in the debate (HC 10 February 2000, cols 457–458). The European Commission's ruling similarly emphasised that medical opinion regarded sexual orientation to be fixed by 16 (European Commission of Human Rights, 1997).

More fluid understandings of sexual subjectivities and identities, placing greater emphasis on the role of culture, were extremely rare in public debates. A comprehensive survey of mainstream national press coverage surrounding the 1994 debate collected by Stonewall (Waites, 1995) revealed only two public interventions challenging emphasis on the fixity of sexual identities: a letter by Davina Cooper (*The Independent*, 24 January 1994, p. 15); and an article by Peter Tatchell (*The Independent*, 24 January 1994, p. 12; cf. Tatchell, 1996b).

Political columnist Matthew Parris, a gay man, waited until after the debate to voice similar objections to the gay lobby's 'dogmatic insistence' that sexuality is unalterable (*The Times*, 26 February 1994).

Though a somewhat lesser emphasis on fixity was evident during 1998–2000, fixity narratives remained influential and attempts to introduce alternative conceptual vocabularies remained markedly absent (Epstein *et al.*, 2000, p. 17). Flurries of discussion on this theme were largely confined to the lesbian and gay press, and 'queer' perspectives showed little sign of permeating mainstream political discourse. One of the most striking features of post-1997 parliamentary debates was the way in which many of the new generation of Labour and Liberal Democrat MPs, who shared similar political outlooks (feminist, progressive, pro-diversity, pro-gay) and passionately supported equality, were also the most confident in asserting the fixity of sexual identities. Openly gay MP Ben Bradshaw (Labour, Exeter) vehemently denied that anyone ever regarded their sexual orientation as a choice (HC 10 February 2000, col. 440). Another example is Oona King MP (Labour, Bethnal Green and Bow), a black woman with a Jewish mother whose burgeoning confidence as a key voice of the ascendant multiculturalist equalities agenda translated into contemptuous laughter and scathing ridicule of those suggesting that sexual identities might be more slippery (cf. field notes from observation in House of Commons public gallery):

Dr. Julian Lewis (New Forest, East)[Conservative]: [...] The only gay boy in my secondary school [...] told me that he started on the road to being a homosexual when he was under-age and was interfered with by an older youth.

Ms. King: [...] most people recognise that people cannot transfer their sexuality if they violently attack someone. People either have a proclivity or they do not. It is ludicrous to suggest that, had I been attacked and sexually assaulted by another woman when I was a 16-year-old girl, I would suddenly have thought, 'Whoops, you know what? I am not a heterosexual: I'm actually a lesbian'. Such arguments are ludicrous. (HC 10 February 2000, col. 473)

The fixity of sexual orientation did not, however, form an entirely decisive parameter or containing logic for mainstream heterosexual supporters of equality. The often impassioned advocacy of 'equality' expressed by many MPs reflected a change of sensibility. For example, Tony Blair in 1994 addressed the hypothetical scenario that the sexual orientation of a small minority might be altered by experiences after the age of 18.

For those who are confused about their sexuality, how does the criminal law help to resolve that confusion? Indeed it merely complicates it. It deters many from seeking the information, advice and help that they need. (HC 21 February 1994, col. 99)

Claims concerning the fixity of sexual orientation that were initially founda-tion stones supporting arguments for legal reform shifted towards becoming convenient 'tools' in the building of a rationale for equality. However, such claims continued to exert a major influence.

Equality supporters were thus able to invoke the support of leading medical authorities for equality at 16 (Stonewall, 1998). Yet neither the BMA nor the RCP offered any systematic account of how processes of sexual identity formation might be relevant to determining appropriate sexual behaviour, or age of consent laws. The positions of these organisations were strategically appropriated by equality campaigners to imply that their knowledge provided an authoritative rationale for reducing the legal age to 16. The BMA, eager to preserve its powerful status as 'voice of the medical profession' (BMA, 1994, p. 3), was content to facilitate this endorsement of its expertise. Pro-gay campaigners pragmatically utilised essentialising biomedical understandings of sexual identity and worked within associated rationales of containment. Medical authority, though explicitly disclaiming some of its own capacity for expertise, was thus nonetheless re-positioned as authoritative, presenting obstacles to the future transformation of attitudes towards homosexuality.

Reductive biomedical understandings of psychological development and the attainment of decision-making competence, critiqued by sociologists of youth and childhood (James, Jenks and Prout, 1998, pp. 1–25; Gillies, 1999), also played a role. This needs to be analysed more independently from the role of narratives of sexual identity-formation than in Epstein *et al.*'s analysis (cf. Epstein, Johnson and Steinberg, 2000, p. 17). The Home Office Policy Advisory Committee which had examined age of consent laws in the late 1970s had emphasised that boys develop relevant forms of maturity 2 years later than girls (PAC, 1981, p. 16; see Chapter 6). Yet arguments about psychological maturity played a diminishing role during the 1990s. In 1994 the Home Secretary Michael Howard referred to the Policy Advisory Committee's conclusions on sex differences, but placed far greater emphasis upon its other arguments concerning the fixity of sexual orientation and homosexuality being 'set apart from society' (HC 21 February 1994, cols 92–97). Arguments premised upon sexual differences in psycho-logical development were inconsistent with an absence of prohibitions against males under 18 having sex with females. By the late 1990s developmental theories of psychological maturity were rarely invoked by campaigners and politicians. This diminution of emphasis partly reflected changes in the evidence of the BMA, whose 1994 report argued that 'There is little solid information on the relationship between emotional and physiological development' (BMA, 1994, p. 5). The BMA had effectively disclaimed its authority to judge the relevance of biological development to the age of consent, bringing it to a similar position as that held by the Royal College of Psychiatrists since 1976 (RCP, 1976). Yet nonetheless, both the BMA and the RCP were invoked as authorities favouring the age of 16 when the issue of psychological development arose.

Biomedical knowledge-claims concerning sexual identity and psychological development were thus appropriated by the lesbian and gay movement to assure mainstream public opinion that the containment of homosexuality could be combined with an equal age of consent, and the granting of privacy, citizenship, liberty and human rights to adults over 16 on an apparently equal basis. Understanding the way in which these fixity-claims concerning sexual identity were sustained to facilitate equalisation of the age of consent requires analysis via engagement with contemporary social and political theory, in the context of analyses of postmodernity and late modernity (Giddens, 1991; Beck, 1992; Beck, Giddens and Lash, 1994; Seidman, 1994; for a more developed version of the following argument, see Waites, 2005). Specifically it requires considering transformations of biomedical and psychological knowledge paradigms in this context. Epistemological trans-formations occurring in late modernity have challenged the hierarchical and exclusionary forms of medical and psychological expertise (Turner, 1995), which increasingly appear to be characterised by greater 'reflexivity' (Giddens, 1991; Beck, 1992; Beck, Giddens and Lash, 1994), responding in part to challenges from critical social science and radical social movements (Seidman, 1994). Medical knowledge paradigms informing debates over homosexuality therefore need to be understood as internally dynamic and heterogeneous.

To understand the implications of these late modern transformations in biomedical knowledge for debates over sexuality, a crucial distinction needs to be drawn between the absence of consensus within the medical profession, and the ways in which medical professionals have maintained a uniform and powerful public voice in public debates. Neither the BMA nor the RCP offered any systematic account of how processes of sexual identity-formation might be relevant to determining appropriate sexual behaviour, or age of consent laws (RCP, 1976; BMA, 1994). Given the deeply contested nature of gay brain and gay gene theories within medical science (Rose, 1996), and fundamental differences between different psychologists and psychoanalytic theorists over the formation of sexual identities (Lane, 1997), it is apparent that profound dispute exists within the medical and psychological sciences over the aetiology of homosexuality. But it is also clear that while there are new forms of reductionism such as in evolutionary psychology (Segal, 1999, pp. 78–115), the concept of homosexuality as a uniform condition is also beginning to be questioned by other medical scientists and practitioners engaging with social science perspectives. While overt engagement with social constructionism and queer theory is lacking, cultural changes leading to the representation of more diverse forms of same-sex behaviour and lifestyle tend to disaggregate understandings of homosexuality. While most medical and psychological professionals retain a conception of sexual orientation as an inherent condition or characteristic of a person, for many such a conception is increasingly abstracted from any definitive or straight-forward understanding of what constitutes, for example, gay or lesbian sexual behaviour or a gay or lesbian 'lifestyle'.

In its interventions in the age of consent debates in the UK the medical profession disclaimed knowledge of any specific theory of the causation of homosexuality and heterosexuality. Yet it nevertheless continued to authoritatively assert that 'sexual orientation' is established by the age of 16 (BMA, 1994). The BMA, eager to preserve its powerful status as 'voice of the medical profession', was content to facilitate its expertise being invoked by others (BMA, 1994, p. 3). Equality campaigners strategically appropriated such medical knowledge-claims, despite widespread scepticism among those activists influenced by gay liberationism. The medical profession, though explicitly disclaiming some of its own capacity for expertise, was thus nonetheless re-positioned as authoritative.

Giddens' optimistic analysis of late modernity tends to suggest growing reflexivity in all areas of social life (Giddens, 1991), but recent responses such as that of Adkins (2002) emphasise that reflexivity can have complex effects, depending on its form and context. In this vein, analysis of debates over 'equalisation' of the age of consent suggests that effects of reflexivity were contextual and derived from the interaction between different paradigms of knowledge and social groups. Though a degree of increased reflexivity is apparent within medical paradigms and institutions, the generalised public uncertainty and doubt associated with late modernity led to a persistence of faith in scientific and professional knowledge-claims in the absence of alternatives. This demand for certainty in late modernity has affinities to what Brown describes as 'reactionary foundationalism', characterised as reactionary by 'its truncated, instrumental link to a foundational narrative; it is rooted not in a coherent tradition but in a fetishized, de-contextualized fragment or icon of such a narrative' (Brown, 1995, pp. 35–36).

In debates over the age of consent, medical knowledge was revalidated in the public sphere. Medical and psychological expertise concerning 'homosexuality' was sought by politicians and the public, but did not offer authoritative certainties. Yet the public status of such expertise was never-theless maintained through an uneasy alliance between professional interests, public demand for authoritative 'scientific' answers, and social movements willing to appropriate dominant expertise.

Increasing internal dispute and conflict is occurring among biomedical authorities over the causes and meaning of 'sexual orientation', simultaneously and in tension with the inclination of the medical profession to maintain its public status, and the willingness of others to endorse this authority. There is extensive conflict over the 'causes' and nature of 'sexual orientation', and conceptions of a homosexual condition are disaggregating, yet fixity claims remain as important markers of the persistence of a homosexual/heterosexual binary. The claim that sexual identities are established by the age of 16 thus remained significant in the UK, a remnant of a particular history of debates over the age of consent since the *Wolfenden Report*. It is a 'fetishized, de-contextualized fragment' of the 'foundational narrative' of modern scientific discourse (Brown, 1995, p. 36), which has been utilised to sustain boundaries between heterosexuality and homosexuality. The uncertainties threatened by increasingly reflexive biomedical knowledge-paradigms, offering a more diffuse conception of homosexuality that is less distinct from heterosexuality, produced a demand for certain boundaries to manage the emergence of new social relationships between heterosexuality and homosexuality. Fixity-claims were rescued from the past and re-articulated because they fulfilled this requirement. They maintained their influence because they were supported by an alliance between the medical and psychological professions and the voices representing 'the lesbian and gay movement'.

This analysis can be developed further in relation to contemporary political theory, since resilient biomedical knowledge-claims find a mutually sustaining relationship with complimentary configurations of liberal political discourse (see Waites, 2005). As Wendy Brown emphasises, developing the theoretical insights of Foucault and Laclau and Mouffe, the articulation of political identities in the public sphere contributes to forms of 'objectification' (Foucault, 1982), producing hierarchically organised social subjects (Brown, 1995, pp. 52–76, esp. p. 55; cf. Laclau and Mouffe, 1985; Mouffe, 1993; Squires, 1999, pp. 124–139). The articulation of fixity-claims in the public sphere thus contributes to sustaining an impermeable heterosexual/homosexual binary (for adults), hence producing discreet social groups which can be addressed by liberalism in the language of equality, while the need to address underlying inequalities is evaded. Contemporary liberal multiculturalist political discourse which approves social 'diversity' (cf. Hall, 2000, p. 210) is underpinned by notions of discrete and bounded communities in ways which conceal persistent cultural hierarchies and evade explicit confrontation or dialogue with radical critiques of mainstream culture. Fixity-claims are thus associated with the operation of liberal rationales of containment, which assume the unthreatened status of heterosexuality. Biomedical knowledge-claims concerning sexual identity have been appropriated to assure mainstream public opinion that the containment of homosexuality can be combined with the granting of legal equality (for further discussion, see Waites, 2005).

Conclusion

The analysis of debates over the 'equalisation' of the age of consent during the 1990s presented in this chapter reveals the persistent heteronormativity of public attitudes, and how this underpinned debates over age of consent laws. The success of the claim for equality at 16 can only be adequately conceptualised in the context of persistent reference to biomedical under-standings of the fixity of sexual identity, operating alongside a renewal of faith in the application of the criminal law and the ambiguous effects of youth welfare expertise. The case for 'equality at 16' which became hegemonic during the 1990s allowed claims for equality, privacy, citizenship, human rights, health promotion and young people's welfare to be forcefully advanced to secure decriminalisation for over-16s, while the debate continued to skirt the issue of sexual identity-formation and the status of young people under 16. 'Equality at 16' was achieved within a rationale that sought to ensure containment of homosexuality, preventing increases in its prevalence. An equal age of consent – equality in law – therefore did not embody equal citizenship in a broad sense.

Subsequent debates over homosexuality suggest that concerns about the fixity of sexual identities have not dissipated in mainstream political debates. Repeal of Section 28 of the *Local Government Act* 1988 was eventually achieved in Scotland in 2000 and in England and Wales in 2003 (Wise, 2000; Moran, 2001; Waites, 2001, 2005); and adoption by same-sex couples was legalised in England and Wales in 2002 (Waites, 2005). However, while conflicts over Section 28 and adoption trespassed further into the dangerous territories of family and childhood by addressing the representation of homosexuality to children of all ages, like the age of consent debates they continued to skirt the issue of sexual-identity formation. Arguments in favour of abolishing Section 28, for example, typically claimed that educational activities are not sufficiently powerful to influence or 'promote' sexual identities, building a case in the political centre ground which continued to work within a logic of containment (Waites, 2005). This suggests that the emphasis upon the fixity of sexual identities evident in the 1990s remains significant in contemporary age of consent debates, and underpinned the Home Office review of sex offences and subsequent reform of age of consent laws in the *Sexual Offences Act* 2003, discussed in the next chapter.

With respect to general relationships between heterosexuality and non-heterosexual sexualities in contemporary society, the analysis in this chapter suggests a disjuncture between developments in the realms of childhood and adulthood. The prevailing emphasis upon the fixity of sexual identity by the age of 16, coupled with the ascendance of claims for equality, citizenship, privacy and human rights, suggests that once homosexuality is seen as a *fait accompli*, the state increasingly seeks to minimise overt discrimination in the lives of adults. Conversely, the analysis suggests a more pessimistic reading of the distinct dynamics applying to under-16s, where the interventions of the criminal justice system and welfare agencies may remain more discrim-inatory. However, the disjuncture is not absolute, since a logic of containment implies continuing differences in the social valuation of non-heterosexuals at all ages which will persist and underlie future conflicts, even where explicitly discriminatory laws have been abolished. Lesbian, gay and bisexual people, beguiled by their new-found public visibility and increasing moves towards equal treatment by the state, should not mistakenly conclude that they are respected and valued as equals in mainstream society.

In contemporary social theory, analyses discern sexual transformations in late modernity, such as Henning Bech's foretelling of 'the disappearance of the modern homosexual' (Bech, 1997, pp. 194–217) or Weeks' view of the grassroots sexual knowledge emerging into the social mainstream (Weeks, 2000, pp. 1–14, 233–245). The analysis presented here, however, suggests a renewal of boundaries between heterosexuality and homosexuality. Emphasis upon the phrase 'gay age of consent' in public debates and the emerging notion of a 'lesbian age of consent' (Waites, 2002a), used without thought of bisexuality or queerness, were indicative of the structuring influence of clearly defined sexual categories.

More generally the age of consent debates of the 1990s reveal an emerging political terrain in which the principle of equality before the law became established; in which human rights operated with growing strength; and in which the expertise of recognised professional authorities represented a crucial source of legitimacy. Professional medical, psychological and welfare expertise concerning 'homosexuality' and 'children's interests' was crucial. My analysis demonstrates, as in the Policy Advisory Committee's review of age of consent laws in the 1970s (discussed in Chapter 6), the persistent role of flawed biomedical and psychological knowledge-claims concerning the development of competence and (especially) the fixity of sexual identities. However, I have also argued through engagement with contemporary social theory that biomedicine and psychology increasingly did not offer authoritative certainties; yet that the public status of their expertise was nevertheless maintained through an uneasy alliance between professional interests, demand from politicians and the public for authoritative 'scientific' answers, and social movements willing to appropriate dominant expertise. This suggests that the rationale for the age of 16 is sustained on increasingly insecure epistemological foundations.

The following chapter moves on to examine the Home Office review of sex offences which was initiated in 1999, partly in response to inconsistencies in the complex framework of age of consent laws revealed by debates over 'equalisation' during the 1990s. The principle of equality which had won acceptance during the long debates of the 1990s was now to be translated into new age of consent laws.

8
New Age of Consent Laws: Adulthood and Childhood

In this chapter, I examine the Home Office review of sex offences in England and Wales initiated in 1999, and the subsequent reform of age of consent laws in England and Wales in the *Sexual Offences Act* 2003. I explore debates over the utilisation of the concepts 'childhood', 'adulthood' and 'abuse' in the formulation of new age of consent laws, focussing in some detail on the contestation of proposed new offences in the policy-making process to reveal the emergence of a new field of political conflict over the regulation of young people's sexuality. The chapter draws on an analysis of submissions made to the Home Office review, and of responses to its consultation paper, obtained from a variety of organisations. I begin by describing the emergence of proposals for an offence of 'Adult sexual abuse of a child', and develop a critique of this proposal through engagement with debates over the definition of boundaries between adulthood and childhood, and the extension of the concept of 'abuse'. I argue that support for this proposal from children's organisations during the review, and its endorsement in the review's consultation paper, reveal worrying protectionist tendencies in contemporary policy-making. I then discuss developments following the Home Office's publication of draft legislation, examining the emergence of a new offence of 'Sexual activity with a child' and the definition of 'Child sex offences committed by children or young persons' in the *Sexual Offences Act* 2003. In the final section, I discuss other features of the *Sexual Offences Act* which have implications for how the notion of an 'age of consent' is conceptualised, including the creation of a uniform definition of consent in sex offences law.

Critiques of the new age of consent laws are discussed. However, in this chapter my focus is upon developing a critical analysis of prevailing political perspectives and forces; my own perspective is outlined in the concluding chapter that follows.

The Home Office review of sex offences

The Home Office review of sex offences, initiated in 1999, involved a wide-ranging examination of sex offences law in England and Wales, in consultation with a variety of interest groups represented on its central Steering Group and External Reference Group. The review was initiated by Home Secretary Jack Straw, in the midst of conflicts over equalisation of the age of consent which revealed the gendered and inconsistent character of existing age of consent laws (see Chapter 7). However, it was also a response to a number of other pressures to reform the law regulating sexual behaviour: public concerns over sex crime; a general desire to 'modernise' sex offences; a desire to ensure sex offences' compliance with the *European Convention on Human Rights,* and a desire to 'give particular priority to the protection of children' (quoting Jack Straw: Home Office, 2000a, p. i; see Stevenson, Davies and Gunn, 2004, pp. 1–7).

The review's provisional recommendations were published in a consultation paper, *Setting the Boundaries,* in July 2000 (Home Office, 2000a,b; for discussion, see Lacey, 2001). After lengthy consideration of responses, in November 2002 the government published proposals for sex offences legislation in a white paper *Protecting the Public,* which largely reflected the conclusions of the review (Home Office, 2002). After parliamentary debates and amendments the *Sexual Offences Act* 2003 was subsequently passed, including new age of consent laws.

The review's consultation paper *Setting the Boundaries* reflected widespread public concern with child protection and child abuse (Home Office, 2000a,b). Its terms of reference emphasised a requirement to produce recommendations that would: 'Provide coherent and clear sex offences which protect individuals, especially children and the more vulnerable, from abuse and exploitation', and 'Enable abusers to be appropriately punished' (Home Office, 2000a, p. iii). In the opening chapter, setting out the review's 'Purpose and Principles', 'Protection' was described as the first key theme, 'part of a wider strategy to enhance protection for children, vulnerable people and victims' (p. 2). Hence a concern to address child abuse and achieve child protection was at the heart of the review process from the outset.

Emerging from this general context, specific proposals for the regulation of young people's sexual behaviour took shape through a clear sequence of developments, outlined in the consultation paper (Home Office, 2000a, pp. 41–57). From the outset the age of 16 formed a non-negotiable parameter for the review; one of the 'basic set of assumptions' was that 'the age of consent must not be lower than 16' (Home Office, 2000a, p. 5). From the review's inception, however, it was also clear that the existing framework of age of consent laws was highly complex, inconsistent and discriminatory, and hence required reform and simplification. As described in previous chapters, a variety of offences operated as age of consent laws applying to different sexual acts, depending on the sex of those involved: 'unlawful sexual intercourse'; 'gross indecency' between males; 'buggery'; 'indecent assault' on a male or a female; and 'indecent conduct towards a young child' (addressing sexual activity which did not involve physical contact and applying only in relation to children under 14) (Home Office, 2000a, p. 34, para. 3.2.1). These offences each had a maximum sentence of two years, except 'indecent assault' for which the maximum sentence was ten years. To address this confused legal framework, calls for simplification were made in many submissions to the review by a variety of organisations.

A variety of views were expressed on the general theme of age of consent laws during public consultation, as described in *Setting the Boundaries* (Home Office, 2000a, pp. 37–39). However, one particular solution came to the fore which responded to the policy agendas of the interest groups which could claim the greatest expertise and authority, the children's organisations. The proposal for a distinct new offence of 'Adult sexual abuse of a child' originated with The Children's Society, a voluntary society of the Church of England, which advanced the idea in its initial submission to the review. This document was not made available to me, despite repeated requests; however, The Children's Society's proposals are clear from the Church of England's submission, which describes and endorses them:

> We believe, with the Children's Society, that there should be harsher penalties for those that perpetrate offences against children and a greater protection of the victim through judicial process. [...] The Board for Social Responsibility would wish to support changes in legislation including a single offence committed by adults against children. [...] It is essential that legislation gives clarity in law and a clear strong message to the public regarding the protection of children and the responsibility of adults. [...] The introduction of an offence of Child Sexual Abuse would greatly strengthen the position of seeking justice for children whilst also emphasising the strength of the message that adults have a responsibility to protect and not to harm children. The abnegation of such a responsibility will be severely punished. [...] A new offence of Child Sexual Abuse carrying severe penalties would strengthen the protection of children. Adults over the age of 18, who have sexual intercourse with a child under 16, where absence of consent was not an issue, would be charged with Child Sexual Abuse. (Church of England, 1999, p. 7)

The Church of England also expressed support for another aspect of The Children's Society's proposals, a distinct offence relating to consensual activity involving under-18s (Church of England, 1999, p. 7).

Other children's organisations did not initially cooperate in proposing these new offences in their submissions to the review; there was no co-ordinated approach. For example, the National Society for the Prevention of Cruelty to

Children (NSPCC) submission (1999) made no such proposal, and neither Barnardo's nor National Children's Bureau made an initial written submission (National Children's Homes (NCH) informed me their submission was not available). However, with The Children's Society represented on the review's External Reference Group, 'Adult sexual abuse of a child' gradually gained support and endorsement. Furthermore, the existing age of 16 received strong endorsement from the NSPCC, represented on the review's central steering group (NSPCC, 1999, p. 3). The NSPCC also rejected age-span provisions to address small age differences on the grounds that these would 'in effect lower the age of consent', and commented: 'Children involved in sexual relations should be treated as victims not offenders, even when they claim to be willingly involved' (NSPCC, 1999, p. 2).

According to *Setting the Boundaries*, the proposal for a single specific offence relating to child sexual abuse received strong support at the review's consultation conference on sexual offences against children – a report which was included as an appendix to the consultation paper (Home Office, 2000b, pp. 297–306). *Setting the Boundaries* comments:

> One of the key issues to emerge from our consultation conference was the need for the law to establish beyond any doubt that adults should not have sex with children, and that this warranted a serious offence to recognise the importance of the crime. The proposal was that there should be an offence of adult sexual abuse of a child, to replace the existing offences of unlawful sexual intercourse and indecency with children, and to offer an increased level of protection against sexual activity between adults and children. Those working with children thought that such an offence would focus attention on the activity of perpetrators, provide greater clarity in law and give a strong message to the public that sexual activity between adults and children is not acceptable. The review accepted the principle of such an offence, and thought that it would clearly define a set of behaviour that was unacceptable and enable the law to treat it with appropriate seriousness. It should also help in the risk assessment of offenders. (Home Office, 2000a, pp. 43–44, para. 3.6.1)

A specific formulation of the offence 'Adult sexual abuse of a child' was subsequently developed by the review group, which would apply to a person of 18 or older who was:

- involved in sexual penetration with a child under 16; or
- who undertook any sexual act towards or with a child under 16; or
- who incited, induced or compelled a child to carry out a sexual act, whether on the accused, another person or the child himself; or
- who made a child witness a sexual act (whether live or recorded) (Home Office, 2000a, p. 44, para. 3.6.4).

The scope of the proposed offence would thus cover the entire spectrum of sexual activity.

It is clear from *Setting the Boundaries* that the decision to advocate an offence of 'Adult sexual abuse of a child' was taken prior to consideration of the law regulating under-18s, and hence shaped the entire legal framework proposed (Home Office, 2000a, pp. 42–45; cf. pp. 51–55). The necessity to address sexual activity between under-18s subsequently led to consideration of various ways to formulate the law, including the possibility that no offence would apply in circumstances where a small age differential existed between partners (Home Office, 2000a, p. 52, para. 3.9.8). Eventually a proposal for an offence of 'sexual activity between minors' was agreed, described repeatedly in the report as a law which would 'mirror' the former offence (Home Office, 2000a, p. 55, paras 3.9.10–12).

Hence the creation of two new gender-neutral offences was initially proposed:

- 'Adult sexual abuse of a child', applying to any sexual act by a person aged 18 or more involved in sexual behaviour with a person under the age of consent, 16, with a maximum sentence of 10 years (recommendation 19; Home Office, 2000a, p. xiii).
- 'Sexual activity between minors' applying wherever a person under 18 is involved in sexual behaviour with a person under 16, with a maximum sentence of 5 years (recommendation 27; Home Office, 2000a, p. xiv).

It is clear that these proposals were profoundly shaped by a general concern among policy-makers to address child sexual abuse by adults, and that this was translated directly into the specific proposed offence of 'Adult sexual abuse of a child'. The simplicity of the proposals' differentiation of adults from children, rather than (for example) introducing the age-span or 'seduction' provisions that are widely used in the US and Europe (Graupner, 2000; Cocca, 2004; see Chapter 3), appealed to policy-makers. Yet there is little evidence in *Setting the Boundaries* that the formulation of proposals was influenced by sustained consideration of other dimensions of government youth policy, for example on sexual health and teenage pregnancy. Significantly, neither the discussion of 'Adult sexual abuse of child' in *Setting the Boundaries* (Home Office, 2000a, pp. 43–45) nor the report from the review's consultation conference (Home Office, 2000b, pp. 297–306) discussed in detail the impact of the new offence on consensual relationships between teenagers and young people, involving 13–16-year olds with other young people aged 18 and above.

The proposal of the Home Office review team for an offence of 'Adult sexual abuse of a child' was later rejected by the Home Office in its proposals for sex offences legislation, where it was replaced by 'Adult sexual activity with a child' (Home Office, 2002); and in the final *Sexual Offences Act* 2003 it was 'Sexual activity with a child' which emerged to address over-18s. Nevertheless, the fact that 'Adult sexual abuse of a child' could be proposed by the review is highly significant. In the following section, therefore, I outline in some detail a critique of 'Adult sexual abuse of a child', as a means to develop a critical analysis of the contemporary field of policy-making and sexual politics relating to young people's sexual behaviour. This critique also serves to illuminate the origins of the new distinction between over-18s and under-18s which was created by the *Sexual Offences Act*. The development of new offences regulating sexual behaviour between under-18s will be discussed later in the chapter.

'Adult sexual abuse of a child'

Under the proposals put forward in *Setting the Boundaries*, 'consent' was not to be legally recognised as existing for children aged under 13 (recommendation 18; Home Office, 2000a, p. xiii). All sexual activity involving physical contact with under-13s was to be encompassed by offences of 'sexual assault' and 'rape'. What was fundamentally at issue in debate on the merits of possible offences to regulate over-18s, therefore, was their impact upon the implementation of existing legal prohibitions against consensual behaviour with teenagers aged 13–16.

Any new offence addressing over-18s would encompass contexts in which there were relatively small age differences between young people: for example, where an 18-year-old male had sex with a 15-year-old female. It would thus apply to a large swathe of young people's conventional sexual behaviour. The first national survey of *Sexual Attitudes and Lifestyles* which collected data in 1990 found that for females aged 13–15 at first intercourse the median age difference from male partners was two years (Johnson *et al.*, 1994, p. 93). The researchers' analysis of age differences, which focussed on the age difference between respondents who had been sexually active in the past year and their most recent sexual partner, found that the median age difference for women aged 16–24 was two years (younger than the male), while the mean difference for these women was 2.96 years (Appendix 3, table A5.5: Johnson *et al.*, 1994, pp. 133, 455). Analyses of qualitative interview data such as that of the Women, Risk and AIDS Project (WRAP) show that teenage girls having sex with older boyfriends is a conventional feature of contemporary heterosexuality (Holland *et al.*, 1998). More generally, qualitative social research on young people's sexual relationships, both heterosexual and same-sex, suggests that age differences in relationships are far from unusual and experienced in a variety of ways.

It is appropriate to contextualise debates over new age of consent laws in relation to existing implementation practices in the criminal justice system. By the time of the review, age of consent laws were not being forcefully implemented. *Setting the Boundaries* records that in relation to unlawful sexual intercourse with a girl under 16, there were relatively few cases reported (1133 in 1998), far less cautions (286 in 1998) and prosecutions (171 in 1998), and the numbers had been declining sharply over the past 15 years (Home Office, 2000a, p. 36, para. 3.2.9). An increasingly prominent objective of some children's organisations from the late 1990s had therefore been to achieve more rigorous implementation of age of consent laws, particularly in circumstances where there was exploitation by adults. This was an issue raised, for example, in the Barnardo's campaign 'Whose Daughter Next?' (with a clear implicit feminist perspective) which focussed on child prostitution but made proposals in relation to the regulation of sexual behaviour more broadly (Barnardo's, 1998). One objection was to the frequently used 'young man's defence' which exempted males under the age of 24 from a charge of unlawful sexual intercourse if they had 'reasonable belief' that a girl was over 16 (*Sexual Offences Act* 1956, s. 3). The review's proposal for an offence of 'Adult sexual abuse of child' was thus in part a response to a previous absence of robust enforcement and particular deficiencies in the existing law.

In relation to under-18s the review group effectively endorsed the shift in implementation practices that had taken place in recent years. Its comments on the proposed offence 'sexual activity between minors' emphasised that prosecutions should only take place in circumstances where behaviour was 'exploitative' or 'coercive', particularly where there was a complaint (Home Office, 2000a, p. 55, para. 3). This marked a significant shift in attitude among mainstream policy-makers, responding to the limitations of the criminal law as an instrument for intervening in young people's sexual lives. However, this emphasis upon discretionary, light-touch implementation with respect to under-18s appears to have been conceived, and was articulated in the report, in explicit contrast to an emphasis upon forceful implementation of the law in the lives of over-18s (Home Office, 2000a, pp. 43–45). 'Adult sexual abuse of child' therefore threatened to introduce novel and repressive principles of regulation where over-18s were involved.

Evaluation of 'Adult sexual abuse of a child' requires consideration of the way in which it represented and categorised sexual behaviour, and of its likely effect on implementation of legal prohibitions against sex with under-16s. What is immediately clear is that the origins of the proposal in an apparent consensus between respected children's organisations created the potential for the offence to be enthusiastically enforced by criminal justice authorities eager to participate in a project of punitively punishing 'child sexual abuse'. The creation of a new offence held the prospect of being interpreted as signalling a major shift in attitudes, in the context of general cultural tendencies towards a protectionist clampdown against those labelled as 'abusers'.

The maximum sentence of ten years for the offence, proposed in *Setting the Boundaries*, marked a significant tightening of the existing legal framework, in which two years was the maximum sentence available for 'unlawful sexual intercourse'. Such an increase had been called for by various organisations working with young people, such as Barnardo's (Barnardo's, 1998). The maximum sentences for buggery and gross indecency, offences applying between males, were also two years; although the maximum sentence for indecent assault on a male or female (for which the consent of under-16s is not a defence) was already ten years (see *Annex Two: Offences and Penalties*, Home Office, 2000a, pp. 143–150). Given that the proposed offence encompassed a range of behaviour by the full age-spectrum of adults, however, the maximum sentence was likely to be interpreted flexibly by the courts.

It was first and foremost the language used in the offence's formulation which made heavy implementation more likely. The concepts 'child' and 'adult' invoke powerful cultural meanings. The concept of 'childhood' has historically been culturally defined as 'pre-sexual', a period of 'innocence' produced in part through a contrast with 'sexuality' (Jackson, 1982; see Chapter 4). Use of the terms 'child' and 'adult' in relation to sexuality therefore has particular sensitive meanings because sexuality is a primary element in broader social definitions of age group categories. Hence use of these concepts in the formulation of sex offences would influence interpretation of the law.

Given that the *Children Act* 1989 defined a child as under 18, echoing the *United Nations Convention on the Rights of the Child* 1989, use of the term 'child' to refer to under-16s was clearly consistent in a broad sense with the existing law. However, particularly in a context where the age of criminal responsibility is 10 in England and Wales, decisions about the use of the term 'child' in the naming of particular offences remained a matter for judgement. The use of the terms 'child' and 'adult' in the offence 'Adult sexual abuse of a child' marked a departure from the language used to name and formulate existing age of consent laws. For example, the full definition of 'unlawful sexual intercourse' used the term 'girl', but not 'child' (see Chapter 4); while 'indecent assault' on a male or on a female made no direct reference to children, although a legal amendment disallowed 'consent' as a defence for a 'child' under 16 (see Chapter 5). Simultaneous use of the terms 'adult' and 'child', juxtaposed to emphasise a contrast, therefore represented a significant symbolic shift, giving age boundaries extra rhetorical impact. This choice of vocabulary, avoiding alternatives such as 'young people' or 'persons under 16', was likely to generate stricter implementation of the law.

However, it was above all the articulation of adulthood and childhood in relation to 'sexual abuse' which gave 'Adult sexual abuse of a child' a severe cultural meaning. The appearance of the concept 'abuse' in the formulation of proposed statutes was a significant distinguishing feature of the Home Office review of sex offences and *Setting the Boundaries*. The term 'abuse' was foregrounded in the review's terms of reference (Home Office, 2000a, p. iii) and was a key theme of the report, particularly in relation to children (Home Office, 2000a, pp. 3, 33). The concept was used in the formulation of several proposed offences: not only 'Adult sexual abuse of child' but also 'persistent sexual abuse of a child' (Home Office, 2000a, p. xiii, recommendation 25), and 'familial sexual abuse' (Home Office, 2000a, p. xv, recommendation 35; for discussion, see pp. 81–96). Yet despite this extensive utilisation, the term 'abuse' was never defined, and its meanings remained uncertain.

The term 'abuse' was already present in sex offences law. It had been utilised in the formulation of age of consent laws in the nineteenth century, which prohibited, for example, that a person should 'unlawfully and carnally know and abuse' a girl under 12 years (*Offences Against the Person Act* 1861, s. 51; see Chapter 4). However, this had been superseded by subsequent legal changes. More recently 'abuse' had been utilised in the name of the offence 'abuse of position of trust' in the *Sexual Offences (Amendment) Act* 2000, prohibiting sexual activity between 16–17-year olds and individuals in an institutional 'position of authority', such as teachers (see Chapter 7). However, in the *Sexual Offences (Amendment) Act*, grammatically, it was the *position of trust* which was the subject of abuse rather than a young person, and hence 'abuse' was held at a distance from particular subjects. By contrast, the proposal to create an offence of 'Adult sexual abuse of a child' would involve introducing the concept of 'sexual abuse' into sex offences law, and defining a child as directly the subject of abuse by an adult.

The meaning of 'abuse' has been contested by a variety of social and political movements, and is a topic of extensive academic debate (Archard, 1999; Scott, 2001, pp. 13–33). Carol Smart has suggested that during the first half of the twentieth century the prevailing meaning of 'abuse' in relation to children and sexuality shifted from an association with moral harm towards an association with psychological harm (Smart, 2000, p. 68). The concepts of 'child abuse' and 'child sexual abuse' which became increasingly used in post-war social policy have tended to be used as if referring to clear and distinct phenomena, in ways which have homogenised the experiences of those involved (Parton, 1991, pp. 52–115). However, the scope of definitions of child sexual abuse utilised in policy-making, research and public discourse has steadily increased in recent decades.

The concept of abuse now carries a heavy burden of representation. Two distinct meanings associated with abuse can be identified. The first is abuse as 'harm', whereby abuse is understood as directly damaging to the victim; frequently psychological harm is referred to. A second meaning associated with abuse, however, is where behaviour places somebody at risk of harm, and/or exploits them in some way. In this context the abuse is of a position of power or trust, and is less directly an abuse of a person; the behaviour is described as abusive to an individual because it is potentially rather than necessarily damaging. This is an increasingly prevalent use of the term, apparent in the creation of 'abuse of trust' laws in the *Sexual Offences (Amendment) Act* 2000. The term 'abuse' as it circulates in public discourse tends to move between and conflate these two meanings.

Homogenising and reductive understandings of the experiences and effects of 'child sexual abuse', associating it with direct psychological harm, are produced and sustained by mainstream psychology. A construct 'child sexual abuse', referred to as 'CSA', has been developed, which crudely homogenises the experiences of young people experiencing sexual activity prior to adulthood. 'CSA' is associated with strong negative experiences, and viewed as a causal factor responsible for intense psychological harm, yet is produced via research which is often based upon biased clinical samples of respondents who have already been referred for psychological treatment, and which homogenises the experiences of young people within a very wide age spectrum, up to the age of 18 (Rind, Tromovitch and Bauserman, 1998; Stainton Rogers and Stainton Rogers, 1999; Reavey and Warner, 2002).

Among feminists, who have led efforts to achieve recognition of child abuse as a political issue, debates have developed over whether to define the existence of abuse in relation to the negative subjective experience of those involved, or to define abuse with reference to the existence of power relations, as advocated by Kelly (1988). Partly in response to feminist campaigning, an increasing tendency to utilise the term 'abuse' in the latter sense is now apparent in mainstream culture and policy-making: for example, in the offence 'abuse of a position of trust' in the *Sexual Offences (Amendment) Act* 2000. However, while many feminists and child protection advocates have sought to extend the scope of the term 'abuse' by defining it to include abuses of power relations, the tendency among policy-makers has been to simultaneously emphasise that abuse is experienced as directly harmful. This creates a problematic tension, increasingly identified in feminist work on abuse engaged with discourse theory and poststructuralism, which questions extensions of the concept (Reavey and Warner, 2002).

Proposals to utilise the term 'abuse' in the formulation of sex offences occurred in this context. The conflation of multiple meanings in a single term inevitably carried problematic implications. While policy-makers are increasingly adopting expanded definitions of abuse, as in the sex offences review, they do so in a context where the term 'abuse' is simultaneously used to signify directly and severely harmful forms of behaviour. The concept is over-extended, and is not flexible enough to perform the many tasks required of it.

The danger concerning 'Adult sexual abuse of a child', therefore, was that its use of the term 'abuse', particularly when combined with the stark juxtaposition of 'adult' and 'child', would exaggerate the severity of some of the offences involved. This analysis is particularly significant in the context of research which documents and critiques the continuing power of the psychological sciences in the legal system (for example: White, 1998).

Mainstream psychology plays a critical role in producing both popular cultural and specifically legal interpretations of the meaning of 'abuse', which would influence the ways in which judges and juries, in particular, would respond to sexual behaviour categorised as 'Adult sexual abuse of a child'.

It may be argued that the concept of abuse is being employed with increasing flexibility in different social contexts, and that individuals are increasingly able to negotiate its multiple meanings. This is apparent to a degree in the emergence of 'abuse of trust' laws, addressing the existence of unequal power relations. However, the utilisation of abuse in the formulation 'Adult sexual abuse of a child' was particularly problematic since it labelled experiences as 'child sexual abuse', which carries an especially heavy implication of severity in contemporary culture. The creation of this new offence would therefore have created a new disposition towards arrests, prosecutions and strict sentencing, even where exploitation did not exist.

Feminists have rightly argued that abuse can be defined by the existence of power relations, rather than the psychological experiences of the individuals involved (Kelly, 1988). However, the extent to which age acts as a proxy indicator of power inequalities sufficient to constitute abuse should not be exaggerated. In relation to age of consent laws, it is not appropriate to apply the category 'abuse' to all illegal activity because the dominant meanings of the concept, influenced by mainstream psychology, associate the existence of 'abuse' with a lack of agency by the younger party, and the experience of negative psychological effects. Power inequalities between over-18s and under-16s are not sufficient to warrant the label 'abuse'. The proposed offence of 'Adult sexual abuse of a child' was therefore fundamentally flawed, since it implied that, unlike a person aged 16–17, any adult over the age of 18 who engaged in sexual activity with a person under 16 was guilty of behaviour which could be labelled 'child sexual abuse'. This set of moral understandings was out of step with young people's own experiences of their social worlds.

How did such a proposal achieve endorsement by the sex offences review? It appears that the proposal gained support because it was centrally addressed to 'children', in a context where children's organisations such as The Children's Society, NSPCC and Barnardo's were the leading recognised sources of expertise in this area of the review's policy-making. Conversely, 'youth' organisations were less involved, the policy-making process failed to adequately conceptualise or consult 'young people', and hence did not integrate their experiences or understandings of age of consent legislation into its conceptual framework (cf. Thomson, 2000, 2004; see Chapter 9). The potentially destabilising term 'young people' was studiously avoided in the review's justification of its proposals, which spoke only of 'adults' and 'children' (Home Office, 2000a, pp. 43–45). Youth organisations oriented to defending the interests of young people aged over 16 were relatively absent from the review: the British Youth Council and the National Youth Agency were not involved in the Steering Group or External Reference Group, nor did they make submissions. Children's organisations such as the National Children's Bureau, more liberal than some of the leading children's charities, were also absent.

The proposal reflected a lack of joined-up thinking by government and policy-makers about young people. Other areas of government youth policy, such as policy on teenage pregnancy and sex education, emphasise the importance of engaging more pragmatically with young people's behaviour in order to make effective interventions. The lack of consideration of these in the review is indicative of the way in which sex offences continue to be viewed by government, as a peculiar and semi-detached area of policy. Greater involvement in the review by the Department of Health might have pushed the review's proposals in a different direction. Similarly, within the children's organisations the emphasis on protection in relation to sexuality is out of step with the rhetoric of respect, participation and rights increasingly utilised in many of their other areas of policy.

After publication of *Setting the Boundaries*, a consultation period facilitated critical responses to its proposals, including 'Adult sexual abuse of a child'. Public debate on the proposed reform of age of consent laws was almost entirely absent in the media. Leading children's charities such as the NSPCC had participated in formulating the proposals, and hence made no response to the white paper. Significant among responses submitted to the Home Office, however, was that from the Independent Advisory Group on Teenage Pregnancy – an independent group of professionals and academics associated with the Teenage Pregnancy Unit in the Department of Health (Independent Advisory Group on Teenage Pregnancy, 2002). This criticised the likely impact of 'Adult sexual abuse of a child' in relation to the government's teenage pregnancy strategy, focussing on the likely deterrent effects upon the uptake of sexual health services by teenagers involved in sexual relationships with over-18s. Barnardo's also belatedly noted the problem that the new offence would have: 'possible implications...for young people who may be involved in relationships which are in no way abusive or exploitative. [...]...if a young woman of 15 has an 18 year-old partner, any form of sexual touching between them would effectively be criminalised' (Barnardo's, 2001, p. 3). However, the organisation commented only that 'there may be times where prosecution would not be an appropriate response', rather than suggesting any alteration to the proposed offence (Barnardo's, 2001, p. 3). During this period, I also published a short critique of 'Adult sexual abuse of child' in the *New Law Journal* and sent copies with accompanying letters to the Home Office and various children's organisations including The Children's Society, Barnardo's and the National Children's Bureau, lobbying for the offence to be reformulated (Waites, 2002b).

In its white paper *Protecting the Public* the Home Office rejected 'Adult sexual abuse of a child' and introduced instead the offence 'Adult sexual activity with a child', thus removing the crucial term 'abuse' (Home Office, 2002, pp. 24–25). The change from 'of' to 'with' implied greater recognition of potential for agency, of young people under 16 as often being active participants rather than passive subjects in sexual behaviour with over-18s. The concept 'abuse' was also removed from the formulation of some other offences in the government's draft *Sexual Offences Bill*, and from all except the existing 'Abuse of a position of trust' in the final *Sexual Offences Act* 2003 (for example, 'Familial sexual abuse of a child' in *Protecting the Public* became 'Sexual activity with a child family member', s. 25), suggesting anxiety concerning the uncertain meanings of 'abuse'. Furthermore, when the *Sexual Offences Bill* was introduced in the House of Lords in January 2003 'Adult sexual activity with a child' had been replaced by 'Sexual activity with a child', further reducing the rhetorical impact of the offence. 'Sexual activity with a child', with a maximum sentence of 14 years, eventually entered the *Sexual Offences Act* 2003 (s. 9), supplemented by other 'Child sex offences' addressing sexual activity where no physical contact occurs: 'Causing or inciting a child to engage in sexual activity' (s. 10; maximum sentence of 14 years); 'Engaging in sexual activity in the presence of a child' (s. 11; maximum sentence of 10 years); and 'Causing a child to watch a sexual act' (s. 12; maximum sentence of 10 years). 'Child sex offences' also included: 'Arranging or facilitating commission of a child sex offence' (s. 14; maximum sentence of 14 years), and 'Meeting a child following sexual grooming' (s. 15; maximum sentence of 10 years).

The precise motivation for the Home Office's decision to reject the proposal for 'Adult sexual abuse of child' in *Setting the Boundaries* is unclear, since various organisations and individuals were involved in lobbying relevant civil servants during the formulation of *Protecting the Public*. However, the implications for contemporary sexual politics are apparent and cause for concern. That the policy-making community responsible for representing children and young people collectively endorsed 'Adult sexual abuse of a child', and that the creation of this offence was only avoided by the decision of David Blunkett's Home Office to ignore the recommendation of *Setting the Boundaries*, is an irony which is worth dwelling upon. David Blunkett is not a noted liberal on criminal justice policy or sex law, having, for example, voted against equalisation of the age of consent for sex between men in 1994. These developments do not paint a happy picture of contemporary policy-making in relation to young people and sexuality.

On the other hand, we should not be too pessimistic. The fact that 'Adult sexual abuse of a child' was abandoned suggests that at least some leading children's organisations must have expressed willingness for the review's proposals to be altered during the drafting of *Protecting the Public*; and the willingness of the Home Office to drop the offence suggests a degree of sensitivity on these issues exists among civil servants working on sex offences. Furthermore, although as I have shown that the formulation of new age of consent laws was led by a desire for a strong law to address all over-18s, it is also apparent that some support for the new framework derived from a more progressive concern to ensure that under-18s were subject to a separate offence facilitating less severe application of legal prohibitions. It should also be recognised that the desire of organisations such as Barnardo's for greater implementation of age of consent laws was informed by a recognition of a lack of intervention by the criminal justice system and the state more generally where many legally consensual sexual relationships involving under-16s are not beneficial to young people, and was not motivated by a desire for punitive implementation of the criminal law in all circumstances (Barnardo's, 2001). In fact what the analysis of the policy-making process suggests is that the agenda for tackling abuse entered the political mainstream without sufficient consideration of respect for young people's agency, but became moderated in the course of events. This is contrary to the perception of some that contemporary policy-making is in every instance increasingly dominated by ever-more one-sided protectionist perspectives. Nevertheless, the law which emerged, 'Sexual activity with a child' and accompanying offences addressing over-18s, introduced a new distinction between over-18s and under-18s which threatened to replace previous discretionary implementation of the law where over-18s were involved with a new universal approach to prosecutions. I shall explore the implications of this offence further in the conclusion to this chapter.

Analysis of these debates facilitates insight into the contemporary field of policy-making and mainstream sexual politics in relation to young people and sexuality. It suggests a more complex picture of policy-making in the area of sex offences than is suggested by left critiques of New Labour's Youth Justice more generally, which focus on the punitive impetus of the government (Goldson, 2000). In relation to the age of consent, as I have shown, initial policy-proposals originated with interest groups rather than government: specifically with The Children's Society, which accumulated support from other leading children's charities regarded as the experts in the field.

Within children's organisations, furthermore, it is clear that feminist approaches to child abuse had obtained significant influence. The redefinition and extension of the concept 'abuse' to encompass behaviour involving unequal power relations had become prevalent, alongside perspectives influenced by radical feminism stressing the extensive and serious character of such abusive behaviour (Kelly, 1988). For example, Sara Swann represented Barnardo's on the review's External Reference Group, having led Barnardo's' campaign on prostitution *Whose Daughter Next?*, in which a feminist analysis was apparent (Barnardo's, 1998); the emphasis on young people as victims of abuse may explain why Barnardo's did not reject 'Adult sexual abuse of child' in its response to the review (Barnardo's, 2001). Liz Kelly, a leading feminist researcher on sexual violence and abuse over many years, was also represented on the External Reference Group (cf. Kelly, 1988).

Particular forms of feminist analysis of sexuality and abuse, influenced by radical feminist approaches, had thus obtained a significant measure of influence within the policy-making field. Consequently, even where the children's organisations were influenced less by traditional conceptions of inherent childhood innocence (a greater tendency with The Children's Society and the NSPCC) and more by work on the ground with young people in which the sexual capacities of young people are recognised (as in Barnardo's prostitution work in Bradford: Barnardo's 1998), the tendency was to interpret young people's experiences through a conceptual framework which justified labelling too broad a range of experiences as abuse.

That the policy-making community concerned with children collectively endorsed 'Adult sexual abuse of a child' at a consultative conference during the review process, and that this was subsequently endorsed in *Setting the Boundaries*, is deeply worrying. In part this can be attributed to a particular unhelpful division between children's organisations and policy-makers and youth organisations and policy-makers during this particular policy review. However, it was fundamentally the consequence of the prevalence of excessively protectionist perspectives advanced by leading children's organisations such as The Children's Society, allied not only to conservative moralism (for example, the Church of England) but also to broader strains of protectionist thought concerning childhood, including feminist perspectives influenced by a moderated radical feminism. Similar alliances have been critiqued before by feminists with a less reductive perspective on sexual relationships in the context of power inequalities (Vance, 1984, 1992; Segal, 1994); and such critiques require renewal to address contemporary circumstances.

'Child sex offences committed by children or young persons'

Having discussed the formulation of the law relating to over-18s, I shall now explore parallel debates over the law relating to under-18s. The objective of children's organisations, accepted by the Home Office review as discussed above, was to introduce a distinction between over-18s and under-18s into sex offences law. This objective was influenced by general shifts in law and policy, notably the *Children Act* 1989 which defined a 'child' as a person aged below 18. Across a range of legal contexts, advocates for children and young people have increasingly been seeking to give under-18s a different status in law, to protect them from the imposition of legal responsibilities often historically conceived with adults in mind. With government apparently immune to pressures from child-policy experts and children's organisations to raise the age of criminal responsibility (Hodgkin, 1998), such advocates in the children's policy field increasingly sought reforms to the law to make distinctions between offences applying to different age groups.

In the sex offences review this resulted in support for the proposal for 'Sexual activity between minors', an offence to apply wherever a person under 18 was involved in sexual behaviour with a person under 16 (recommendation 27; Home Office, 2000a, p. xiv). This offence, with the same maximum sentence of five years proposed in *Setting the Boundaries*, was endorsed in *Protecting the Public*. However, when the *Sexual Offences Bill* was introduced to parliament, 'Sexual activity between minors' was replaced by an offence addressing 'children and young persons', a phrase carrying a more flexible cultural meaning. In the *Sexual Offences Act* 2003 that emerged, the offence of 'Child sex offences committed by children or young persons' addressed sexual activity involving under-18s with under-16s (s. 13). Under this offence, under-18s were to be prohibited from the same range of sexual activity with under-16s as over-18s, as defined in 'Sexual activity with a child' (s. 9) and other child sex offences addressing situations without physical contact (ss. 10–12), described in the previous section. However, the maximum sentence was lower at five years. This new offence encompassing behaviour between under-18s and under-16s became a focus of criticism from some liberals and children's advocates as the *Sexual Offences Bill* passed through parliament, due to its criminalisation of young people involved in non-coercive consensual activity as offenders.

Reforms to the basic age of consent laws should be seen in the context of other changes related to the regulation of young people's sexual behaviour, proposed in *Setting the Boundaries* and enacted in the *Sexual Offences Act* 2003, involving a general tendency towards extensions of prohibitions, and a shift from the employment of 16 as an age boundary to 18 in several selected contexts (Stevenson, Davies and Gunn, 2004). A new offence of 'sexual grooming' was proposed in *Protecting the Public*, and developed into the offence 'Meeting a child following sexual grooming' in the eventual *Sexual Offences Act* (s. 15); this criminalised a person over 18 who meets with a person under 16 with intent to commit a sexual offence. In relation to sexual activity within families, the new act (unlike previous incest laws) prohibited only activity involving under-18s, utilising the term 'child' to refer to these (ss. 25–26). The offence 'Indecent photographs of persons aged 16 or 17' criminalised taking 'indecent' photographs of under-18s, in the absence of marriage or living as 'partners in an enduring family relationship' (s. 45) (previously illegal when involving under-16s under the *Protection of Children Act* 1978). And offences relating to prostitution and pornography also prohibited behaviour involving under-18s, and employed the term 'child' to describe under-18s (ss. 47–51). This widespread use of the age 18 as a boundary in particular contexts was discrepant with the basic age of consent of 16, but consistent with the distinction between under-18s and over-18s in the new age of consent offences.

A significant issue concerning the reforms was whether children and young people were to be positioned as sex offenders or innocent victims by the law. In the previously existing legal framework the offence of 'unlawful sexual intercourse' had positioned females under 16 as innocent victims, guilty of no offence when engaging in sexual intercourse with a male, whereas a male was held legally responsible (see Chapter 4). In the reform of sex offences required to equalise the age of consent for sex between males (see Chapter 7), equality campaigners had successfully lobbied to amend the law to decriminalise males under 16 involved in illegal sexual activity with over-16s (cf. *Sexual Offences (Amendment) Act* 2000, s. 2); although the fact that this did not decriminalise sexual activity between males under 16 was defended by the Home Office ministers during parliamentary debates. However, 'indecent assault', on a male or on a female, continued to be an offence which under-16s could commit (Hall, 1996). The sex offences review, and subsequently government, was thus faced with a situation where a shift to gender-neutrality required either greater criminalisation of some under-16s (females) or decriminalisation of others. An extension of criminalisation was the option selected. For some this raised questions as to why young people under 16, not judged old enough to be legally permitted to engage in sexual behaviour with each other, should be held criminally responsible for such behaviour: did this imply responsibilities without rights? (for criticism, see Bennion, 2003, p. 18).

Government responded however, by emphasising that the discretionary implementation of the law by the police and prosecuting authorities was intended when dealing with behaviour between young people. This emphasis upon discretionary implementation emerged as a central and distinctive feature of the new approach to the age of consent with respect to under-18s. This was explicit in the recommendations of *Setting the Boundaries*, which emphasised that prosecutions should only take place in circumstances where behaviour was 'exploitative' or 'coercive', particularly where there was a complaint (Home Office, 2000a, p. 55, para. 3, September 11). *Protecting the Public* subsequently commented:

> While it is recognised that much sexual activity involving children under the age of consent might be consensual and experimental and that, in such cases, the intervention of the criminal law may not be appropriate, the criminal law must make provision for an unlawful sexual activity charge to be brought where the sexual activity was consensual *but was also clearly manipulative*. (Home Office, 2002, p. 25; italics added)

The white paper also drew explicit attention to the discretionary role of the Crown Prosecution Service in deciding whether any prosecution is in the 'public interest' (Home Office, 2002, pp. 17–18). This emphasis on discretion was noted approvingly by the Conservative opposition spokesperson Baroness Noakes when the *Sexual Offences Bill* was introduced to parliament, in the context of comments on the dangers of 'over-criminalisation' (HL 13 February 2003, col. 778). It is apparent that a new mainstream consensus had emerged in debates over the age of consent, encompassing leading children's organisations, the Labour government and the Conservative party, in which the continuing existence of legal prohibitions below the age of 16 was to be accompanied by a newly explicit and government-sanctioned strategy of light-touch implementation, in which social welfare agencies would take a more leading role than criminal justice authorities in the regulation of under-16s sexual behaviour, while continuing to operate under the criminal law umbrella (see also Barnardo's, 2001, p. 3). Prosecution would, it was claimed, be reserved for circumstances judged to involve manipulation, exploitation or excessive power inequalities.

Such assurances did not satisfy all critics however. A detailed critique of the *Sexual Offences Bill*, focussing particularly upon its implications for the regulation of sexual behaviour involving children and young people, was produced immediately after the Bill's publication by the prominent Barrister and parliamentary drafter Francis Bennion (2003). Bennion's critique, founded in a liberal humanist philosophy, not only can be seen as reflecting a libertarian strand of thinking on sex among some Conservative social liberals, but can also be taken as representative of broader libertarian currents of opinion, resonating with some work in sociology and libertarian sexual politics which is critical of regulation of young people's sexual behaviour (for example: Corteen and Scraton, 1997; Lind, 1998; Tatchell, 2002). Bennion described the Bill as a 'Sex Hate Bill' which was 'deeply flawed' and a 'pathetic effort', criticising it for reflecting an absence of 'happy acceptance of human sexuality' in society, and being 'fuelled by public hysteria' (Bennion, 2003, p. 6). Tendencies towards similar attitudes, blurred with patriarchal conservatism and disinterest in children's sexual experiences, are apparent in comments from the right-wing broadsheets which Bennion cites: *The Times* expressed antipathy towards new offences of 'grooming a child for sex' and the criminalisation of prostitution and pornographic photography involving 16–17-year olds; *The Telegraph* calling the bill 'unnecessary and uncalled-for' (Bennion, 2003, p. 35).

Bennion commented that the Bill implied a view '. . . that children if merely touched by sex, are somehow thereby irredeemably scarred and marred. Yet the truth is that children are far more robust than that. [. . .] . . . what truly mars many children who encounter sex even in a non-violent, consenting, way is the horrified attitudes to this occurrence of the adults around them. [. . .] Sex hate is the cause of their suffering' (Bennion, 2003, pp. 7–8). Bennion thus grounded his objections to 'Adult sexual activity with a child' and 'Sexual activity between minors' in assertions that an adolescent under 16 is a 'highly sexual being'. In relation to 'Sexual activity between minors' he commented: 'I find it incredible that the Government should really think this is the right way to proceed when laying down our sex laws . . . Anyone knows who remembers their own childish consensual sex play, and sexual experimenting and exploring with age mates, that such activities are a universal and important part of everyone's growing up. The criminal law should not interfere with it' (Bennion, 2003, p. 13). Furthermore, 'a child is incomplete without awareness of its sexuality' (Bennion, 2003, p. 15). In response to the government's emphasis upon discretionary enforcement by the police and Crown Prosecution Service, Bennion argued that this should not be relied upon (Bennion, 2003, p. 17). Similar attitudes were expressed by J.R. Spencer, QC and Professor of Law at Cambridge, who criticised the *Sexual Offences Bill*'s criminalisation of consensual acts between children (Spencer, 2003), and in Peter Tatchell's earlier calls for an equal age of consent at the age of 14 (Tatchell, 2002).

Objections were also made by other critics during the *Sexual Offences Bill*'s passage through parliament, but typically were expressed by women and framed in terms of concern for children's best interests, rather than via invocation of liberal or libertarian philosophy associated with male critics outside parliament. Concerns were expressed about comprehensive criminalisation of young people's sexual behaviour. For example, in the first parliamentary debate over the bill at its second reading in the House of Lords, Baroness Gould of Potternewton (Labour) asked: 'is it right to criminalise what are innocent consensual relationships rather than addressing the issues through the child protection system?' (HL 13 February 03, col. 786). In relation to the proposed offence prohibiting 'Child sex offences committed by children or young persons', the Baroness commented:

> While I appreciate that there has to be a criminal offence to deal with young people who commit serious sexual offences, will my noble and learned friend the Minister consider that the Bill provides the opportunity to introduce a strategic approach to children and young people who display signs of sexually harmful behaviour by ensuring the co-ordination of assessment, referral and treatment services and the provision of coun-selling services? It is important that children who sexually abuse must be treated as children first and foremost. (HL 13 February 03, col. 786)

Baroness Walmsley, speaking for the Liberal Democrats, commented more forcefully:

> It is the way in which the Bill deals with young people who are accused of sexual offences that concerns us most. I think that it boils down to the danger of over-criminalisation and the lack of clarity about where profes-sional assessment and treatment come into the picture. [...] I think these matters should be dealt with through the child protection system and not through the criminal justice system. [...]. A balance needs to be struck between dealing appropriately with a range of coercive behaviour without criminalising mutually agreed behaviour. [...] It sends out the wrong message to young people by turning early sexual exploration from something normal to be enjoyed into furtive activities punishable by

a gaol term. By doing so, it will deter young people from seeking advice and professionals from giving it. [...] the Bill omits any reference to a strategic, multi-agency approach to children and young people who display sexually harmful behaviour, to ensure the co-ordination of assessment, referral and therapeutic treatment services. [...] The solution to all that seems to be that the Bill should deal with those under 18 separately, punishing only behaviour that is aggressive or non-consensual. (HL 13 February 2003, cols 869–871)

Parliamentary debates thus show that the universal criminalisation approach was questioned in the political mainstream, especially by Labour and Liberal Democrat members of the House of Lords and House of Commons, and also by a few Conservatives (such as Lord Skelmersdale: HL 13 February 03, col. 797). Criticism was also made of the Bill for placing under-18s on the national Sex Offences Register, together with other sex offenders (Baroness Walmsley: HL 13 February 2003, cols 870–871). Yet in the context of the preceding sex offences review in which children's organisations had played a formative role, the government was unwilling to drop the universal criminalisation approach. The government's position was expressed by Lord Falconer:

We are keen to ensure that proper protection be given [...] to children [...]. That will mean, as it does now in relation to current offences, that one must criminalise certain activities that, on the facts of a particular case, would never merit a prosecution because it would not be in the public interest for there to be one. [...] As noble Lords all around the House have said, it is a delicate balance. We believe that we have got the delicate balance right. (HL 13 February 2003, col. 876)

Considerable concern was apparent during the House of Lords committee stage (HL 1 April 03). Baroness Noakes (Conservative) moved an amendment (no. 64) which would have decriminalised consensual sexual acts between under-18s and 13–16-year olds, commenting: 'I do not believe that it is always necessary to criminalise activities where it would not be in the public interest to prosecute. Indeed, I think that it is dangerous for the criminal law to be written in a way which criminalises activities that are regarded as normal activities' (HL 1 April 03, col. 1211). This was rejected on the grounds that it would constitute 'removing the age of consent' (Baroness Blatch, Conservative: HL 1 April 03, col. 1213). Baroness Noakes also unsuccessfully proposed that the government's Attorney-General be required to issue guidance to the Crown Prosecution Service on the circumstances in which prosecutions of under-18s should be undertaken; this was supported by the Law Society and some children's charities (HL 1 April 03, col. 1213). At the bill's report stage Baroness Walmsley attempted to remove the clause addressing 'Child sex offences committed by children or young people' from the bill in order to force a complete rethink of the law (HL 2 June 2003, col. 1103). She made further attempts to decriminalise consensual sexual activity at the bill's third reading, again without success (HL 17 June 2003, col. 683). Similar concerns about the criminalisation of all forms of sexual activity for under-16s were raised in the House of Commons, where various amendments were tabled at the bill's report stage by Annette Brooke (Liberal Democrat), Lynne Jones (Labour) and Dominic Grieve (Conservative), suggesting measures such as age-span provisions applying to particular forms of activity (HC 3 November 2003, cols 614–620).

Concerns about the effects of criminalisation upon under-16s thus increasingly came to the fore, but because they had been of limited interest to children's organisations earlier in the policy-making process they made no impact. Nevertheless, analysis of parliamentary debates shows that calls for the reduction of the age of consent when involving under-18s, for age-span provisions, and/or for a reformulation of the law to decriminalise 13–16-year olds involved in non-coercive activity, have been made in the political mainstream. Calls for a reformulation of the legal framework by figures such as Baroness Walmsley show that such measures command significant support among policy-makers concerned with children and young people, and are no longer the preserve of the radical fringe of sexual politics.

The debates suggest that a more measured and detailed consideration of how to formulate the law applying to under-16s could have produced a different outcome. However, because children's organisations' objectives at the outset of the Home Office review of sex offences were focussed upon achieving standardisation and simplification of a confused legal framework, and upon strengthening legal prohibitions applying to over-18s the review did not focus in sufficient detail upon how the law should address under-18s. Once legislation was introduced, in the light of the preceding review, government was unwilling to undertake a fundamental revision of the age of consent or the universal criminalisation of under-16s. Parliamentary debates and committees provided insufficient scope for the complex debate required to take place, but considerable discontent was apparent from MPs concerned with child welfare.

The merits of the new age of consent laws created will be discussed further in the final chapter, which outlines my own perspective on contemporary age of consent debates. However, before concluding this chapter it is appropriate to comment briefly on some other general features of the *Sexual Offences Act* 2003 which changed the legal context in which the concept 'age of consent' can be utilised.

Consent in the *Sexual Offences Act* 2003

The *Sexual Offences Act* marked a move towards a more consistent framework of sexual offences. One important aspect of this was that the regulation of non-consensual behaviour was reformed. Offences of 'indecent assault on a male' and 'indecent assault on a female' (*Sexual Offences Act* 1956) were replaced by 'Assault by penetration' (*Sexual Offences Act* 2003, s. 2) and 'Sexual assault' (s. 3). This removed the requirement for 'indecency', historically associated with the conception of 'indecent assault' as a public offence, and hence embodied a general principle of regulation of all assaults. Like 'Rape' (s. 1), but unlike the previous 'indecent assault' laws, the new assault offences are formulated to be conditional upon absence of consent. Rape was also reformed to remove the defence of genuine or mistaken belief in consent (described in Chapter 6; Stevenson, Davies and Gunn, 2004, pp. 5, 31–37; cf. Jamieson, 1996). Gaps in prohibitions against non-consensual behaviour were thus removed and consent emerged as a more consistent principle in the formulation of the law in this respect.

Another very significant reform was the introduction of a new statutory definition of 'consent' to apply throughout the Act wherever consent is at issue: 'For the purposes of this Part, a person consents if he agrees by choice, and has the freedom and capacity to make that choice' (*Sexual Offences Act*, s. 74; see Stevenson, Davies and Gunn, 2004, pp. 9–29). This implies greater consistency between areas of sex offences law. However, the restricted scope of this definition does not address continuing inconsistencies in the meaning of consent in the criminal law more broadly, which remain to be addressed. The uncertainties created by the *Brown* ruling, and the circumscribed circumstances in which it implies consent to be a sufficient condition for legal sexual behaviour, remain (see discussion in Chapter 7).

In general, the *Sexual Offences Act* 2003 thus witnessed some movement towards consent operating as a more consistent principle in defining the legality of sexual behaviour. I will not discuss these issues further here (for more detail and discussion, see Stevenson, Davies and Gunn, 2004). It is apparent that this alters the way in which the notion of an 'age of consent' can be used and conceptualised. However, it is also clear that wider inconsistencies in the scope and definition of consent in law (cf. *Brown*) mean that age of consent laws do not embody clear or universal legal principles of respect for consent between sexual partners. Furthermore, continuing differences in the ages applying to different forms of sexual behaviour (18 as the age for prostitution, photography, familial sexual activity, 'abuse of a position of trust', etc.) confound expectations among some of the public that the age of 16 applies universally as an age of consent to all forms of sexual behaviour.

Conclusion

The Home Office review and subsequent reform of age of consent laws took place within the 'logic of containment' concerning same-sex sexualities described in Chapter 7. The hegemony of 'equality at 16' established during the 1990s was a major factor in stalling reconsideration of the 'heterosexual' age of consent, which was explicitly ruled out of the review's terms of reference. The rationale which underpinned equality at 16 constrained attempts to lower the age of consent, in a context where moralists express horror at the possibility of gay sex being legal at 14 (cf. 'Legalise sex at 14 plan', *Daily Mail*, 25 August 1998, pp. 1–2). But more generally, reluctance to questioning the criminalisation of all sexual behaviour for under-16s was a consequence of the attitudes prevailing among children's organisations, combined with the New Labour government's faith in the criminal law as an effective instrument of policy in addressing young people.

In the first part of the chapter, I demonstrated how the new legal framework addressing over-18s was shaped by protectionist agendas. Because 'Adult sexual abuse of a child', was reformulated as 'Sexual activity with a child', the danger of heavy implementation has been ameliorated. However, the consequences of the decision of the sex offences review and the government to introduce different offences to address over-18s and under-18s still appear likely to be undesirable in their effects on many young people over 18. The creation of distinct offences applying to over-18s, with a maximum sentence of 14 years for 'Sexual activity with a Child', appears likely to create an approach favouring prosecution of over-18s among police and prosecutors – particularly given the government's contrasting emphasis upon discretionary implementation of 'Child sex offences committed by children or young persons'. Consequently, where commonplace sexual behaviour between 18- and 15-year olds was often previously addressed with police warnings, it now appears much more likely to result in court cases.

The hope is that, by contrast, the creation of a distinct offence applying to legally consensual behaviour between under-18s, 'Child sex offences committed by children and young persons', will facilitate a spectrum of discretionary responses, and that prosecutions will not be undertaken in circumstances which are not exploitative, coercive or abusive. However, such behaviour remains universally criminalised, and no new guidelines are to be issued by government to prosecuting authorities; hence the legal situation of under-18s has not fundamentally changed. Therefore, whether the benefits of a specific offence applying to under-18s are sufficient to outweigh the negative impact of more widespread prosecutions against young people over 18 in circumstances where there is no coercion is unclear. The police and courts appear likely to interpret both offences too severely and become too disposed towards jail sentences. Importantly, for all age groups, how appropriate circumstances for police intervention are defined (exploitation, coercion, abuse, etc.), and with reference to what kinds of expertise, remains a contested issue.

The obvious alternative to the newly created age of consent laws would have been a single, simple age of consent offence formulated in terms such as 'Sexual activity with a child', addressing all over-16s in the same terms.

The children's organisations' support for the introduction of a distinction between over-18s and under-18s was motivated to a considerable degree by a desire to use the law to send a moral message that sexual activity between over-18s and under-16s is always deeply wrong. Ultimately this attitude is simply out of step with the everyday experiences of many young people. In seeking to use the law to convey such messages to police, prosecutors and society, the children's organisations fell into the common trap of focussing on law as a clear and visible instrument of policy, rather than on influencing existing law enforcement practices within the criminal justice system, and on broader measures in social policy to support young people. The consequence appears likely to be an unhelpful and excessively punitive new tendency in the enforcement of age of consent laws against young people over 18. While a distinction between over-18s and under-18s may be acceptable to retain, as I suggest in the final chapter, the interpretation of this distinction which led to its creation, and the resulting tendency towards punitive implementation in relation to all over-18s, is misguided.

The analysis of the policy-making field in this chapter shows the need to overcome crude divisions between 'children' and 'young people' in policy-making. It also suggests the urgent need to address unresolved tensions between agendas for 'child protection' and agendas to promote 'children's rights and participation'. Children's organisations utilise both discourses simultaneously in different areas of policy; but sexuality is invariably defined as a realm for protection, leading to an incoherent approach to policy-making.

In debates over contemporary youth justice policy, many sociologists and criminologists have been fiercely critical of New Labour's renewal of faith in the criminal law as an effective instrument of policy (see various contributions in Goldson, 2000). Such perspectives might suggest that New Labour would be agenda-setting; yet analysis of the sex offences review suggests otherwise. The proposal for 'Adult sexual abuse of a child' clearly derived from children's organisations, not from government; and to a considerable extent the child protection agendas informing the agendas of children's organisations such as Barnardo's derive from progressive and feminist perspectives rather than more traditional forms of protectionism. 'Adult sexual abuse of a child' might have been expected to appeal to the protectionist, paternalistic and moralistic tendencies of the New Labour Home Office, particularly the Home Secretary David Blunkett; yet in fact the government rejected a proposal initially advanced by the children's organisations and supported by the sex offences review group. This suggests that the political field cannot be adequately conceptualised with reference to a moralistic and punitive government agenda; policy is being determined in a far more complex context.

The implication is that critical attention in the field of youth policy on sexuality should focus a little less on attacking government moralism and punitivism, and a little more on the unresolved tensions and disputes over the correct relationship between 'rights' and 'protection', and the appropriate definition of abuse, which exist among those influencing policy more generally. Contemporary policy-making can only be understood if it is recognised that previously radical and marginal political movements concerned with supporting the interests of children and addressing gender inequality, which emerged in the 1960s and 1970s (see Chapter 6), have now reached centre-stage in policy-making. Child advocates, including some feminists, have to a significant degree become the new recognised experts. Because longstanding tensions among progressives and radicals remained without sufficient dialogue, and because young people's voices were not adequately represented, protectionist perspectives gained excessive influence and ill-judged proposals emerged. In the final chapter that follows, I develop a response to these mainstream policy debates and the new legal framework by exploring the fundamental rationale for age of consent laws, and put forward my own proposal for reform of the law.

9
Rethinking the Age of Consent

What is the rationale for age of consent laws? Should we have an age of consent at all? Is the current age of consent of 16 in Great Britain appropriate? In this final chapter, I return to these fundamental questions, raised in the opening chapters. I begin by reflecting on the history of age of consent debates outlined in the book, synthesising my analysis of the conceptual underpinnings of the current legal age of 16 in Great Britain (that is, England, Wales and Scotland; in Northern Ireland the age is 17). I demonstrate that a re-evaluation of the age of consent is warranted. I then reconsider the British situation in the light of empirical evidence on young people's sexual behaviour, and the international comparative survey provided in Chapter 3; and following from this suggest that there is a case for lowering the age of consent. To explore the issue further, I examine research evidence on young people's own attitudes towards age of consent laws. I then return to conceptual issues concerning the appropriate rationale for age of consent laws, beginning with the meaning of citizenship in relation to sexuality and childhood. This theoretical discussion develops from the British context but has wider international relevance. I develop an account of the rationale for age of consent laws via critical engagement with libertarian perspectives on the regulation of sexuality, and moralist, utilitarian and radical conceptions of the function of criminal law; and via discussion of themes including the role of the youth justice system, the significance of individual consent and vulnerability, and the socially mediated relationship between individuals and the law. I conclude by making an argument for what I believe would be an appropriate change in the law.

I do not attempt to engage fully with the extensive empirical research available on young people's sexuality, as would be required for a comprehensive evaluation of current age of consent laws. Rather, the main focus of my contribution is to develop a critique of the conceptual and theoretical approaches employed in current contributions to debates over age of consent laws, and advocate a way forward in this respect.

The history of age of consent laws in the UK

My analysis of the history of debates over age of consent laws (Chapters 4–8) has demonstrated that the current age of 16 in Great Britain is a legacy of nineteenth-century attitudes towards gender and childhood, given new credence in recent decades by reference to the flawed knowledge-claims of developmental psychology and biomedical science.

In Chapter 4 I showed that an increase in the age of consent for a girl to engage in sexual intercourse to 16 in 1885 was informed by beliefs in girlhood as a natural state of sexual innocence. Prevailing bourgeois conceptions of childhood and gender, emphasising the inherent vulnerability of young female bodies, combined with patriarchal conceptions of women and children as male property to produce an emphasis upon 'protection'. The age of 16 was not equated with attainment of the same degree of competence in decision-making associated with male citizenship in the public sphere; rather, it was understood to reflect bodily vulnerability and a much more limited degree of psychological competence.

As discussed in Chapter 5, the age of 16 was later replicated in the reform of the law on 'indecent assault' in the 1920s, which was increasingly interpreted during the twentieth century to provide a minimum age of 16 for sexual activity other than intercourse, including sex between women. In Chapter 5 I also examined the creation of a minimum age of 21 for sexual activity between men when this was partially decriminalised within a tightly defined private sphere in 1967. The rationale for decriminalisation provided by the *Wolfenden Report* emphasised the hope that medical treatments would lead to the eradication of homosexuality; hence the decriminalisation of homosexuality illustrates that an age of consent does not necessarily imply straightforward liberty for individuals above a specified age. The chapter demonstrated that the male homosexual age of consent embodied profound inequality, which became contested in subsequent campaigns for equalisation of age of consent laws.

In Chapter 6 I examined the emergence of movements for sexual liberation from the 1960s, which transformed debates over age of consent laws, and explored the impact of these on a major review of age of consent laws by a Home Office Policy Advisory Committee in the late 1970s. I demonstrated that in this review new forms of biomedical knowledge-claim came to the fore. Medicalised understandings of female adolescence were prominent in the new rationale adopted to underpin the age of consent of 16 for sexual intercourse, which argued that a lower age of consent would encourage earlier sexual activity and emphasised a direct link between this sexual activity and various consequences (pregnancy, abortions, cervical cancer, emotional harm, etc.). Developmental psychology was also invoked, though more prominently to justify advocacy of a higher age for sex between men. Relative to the nineteenth century, the rationale for the age for sexual intercourse shifted from moral protectionism and an emphasis upon the inherently non-sexual nature of female bodies under 16 towards new forms of medicalisation which allowed for greater female desire while simultaneously emphasising risks deriving from biology. There was also a greater emphasis on the age of consent being equated with individual psychological competence, also linked to greater emphasis upon other dimensions of female citizenship above 16 (such as the school-leaving age being 16). I argued that these invocations had limited coherence and sophistication, and were clearly politically strategic to a considerable degree, yet the rise to prominence of medical and psychological sciences in the public sphere nevertheless reflected broader social tendencies (cf. Rose, 1999). A further important element of the prevailing approach was a belief in a relatively direct relationship between the law and the young people's utilisation of it in their sexual negotiations: 'The present law assists them [girls] to refuse sexual intercourse' (PAC, 1981, p. 7, para. 18). By contrast the committee gave little attention or credence to arguments that the law impeded effective safer sex education and sexual health promotion strategies to address under-16s.

In Chapter 7 I discussed debates over the 'gay age of consent' during the 1990s, culminating in 'equalisation' of the age of consent in 2000. In these debates developmental psychology continued to be invoked, but after the 1994 debate played a diminishing role. However, biomedical knowledge-claims concerning the age at which sexual identities become fixed, appropriated from the *Wolfenden Report* and rearticulated by equality campaigners, played a fundamental role in facilitating the emergence of a new hegemony in age of consent debates supporting 'equality at 16'. Claims that sexual identities are established before the age of 16 enabled equalisation of the age of consent to be achieved alongside the persistence of mainstream cultural assumptions of the preferential status of heterosexuality.

In Chapter 8, finally, I examined the Home Office review of sex offences that was initiated in 1999, and subsequent debates over the *Sexual Offences Act* 2003. In these, I showed that the age of 16 was never open to question. The agenda for reform of age of consent laws was set by children's organisations advancing protectionist perspectives. These placed excessive emphasis on the abusive character of sexual relationships in which age differences existed between partners, and thus misrepresented young people's experiences, yet influenced the creation of new age of consent laws which introduced a distinction between offences regulating over-18s (including 'Sexual activity with a child') and under-18s ('Child sex offences committed by children or young persons'). This distinction, while intended to achieve the positive outcome of more selective and discretionary implementation of prohibitions in relation to under-18s, is likely to result in excessively punitive implementation of the law against over-18s having sex with teenagers under 16, where use of police reprimands would be more appropriate in many cases.

This history reveals the deeply problematic conceptual basis on which the current age of consent has been founded. The age of 16 originates in a nineteenth-century context dominated by outdated assumptions about gender and childhood, in which the nature of female children was characterised as being inherently non-sexual. This age was reaffirmed in the late 1970s review with reference to reductive invocations of biomedical and psychological knowledge, which assumed that the legal age for sexual activity could be fixed at an age defined by biological and associated psychological development. In subsequent debates over 'equalisation' of the age of consent during the 1990s, biomedical knowledge-claims concerning the fixity of sexual identities played a crucial role, underpinning the new hegemony of equality at 16. The age of consent is therefore built on shaky foundations, rationalised via arguments that misrepresent the individual and seek to short-cut the complex socially mediated relationships between the individual, the law and the society, which a more sociologically informed perspective can help to clarify.

My analysis has also demonstrated, however, that the forms of biomedical and psychological knowledge-claim prevailing in recent decades have not represented straightforward assertions of expertise by confident authorities. Rather, as I showed in Chapters 6 and 7, policy-makers and politicians have strategically and selectively employed 'science' in the public sphere to manage conflicts over age of consent laws. In the context of analyses of postmodernity and late modernity which suggest tendencies towards a degree of greater reflexity in biomedical knowledge, my analysis suggests that the persistent invocation of biomedical and psychological authorities occurs in the context of significant heterogeneity and conflict within biomedical and psychological knowledge paradigms, and is a product of appropriation by policy-makers and social movements such as the lesbian and gay movement, rather than simply reflecting the institutionalised power of biomedicine (see also Waites, 2005). This suggests scope for a shift in the terms of debate if critical perspectives are advanced and engaged in the public sphere.

My analysis has also emphasised the heteronormativity of recent debates over age of consent laws, showing how laws applying to same-sex behaviour have been brought into line with an assumed heterosexual norm at the age of 16 (see especially Chapter 8). This critique raises the question of what it would mean to think about age of consent laws beyond heteronormativity. Should we in fact have a single age of consent for both male/female and same-sex behaviour? It might be argued that there are differences in the character of same-sex sexual relationships from heterosexual relationships: for example some strands of lesbian feminist writing have tended to emphasise that sexual relationships between women tend to be characterised by a greater sense of equality between partners than in other relationships. However, there are a variety of forms of inequality and power differential that exist in both heterosexual and same-sex contexts, including those related not only to age, but also to factors such as economic power, class, 'race' and ethnicity; and same-sex relationships are not impervious to the effects of gendered power. In this context my view is that a universal and gender-neutral approach to the formulation of the law itself is certainly appropriate; and hence I assume this in the discussion that follows. However, it is nevertheless necessary to give attention to the particular forms and circumstances of same-sex behaviour in interpreting whether or how the law should be implemented. Equality in law and political discourse should not be translated into expectations of 'sameness' among the police and criminal justice authorities with respect to the implementation of the law in same-sex contexts – as I have commented previously (Waites, 2002a). For example, it may be appropriate to expect that fewer sexual relationships between women will be prosecuted. We should be wary of how the police and courts will interpret the new law.

The contemporary context

In the remainder of this chapter, I will develop my own argument about the way forward in debates over age of consent laws. I will begin in this first section by commenting on some of the relevant empirical evidence on young people's sexual development and behaviour, and on international comparative evidence about the law.

The starting points for future debates, then, are clear. Reductive assumptions that biological development is straightforwardly linked to competence in sexual decision-making, which have previously supported the age of 16, are being undermined even by developments in biological research. Whereas the Policy Advisory Committee of the 1970s accepted evidence that puberty occurred on average at the age of 14, recent research by Professor Jean Golding shows puberty to be occurring earlier, with the average age of menarche in girls now 12 years 10 months.[1] If the appropriate age for sexual activity were defined by physiological development, then we could infer that earlier sexual activity is appropriate. But an entirely different type of analysis is needed.

Reappraising age of consent laws requires a movement away from bio-logising and developmentalist understandings of young people's sexual competence and sexual identity. Within psychology this demands an appre-ciation of the socially determined, rather than biologically given, nature of subjectivity and competence. Critiques of developmentalist assumptions and the medicalisation of adolescence need to be pursued (Griffin, 1997; James, Jenks and Prout, 1998; White, 1998; Gillies, 2000). In the debates over new age of consent laws in the *Sexual Offences Act* 2003, discussed in Chapter 8, there were signs that these shifts were occurring in the political mainstream: there was little attempt to link the law straightforwardly to individual development, and an increasingly nuanced discussion among MPs of issues of sexual behaviour and sexual health.

Nevertheless, the agenda for the debate, as I have shown, was set by child protectionists who tended to assume the efficacy of age of consent laws in influencing behaviour, and who did not allow the question of whether a lower age of consent would be appropriate to be debated. What remained absent from debate among key policy-makers during the Home Office review was a full engagement with arguments for a lower age of consent, and/or the decriminalisation of children under 16 who are involved in sexual activity – although such arguments were subsequently voiced by some liberal dissidents in parliament during debates over the *Sexual Offences Act*.

Several contemporary social trends suggest the desirability of reappraising the age of consent, and seriously considering whether it should be lowered. It is apparent that as a society we are failing to support young people sufficiently in relation to sex, and that the current approach to sex and relationship education and sexual health is not working adequately. In general, qualitative research reveals a picture of many young people negotiating sexual behaviour in a context of secrecy, constrained by power relationships while lacking confidence, resources and support (for example: Holland *et al.*, 1998). More specifically, as a result of inadequate contraception there are increasing rates of infection with HIV/AIDS and other sexually transmitted diseases among young people (Department of Health, 2001; Fenton *et al.*, 2001; Johnson *et al.*, 2001; Health Protection Agency, 2004). Research suggests Chlamydia infection rates up to 12 per cent among women in some areas, with infections rising particularly sharply among teenagers since the 1990s and more than 1.3 per cent of females and 0.9 per cent of boys aged 16–19 infected in the UK; and Chlamydia in females is associated with cervical cancer and pelvic inflammatory disease which lead to ectopic pregnancy and infertility (Department of Health, 2001, pp. 5–6; Health Protection Agency, 2004, pp. 26–29). While the numbers of unwanted teenage pregnancies among under-18s should not be exaggerated as contemporary government discourse tends to do (Monk, 1998b; cf. Social Exclusion Unit, 1999), the UK does have a high rate of teenage pregnancies by international standards. Over a quarter of 14–15-year olds think the pill prevents sexually transmitted infections (Department of Health, 2001, p. 8). Too much sexual activity is occurring without appropriate knowledge and skills, as government is increasingly recognising and seeking to address (Department of Health, 2004). As Jackie West concluded from an empirical study of young people's experiences of sex education and sexual health provision, focussing on sexual health clinics in Avon via 400 questionnaires and 147 interviews with young people aged 14–21, what is central is a 'need for greater opportunities to talk about sex and relationships', in a context where such opportunities are limited by attitudes to youth (West, 1999, pp. 526–527). In this context it is argued by some sexual health professionals that the age of consent should be lowered, especially for sex between young people (under-18s), to facilitate more effective support from health and education services.

The current law should also be evaluated in the context of a realistic recognition of the extent to which it is ignored by young people. According to the first National Survey of Sexual Attitudes and Lifestyles (NATSAL), which collected data up to 1990, the average age of first heterosexual intercourse was 17, but was falling among young people (Johnson *et al.*, 1994). However, in the more recent NATSAL survey, which interviewed people aged 16–44, it was found that among those aged 16–19 at interview, the median age was 16 for both males and females. The proportion reporting first heterosexual intercourse under 16 was 30 per cent for men and 26 per cent for women; and this proportion increased during the 1980s up to but not after the mid-1990s (Wellings *et al.*, 2001, p. 1843). However, a much higher proportion of young people engage in other forms of sexual activity prohibited by the law; in the first NATSAL survey the average age of first 'sexual experience', including mutual masturbation, oral sex and so on, was found to be 14 (Johnson *et al.*, 1994; analysis of data on experiences other than intercourse has yet to be published from the second NATSAL survey). Other recent research reveals 'an increasing proportion of young people are sexually active below the age of consent' (Wertheimer and Macrae, 1999, p. 19). This also suggests that a serious reconsideration of the current legal age of 16 is justified.

Many young people, especially girls, express dissatisfaction and 'regret' about their first sexual experiences with hindsight: among 16–24-year olds who had first intercourse aged 13 or 14, 42 per cent of males and 84 per cent of females expressed 'regret', defined as the wish that they had 'waited longer'. However, among those who had first intercourse aged 15, 26 per cent of males and 49 per cent of females expressed this view (Wellings *et al.*, 2001, p. 1847). Since more than 50 per cent of young people aged 16–24 do not express regret about having sexual activity below the age of consent, this tends to suggest the need to improve the quality of negotiations and relationships, rather than that sexual activity below the current legal age is always later recognised as misguided. Qualitative research also suggests much dissatisfaction with 'first sex' in a heterosexual context, especially among females (Holland *et al.*, 1998); but we should be wary of assuming that empirical data showing negative experiences of 'first sex' reflects experiences of early sexual behaviour more generally.

An international comparative analysis, provided in Chapter 3, suggests that the current age of consent in the UK remains high by the standards of western Europe. According to Helmut Graupner's survey, in Europe sexual intercourse with 14-year olds is legal in 51 per cent of states, and with 15-year olds in 72 per cent; and the age of 15 appears most common in the European Union (Graupner, 2000, pp. 416, 424). While the age is generally 16 or higher for sexual intercourse in the various states of the US, for example, historical analysis suggests that this reflects the greater impact of social purity movements in the late nineteenth and early twentieth century than in much of western Europe (Cocca, 2004). The influence of social purity movements is not a sound basis for the current law.

Together with my historical critique, these empirical observations and international comparisons indicate there is a clear case for lowering the age of consent to 15 or 14 to facilitate young people receiving improved sex and relationship education, sexual health service provision and wider forms of support and guidance, which research shows to remain inadequate (Thomson and Blake, 2002; Hirst, 2004). Decriminalising behaviour would make it easier for young people to come forward and talk about what they are doing, and for adults to talk to them. But to evaluate such a move requires a broader conceptual analysis. Before moving onto this I will first explore evidence on young people's own views and perspectives on age of consent laws.

Young people's views of age of consent laws

Historically, debates over the age of consent have not been well informed by empirical research on young people's own views and experiences in relation to sexuality and the law, and have tended to draw primarily upon quantitative data relating to young people's sexual behaviour (for example: Johnson *et al.*, 1994; Wellings *et al.*, 2001). However, qualitative research into young people's sexual behaviour is proliferating (for example: Holland *et al.*, 1998; Hirst, 2004), and research on attitudes towards age of consent laws has also begun to emerge – although as Jackie West has commented, much contemporary research on young people's sexuality continues to lack a systematic or theorised examination of age or generation as a social dynamic (West, 1999, p. 526), and even in youth research a precise focus on age differences often remains lacking.

The *Youth Values: Identity, Diversity and Social Change* research project (aka '*Respect*'), funded by the UK's Economic and Social Research Council, examined the values of approximately 1800 11–16-year olds from a selection of eight schools (four in Northern Ireland, four in England), producing data on attitudes towards a wide range of subjects including sex and age of consent laws (Holland and Thomson, 1999). The first phase of the study involved a structured questionnaire, from which quantitative attitudinal data has been published on issues including 'sexual intercourse under the age of 16', 'sex outside marriage', 'unsafe sex' and 'homosexuality' (McGrellis *et al.*, 2000). According to this only 30 per cent of boys and 37 per cent of girls in the study believed sexual intercourse under the age of 16 is always wrong (McGrellis *et al.*, 2000, p. 14). The second phase of the study involved focus-group interviews, three of which I was involved in myself as a facilitator, with questions which included specific reference to age of consent laws. Rachel Thomson has analysed the data on this issue (Thomson, 2000, 2004).

In these focus group discussions, according to Thomson, many young people expressed support for an age of 16, and an increase to 18 was more popular than a reduction to 14. However, as discussion developed, many also rejected the idea that law alone defined whether sex is legitimate (Thomson, 2004, p. 137). In general the research suggests that young people tend to value age of consent laws as a 'safety net', perceiving them as able to offer protection in a minority of circumstances involving sexual activity where things go wrong:

> although they [young people] did not recognize the authority of the law to determine their sexual practices they did, grudgingly, accept that the law could lend support when under pressure...[...] The law then becomes a resource on which they can draw when they need support. (Thomson, 2004, p. 140)

These empirical findings suggest diminishing respect for legal proscriptions about personal behaviour, and show the willingness of young people to break the law in accordance with their own moral judgements (Thomson, 2004, p. 140). My interpretation is that the initially prominent narratives of support for legal authority represent young people to an extent reproducing conventional forms of moral discourse which they perceive as 'expected' in the particular form of public sphere constituted by the focus group interview method; but Thomson's reported data (2004) shows how judgements became more ambivalent as discussion progressed. Nevertheless, young people do appear to maintain a perception of age of consent laws as conveying moral messages from society about appropriate sexual activity. In a sense, young people tend to be legal moralists in their understanding of how law functions – viewing it as attempting to communicate a moral message about appropriate behaviour, rather than pragmatically adjusting to actual behaviour – while also actively negotiating their relationship to it, in some cases with degrees of self-conscious 'resistance'. However, the interviews suggest that what determines whether sexual activity takes place is much more influenced by young people's own sexual cultures, the gendered power relationships within these, and how these influence what is experienced as 'timely' sex or 'readiness' for sex (Thomson, 2004). Many young people are willing to reject age of consent laws when they conflict with their own moral judgements, as large-scale quantitative research confirms (Wellings *et al.*, 2001), and do not expect the law to intervene in 'normal' teenage sex.

This research evidence suggests a need for the law and the criminal justice system to regulate major power imbalances, especially where age differences are involved, to serve the protective umbrella function young people desire (cf. Thomson, 2004, p. 140). But despite young people's wariness of reducing the age of consent, which reflects more general popular beliefs in the efficacy of criminal law as an instrument of policy, their comments on the conventionality of under-age sex provide little support for the criminalisation of all sexual behaviour involving under-16s.

Nevertheless, the fact that the law is perceived as signalling what is a desirable standard of behaviour, and as providing a protective umbrella, suggests it would be unwise to dismiss entirely the idea that it has any function in constituting social norms of behaviour, even if we acknowledge that many young people transgress it. Advocates of lower age of consent laws tend to point to evidence of many young people flouting the law as relatively straightforward evidence that it is ill-founded (for example, Tatchell, 2002), and certainly this behaviour shows that the law is not working as traditional legal moralism desired: the law's 'moral message' is not being straightforwardly heeded. But the fact that there is a significant level of illegal behaviour does not imply that the law is absolutely failing to perform any role in constituting social norms – even if other factors shaping some young people's sexual cultures are more powerful.

The law still has some socially constitutive role to play in preserving the collective welfare and interests of young people, certainly unless and until sex and relationship education can much more consistently and effectively communicate a message about why and how to abstain from risky sexual activity at particular ages. For those who are not aware of the age of consent, part of the answer is better education about the law, not its abolition. We should maintain a limited but nonetheless significant sense of the constitutive role of law in defining social norms and shaping sexual behaviour in society. The law may not exert much direct influence on the agency of young people, but it does play a more indirect role in defining a framework of expectations and norms for parents and professionals working with young people, which informs how they seek to shape and influence young people's behaviour. In an era when respect for the law and traditional institutions has declined, when there is greater acceptance of cultural diversity, and when young people are increasingly confident in asserting their own values, we should maintain a sense of the age of consent continuing to provide one of the clear boundaries which young people need and can negotiate their lives in relation to; as enabling in this sense, rather than only constraining.

Having engaged with young people's own views on the issue, I will now move on to develop my theoretical analysis of the rationale for age of consent laws *per se*, first by returning to the theme of citizenship.

Citizenship, sexuality and childhood

Academic discussions of the relationship between sexuality and citizenship (cf. Evans, 1993; Plummer, 1995; Waites, 1996; Weeks, 1998b; Bell and Binnie, 2000; Richardson, 2000a; Stychin, 2003) and the relationship between childhood and citizenship (Alderson, 1992c; Economic and Social Research Council, 1998; James, Jenks and Prout, 1998), introduced in Chapter 2, help to make sense of recent public debates over age of consent laws. There has been a historical shift from a situation in which only adults (initially only males, and also defined by class and 'race') were conceptualised as citizens with particular rights and responsibilities, and in which children were regarded as the property of others, to a situation in which children are regarded as a particular type of person also deserving of certain rights and carrying particular responsibilities (though the latter is less discussed). Current debates over childhood focus on whether children should have the same form of rights and responsibilities as adults, or distinct forms (Archard, 1993); but it is widely accepted that children deserve at least some rights as individuals. In parallel there has been a shift from an assumed model of sexuality informing conceptions of citizenship (for example, the origin of the right to 'privacy' in conceptions of a male citizen with legitimate sexual access to his wife within the family) to thinking explicitly about the relationship between sexuality and citizenship, and towards viewing each individual as having certain sexual rights (Petchesky, 2000). The history of age of consent laws can be situated and understood in this context: whereas original age of consent laws were conceived as protecting girls' virginity as the property of their fathers, contemporary conflicts over age of consent laws are located in debates over the appropriate form of rights for children in relation to sexuality (cf. Waites, 1999b).

However, contemporary attempts to think about the relationship of citizenship and rights to issues related to the sexuality of children and young people raise as many problems as they solve. In thinking about what the rights of children and adults might be in relation to sexuality, the tendency is to conceptualise the rights of adults by drawing on notions of individual bodily integrity to advocate a right to engage in consensual sexual behaviour; whereas by contrast the rights of children are conceived first and foremost in terms of rights to protection, as is apparent in the focus of the *United Nations Convention on the Rights of the Child* on rights to protection against sexual exploitation and abuse (discussed in Chapter 3). Consequently the introduction of concepts of citizenship and rights into debates over age of consent laws tends to exacerbate rather than mediate the tensions between childhood and adulthood and, if used without other conceptual reference points, is an unhelpfully restrictive vocabulary to address these issues. But understanding this context helps to understand some of the processes heightening antagonism in contemporary age of consent debates.

There is no necessary benefit to thinking about the age of consent in relation to citizenship *per se*, or linking the issue to wider citizenship discourses. Contemporary uses of the concept in relation to young people in public and political discourses have various problematic implications. In the UK the idea of young people's citizenship has been associated with campaigns to lower the voting age from 18 to 16, recently debated but rejected as a potential policy for the 2005 general election manifesto by the Labour Party. This potentially valuable measure, which would bring the voting age into line with the school-leaving age, is often advocated with reference to the purported benefits of 'joined-up' policy-making. Association of the age of consent with this discourse of citizenship among policy-makers is problematic in this context, since it could frustrate attempts to debate lowering the age of consent below 16. The age of consent should be determined primarily through consideration of the circumstances experienced by young people in their sexual behaviour, which may not imply boundaries corresponding to those applying in other areas of their social lives, or appropriate to other dimensions of their transitions to adulthood.

Nevertheless, thinking about the themes of academic debates on citizenship, sexuality and childhood is beneficial. The literature on citizenship signals that we need to think about age of consent laws in relation to the emergence of understandings of children as individuals with certain rights and responsibilities (Alderson, 1992c; Archard, 1993; Lansdown, 1994). These may, however, be different rights and responsibilities from those of adults. Rather than a universal model of citizenship, a differentiated model of citizenship is appropriate, in which particular groups such as children and young people have a particular status. If this is accepted, it raises profound questions about the way young people are addressed by the law and the criminal justice system.

Children and young people defined in law as criminally responsible have historically been addressed by the criminal justice system and the criminal law in largely the same way as adults, and by the same system. This is changing, but it has not changed sufficiently, as I discuss later in the chapter. My view is that age of consent laws need to be reconceptualised in a context where one of the central objectives of institutions regulating young people's behaviour is to support the interests and welfare of those children, unlike traditional criminal law which focusses upon providing redress against harm to others via punishment. In short, age of consent laws can be defended alongside advocacy of a major social, cultural and philosophical shift in attitudes towards the role of regulatory agencies and institutions addressing young people. Many of the objections to age of consent laws derive from a concern over the ideas of punishment and retribution associated with criminal law; if institutions addressing children and young people had a different conception of the implications of responsibility for children from the implications of responsibility for adults, and were centrally oriented towards the welfare of all children including both 'victims' and 'offenders', these objections could be addressed.

Before discussing this issue of how the criminal justice system addresses young people further, I will now engage with libertarian and liberal critiques of age of consent laws. My general sympathies, it should be clear by now, lie with those who are critical of mainstream child protectionism, and who view the current operations of the criminal justice system to prohibit all sexual behaviour by under-16s with scepticism. I have suggested there are strong reasons to consider lowering the age of consent to 15 or 14. However, engaging critically with libertarians and liberals helps to clarify some of the principles at stake.

Libertarian and liberal critiques of age of consent laws

Contemporary arguments for the lowering or abolition of age of consent laws can collectively be labelled as 'libertarian' (Levine, 2002; Tatchell, 2002; Sawyer, 2003), but only if it is understood that they are not typically characterised by the 'anything goes' morality often associated with the term in mainstream public discourse. Typically these recent arguments do not present themselves as placing absolute priority on individual freedom or 'children's rights' as values; rather they advocate lowering or abolition of age of consent laws in the context of socially contextualised analyses which take explicit account of social hierarchies and power relations associated with age, gender and other factors. They advocate lowering age of consent laws not necessarily or only to extend the scope of pleasurable activity, but as a means to avoid unwanted pregnancies, sexually transmitted infections (STI's) and 'bad sex' via education and health promotion. Furthermore it is apparent from parliamentary debates discussed in the previous chapter that significant sections of liberal opinion in the political mainstream, including prominent campaigners for children's interests and sexual health, support at least some selective decriminalisation of sexual activity between young people under 16. Hence a view which is dismissed as libertarian extremism when advanced from one source may carry respectability in a different context.

In the UK context, overtly libertarian arguments for a lower (and equal) age of consent emerged in the early 1970s, leading to groups such as the Sexual Law Reform Society and the National Council for Civil Liberties (NCCL – now Liberty) proposing an age of 14 (Sexual Law Reform Society, 1974; National Council for Civil Liberties, 1976; see Chapter 6). Queer activist Peter Tatchell's arguments for equality at 14 since the mid-1990s (Tatchell, 1996a), supported by the Queer direct action group Outrage for a period in the mid-1990s (Lucas, 1998, pp. 214–215) and published more recently by the Libertarian Alliance (Tatchell, 2002), represent an inheritance of these earlier positions, as have writings by former NCCL activists (Pollard, 1993). Other voices raised against the current legal framework, such as that of the liberal humanist Francis Bennion, also appear influenced by this political history, while not subscribing to libertarian philosophy or ideology (Bennion, 2003).

More generally in academic work, particularly in sociology, writing on sexuality from various perspectives has questioned the extent of prohibitions on sexual activity involving children. From contemporary critical social psychology, Wendy and Rex Stainton Rogers have raised the question 'What is good and bad sex for children?' and emphasised the harmless character of much sexual activity between children (Stainton Rogers and Stainton Rogers, 1999). Despite being highly exceptional among feminists, Gayle Rubin's work defending paedophilia is well known (Rubin, 1984); leading second wave feminists such as Kate Millett also explored the possibility of legitimate child/adult sexual relations (Millett, 1984). There has also been a particular stream of writing by gay men since the 1970s which has empha-sised evidence that some adult/child sexual contact between males does not have harmful psychological effects (Gay Left Collective, 1980b; Sandfort, 1982a,b; Evans, 1993, pp. 209–239; Lind, 1998), and in some cases called for the abolition of age of consent laws (Gough, 1980; Tsang, 1981; Geraci, 1997). French radical philosophers and activists Michel Foucault and Guy Hocquenghem, for example, organised a petition campaigning for measures including 'the decriminalization of relations between minors and adults below the age of fifteen' (Hocquenghem, quoted in Foucault *et al.*, 1978, pp. 272–273).

In the US, journalist and activist Judith Levine's *Harmful to Minors: The Perils of Protecting Children from Sex* has recently presented one of the most sustained and powerful polemics against the legal regulation of children's involvement in sexual activities (Levine, 2002). In an expansive overview of US debates, engaging with empirical evidence of children's experiences, Levine attacks censorship of children's access to the media, the deficiencies of conservative sex education, and pathologising understandings of children's sexual activity and definitions of 'abuse' in therapy. In relation to age of consent laws she concludes that:

> Legally designating a class of people categorically unable to consent to sexual relations is not the best way to protect children . . . Criminal law which must draw unambiguous lines, is not the proper place to adjudicate family conflicts over youngsters sexuality. (Levine, 2002, p. 88)

If such laws are to exist, Levine suggests, an appropriate model would be the legal framework that existed in the Netherlands during the 1990s, now abolished, which required a complaint from a parent or other authority to pursue a prosecution where 12–15-year olds were involved (Levine, 2002, p. 89; see Chapter 3). However, the thrust of her argument is towards abolition, and she provides no systematic account of what the rationale for age of consent laws should be.

A similar position was recently advanced in the UK by journalist Miranda Sawyer in a Channel 4 documentary *Sex before 16: Why the Law is Failing* (16 November 2003, 9–10 p.m.) and an accompanying newspaper article, which argued that the criminalisation of all sexual activity for under-16s is 'laughably unrealistic' and that the age of consent should be lowered to 12 (Sawyer, 2003). Sawyer, whose background is in journalism on music and youth culture, can be seen as representing a generation of women who grew up after the women's liberation movement: she subscribes to a version of feminism favouring women's autonomy rather than protection. Her difficulty in discerning a rationale for prohibitions against consensual behaviour is thus indicative of broader tendencies which I have experienced in my discussions over age of consent laws: liberals and progressives, including many young people, find it hard to articulate any justification for prohibitions on consensual behaviour. A popular libertarianism has considerable influence.

Contemporary libertarian and radical liberal writers typically present their arguments in opposition to a 'panic' over child abuse in contemporary culture, which they view as pervasive and dominant in the cultural mainstream (Pollard, 1993; Levine, 2002; Bennion, 2003). Writing in the US context, Levine characterises this tendency as 'the sexual politics of fear' (Levine, 2002, p. xxi). It seems to me, however, that this view of contemporary developments exaggerates the pervasiveness of conservative attitudes, particularly in the UK, and underestimates the extent to which a growth of concern about child sexual abuse in recent decades has been well founded. To characterise the contemporary politics of children's sexuality in this way underestimates the complexity of the emerging situation in the UK, as I sought to demonstrate in Chapter 8. Writings by libertarian and radical liberal writers on children's sexuality, such as Levine and Bennion, tend to reproduce an unhelpful picture of dichotomised political positions; and also tend to remain reactively anti-regulation (Levine, Pollard, Tatchell, Sawyer), rather than attempting to construct positive accounts of the basis on which any form of regulation could be justified (although Bennion attempts this).

How are these libertarian and radical liberal perspectives to be evaluated? To begin with I will focus on critically analysing tendencies in the discourses employed and the way arguments are formulated, rather than their substantive conclusions. The basic problem is that libertarians place too much emphasis on the sheer pleasure and harmlessness of much child and adolescent sex, and present their arguments in a way that implies a case for removing age of consent laws follows directly from this. For example, Judith Levine emphasises the existence of children's capacities for sexual pleasure and desire, and draws the conclusion that sex is a 'crucial' part of growing up (Levine, 2002, cover). Francis Bennion (2003, p. 13) places emphasis on the fact that children are 'sexual beings', and tends to view this in itself as making legal prohibitions unjust; Craig Lind focusses on critiquing perceptions of 'sexual innocence' (Lind, 1998); Miranda Sawyer emphasises that 'we have sexual feelings from a very early age' and that sex is 'natural behaviour' (Sawyer, 2003, p. 2). Similarly, but focussing on love rather than sex, Peter Tatchell invokes Romeo and Juliet, aged 14 and 13, as 'one of the greatest love stories of all time' (Tatchell, 2002). From this type of perspective, if specific instances of behaviour are pleasurable and harmless to participants, there can be no justification for prohibitions.

However, the way such commentaries emphasise the sheer pleasure and harmlessness of much child and adolescent sex, or the strength and sincerity of the feelings involved, does not take the argument far forward. While libertarians perpetually insist they are countering a pervasive cultural sex panic and sexual moralism that denies the sexuality of children (Levine, 2002; Bennion, 2003), a more realistic view is that recognition of children's sexual capacities and potential is now widespread, particularly in the context of pervasive sexualisation of adolescence in the media (McNair, 2002). The capacities of teenagers for sexual pleasure are surely apparent by now; but this in itself is not sufficient justification for removal of legal prohibitions on all consensual activity. To believe that the existence of adolescent capacities for sexual pleasure in itself requires that sexual behaviour be initiated (cf. Bennion, 2003) is in fact a form of essentialist thinking which implies that adolescence without such activity is an 'unnatural' state (influenced by masculinist sexological narratives of the necessity of sexual release), rather than simply involving a different embodied experience of being in the world. Here variants of liberal humanism and libertarianism draw on particular biologically determined conceptions of human development which should be challenged in the light of anti-essentialist approaches to sexuality (for example: Weeks, 1985). Sex is not a 'crucial' part of growing up for children (cf. Levine, 2002); young people's *desires*, which significantly many sex radicals conclude their arguments by asserting (Evans, 1993, p. 239; Levine, 2002, p. 225), cannot serve as a foundation for our conclusions; nor can love, since love does not require sex for its expression (and being in love, in any case, is unreliable as a basis for anything). What is required instead is a socially contextualised assessment of the costs and benefits, the pleasures and pains involved in prohibiting sexual behaviour. Philosophically, if it is not accepted that sexual activity is determined to be necessary or vital by human nature, even for post-pubescent adolescents, then it becomes difficult to ground an approach to the law in a deontological ethics focussing on the individual, and a more collectively oriented approach appears appropriate.

Critics of age of consent laws, such as Levine, typically focus on individual cases, and hence implicitly prioritise individual interests over the collective interests of young people, and this is reflected in their approach to empirical research and its presentation. There is a tendency to investigate particular cases of the law's application, demonstrate negative consequences for specific individuals, and to conclude from this that age of consent laws cannot be justified. For example, Judith Levine's discussion of statutory rape laws focusses in depth on the case of Dylan Healy, 21, and Heather Kowalski, 13, and demonstrates how this loving relationship was ruined by parental and legal intervention, resulting in a sentence of 12–24 years imprisonment for Dylan for sexual assault (Levine, 2002, pp. 68–89). Yet while Levine is absolutely right to challenge punitive sentencing and the harsh way the justice system deals with such cases (see my discussion of this below; and she is also right to challenge pervasive approaches to sexual activity between children in therapy, and much else), her focus on a single case to make an argument against age of consent laws fails to address their collective effects in society as a whole. Methodologically and philosophically, particular cases do not provide a sound basis for overall conclusions. There is no balance sheet weighing the negative effects of legal intervention against any negative consequences of the law *not* intervening where young people are above the age of consent. Levine asks only: 'Do statutory rape prosecutions have any constructive effect on the "perpetrator", the "victim" or her family?'; she shows little recognition that some young people do enter sexual relationships which, although it would be undesirable to legally define them as non-consensual, can be abusive, coercive and damaging; and hence some prosecutions are beneficial. But she also fails to ask whether the existence of the law has any positive effects for the majority of young people who are never prosecuted.

Another problem with libertarian arguments is an insufficiently integrated analysis of the implications of gendered power relations. If negative effects of early sexual activity were more explicitly weighed – such as unwanted pregnancy, HIV-infection, widespread later experiences of 'regret' empirically documented in the NATSAL survey (especially among girls: Wellings *et al.*, 2001), and girls' ambivalence about early sex shown in feminist qualitative research (Holland *et al.*, 1998; Thomson, 2004) – then the particular gendered impact of age of consent laws would become clearer. Typically libertarians acknowledge gender inequality in experiences between young males and females in heterosexual contexts, including the disproportionate extent of female regret (Levine, 2002, pp. xxxiii, 135–136, 155), but do not integrate recognition of the extent of this discrepancy fully into their analyses (Levine, 2002; Tatchell, 2002). Yet in my view sustained attention to gendered power relations lends weight to the case for prohibitions; and attention to collective patterns of experience tends to bring these to the fore.

The fundamental conceptual problem with libertarian arguments such as Levine's is that their analysis is individualising: there is no theorisation or acceptance of a role for the law in acting for the collective good of young people, and particularly in producing and sustaining social norms of behaviour. For libertarians, in general, the assumption is that if no harm occurs to particular individuals, no law can be justified (see also Sawyer, 2003). Peter Tatchell comments that 'although the number of young people under 16 arrested for consenting sex is small, that is no consolation to those who are arrested. One unjust arrest is one too many' (Tatchell, 2002). This represents a philosophical approach to jurisprudence in which individual desires need not be set aside for the good of the collective.

This tendency is reflected in much recent academic work on the legal regulation of sexual behaviour. In law, especially but not only in the UK, philosophical debate has historically been dominated by the debate between legal moralists (Devlin, 1959) and utilitarians (Hart, 1963); this was the focus of debates over the *Wolfenden Report* in the 1950s (see Chapter 5), and over 'permissive' legislation in the 1960s and 1970s. Much of the new writing on sex law which has emerged since the 1970s, influenced by feminism and radical sexual movements, has tended to remain influenced (with or without explicit theorisation) by a liberal utilitarian approach to criminal law which emphasised that legal prohibitions should only extend where their enforcement could be fully justified by the damaging consequences of behaviour in each individual case. On the one hand, radicals contested laws which extended excessively into individual decision-making (for example, prohibitions on same-sex behaviour); on the other hand, feminists argued legal prohibitions should extend and apply to all non-consensual activity (for example, rape in marriage). While radical theorists such as Foucault challenged utilitarian legal philosophies in many respects, emphasising law's role in constituting categories of deviance (Foucault, 1977; Foucault *et al.*, 1978; Smart, 1989), Foucault and other sceptics nevertheless tended to share utilitarian objections to legal restrictions on the individual based on collective interests – and this remains the tendency among many radical writers on sexuality and law. But while liberal utilitarians have emphasised that people will persist with certain types of behaviour irrespective of the law, Foucault often emphasised the extent to which individual behaviour is relational to the law, whether compliant or transgressive, and that law plays a role in constituting and producing social norms of behaviour.

In my view, an approach refuting any legal restrictions on individuals to serve the collective interests of children and young people is inadequate to think about the social role of the law in relation to them. We therefore need to reconsider aspects of the legal moralist tradition, to challenge individualism in the light of collectivist political and philosophical traditions including socialism, feminism and communitarianism, and defend the legitimacy of age of consent laws as instruments through which society can defend the collective interests of young people. The justification for prohibitions against particular instances of sexual behaviour which are harmless, pleasurable and consensual is that such behaviour in general entails unacceptable risks of negative consequences for those involved, and that to a limited extent law can play some legitimate role in enforcing social norms to the benefit of vulnerable groups, and can also operate as a 'protective umbrella' facilitating interventions by state agencies in particular cases. This can only be the case, however, if the law regulating childhood is conceptualised in a different manner from traditional criminal law, which is primarily concerned with punishment, and adopts a central and genuine concern with promoting children's welfare.

Broadly speaking, the utilitarian critique of legal moralism is convincing when considered with respect to age of consent laws, in the sense that legal prohibitions have little direct impact on people's immediate decisions about sexual behaviour. However, the law can and does play a limited role in defining social norms of behaviour, particularly indirectly through influencing what parents and schools regard as appropriate time-scales for sexual behaviour, and hence influencing general social expectations. Where the utilitarian perspective is more profoundly flawed, however, is in its specific emphasis that good law is law which is possible to rigourously and consistently apply. While this may be a sound principle of law in many contexts, consideration of the age of consent issue suggests it is not appropriate in relation to vulnerable groups such as children. Such a philosophy militates against maintaining age of consent laws as a protective umbrella, to be applied only rarely and sparingly; yet this is an appropriate approach to the criminal law in this respect.

Responding to current dilemmas in the UK, liberal child welfare campaigners have continued to focus their concern on reducing the scope of the law (for example, Baroness Walmsley, discussed in Chapter 8). Some have argued that the law should be reformulated to decriminalise consensual sexual activity between children and young people, or at least certain types of non-risky sexual activity (such as mutual masturbation). Policy-makers have struggled to find ways to do this: Home Secretary David Blunkett referred to this problematic as a 'conundrum' during debates over the *Sexual Offences Act* 2003 before concluding it impractical. Distinguishing between types of behaviour might seem appealing: mutual masturbation involves no risk of STDs or pregnancy; oral sex does not necessarily lead on to intercourse when understood in the context of young people's sophisticated sexual cultures and particular sexual scripts (see Hirst, 2004, p. 119). However, while one type of activity does not automatically lead to progression to another, it is doubtful whether making such distinctions in law could provide the clear framework which young people require. Alternatively the idea of criminalising only forms of behaviour which are exploitative or abusive, and decriminalising other consensual behaviour between young people might initially appear attractive, but aside from the problem of how to define such a select category of problematic behaviour in law, this approach would fail to provide young people with the clear boundaries and framework they need.

I would suggest that the problem is not with the fact that age of consent laws encompass a significant amount of sexual activity that is consensual, harmless and pleasurable, as an evaluation by the standards of a jurisprudence excessively concerned with the individual would imply. Rather, debates over age of consent laws reveal problems with the excessive concern for the individual in liberal utilitarian conceptions, and many radical conceptions, of the function of criminal law when adopted in relation to childhood. In conceptualising the philosophical basis of the law in relation to childhood, we need to accept that it can legitimately operate as a protective umbrella in the collective interest of children. Like other legal theorists concerned with childhood, such as Marinos Diamantides (1999), I believe that concepts such as 'children's rights', 'autonomy', 'self-determination' and 'consent' are insufficient, and that a more collectively oriented approach is required to protect the vulnerable. Although from a feminist perspective I do not favour Diamentides' advocacy of a renewal of 'paternalism' to achieve this, the concept of protection should not be abandoned to become the sole preserve of conservative moralists.

A metaphor may serve to illustrate. Drivers face low speed limits in urban areas, which can be thought of as akin to laws requiring teenagers to abstain from sex and stick to 'snogging'. Most people who break speed limits do not directly do anyone any harm. But we have laws against speeding to enforce social norms which are beneficial to all because speeding will on occasion have serious consequences for others, and may also for ourselves. Similarly much under-age sex is harmless and pleasurable, but age of consent laws enforce a collective cultural practice of sexual abstinence which benefits young people as a whole, any of whom in a particular case might be unlucky and experience (for example) unwanted pregnancy, condoms breaking, or exploitation by an older party. If the criminal justice system were reformed appropriately to embody a focus on child and youth welfare, young people could view age of consent laws as embodying a collective moral project, requiring them to protect one another through abstention. Returning to the driving metaphor, having the patience to keep to the speed limit is worth it if you know that you can put your foot down when you hit the motorway.

Youth justice

What is crucial, however, is that prohibitions criminalising young people engaging in illegal sexual behaviour with other young people are enforced in a profoundly different way from those applying to adults, and in most cases with an extremely light touch. Inseparable from, and equally important to, the argument that age of consent laws are defensible must be the argument that the criminal justice system and the law addressing children should operate in a way that recognises them as having a specific social and cultural status. English law, as it evolved historically, applied criminal law in largely the same form to criminally responsible children as to adults. Yet the expansion of the concept of childhood in our culture such that a 'child' has been defined as a person under 18 in the *Children Act* 1989, and the extension of young people's transitions to adulthood, require fundamental changes in the way the criminal law addresses young people. While there are good arguments that the age of criminal responsibility (10 in England and Wales, 8 in Scotland) should be raised (Bandalli, 2000, p. 90), some form of criminal responsibility is required to address many teenagers under 16; but a more systematic distinction needs to be drawn between the ways in which the criminal justice system addresses adults and children recognised as having legal capacity.

In some respects, New Labour's 'New Youth Justice', involving a radical overhaul of the youth justice system in England and Wales, has moved in this direction, but in others it has had negative effects (Goldson, 2000a). Labour's creation of a Youth Justice Board – with responsibility for the central direction of youth justice policy in England and Wales (Pitts, 2000, p. 6) – the new Youth Offending Teams, and the renewal of the youth courts (Monaghan, 2000) have aimed to create a more integrated 'joined-up' approach to young people, focussing on their specific circumstances as distinct from adults. But such 'joined-up' approaches can homogenise groups of young people with excessively punitive effects, insensitive to their particular ages and circumstances. Hence, as I have discussed in the previous chapter, the move to distinguish between age of consent laws addressing over-18s and under-18s was to a degree motivated by a helpful move towards treating under-18s differently, but in its broader context is likely to be unhelpfully interpreted and implemented, creating a rigid and punitive approach to relationships involving limited age differences (such as between 18-year olds and 15-year olds).

In any case, a joined-up approach is not evident in some areas where greater consistency would be helpful: children above the age of criminal responsibility in England and Wales can still be tried in Crown Courts rather than youth courts for serious crimes (Bandalli, 2000, p. 89). A more synthesised and integrated approach is needed to the way in which under-16s and/or under-18s are dealt with by the police, the courts and the offender institutions – an approach clearly distinct from that for dealing with adults. Importantly the youth justice system, and the law as it applies to young people, needs to be culturally perceived and politically represented as clearly distinct from the system applying to adults; this would encourage changes in the cultural perceptions of young people who break the law. This approach could bridge the gap in young people's experiences between the more sensitive and contextual way they experience punishment at school or in the home, and the way they are subject to the criminal law, experienced as more absolutist.

New Labour's reforms of the youth justice system in England and Wales and its discourses on youth crime have worrying implications in relation to young people's sexual behaviour. Advocacy of an ethos of 'zero tolerance' on the basis that minor crime leads to major crime (Muncie, 2000, pp. 23–25), an emphasis on 'early intervention' involving abandonment of diversionary strategies such as informal police cautions in favour of formal reprimands (Goldson, 2000b, p. 35), and a tendency away from community supervision towards incarceration (Moore, 2000) all tend to work against the extremely light touch approach which is required to address most sexual behaviour between children, even while the police and Crown Prosecution Service exercise discretion and limit the number of prosecutions. While there are important benefits of interventionist approaches in addressing the minority of 'young sexual abusers', tendencies towards approaching all sexual activity between children via such categories, which significantly emerged in literature for practitioners working with sex offenders, are unhelpful (Brownlie, 2001, pp. 520–521). The tendency of Youth Offender Panels to be oriented towards punishment rather than children's welfare is undesirable (Haines, 2000). A more sensitive, light touch approach is needed which can mediate between the 'leave kids alone' approach of pre-1990s juvenile justice movements and the contemporary excesses of interventionism. For England and Wales there may be much to learn from Scotland, which has a system of children's hearings in non-adversarial tribunals to avoid the criminal courts (Bandalli, 2000, pp. 84, 90). But for most sexual behaviour between post-pubescent children, what is required is a prohibition which is minimally and sensitively enforced by child welfare professionals offering education about the social and moral reasons why under-age sexual behaviour is prohibited because of its risks. For pre-pubescent children below the age of criminal responsibility, meanwhile, much activity which is commonly described as 'sexual' (touching genitals, etc.) involves very low risk and is harmless (cf. Stainton Rogers and Stainton Rogers, 1999).

Of course, even if the approach to children with legal capacity that I have outlined were fully adopted, questions would remain to be addressed about the forms of knowledge concerning 'children's best interests' and 'child welfare' that would prevail, and the disciplinary effects of institutionalised practices. These have been analysed in existing child-welfare institutions and regimes by commentators influenced by Foucault and his understanding of 'governmentality' (Bell, 1993; Monk, 1998a,b, 2004; Brownlie, 2001). But such analyses, while important in problematising the operations of current institutions, do not present a case against the existence of age of consent laws and such institutions *per se*.

Having argued against libertarian approaches, and hence having provided a general rationale for the continuing existence of age of consent laws if contextualised in relation to reform of the criminal justice system, it remains to engage in more detail with the questions of how the age of consent should be conceptualised, and what the age of consent should be.

Consent and vulnerability

The invocation of reductive forms of biomedical and psychological authority to provide rationales for age of consent laws, described in preceding chapters, requires critique in two crucial respects. First, it is necessary to rethink the nature of the subject with respect to both understandings of competence required for decisions about sexual behaviour, and understandings of sexual identity. Secondly, it is necessary to rethink the social relationship between subjects and the law. Theoretical work in socio-legal studies on childhood, law and competence in recent years has addressed both of these issues, but

I would suggest that the recent emphasis upon rethinking the subject has sometimes been at the expense of a sustained sociological understanding of the subject's location within social relations.

In the literature on age of consent laws, as in socio-legal literature on law, sexuality and sex offences more generally including the expansive literature on rape and sexual assault, the quest by critical scholars for new rationales for sex laws has led to a focus on the question of sexual consent (for example: Archard, 1998; Reynolds 2002/2003; Cowling and Reynolds, 2004). Rejecting traditional laws based on patriarchal assumptions or presumptions of childhood as a period of sexual innocence, the focus has shifted to thinking about what constitutes 'real consent', in the hope that this can provide a basis for new approaches to law. While feminist work, in particular, has challenged assumptions that consent is always clear-cut, much feminist work remains focussed on revising understandings of what constitutes significant consent, concerned with the individual's competence and understanding of the world (Reynolds, 2002/2003; Corteen, 2004; Moore and Reynolds, 2004). It is appropriate and necessary to maintain a view of 'consent' as a valid criteria for legality in relation to sex between adults, rather than question the significance of consent as some radical feminists such as Catherine Mackinnon have sought to do in relation to prostitution in particular (Mackinnon, 1989; Moore and Reynolds, 2004; Sullivan, 2004). But while consent is an appropriate central principle for regulating sex between adults, rape and sexual violence, competence and consent are not adequate concepts to address debates over the law regulating childhood. A preoccupation with consent can lead to an inadequate conceptualisation of the relationship between the individual and the law in their social context, even when subjectivity and psychology are understood as subject to substantial social influence. Sociological and social theory is also required.

It is certainly the case that sociological thinking has had a limited impact upon the small amount of literature which explicitly addresses the rationale underpinning age of consent laws. For example, David Archard's recent book *Sexual Consent* is conscious of issues raised by feminism, sexual liberation and movements for children's rights (Archard, 1998). Yet his discussion of age of consent laws equates the minimum legal age for sexual behaviour with an age at which competence to make decisions concerning sexual behaviour is acquired by a subject (Archard, 1998, pp. 116–129). He assumes that any legal age is an age at which 'capacity' is recognised, 'above which are adults presumed capable of consent and below which are children presumed incapable of consent' (p. 116). He argues that the correct basis for age of consent laws is the attainment of 'maturity': 'a certain level of cognitive development – that is an ability to understand the relevant facts, a certain degree of acquired knowledge, and a certain level of temperamental maturity' (p. 124). He recognises that education will be an important influence on the attainment of these capacities, and makes a gesture towards the wider 'social picture' also being important (pp. 124–126), but the emphasis is still very much on equating the law with individual cognitive development. Archard's description of legal age boundaries with the phrase 'age of majority' also tends to suggest that the law reflects recognition of certain forms of citizenship and competence (p. 116).

Archard also assumes that age of consent laws necessarily imply a denial of children's sexuality – in sex with an older party they 'refuse to acknowledge the expressed sexuality of one party to the activity' (Archard, 1998, p. 120). Conversely, however, he regards age of consent laws as denying the validity of a child's consent, and characterising all behaviour below a legal age as 'non-consensual' (p. 119). Yet while this may be the case in the formulation of some laws (such as those defined as 'statutory rape laws' in the US), it is not necessarily the case for all rationales for legal age boundaries, as the distinction between UK laws on 'indecent assault' and 'unlawful sexual intercourse' prior to 2003 illustrates (cf. *Sexual Offences Act* 1956; see Chapters 4 and 5). In the *Sexual Offences Act* 2003, only offences applying to under-13s assume a child's consent not to exist (see Chapter 8). Age of consent laws, then, are not necessarily all premised on assumptions that those below a legal age are not sexual or cannot consent; and it cannot be assumed that they should be.

A key problem with Archard's perspective is that the issue of an individual's competence needs to be distinguished from the role of the law in a broader social context. Prohibitive laws may be legitimate as limits against social forces which act upon subjects independently of their agency or competence. The task of theorising the basis of age of consent laws demands analysis of the mediated relationships between individual subjectivity and competence and the role of the law with reference to social and sociological theory. We need to appreciate the complex relationship between individual competence and the law, taking into account the effects of the law upon young people collectively. Archard's approach reflects a cognitive focus in the conception of competence, a privileging of the individual and an under-theorisation of the social apparent in a tendency to assume that legal regulations upon subjects should straightforwardly mirror the age at which subjects acquire relevant competence. The focus on the individual's understanding of the world is characteristic of much recent work focussing on consent and sexual consent in law and socio-legal studies more generally. We need to move beyond this dominant conceptual framework.

In relation to the subject, we need to avoid the legacies of developmental thinking, as Archard acknowledges (Archard, 1998, p. 124). However, a socio-logised conception of the subject's competence need not imply that competence is highly susceptible to short-term transformation through agency, as some other commentators have tended to assume. When critiques of developmentalist understandings of subjectivity and competence are made, the consequence is often the suggestion that regulations be reduced to allow children to make decisions. This is the case, for example, with Priscilla Alderson's work on children's participation in health-care decision-making, in areas including sexual health (Alderson, 1990, 1992a; Alderson and Montgomery, 1996a). If the logic of such work were pursued with respect to sexual decision-making, it might well suggest reductions in the age of consent. Some sexual libertarians adopt similar arguments (although many paedophiles emphasise the sexual innocence and natural immaturity of children alongside the harmlessness of sexual activity, rather than children's competence to understand the activity: Geraci, 1997). Yet arguments such as Alderson's, emphasising the potential of children to develop competence to make judgements about sex if given appropriate education and resources, can nevertheless underestimate the complexity of the risks and structural forces operating in a particular social context which require assessment by subjects: and/or underestimate the severity of potential consequences of decisions which require protection. Children's embodied vulnerability as experienced in (and in part constituted in) its social context as well as children's competence must be taken into account.

With respect to the relationship between the subject and the law, it is necessary to question the assumed equation between the law and what is implied to be the average age at which relevant competence is acquired among individuals. Analyses such as Archard's effectively assume that age of consent laws are optimally fixed at the age when an average subject acquires sufficient competence in assessing the pleasures and dangers in its environment, so as to be able to judge whether participation in sexual behaviour is wise or beneficial. At a given point the development of the subject's competence will enable it to make an informed judgement about its social circumstances, balancing risks and benefits, and this is the point at which age of consent laws and other similar regulations should be fixed. This form of thinking assumes that an optimal age of consent will exist at an age when the competence of the (implicitly average) subject is ideally matched to the realities of the social structure. Competence in judging risks is seen as the only issue, without distinction from the issue of protection from the effects of risks which may have disproportionately serious consequences for younger people. But this conceptualisation does not allow for a possible disjuncture between the social forces generating the (average) subject's competence and the social forces generating risks. A disjuncture may exist because however much we may improve the competence of young people to make decisions, by equipping them with skills and resources, the degree of dangers given the risks involved if something goes wrong (such as condoms breaking or becoming involved with an abusive partner) can be too great. Given the ever-present possibility that things go wrong, the age of consent must be determined at a level when the seriousness of the potential negative consequences of sexual activity and relationships are reduced by the social consequences of reaching a higher age.

So we need to think about children's vulnerability. In discussing this, Gerison Lansdown helpfully draws a distinction between children's 'inherent vulnerability' and their 'structural vulnerability' in the context of social relations (Lansdown, 1994, pp. 34–35). As Lansdown argues there is a general cultural tendency to exaggerate the former due to a failure to conceptualise the latter; and structural vulnerability can be ameliorated to a degree by granting children rights and resources. The most radical of child liberationists go further, tending to minimise the extent to which children are inherently more vulnerable than adults due to their biology, while emphasising that children's structural vulnerability is itself largely a product of the way in which society produces a particular cultural conception of childhood as a period of innocence distinct from adulthood. By this type of argument, if we were to stop imagining childhood as a period of sexual innocence and grant children rights in relation to sexuality, children with the necessary education and resources would be able to negotiate sexual activity safely, and hence their structural vulnerability would dissipate. But this approach, evident to some extent in Lansdown's focus on civil rights, is unrealistic in its minimisation of children's inherent vulnerability, and its exaggeration of the extent to which rights and associated resources are sufficient to ameliorate children's structural vulnerability.

A few examples help to demonstrate limits to the extent that a young person can ameliorate both bodily and structural effects. A young person's physical body places them in certain determinate relationships to older people who tend to be stronger, independent of their sexual negotiating skills. Young people's lack of independent financial resources places them in a determinate relation to older individuals. Regardless of a young person's skills and resources for negotiating safe sex, the consequences of becoming pregnant or HIV positive are likely to be experienced as more serious for younger age groups (over the long term, though perhaps not immediately); and while this vulnerability is in many ways a consequence of children's social experience, rather than biological, it is unrealistic to think that the social meanings which generate such experiences could entirely be transformed through providing rights, education and resources. Irrespective of whether or not a young person receives a good sex education or develops competence in sexual negotiations, there remain certain social forces which act upon them determined by their youth: they remain subject to certain patterns of risk determined by their embodiment, their social and material context, financial and institutional circumstances.

From a perspective informed by sociological theory, individuals participating in sexual behaviour can thus be conceptualised as being located in social structures which imply stratified levels of risk acting upon them; and age of consent laws can be understood as intervening in this context seeking to mitigate such risks. In debates in sociological theory over the relationships between the individual and society, and between structure and agency, most sociologists accept the analytical necessity of maintaining conceptual distinctions between agency and structure, and avoiding 'conflationism' (Mouzelis, 1995). Similarly in conceptualising the relationship between the individual's consent and the rationale for age of consent laws, we need to avoid the analytical conflation of agency and structure, and maintain a sense that the average young person's understanding of their social context may not be well matched to the way in which their social context situates and impacts upon them.

It is highly unlikely, though hypothetically conceivable, that an age of consent law could be fixed at an age where the average subject's competence in judging risks equated perfectly with the optimal age at which the law offered a suitable level of protection to young people collectively from the risks of 'things going wrong'. It therefore seems likely that age of consent laws should not be conceived primarily with reference to young people's own competence in assessing risks, as much existing literature on age of consent laws emphasises, but should also take considerable account of the consequences of their sexual behaviour and relationships. In this light the age of consent should be fixed, through consideration of young people collectively, at an age which can contribute to reducing risks and potential negative consequences to an acceptable level. In theorising age of consent laws, greater attention should thus be given to the effects of social structure – the systematic social forces which impose risks upon young people. However, this focus on the impact of structural effects at a collective level should not preclude a recognition of the agency of many young people who do develop competence and negotiate their circumstances skilfully, which much contemporary government research on teenage pregnancy (employing quantitative methods) tends to obfuscate with its language of 'risk factors' (Social Exclusion Unit, 1999). The rationale for an age of consent is not that such risks are far greater below a particular age, or that they have a uniform impact or cannot be successfully negotiated by some individuals; but merely that they have to address general patterns affecting young people collectively, taking particular account of the most vulnerable.

To summarise, the drift of much recent literature on the legal regulation of childhood and children's sexuality has been towards an emphasis on the individual's capacity and consent. Combined with critiques of developmentalism and a growing emphasis on children's capacities to acquire competence and understanding of their worlds (Alderson, 1990, 1992a,c; Alderson and Montgomery, 1996a), this has tended to suggest a lowering of age of consent laws. This needs to be questioned with reference to sociological perspectives which foreground a distinction between individuals' understanding of their worlds and the way in which social worlds impact on individuals. The preoccupation with sexual consent reflects an unwillingness to grasp that law needs to address the collective structural position of children as a vulnerable group. While structural effects do not act deterministically or equally upon all individuals, their general patterns should be taken into account in determining age of consent laws.

A proposal for reform of the age of consent

I have argued that the epistemological basis upon which the current age of consent in Great Britain is founded is profoundly flawed; that contemporary evidence of young people's sexual behaviour shows many are criminalised by the current law; and that international comparative evidence on the law in other states suggests a lower age of consent should be considered. A lowering of the age of consent was not fully considered or admitted as a real possibility during the review of sexual offences which preceded the formulation of the *Sexual Offences Act* 2003, yet the need for consideration of such a move is strongly suggested by a variety of evidence. Serious consideration should be given to a change in the law to facilitate more effective support and guidance for the many young people who are currently criminalised.

I have also argued, however, that there is a clear rationale for legal prohibitions upon some of children's sexual behaviour that is recognised in law as consensual. The rationale for prohibitions derives from the legitimate role of the law in enforcing patterns of behaviour which protect the interests of children as a vulnerable social group. This rationale becomes clear from a focus upon the long-term interests of particular children who are likely to experience risks if they engage in sexual behaviour over time, rather than a focus on isolated examples of behaviour perceived as harmless; and it also derives from a focus on the collective interests of children rather than a prioritisation of individual interests.

What is the potential in contemporary mainstream policy debates in the UK for rethinking age of consent laws in the future? There may be increasing opportunities for theorising the age of consent in a more sociologically informed way, especially if or when a new review of age of consent laws occurs, although this is unlikely in the next few years given the extensive consultation and debate that preceded the *Sexual Offences Act* 2003. More conceptually sophisticated perspectives are gaining some influence in policy-making circles, and increasingly throw knowledge deriving from biomedicine and developmental psychology into question, although even in social research informing policy there is a worrying focus on quantitative methods, and the discourse on 'risk factors' presents early sexual behaviour as straightforwardly causing negative consequences in later life (Social Exclusion Unit, 1999). Mainstream policy debates have their own dynamics, and academic theory is often not able to inform policy-making. However, the prevailing paradigms of knowledge which structure contemporary policy-making and mainstream political debates can be positively influenced by wider developments in the social sciences, and interest groups involved in policy-making should seek to critically appraise the expertise on which they draw in this light.

The issue of the age of consent raises broader dilemmas about the balance between individual freedom and the protection of vulnerable groups in society. The argument I have sought to make in this chapter is that an excessive preoccupation with 'freedom', understood as absence of state regulation, is not in the interests of young people as a whole. The challenge for liberals, progressives and radicals in conceptualising these issues is to move away from an exclusive focus on the individual and their consent as a governing principle in relation to the law addressing childhood, and to renew a sense of the legitimacy of the law intervening to constitute social norms which are in the collective interest of young people, and to exist as an umbrella facilitating state intervention in particular young people's lives when this proves necessary. We need to recognise that to live within such a framework is positive and enabling for children rather than purely restrictive.

What does this imply in concrete terms? The present situation, with a universal age of consent of 16, encompasses too much of young people's sexual behaviour. The average age of first sexual experience with another person is 14 (Johnson *et al.*, 1994), and 30 per cent of boys and 26 per cent of girls have heterosexual intercourse below 16 (Wellings *et al.*, 2001, p. 1843). A realistic recognition of young people's actual sexual behaviour is needed, and the law is currently out of step with this. Research on young people's attitudes and behaviour shows that despite their sympathy for maintaining an age of 16, in practice many, perhaps most, do not experience the law as a major direct influence in their decisions about whether to engage in sexual behaviour. In general the law has limited effect in stopping people having sex. If those young people who express 'regret' about early sexual activity are to be enabled or encouraged to defer sex until later, the effective way to do this is through education and discussion, both in school and at home, which will influence their interpretation of what constitutes their own 'readiness' for sex and what makes it 'timely' (cf. Thomson, 2004, p. 142), and give them the skills and confidence to negotiate power relations related to gender, age and other sources of inequality.

At the time of writing, the government is launching a major new national public information campaign addressing sexually transmitted diseases; yet how are young people to discuss their behaviour openly if it is to remain criminal? The appalling statistics on sexually transmitted infections (Health Protection Agency, 2004), and the considerable levels of regret about early sexual experiences evident among young people, show that present sexual health and education interventions remain inadequate, and more broadly that parents and society as a whole are not confronting the realities of young people's sexual behaviour. Young people will not adhere to laws they perceive as out of touch with their experiences.

A starting point for discussion of possible changes to the law is the need to address the distinction between over-18s and under-18s that currently exists in age of consent legislation. In the previous chapter, I argued that the introduction of this distinction was driven by a protectionist agenda, and likely to lead to excessively punitive implementation of 'Sexual activity with a child' in the many instances where there are small age differences between partners (for example, those aged 15–18). However, as I have argued in this chapter, it is also important that the law and criminal justice system adjust to address criminally responsible children and young people in different ways from adults, and the over-18/under-18 distinction provides a way to do this in a way that corresponds to other major contours of the law, especially the *Children Act* (1989). Therefore if the protectionist motivations behind the introduction of this distinction can be moderated, maintaining sexual offences specific to over-18s and under-18s should be acceptable. For this to be the case, the police and courts need to adopt a careful and flexible approach to implementing 'Sexual activity with a child', rather than the universalist and punitive approach apparent in the process of its formulation. However, for the purposes of discussion of possible changes to age of consent laws I will assume this distinction is retained.

Three possible alternatives to the present formulation of age of consent laws have been most widely canvassed as means to reduce the criminalisation of under-16s. The first, proposed for example by Peter Tatchell, calls for a reduction of the age of consent to 14 (Tatchell, 2002). The age 14 is the most widely debated lower alternative age of consent and would appear to represent a significant enough change from the current age of 16 to be worthwhile, especially if we acknowledge that the consistency of 16 with the school-leaving age represents an advantage compared to 15. An age of 14 would help to ensure that there was not excessively punitive implementation of 'Sexual activity with a child' and allied offences in circumstances of small age differences (such as three years between 18- and 15-year olds), which is a current danger. However, since adults of all ages could have sex legally with 14-year olds, the disadvantage would be that more legally consensual but nevertheless systematically exploitative, abusive and damaging behaviour, especially by adult men with both girls and boys, would be beyond the scope of police intervention. This proposal underestimates the extent of such exploitative and abusive behaviour, which is being renewed and taking new forms in the context of 'cultural sexualization' (McNair, 2002), and the structuring effects of age and gender in defining power relations in this respect. Qualitative research evidence on young people's views suggests approval for the law facilitating intervention in circumstances where major power imbalances exist (Thomson, 2004), and whether adults over 18 are involved is a significant indicator of this.

A more widely debated proposal during passage of the *Sexual Offences Act* 2003 through parliament was to decriminalise 'Child sex offences committed by children or young persons' altogether; that is, all behaviour between those aged 13 and above with under-18s (sexual activity with under-13s is legally defined as non-consensual) (see Chapter 8). The possible advantage of this proposal relative to a reduction of the age of consent to 14 would be that, since adults (over-18s) would remain prohibited from any behaviour with under-16s, more abusive behaviour by adults could be prevented by the criminal justice system. The disadvantage, however, would be that such abusive behaviour between all young people aged 13–17 would be beyond the scope of intervention. In this case the problem with the proposal to abolish 'Child sex offences committed by children or young persons' is that it focusses excessively on what is legally defined as consensual, rather than recognising that the law has a limited but legitimate role in constituting social norms of behaviour, and a legitimate role in protecting children collectively as a vulnerable group by facilitating state intervention in their lives where necessary. It tends not to recognise the existence of consensual but abusive or excessively risky behaviour among young people (Brownlie, 2001), which makes facilitating the possibility of state intervention desirable in certain cases. It fails to learn the lessons of debates over consent, especially feminist debates over consent in heterosexual sex, which suggest that we draw a distinction between what is recognised as consent in law and what we believe is a desirable standard of consent; and hence that legally recognised consent does not imply the absence of a damaging or abusive relationship which should be prohibited by law in a child's interests.

A further alternative possibility which has also been discussed would be to retain the age of 16 as the legal age for sexual behaviour, but to formulate the law such that no person under 16 would be criminalised. This would represent a return to the original nineteenth-century conception of an 'age of consent', embodied in the *Criminal Law Amendment Act* 1885 which defined the age of consent for sexual intercourse as an age below which girls were not seen as morally or criminally responsible. To universalise this approach to children of both sexes, and to all forms of sexual behaviour, could be argued to be an appropriate way to embody 'protection' of children as a vulnerable group in the law, by contrast to criminalisation. The problem with this approach, however, is that it would not effectively deter sexual behaviour between under-16s as intended; and hence it fails to adequately conceive the role of law enforcement. As with the previous proposal, furthermore, it would make it impossible to prosecute children aged 13–15 who behave in a sexually abusive way with other children over 13 where behaviour was legally defined as consensual.

The solution that I suggest, therefore, is that the age of consent should be reduced to 14 (via a redefined version of 'Child sex offences committed by children or young persons'), but with a two-year 'age-span provision' applying until the age of 16. This would mean that 14-year olds could legally have sex with those aged 14–16; 15-year olds with those aged 14–17; and 16-year olds with anyone aged 14 or above, including all adults. The age of consent would thus remain 16 in relation to adults over 18 and 'Sexual activity with a child' (and associated 'Child sex offences': *Sexual Offences Act* 2003).

A two-year age-span, unlike a three-year age-span, would not imply that 15-year olds under the current age of consent could legally have sex with over-18s – an advantage if the distinction between over-18s and under-18s is to be retained. A reduction of the age of consent to 14 combined with a two-year age-span (i.e. two years maximum between partners' birthdays) would imply recognising that children under 16 can in some circumstances legitimately have sex with their peers, but not with adults. It should be accompanied by redoubled efforts to extend and improve the provision of sex and relationship education, sexual health promotion, and skills, resources and support of many kinds to young people, to enable them to make decisions about whether and how to have sex more confidently and effectively.

My solution implies a conception of young people's citizenship which repudiates the prevailing stark dichotomy whereby childrenn's sexual citizenship is equated entirely with 'protection', understood as legal prohibition, and defined in stark contrast to adult sexual citizenship, defined by sexual 'autonomy' (understood as the absence of legal prohibitions). The proposal recognises the complexity involved in defining a legal framework which can embody sexual citizenship for young people. By legalising some sexual activity for 14–15 year-olds this proposal challenges the idea that childhood and sexuality are mutually exclusive, and advances a conception of children and young people's citizenship which refutes this.

Age-span provisions were introduced in most states in the United States between 1971 and 1998 – 43 out of 50 had such provisions by 1999 (Cocca, 2004, pp. 36, 38). They are less common elsewhere in the world, although much of Europe also supplements minimum age limits in a different way, by employing 'seduction' provisions which make sexual activity of a particular character illegal (Graupner, 2000, pp. 441, 454; see Chapter 3). Age-span provisions have not been given full consideration in reviews of age of consent laws in England and Wales; comparative evidence on how they operated in other states such as the United States was not engaged with in the reports of the Policy Advisory Committee of the 1970s (PAC, 1979, 1981; cf. Chapter 6). In the most recent Home Office review, discussed in Chapter 8, the report *Setting the Boundaries* briefly surveyed international evidence including the recommendation of the federal Australian Model Criminal Code Officers Committee (MCCOC) in 1999 that Australian states should adopt a 'similarity of age defence' to apply where the accused was within 2 years in age of the complainant (Home Office, 2000a, p. 40; cf. pp. 39–40). At the review's consultation conference on sex offences against children, discussion groups of experts suggested that 'a two-year age gap might be acceptable' to recognise peer activity as less serious (Home Office, 2000b, Appendix H4, p. 302). However, due to the prevalence of protectionist perspectives, a lower age of consent was ruled off the Home Office review's agenda, and its report did not engage with such arguments for age-span provisions (Home Office, 2000a, pp. 41–49).

Significantly a two-year age-span has recently been proposed in the draft Criminal Code for Scotland written by senior Scottish academic lawyers, currently being debated (Clive *et al.*, 2003; see Part 3, Sexual Offences, section 65 'Unlawful sexual activity with a young person'). However, this would apply to activity with a minor (aged 12–15 inclusive) only for forms of sexual touching other than 'sexual intercourse' defined as 'penetration of the genitalia, anus or mouth by the penis', for which 16 would remain the legal age (s.64, s.66). This reform would thus be a move in the right direction, but not far enough.

Although age-span provisions can leave teenagers criminalised for sex with individuals only a little older than other legal partners, they are preferable to comprehensive prohibitions. My proposed change would recognise the extent to which the present law is ineffective in constituting social norms of behaviour between young people, and inappropriate in the context of the extensive sexual activity of under-16s which occurs. The new legal framework would, however, continue to provide the protective umbrella for children as a vulnerable group which they see as particularly necessary in relation to adults (cf. Thomson, 2004, p. 140), and play a role in preserving particular social norms of behaviour between adults and children by informing education and general cultural expectations. Prohibitions would however need to be more sensitively and flexibly implemented than at present, taking more account of the nature of relationships in individual cases, particularly in circumstances of small age differences between partners. In relation to adults, on the one hand the police should not turn a completely blind eye to men who systematically seek out girls under 16 to abuse and exploit, as they often have; on the other hand, interventions should be measured and flexible, not driven by exaggerated public fears of paedophilia.

This approach is informed by consideration of the different capacities of the law to influence social norms of sexual behaviour among adults and among young people. I have suggested a broad sympathy for liberal utilitarian critiques of legal moralism in relation to sexual behaviour, which emphasise that the law will have limited impact on what people do. However, the law appears to have less capacity to influence decisions about sexual behaviour among children than among adults; and the extent to which it is desirable to hold these groups morally and criminally responsible also differs. To lower the age of consent to 14 and introduce a two-year age-span provision would recognise the considerable extent to which sexual behaviour among 14–15-year olds will occur irrespective of the law; whereas the law is a more realistic tool for proscribing adult sexual behaviour.

Such an approach draws some support from the statistics on young people's sexual behaviour, but given the extent of later 'regret' we cannot draw direct conclusions about the implications of these: it is unclear whether improved education and support would lead to young people deferring sex for longer, or having happier, safer sex earlier. Age of consent laws cannot be decided by simply adjusting to what young people currently do; they need to be decided in a way that contributes to creating a framework which can enable young people to live better, happier, more satisfied lives. Nor should the extent to which age of consent laws obstruct sex education and sexual health promotion be exaggerated. Plenty of current initiatives demonstrate that to a considerable extent it is possible for adults to reach out to young people and work with them within the current legal framework; where this is not happening it could happen much more. The problem with an excessively high age of consent in relation to health and education is perhaps more specific, that it is obstructive in preventing some sexually active young people from taking the initiative in seeking advice and support from adults when they need it. And those who fear the law are likely to be those most in need.

What is abundantly clear is that the current age of consent is unsatisfactory and needs rethinking. In contemporary Britain, favouring an age of consent of 16 applying to all sexual behaviour implies faith in a wistful fantasy that young people will abstain. There is a need instead to admit the limited direct impact that law has on young people's sexual behaviour, and to confront the realities of their situations and experiences. But reform should not only be motivated by public health pragmatism and the desire to enable provision of better support and guidance; it should also be driven by recognition of the extent to which sexual activity is an integral and positive part of many young people's social experience, through which valuable feelings can find expression, and through which the self can flourish through relationships with others. The political challenge for government, the main political parties and all interest groups and individuals concerned with young people's sexuality, is to facilitate and engage in a full public debate over the strong case for reforming the present law.

Notes

4 Heterosexuality and the age of consent

1. My general approach to the law is to reject legal positivism and proceduralist conceptions of criminal law as a coherent unitary system, in favour of a critical, interpretative approach which is sociologically and historically informed, and hence able to recognise the inconsistencies and disjunctures in law that have existed (for an introduction to this view of criminal law, see Lacey and Wells, 1998).

5 Homosexuality and the age of consent

1. Some references to this and other reports include paragraph numbers, given in the form (CHOP, 1957, p. 1, #1).
2. 'Wolfenden Debate', editorial, *The Guardian*, 26 November 1958.
3. 'What they say about the Vice Report', *Evening News*, 5 September 1957.
4. According to the documentary *A Bill Called William*, Channel Four, 3 July 1997, 9–10 p.m.
5. See also the records of the Homosexual Law Reform Society in the Hall-Carpenter Archive, Library of the London School of Economics and Political Science.
6. It has been claimed that the leading Conservative Lord Robert Boothby and Labour MP Tom Driberg, both known homosexuals, were protected from the press and police by a cross-party agreement when their links to gangland killers the Kray twins emerged in 1964. Boothby was involved in a friendship, possibly a sexual relationship, with Ronnie Kray, while also the lover of Lady Dorothy Macmillan, the wife of former Conservative Prime Minister Harold Macmillan. The events were discussed in a Channel Four documentary *Secret History: Lords of the Underworld*, 23 June 1997, 9–10 p.m. See also *Independent on Sunday*, 15 June 1997, magazine; *Pink Paper*, 20 June 1997, p. 2.
7. Leo Abse, quoted in interview for *A Bill Called William*, ibid.
8. The enduring influence of these positions in structuring debates over law in the UK is evident in the inclusion of a philosophical summary framed in these terms as an appendix to the Law Commission's consultation paper *Consent in the Criminal Law* (Law Commission, 1995, Appendix C).
9. This led to Home Office–funded electric-shock 'treatment' programmes being inflicted upon homosexual prisoners: 'Gay prisoners given shock treatment, papers reveal', *The Guardian*, 28 November 1997, p. 1.
10. A further recent study of the Wolfenden committee by Patrick Higgins has also been presented as a critique of liberal commentaries on the report, claiming that 'Commentary on the report has tended to be favourable to its contents, accepting a liberal spin, and has tended to elevate the importance of Wolfenden. . . . By the time of his death in 1985, Wolfenden had been elevated to the status of a liberal saint, the emancipator of the British homosexual' (Higgins, 1996, p. 12). Yet Higgins provides no references to his 'liberal' targets, other than Sir John Wolfenden himself; nor does he engage with existing critiques of liberal readings of Wolfenden (Weeks, 1977, 1989; Bland, McCabe and Mort, 1979; Hall, 1980;

Mort, 1980). Consequently Higgins tends to reproduce the liberal mythology he is ostensibly against, and in fact gives a more liberal reading of the motives for instigating Wolfenden and of the committee's report than these existing commentaries.

11. However, it is noteworthy that radical critiques of the *Wolfenden Report* have been primarily concerned with addressing public assumptions rather than other academic commentaries; liberal interpreters of the report have not been easy to find for radical critics. In an extensive review, Tim Newburn has identified several writers who he describes as providing 'liberal-historical' interpretations of legislation and social trends associated with 'permissiveness' in the 1950s and 1960s, yet characterises their commentaries, in contrast to conservative interpretations, as 'generally more sceptical of the extent of permissiveness' (Newburn, 1992, p. 7). He is unable to identify liberal theorists who argue that the *Wolfenden Report* and subsequent legislation represented a wholehearted endorsement of individual freedoms.

12. 'Sutherland vs. the United Kingdom: Report of the European Commission of Human Rights', application 25186/94, 1 July 1997.

13. Quoted from a filmed interview in *A Bill Called William*, Channel Four, 3 July 1997, 9–10 p.m.

6 Sexual liberationism and the search for new sexual knowledge

1. Records of GLF's activities are held in the national lesbian and gay Hall-Carpenter Archive, at the British Library of Political and Economic Science, London. For GLF papers, diaries, correspondence, photos and memorabilia, see the Gay Liberation Front files and the John Chesterman papers. See also gay periodicals: London GLF's journal *Come Together*, issues 1–16 (HCA file 253); *Gay News*, July 1972 to July 1974, issues 1–50 (HCA file 294); *Gay International News* (HCA Chesterman file 8).

2. For example: 'Age of consent: A vital issue', letter from CHE chairman, *Gay News*, no. 14, 1973, p. 9.

3. 'Age of consent', *Come Together*, issue 8, August 1971, p. 1 (HCA file 253); 'GLF Youth Group', flyer describing group and its basic aims (HCA GLF file 3).

4. For the debate in *Gay News* over Paedophilia, see Peter Kelsey 'Pederasty', *Gay News*, no. 8, p. 8; 'Pederasty and you' – letters, *Gay News*, no. 10, p. 7; Mark Adams, 'Re-building the image – views on boy-lovers', *Gay News*, no. 12, p. 10; 'Of men and little boys' and 'The body politic affair', *Gay News*, no. 14 (New Year 1973), p. 7; Letters, *Gay News*, no. 16, p. 2; 'Boys for sale in New York: All prices, all ages', *Gay News*, no. 18, pp. 7, 10; 'Hello young lovers', editorial, *Gay News*, no. 49, p. 2.

5. The situation in Scotland was subsequently changed by the *Age of Legal Capacity (Scotland) Act* 1977, which set the age of legal capacity at 16. The *Marriage (Scotland) Act* 1977 gave young persons aged 16 the capacity to marry without parental consent.

6. 'Age-of-consent idea "naive" ', *Sunday Times*, 26 May 1974; 'Row over call for "consent at 12" ', *The Scotsman*, 28 May 1974; 'CHE sack Vice-President', *Gay News*, no. 48, 6 June 1974. The CHE's Working Party on Law Reform had recommended a basic age of consent of 16, but 12 in cases where a defendant could prove the existence of meaningful consent; see 'CHE Report angers reformers', *Gay News*, no. 46, 9 May 1974, p. 3.

7. On the internal debate, and review by the CHE's Working Party on Law Reform, see 'CHE Report angers reformers', *Gay News*, no. 46, 9 May 1974, p. 3.
8. See 'Equal means sixteen', report on CHE's Malvern Conference, *Gay News*, no. 48, 6 June 1974, p. 1; on the conference see also 'A new pride', editorial, p. 2; 'Don't ask-demand!: The theme of Malvern', p. 3; 'New sex laws', p. 5. Internal debates over a lower target nevertheless persisted into the 1980s (CHE Law Reform Committee, 1980).
9. During the campaign the three main party leaders, Jeremy Thorpe (Liberal), Edward Heath (Conservative) and Harold Wilson (Labour), were interviewed by *Gay News* on equality issues including the age of consent. Each gave non-committal answers, emphasising that homosexuality was an issue for individual MPs, not party policy, see *Gay News*, no. 41, 28 February 1974, p. 3.
10. On the campaign launch, see 'Homosexuals to seek further reforms', *The Times*, 3 July 1975.
11. See criminal statistics in England and Wales for 1975–1977, provided in the Attorney General's Written Answer to a parliamentary question (HC 22 January 1979, cols 18–20).
12. 'Quakers make 14 age of consent', *Sunday Express*, 16 April 1972.
13. 'Dr. Robinson puts case for age of consent to be 14', *The Times*, 6 July 1972; 'Consent to what?', editorial, *New Law Journal*, Vol. 122, no. 5554, 13 July 1972, pp. 621–622.
14. Antony Grey continued to advocate the Sexual Law Reform Society's solution for many years, see A. Grey 'Free to choose sex', letter, *New Statesman and Society*, 30 June 1995, p. 28.
15. The Policy Advisory Committee subsequently referred to public controversy over campaigns by the SLRS and CHE in contextualising its own creation (PAC, 1979, p. 1, #3). For criticism of the decision to set up the inquiry, see Ronald Butt 'Who really wants a change in the age of consent?', *The Times*, 22 January 1976.
16. Quoted by Boris Johnson 'The final twiumph', *The Daily Telegraph*, 22 July 1998, p. 22.
17. On the wider political and social context structuring debates over sexuality during the 1970s and early 1980s (Weeks, 1989, pp. 273–306; Durham, 1991; Jeffery-Poulter, 1991, pp. 109–175).
18. The occupations of members are listed in CLRC, 1984, Appendix A.
19. These submissions provide vital evidence, given that standing committees (at this time) received no oral evidence (Grey, 1997, p. 50). For a list of those who made written submissions, see PAC, 1981, Annex II. Press reports from the Hall-Carpenter Archive provide a rich source of data on written submissions received by the Policy Advisory Committee from various interest groups, and public responses to their work, in a context where access to committee records is prohibited due to the 'thirty-year rule' governing the availability of official documents. The Hall-Carpenter Archive press-cuttings collection is based at the Art and Design Library, Middlesex University (Cat Hill campus).
20. Margrit Schwarz (Secretary, The Josephine Butler Society), 'The age of consent', letter to *The Times*, 30 January 1976.
21. Police Superintendents Association of England and Wales (1975), submission to the Criminal Law Revision Committee; quoted in 'Liberalism has gone much too far', *Police Review*, 12 December 1975, p. 1581.
22. 'BMA against change in age of consent', *Ipswich Evening Star*, 16 August 1976.
23. 'Lower age of consent for gays', *The Guardian*, 15 May 1976.

24. For critical right-wing responses, see comments by Conservative Rhodes Boyson MP in 'Permissive society nonsense', *Methodist Recorder*, 18 March 1976; 'Sexual Subversion', editorial, *Daily Telegraph*, 10 March 1976; Russell Lewis, 'The crusaders for sexual licence', *Daily Telegraph*, 20 April 1976; and 'Make sex legal for girls of 14', *Daily Express*, 9 March 1976.

25. It is noteworthy that Patricia Hewitt, Secretary of State for Trade and Industry and Minister for Women in the current Labour government (2004), was General Secretary of the National Council for Civil Liberties at the time of the report's publication. The current Solicitor General, Harriet Harman, also worked for the organisation.

26. 'The Lolita Charter is Kicked Out: Home Office says no to "sex at 14" demands', *The Sun*, 29 June 1979, p. 7.

27. For press coverage, see, for example, 'Age of consent should remain 16, says study group', *The Daily Telegraph*, 29 June 1979; 'The Lolita Charter', *The Sun*; 'Call to reduce gay consent age to 18' (p. 1) and editorial 'The ages of consent and wisdom' (p. 12), *The Guardian*, 29 June 1979.

28. Melanie Phillips 'Abolish age of consent, says report', *The Guardian*, 12 September 1979.

29. The *Indecency with Children Act* 1960 stated:

> 1 (1) Any person who commits an act of gross indecency with or towards a child under the age of fourteen, or who incites a child under that age to such an act with him or another, shall be liable on conviction on indictment to imprisonment for a term not exceeding two years, or on summary conviction to imprisonment for a term not exceeding six months, to a fine not exceeding one hundred pounds, or to both.

> This legislation had been introduced to address instances where a person 'passively' invites sexual contact without committing an 'assault', or performs a sexual act that does not involve physical contact, such as self-masturbation in front of another person. Court cases had appeared to reveal this as a loophole in existing legislation, although subsequent judgements ruled that such acts fell within a revised definition of 'indecent assault' (Lacey and Wells, 1998, p. 405). In Scotland, the *Sexual Offences (Scotland) Act* 1976 Section 5 similarly created the offence of 'Indecent behaviour towards a girl between 12 and 16', prohibiting 'lewd, indecent or libidinous' behaviours regardless of consent (later recodified as Section 6 of the *Criminal Law (Consolidation) (Scotland) Act* 1995).

30. For indicative responses, see 'The young love charter', *Evening Standard*, 11 September 1979, pp. 1–2; 'Sex, sin and society: A challenging Express series answering the questions that every worried parent is now asking', *Daily Express*, 26 September 1979; Teddy Taylor, 'The sickness which could destroy us all', *Sunday Mail* (Scotland), 16 September 1979.

31. 'Consent age to stay, says Mrs. Thatcher', *Daily Telegraph*, 5 October 1979.

32. See 'Homosexual age of consent should be lowered to 18, says report', *The Guardian*, 10 April 1981.

33. 'Fury over shake-up in sex law', *Daily Express*, 6 April 1981, p. 1; 'Too young' – editorial, *The Sun*, 7 April 1981.

34. 'What ages of consent?' – editorial, *The Guardian*, 10 April 1981.

35. Contrasting attitudes were evident in 'Resolution 756 on discrimination against homosexuals' passed by the Parliamentary Assembly of the Council of Europe,

1 October 1981, which urged member states 'to apply the same minimum age of consent for homosexual and heterosexual acts' (s. 7.ii).

36. For media responses, see 'Insistent husband "should risk prosecution for rape"', *Daily Telegraph*, 6 November 1980; 'Top lawyers recommend changes in sex laws', *The Guardian*, 6 November 1980.

37. For press coverage, see 'Sex law changes urged by judges', *The Guardian*, 13 April 1984; 'Fury over call for sex law shake-up', *Daily Express*, 13 April 1984; 'The sex revolution', *Daily Mirror*, 13 April 1984.

38. Campaign for Homosexual Equality 'Report of the Criminal Law Revision Committee – "disappointing and inconsistent"', press release, April 1984.

39. As a former Home Office civil servant, Hindley was able to achieve special access to study the medical submissions made to the committee, the only significant exception being the evidence of the BMA, which is in any case discussed in the PAC report (PAC, 1981, pp. 16–17, #42; Hindley, 1986, pp. 595, 598).

40. This statement presented to the Criminal Law Revision Committee in June 1976 was reiterated as BMA policy in response to the Criminal Law Revision Committee's working paper in 1981, and its final report in 1984 (CLRC, 1981, 1984). It was only reconsidered and changed in 1994 (BMA, 1994).

7 Equality at last? Age of consent debates in the 1990s

1. This occurred in the context of clear moves by the European Court towards ruling unequal ages of consent illegal (Helfer, 1990). The case was subsequently continued by Euan Sutherland, on whose case a ruling was eventually made, and Chris Morris.

2. 'MPs to vote on allowing gay sex at 18', *The Times*, 22 December 1993, p. 1.

3. For background on the formation and organisational form of Stonewall, and also of Outrage (discussed below), see Rayside (1998, pp. 47, 52–60).

4. *The Times*, 16 February 1994, p. 14.

5. Dr David Starkey, *The Independent*, 21 February 1994, p. 15.

6. Simon Hughes MP also proposed an amendment (clause 6) in support of equality at 17, but this never became a serious option in the debate. All amendments sought to equalise the law in England, Wales and Scotland. A subsequent government amendment to the same bill in April 1994 brought the age of consent down to 18 in Northern Ireland (Rayside, 1998, p. 52).

7. Also in February 1994, by contrast, the European Parliament passed a resolution in favour of sexual equality for lesbians, gay men and bisexuals by 159 votes to 96; see 'A Gay MP looks towards Europe', *Our View: The News and Current Affairs Magazine for Lesbians and Gay Men*, no. 4, April–May 1994, pp. 9–11.

9 Rethinking the age of consent

1. 'One girl in six hits puberty by age of eight', *The Observer*, 18 June 2000, pp. 1–2; 'Too much too young', *The Observer*, 18 June 2000, Review, pp. 1, 4; 'Sex from 8 to 18', Channel 4, Tuesday 27 June 2000, 9 p.m.

Bibliography

Aapola, S. (1997) 'Mature Girls and Adolescent Boys? Deconstructing Discourses of Adolescence and Gender', *Young: Nordic Journal of Youth Research*, Vol. 5, no. 4, pp. 50–68.

Abbott, P. and Wallace, C. (1992) *The Family and the New Right* (London: Pluto Press).

Abelove, H., Barale, M.A. and Halperin, D.M. (eds) (1993) *The Lesbian and Gay Studies Reader* (London: Routledge).

Adam, B.D. (1987) *The Rise of a Gay and Lesbian Movement* (Boston: Twayne Publishers).

Adam, B.D., Duyvendak, J.W. and Krouwel, A. (eds) (1999) *The Global Emergence of Gay and Lesbian Politics: National Imprints of a Worldwide Movement* (Philadelphia: Temple University Press).

Adkins, L. (2002) *Revisions: Gender and Sexuality in Late Modernity* (Buckingham: Open University Press).

Ageofconsent (2004) *Age of Consent*, http://www.ageofconsent.com/(28 June 2004).

Ainley, R. (1995) *What is She Like? Lesbian Identities from the 1950s to the 1990s* (London: Cassell).

Alderson, P. (1990) 'Consent to Children's Surgery and Intensive Medical Treatment', *Journal of Law and Society*, Vol. 17, no. 1, pp. 52–65.

——(1992a) 'In the Genes or in the Stars? Children's Competence to Consent', *Journal of Medical Ethics*, Vol. 18, no. 3, pp. 119–124.

——(1992b) 'Did Children Change, or the Guidelines?', *Bulletin of Medical Ethics*, no. 80, pp. 21–28.

——(1992c) 'Rights of Children and Young People', in A. Coote (ed.) *The Welfare of Citizens: Developing New Social Rights* (London: Institute for Public Policy Research/Rivers Oram Press), Chapter 8, pp. 153–180.

——(1994) 'Researching Children's Rights to Integrity', in B. Mayall (ed.) *Children's Childhoods: Observed and Experienced* (London: Falmer Press).

——(1995) 'Consent and the Social Context', *Nursing Ethics*, Vol. 2, no. 4, pp. 347–350.

Alderson, P. and Mayall, B. (eds) (1994) *Children's Decisions in Health Care and Research: Edited Conference Proceedings* (London: Institute of Education, Social Science Research Unit).

Alderson, P. and Montgomery, J. (1996a) *Health Care Choices: Making Decisions with Children* (London: Institute for Public Policy Research).

——(1996b) 'Health Care Choices: Making Decisions with Children – Summary of Conclusions and Recommendations', *Bulletin of Medical Ethics*, no. 117, pp. 8–11.

Alldred, P. (1998) 'Ethnography and Discourse Analysis: Dilemmas in Representing the Voices of Children', in J. Ribbens and R. Edwards (eds) *Feminist Dilemmas in Qualitative Research* (London: Sage), pp. 147–170.

Althusser, L. (ed.) (1971) 'Freud and Lacan', *Lenin and Philosophy and Other Essays* (London: New Left Books).

Altman, D. (1971/1974) *Homosexual: Oppression and Liberation* (London: Allen Lane).

——(ed.) (1980) 'What Changed in the Seventies?', in Gay Left Collective *Homosexuality: Power and Politics* (London: Allison & Busby), pp. 52–63.

——(1993) *Homosexual Oppression and Liberation* (with new Introduction by J. Weeks and Afterword by D. Altman) (London: Serpents Tail).

——(1998) 'Globalization and the "AIDS industry"', *Contemporary Politics*, Vol. 4, no. 3, pp. 233–245.

——(1999a) 'Globalization, Political Economy and HIV/AIDS', *Theory and Society*, Vol. 28, no. 4, pp. 559–584.

——(1999b) 'The Internationalization of Gay and Lesbian Identities', in D. Epstein and J.T. Sears (eds) *A Dangerous Knowledge: Sexuality, Pedagogy and Popular Culture* (London: Cassell), pp. 135–149.

——(2001) *Global Sex* (Chicago: University of Chicago Press).

Andrews, G. (ed.) (1991) *Citizenship* (London: Lawrence & Wishart).

Archard, D. (1993) *Children: Rights and Childhood* (London: Routledge).

——(1998) *Sexual Consent* (Oxford: Westview Press).

——(1999) 'Can Child Abuse be Defined?', in M. King (ed.) *Moral Agendas for Children's Welfare* (London: Routledge), pp. 74–89.

Ariès, P. (1962) *Centuries of Childhood* (London: Cape).

Baker, C. (1983) 'The "Age of Consent" Controversy: Age and Gender as Social Practice', *Australian and New Zealand Journal of Sociology*, Vol. 19, no. 1, pp. 96–112.

Bandalli, S. (2000) 'Children, Responsibility and the New Youth Justice', in B. Goldson (ed.) *The New Youth Justice* (Dorset: Russell House Publishing), Chapter 5, pp. 81–95.

Banks, O. (1981) *Faces of Feminism: A Study of Feminism as a Social Movement* (Oxford: Martin Robertson).

Barbalet, J.M. (1988) *Citizenship: Rights, Struggle and Class Inequality* (Milton Keynes: Open University Press).

Barnardos (1998) *Whose Daughter Next? Children Abused Through Prostitution* (Basildon: Barnardos' Child Care Publications).

——(2001) *Setting the Boundaries: Reforming the Law on Sexual Offences – Barnardos Response*, unpublished paper.

Barrett, M. (1991) *The Politics of Truth: From Marx to Foucault* (Cambridge: Polity Press).

Bartlett, N. (1988) *Who Was That Man? A Present for Mr. Oscar Wilde* (London: Serpent's Tail).

Bartlett, P. (1997) 'Sodomites in the Pillory in Eighteenth-Century London', *Social and Legal Studies*, Vol. 6, no. 4, pp. 553–572.

Bauserman, R. (1990) 'Objectivity and Ideology: Criticism of Theo Sandfort's Research on Man–Boy Sexual Relations', *Journal of Homosexuality*, Vol. 20, nos 1/2, pp. 297–311.

Bauserman, R. and Rind, B. (1997) 'Psychological Correlates of Male Child and Adolescent Sexual Experiences with Adults: A Review of the Nonclinical Literature', *Archives of Sexual Behaviour*, Vol. 26, no. 2, pp. 105–141.

Bech, H. (1997) *When Men Meet: Homosexuality and Modernity* (Cambridge: Polity Press).

Beck, U. (1992) *Risk Society: Towards a New Modernity* (London: Sage).

——(2000) 'The Cosmopolitan Perspective', *British Journal of Sociology*, Vol. 51, no. 1, pp. 79–105.

Beck, U., Giddens, A. and Lash, C. (1994) *Reflexive Modernization: Politics, Tradition and Aesthetics in the Modern Social Order* (Cambridge: Polity).

Bell, D. and Binnie, J. (2000) *The Sexual Citizen: Queer Politics and Beyond* (Cambridge: Blackwell).

Bell, R. and Jones, G. (2000) *Balancing Acts: Youth, Parenting and Public Policy* (York: Joseph Rowntree Foundation).

——(2004) *Youth Policies in the U.K.: A Chronological Map*, http://www.keele.ac.uk/depts/so/youthchron/(7 July 2004).

Bell, V. (1993) 'Governing Childhood: Neo-liberalism and the Law', *Economy and Society*, Vol. 22, no. 3, pp. 390–405.

Benhabib, S. (1992) *Situating the Self: Gender, Community and Postmodernism in Contemporary Ethics* (Cambridge: Polity Press).

Bennion, F. (2003) *Sexual Ethics and Criminal Law: A Critique of the Sexual Offences Bill 2003* (Oxford: Lester Publishing).

Berlant, L. and Warner, M. (1998) 'Sex in Public', *Critical Inquiry*, Vol. 24, no. 2, Winter, pp. 547–566.

Bernard, F. (1997) 'The Dutch Paedophile Emancipation Movement', in J. Geraci (ed.) *Dares to Speak: Historical and Contemporary Perspectives on Boy-Love* (Swaffham, Norfolk: Gay Men's Press), pp. 34–49.

Bhatt, C. (1997) *Liberation and Purity: Race, New Religious Movements and the Ethics of Postmodernity* (London: UCL Press).

Birch, K. (1988) 'A Community of Interests', in B. Cant and S. Hemmings (eds) *Radical Records: Thirty Years of Lesbian and Gay History* (London: Routledge), pp. 51–59.

Bland, L. (1992) 'Feminist Vigilantes of Late-Victorian England', in C. Smart (ed.) *Regulating Womanhood: Historical Essays on Marriage, Motherhood and Sexuality* (London: Routledge), pp. 33–52.

——(1995) *Banishing the Beast: English Feminism and Sexual Morality 1885–1914* (London: Penguin).

Bland, L., McCabe, T. and Mort, F. (1979) 'Sexuality and Reproduction: Three "Official" Instances', in M. Barrett, P. Corrigan, A. Kuhn and J. Wolff (eds) *Ideology and Cultural Production* (New York: St. Martin's Press), pp. 78–111.

Bowley, M. (1997) 'More Power to Their Elbows', *New Law Journal*, Vol. 147, no. 6807, 12 September 1997.

Brannen, J. and Edwards, R. (1996) 'Introduction: From Parents to Children – The Generation of a Research Programme', in J. Brannen and R. Edwards (eds) *Perspectives on Parenting and Childhood: Looking Back and Moving Forward* (London: South Bank University), pp. 1–10.

Bravmann, S. (1996) 'Postmodernism and Queer Identities', in S. Seidman (ed.) *Queer Theory/Sociology* (Oxford: Blackwell), pp. 333–361.

Brierley, J. (1993) *Growth in Children* (London: Cassell).

British Medical Association (1994) *Age of Consent for Homosexual Men: A Scientific and Medical Perspective*, Report to the Council of the British Medical Association from the Board of Science and Education (London: British Medical Association).

British Paediatric Association (1992) 'Guidelines for the Ethical Conduct of Medical Research Involving Children', *Bulletin of Medical Ethics*, no. 80, pp. 13–20.

Bronitt, S. (1994) 'Spreading Disease and the Criminal Law', *Criminal Law Review*, no. 21.

Brown, L. (ed.) (1993) *The New Shorter Oxford English Dictionary* (Oxford: Clarendon Press).

Brown, W. (1995) *States of Injury: Power and Freedom in Late Modernity* (Princeton: Princeton University Press).

Brownlee, I. (1998) 'New Labour – New Penology? Punitive Rhetoric and the Limits of Managerialism in Criminal Justice Policy', *Journal of Law and Society*, Vol. 25, no. 3, pp. 313–335.

Brownlie, J. (2001) 'The "Being-Risky" Child: Governing Childhood and Sexual Risk', *Sociology*, Vol. 35, no. 2, pp. 519–537.

Bulmer, M. and Rees, A.M. (eds) (1996) *Citizenship Today: The Contemporary Relevance of T.H. Marshall* (London: UCL Press).

Butler, J. (1990) *Gender Trouble: Feminism and the Subversion of Identity* (New York: Routledge).

Butler, J. and Scott, J. (1992) *Feminists Theorize the Political* (London: Routledge).

Campaign for Homosexual Equality (1976) *Submission to the Criminal Law Revision Committee* (Manchester: Campaign for Homosexual Equality), May.

Campaign for Homosexual Equality Law Reform Committee (1980) *The Law Relating to Consensual Sexual Acts*, unpublished paper (London: Campaign for Homosexual Equality).

Cant, B. and Hemmings, S. (eds) (1988) *Radical Records: Thirty Years of Lesbian and Gay History* (London: Routledge).

Card, R. and Ward, R. (1998) *The Crime and Disorder Act 1998: A Practitioner's Guide* (Bristol: Jordans).

Carver, T. and Mottier, V. (eds) (1998) *Politics of Sexuality: Identity, Gender, Citizenship* (London: Routledge).

Castells, M. (1997) *The Power of Identity* (Oxford: Blackwell).

Chalmers, J. (2003) 'Is Underage Intercourse Shameless Indecency?', *Scots Law Times*, no. 14, pp. 123–127.

Chauncey, G. (1995) *Gay New York: The Making of the Gay World, 1890–1940* (London: Flamingo, HarperCollins).

Christian Institute (1999) *Age of Consent: The Case Against Change* (Newcastle upon Tyne: Christian Institute).

Church of England, Board for Social Responsibility (1999) *Submission to the Home Office Sex Offences Review Team*, unpublished paper.

Clarke, P.B. (1994) *Citizenship* (London: Pluto Press).

Clive, E., Ferguson, P., Gane, C. and McCall Smith, A. (2003) *A Draft Criminal Code for Scotland with Commentary* (Edinburgh: Scottish Law Commission).

Cocca, C.E. (2002a) 'From "Welfare Queen" to "Exploited Teen": Welfare Dependency, Statutory Rape, and Moral Panic', *National Women's Studies Association Journal*, Vol. 14, no. 2, Summer, pp. 56–79.

——(2002b) 'Prosecuting Mrs. Robinson? Gender, Sexuality and Statutory Rape Laws', *Michigan Feminist Studies*, Vol. 16, pp. 1–25.

——(2002c) 'The Politics of Statutory Rape Laws: Adoption and Reinvention of Morality Policy in the States, 1971–1999', *Polity*, Vol. XXXV, no. 1, Fall, pp. 51–72.

——(2004) *Jailbait: The Politics of Statutory Rape Laws in the United States* (New York: State University of New York Press).

Cocks, H.G. (1998) *Abominable Crimes: Sodomy Trials in English Law and Culture, 1830–1889*, PhD thesis Department of History, University of Manchester.

Cohen, E. (1993) *Talk on the Wilde Side: Toward a Genealogy of a Discourse on Male Sexualities* (London: Routledge).

Cohen, S. (ed.) (1971) *Images of Deviance* (Harmondsworth: Penguin).

——(1972) *Folk Devils and Moral Panics* (London: MacGibbon and Kee).

Committee on the Age of Majority (1967) *Report of the Committee on the Age of Majority*, Cmnd. 3342 (London: HMSO).

Committee on Homosexual Offences and Prostitution, Home Office and Scottish Home Department (CHOP) (1957) *Report of the Committee on Homosexual Offences and Prostitution*, Cmnd. 247 (London: HMSO).

Connell, R.W. (1995) *Masculinities* (Cambridge: Polity Press).

Cooper, D. (1994) *Sexing the City: Lesbian and Gay Politics Within the Activist State* (London: Rivers Oram Press).

Corteen, K. (2004) 'Beyond (Hetero)Sexual Consent', in M. Cowling and P. Reynolds (eds) *Making Sense of Sexual Consent* (Aldershot: Ashgate), Chapter 10, pp. 171–194.

Corteen, K. and Scraton, P. (1997) 'Prolonging "Childhood", Manufacturing "Innocence" and Regulating Sexuality', in P. Scraton (ed.) *'Childhood' in 'Crisis'?* (London: UCL Press), pp. 76–100.

Cowling, M. and Reynolds, P. (eds) (2004) *Making Sense of Sexual Consent* (Aldershot: Ashgate).

Crane, P. (1982) *Gays and the Law* (London: Pluto Press).

Cretney, S.M. and Masson, J.M. (1997) *Principles of Family Law*, sixth edition (London: Sweet & Maxwell).

Cretney, S.M., Masson, J.M. and Bailey-Harris, R. (2002) *Principles of Family Law*, Seventh edition (London: Sweet & Maxwell).

Cretney, S.M., Masson, J.M. and Bailey-Harris, R. (2002) *Principles of Family Law*, seventh edition (London: Sweet&Maxwell) Criminal Law Revision Committee (CLRC) (1980) *Working Paper on Sexual Offences* (London: HMSO), October.

——(1982) *Working Paper on Offences Relating to Prostitution and Allied Offences* (London: HMSO), December.

——(1984) *Sexual Offences*, fifteenth report Cmnd. 9213 (London: HMSO), April.

Crompton, L. (1980) 'The Myth of Lesbian Impunity: Capital Laws from 1270–1791', *Journal of Homosexuality*, Vol. 6, nos 1–2.

Cruikshank, M. (1992) *The Gay and Lesbian Liberation Movement* (London: Routledge).

David, H. (1997) *On Queer Street: A Social History of British Homosexuality 1895–1995* (London: HarperCollins).

Davies, C. (1975) *Permissive Britain: Social Change in the Sixties and Seventies* (London: Pitman).

——(1980) 'Moralists, Causalists, Sex, Law and Morality', in W.H.G. Armytage, R. Chester and J. Peel (eds) *Changing Patterns of Sexual Behaviour* (London: Academic Press), pp. 13–43.

de Lauretis, T. (1991) 'Queer Theory: Lesbian and Gay Sexualities', *Differences*, no. 3, pp. iii–xviii.

Delanty, G. (2000) *Citizenship in a Global Age* (Buckingham: Open University Press).

Dempsey, B. (1998) 'Piecemeal to Equality: Scottish Gay Law Reform', in L.J. Moran, D. Monk and S. Beresford (eds) *Legal Queeries: Lesbian, Gay and Transgender Legal Studies* (London: Cassell), pp. 155–166.

Department of Health (2001) *The National Strategy for Sexual Health and HIV* (London: Department of Health).

——(2004) *Choosing Health: Making Health Choices Easier*, Public Health White Paper, November, Cm. 6734 (London: Department of Health).

Devlin, P. (1959) *The Enforcement of Morals: Maccabean Lecture in Jurisprudence* (London: OUP).

Diamentides, M. (1999) 'Meditations on Parental Love: The Transcendence of the Rights/Welfare Debate', in M. King (ed.) *Moral Agendas for Children's Welfare* (London: Routledge).

Dine, J. and Watt, B. (1998) 'The Transmission of Disease During Consensual Sexual Activity and the Concept of Associative Autonomy', *Web Journal of Current Legal Issues*, no. 4.

Doan, L. (1997) ' "Gross Indecency between Women": Policing Lesbians or Policing Lesbian Police?', *Social and Legal Studies*, 'Legal Perversions' special issue, Vol. 6, no. 4, December, pp. 533–551.

——(2001) *Fashioning Sapphism: The Origins of a Modern English Lesbian Culture* (Columbia: Columbia University Press).

Dollimore, J. (1997) 'Bisexuality', in A. Medhurst and S.R. Munt (ed.) *Lesbian and Gay Studies: A Critical Introduction* (London: Cassell), pp. 250–260.

DuBois, E.C. and Gordon, L. (1984) 'Seeking Ecstasy on the Battlefield: Danger and Pleasure in Nineteenth-century Feminist Sexual Thought', in C.S. Vance (ed.) (1984/1992) *Pleasure and Danger: Exploring Female Sexuality* (London: Pandora Press), pp. 31–49.

Duff, A. (ed.) (1997) *The Treaty of Amsterdam: Text and Commentary* (London: Federal Trust).

Durham, M. (1991) *Sex and Politics: The Family and Morality in the Thatcher Years* (London: Macmillan).

——(1994) 'Major and Morals: Back to Basics and the Crisis of Conservatism', *Talking Politics*, Vol. 7, no. 1, Autumn, pp. 12–16.

Dworkin, A. (1981) *Pornography: Men Possessing Women* (London: Women's Press).

Eadie, J. (1993) 'Activating Bisexuality: Towards a Bi/Sexual Politics', in J. Bristow and A.R. Wilson (eds) *Activating Theory: Lesbian, Gay, Bisexual Politics* (London: Lawrence & Wishart), pp. 139–170.

Economic and Social Research Council (ESRC) (1997) *Children 5–16: Growing into the 21st Century – An Economic and Social Research Council Research Programme*, information pack (Swindon: ESRC).

——(1998) *Youth, Citizenship and Social Change – An Economic and Social Research Council Research Programme*, information pack (Swindon: ESRC).

Edwards, A. (1996) 'Gender and Sexuality in the Social Construction of Rape and Consensual Sex: A Study of Process and Outcome in Six Recent Rape Trials', in J. Holland and L. Adkins (eds) *Sex, Sensibility and the Gendered Body* (London: Macmillan), pp. 178–201.

Edwards, S. (1981) *Female Sexuality and the Law* (London: Robertson).

——(1996) *Sex and Gender in the Legal Process* (London: Blackstone Press).

Ellis, S.J. and Kitzinger, C. (2002) 'Denying Equality: An Analysis of Arguments against Lowering the Age of Consent for Sex between Men', *Journal of Community and Applied Psychology*, Vol. 12, pp. 167–180.

Ellmann, R. (1987) *Oscar Wilde* (London: Hamish Hamilton).

Epstein, D. and Johnson, R. (1998) *Schooling Sexualities* (Buckingham: Open University Press).

Epstein, D., Johnson, R. and Steinberg, D.L. (2000) 'Twice Told Tales: Transformation, Recuperation and Emergence in the Age of Consent Debates 1998', *Sexualities*, Vol. 3, no. 1, pp. 5–30.

Epstein, S. (1987) 'Gay Politics, Ethnic Identity: The Limits of Social Constructionism', *Socialist Review*, nos 93/94, May–August, pp. 9–54; reprinted in E. Stein (ed.) (1992) *Forms of Desire: Sexual Orientation and the Social Constructionist Controversy* (London: Routledge), pp. 239–293.

——(1996) 'A Queer Encounter: Sociology and the Study of Sexuality', in S. Seidman, (ed.) *Queer Theory/Sociology* (Oxford: Blackwell), pp. 145–167.

——(1999) 'Book Review: Steven Seidman (1997) *Difference Troubles: Queering Social Theory and Politics*' (Cambridge: Cambridge University Press), *Sexualities*, Vol. 2, no. 2, May, pp. 270–272.

Eschle, C. (2001) *Global Democracy, Social Movements and Feminism* (Boulder: Westview Press).

European Commission of Human Rights (1997) Application no. 25186/94, Euan Sutherland against the United Kingdom: Report of the Commission, adopted 1 July 1997.

Evans, D. (1993) *Sexual Citizenship: The Material Construction of Sexualities* (London: Routledge).

——(1995) '(Homo)Sexual Citizenship: A Queer Kind of Justice', in A.R. Wilson (ed.) *A Simple Matter of Justice: Theorizing Lesbian and Gay Politics* (London: Cassell), pp. 110–145.

Faderman, L. (1981) *Surpassing the Love of Men: Romantic Friendship and Love between Women from the Renaissance to the Present* (London: Junction Books).

——(1985) *Scotch Verdict* (London: Quartet Books).

Faraday, A. (1985) *Social Definitions of Lesbians in Britain 1914–1939: 'Subject to Query'*, PhD thesis, Department of Sociology, University of Essex.

——(1988) 'Lesbian Outlaws: Past Attempts to Legislate against Lesbians', *Trouble and Strife*, Vol. 13, pp. 9–16.

Faulks, S. (ed.) (1996) 'Jeremy Wolfenden', *The Fatal Englishman: Three Short Lives* (London: Hutchinson), pp. 209–309.

Fenton, K.A., Korovessis, C., Johnson, A.M., McCadden, A., McManus, S., Wellings, K., Mercer, C.H. *et al.* (2001) 'Sexual Behaviour in Britain: Reported Sexually Transmitted Infections and Prevalent Genital *Chlamydia Trachiomatis* Infection', *The Lancet*, Vol. 358, no. 9296, 1 December, pp. 1851–1854.

Fernbach, D. (1998) 'Biology and Gay Identity', *New Left Review*, no. 228, pp. 47–66.

Finkelhor, D. (1990) 'Response to Bauserman', *Journal of Homosexuality*, Vol. 20, nos 1/2, pp. 313–315.

Firestone, S. (1971) *The Dialectic of Sex* (London: Cape).

Fortin, J. (1998) *Children's Rights and the Developing Law* (London: Butterworths).

Foucault, M. (1967) *Madness and Civilisation* (London: Tavistock).

——(1970) *The Order of Things: An Archaeology of the Human Sciences* (London: Tavistock Publications).

——(1972) *The Archaeology of Knowledge* (London: Tavistock Publications).

——(1977) *Discipline and Punish* (London: Allen Lane, Penguin Press).

——(1980) *Power/Knowledge: Selected Interviews and Other Writings 1972–1977*, ed. C. Gordon (London: Harvester Wheatsheaf).

——(1981) *The History of Sexuality, Volume One: An Introduction* (London: Penguin).

——(1982) 'The Subject and Power', in H.L. Dreyfus and P. Rabinow (ed.) *Michel Foucault: Beyond Structuralism and Hermeneutics* (Brighton: Harvester Press Ltd), pp. 208–216.

Foucault, M., Hocquenghem, G. and Danet, J. (1978) 'Sexual Morality and the Law', in L.D. Kritzman (ed.) *Michel Foucault: Politics, Philosophy, Culture – Interviews and Other Writings 1977–1984* (London: Routledge).

Fuss, D. (1989) *Essentially Speaking: Feminism, Nature and Difference* (London: Routledge).

Gagnon, J. and Simon, W. (eds) (1967) *Sexual Deviance* (New York: Harper & Row).

——(eds) (1970) *The Sexual Scene* (New Jersey: Transaction Books).

Gamson, J. (1997) 'Messages of Exclusion: Gender, Movements and Symbolic Boundaries', *Gender and Society*, Vol. 11, no. 2, pp. 178–199.

Gatter, P. (1999) *Identity and Sexuality: AIDS in Britain in the 1990s* (London: Cassell).

Gay Left Collective (eds) (1980a) *Homosexuality: Power and Politics* (London: Allison & Busby).

——(1980b) 'Happy Families? Paedophilia Examined', in P. Mitchell (ed.) *Pink Triangles: Radical Perspectives on Gay Liberation* (Boston: Alyson Publications Inc.).

Gay Liberation Front (1971) *Gay Liberation Front Manifesto* (London: Gay Liberation Front); reprinted in L. Power (1995) *No Bath But Plenty of Bubbles: An Oral History of the Gay Liberation Front 1970–1973* (London: Cassell), pp. 316–330.

——(1973) *Psychiatry and the Homosexual*, Gay Liberation Front Pamphlet 1 (London: Gay Liberation Front).

Geoghegan, V. (1981) *Reason and Eros: The Social Theory of Herbert Marcuse* (London: Pluto Press).

Geraci, J. (ed.) (1997) *Dares to Speak: Historical and Contemporary Perspectives on Boy-Love* (Swaffham, Norfolk: Gay Men's Press).

Giddens, A. (1971) *Capitalism and Modern Social Theory* (Cambridge: Cambridge University Press).

——(1990) *The Consequences of Modernity* (Cambridge: Polity Press).

——(1991) *Modernity and Self-Identity: Self and Society in the Late Modern Age* (Cambridge: Polity Press).

——(1992) *The Transformation of Intimacy* (Cambridge: Polity Press).

——(1994) 'Living in a Post-Traditional Society', in U. Beck, A. Giddens and S. Lash (eds) *Reflexive Modernization: Politics Tradition and Aesthetics in the Modern Social Order* (Cambridge: Polity Press), pp. 56–109.

——(1998) *The Third Way: The Renewal of Social Democracy* (Cambridge: Polity Press).

——(1999) *Runaway World* (London: Profile).

——(2000) *The Third Way and Its Critics* (Cambridge: Polity Press).

——(ed.) (2001) *The Global Third Way Debate* (Cambridge: Polity Press).

Gillies, V. (2000) 'Young People and Family Life: Analysing and Comparing Disciplinary Discourses', *Journal of Youth Studies*, Vol. 3, no. 2, pp. 211–228.

Gillies, V., with Ribbens McCarthy, J. and Holland, J. (1998) *Young People and Family Life: Analysing and Comparing Disciplinary Discourses*, Occasional Paper no. 3, Centre for Family and Household Research (Oxford: Oxford Brookes University).

Gilligan, C. (1982) *In a Different Voice* (Cambridge, Mass.: Harvard University Press).

Glaser, D. and Frosh, S. (1993) *Child Sexual Abuse*, second edition (London: Macmillan).

Goffman, E. (1968) *Asylums* (London: Penguin).

Goldson, B. (ed.) (2000a) *The New Youth Justice* (Dorset: Russell House Publishing).

——(ed.) (2000b) 'Wither Diversion? Interventionism and the New Youth Justice', *The New Youth Justice* (Dorset: Russell House Publishing), Chapter 3, pp. 35–57.

Gordon, G.H. (1978) *The Criminal Law of Scotland* (Edinburgh: Green & Son).

Gough, J. (1980) 'Childhood Sexuality and Paedophilia', in P. Mitchell (ed.) *Radical Perspectives on Gay Liberation* (Boston: Alyson Publications Inc.).

Gouldner, A.W. (1970) *The Coming Crisis of Western Sociology* (London: Basic Books, 1970).

——(ed.) (1973) 'Anti-Minotaur: The Myth of a Value-Free Sociology', *For Sociology: Renewal and Critique in Sociology Today* (London: Allen Lane).

Gramsci, A. (1971) *Selections from the Prison Notebooks 1929–1935* (London: Lawrence & Wishart).

Graupner, H. (1996) ' "Corruption of Minors" Repealed in Spain', *ILGA Euroletter*, no. 39, February (Copenhagen: International Lesbian and Gay Association).

——(1997a) *Sexualität, Jugendschutz & Menschenrechte: Über das Recht von Kindern und Jugendlichen auf sexuelle Selbstbestimmung* (Frankfurt/M: Peter Lang Publishing Group), Vol. 1.

——(1997b) *Sexualität, Jugendschutz & Menschenrechte: Über das Recht von Kindern und Jugendlichen auf sexuelle Selbstbestimmung* (Frankfurt/M: Peter Lang Publishing Group), Vol. 2.

——(1997c) Extract from 'Portugal De-equalised Age of Consent in 1995', *Euro-Letter, no. 55*, November (ILGA-Europe: Brussels), p. 7; reprinted in G. Diniz and H. Graupner, 'Portugal', in ILGA-Europe (1998) *Equality for Lesbians and Gay Men: A Relevant Issue in the Civil and Social Dialogue* (Brussels: ILGA-Europe).

——(1998) contributions to *Odysseus 98/99* (Washington, USA: Odyssesus Enterprises Ltd).

——(1999) 'Love versus Abuse: Crossgenerational Sexual Relations of Minors: A Gay Rights Issue?', *Journal of Homosexuality*, Vol. 37, no. 4, pp. 23–56.

——(2000) 'Sexual Consent: The Criminal Law in Europe and Overseas', *Archives of Sexual Behavior*, Vol. 29, no. 5, pp. 415–461.

——(2003) 'Sexuality, Youth Protection and Human Rights – A European Priority Area', http://members.aon.at/graupner/e/index.htm (20 August 2003).

Graupner, H. and Bullough, V.L. (eds) (forthcoming, 2005) *Adolescence, Sexuality and the Criminal Law: Multidisciplinary Perspectives* (New York: Haworth Press).

Green, R. (1997) 'The United States', in D.J. West and R. Green (eds) *Sociolegal Control of Homosexuality: A Multi-Nation Comparison* (New York: Plenum Press), pp. 145–167.

Greenwood, V. and Young, J. (1980) 'Ghettos of Freedom: An Examination of Permissiveness', in National Deviancy Conference (ed.) *Permissiveness and Control: The Fate of the Sixties Legislation* (London: Macmillan), pp. 149–174.

Greer, A., Barbaree, H. and Brown, C. (1997) 'Canada', in D.J. West and R. Green (eds) *Sociolegal Control of Homosexuality: A Multi-Nation Comparison* (New York: Plenum Press), pp. 169–177.

Greer, G. (1971) *The Female Eunuch* (London: Paladin).

Grey, A. (1992) *Quest for Justice: Towards Homosexual Emancipation* (London: Sinclair-Stevenson).

——(1997) *Speaking Out: Writings on Sex, Law, Politics and Society 1954–1995* (London: Cassell).

Griffin, C. (1997) 'Troubled Teens: Managing Disorders of Transition and Consumption', *Feminist Review*, no. 55, pp. 4–21.

Haines, K. (2000) 'Referral Orders and Youth Offender Panels: Restorative Approaches and the New Youth Justice', in B. Goldson (ed.) *The New Youth Justice* (Dorset: Russell House Publishing), Chapter 4, pp. 58–80.

Hall, J. (1996) 'Can Children Consent to Indecent Assault?', *Criminal Law Review*, pp. 184–188.

Hall, S. (1974) 'Deviance, Politics and the Media', in P. Rock and M. McIntosh (eds) *Deviance and Social Control* (London: Tavistock Publications), pp. 261–305; reprinted in H. Abelove, M.A. Barale and D.M. Halperin (1993) *The Lesbian and Gay Studies Reader* (London: Routledge), pp. 62–90.

——(1980) 'Reformism and the Legislation of Consent', in National Deviancy Conference (ed.) *Permissiveness and Control: The Fate of the Sixties Legislation* (London: Macmillan), pp. 1–43.

Hall, S. (2000) 'Conclusion: The Multi-cultural Question', in B. Hesse (ed.) *Un/settled Multiculturalisms: Diasporas, Entanglements, Transruptions* (London: Zed Books), pp. 209–255.

Hart, H.L.A. (1963) *Law, Liberty and Morality* (London: OUP).

Hauser, R. (1962) *The Homosexual Society* (London: Bodley Head).

Health Protection Agency (2004) *HIV and Other Sexually Transmitted Infections in the United Kingdom in 2003*, Annual Report November 2004 (London: Health Protection Agency).

Heaphy, B., Donovan, C. and Weeks, J. (1998) ' "That's Like my Life": Researching Stories of Non-heterosexual Relationships', *Sexualities*, Vol. 1, no. 4.

Heinze, E. (1995) *Sexual Orientation: A Human Right* (Dordrecht: Martinus Nijhoff).

Held, D. (1995) *Democracy and the Global Order: From the Modern State to Cosmopolitan Governance* (Oxford: Polity Press).

Held, D., McGrew, A., Goldblatt, D. and Perraton, J. (1999) *Global Transformations: Politics, Economics and Culture* (Cambridge: Polity Press).

Helfer, L.R. (1990) 'Finding a Consensus on Equality: The Homosexual Age of Consent and the European Convention on Human Rights', *New York University Law Review*, Vol. 65, no. 4, pp. 1044–1100.

Hemmings, C. (1993) 'Resituating the Bisexual Body', in J. Bristow and A.R. Wilson (eds) *Activating Theory: Lesbian, Gay, Bisexual Politics* (London: Lawrence & Wishart), pp. 118–138.

Herdt, G. (1994) 'Interview', *Paedika: The Journal of Paedophilia*, Vol. 3, no. 2 (Winter); reprinted in J. Geraci (ed.) (1997) *Dares to Speak: Historical and Contemporary Perspectives on Boy-Love* (Swaffham, Norfolk: Gay Men's Press).

——(1997a) *Same Sex, Different Cultures: Exploring Gay and Lesbian Lives* (Oxford: Westview Press).

——(1997b) *Sexual Cultures and Migration in the Era of AIDS* (Oxford: Clarendon Press).

Herdt, G. and Boxer, A. (1993) *Children of Horizons: How Gay and Lesbian Teens are Leading a New Way Out of the Closet* (Boston: Beacon Press).

Herek, G.M. (ed.) (1998) *Stigma and Sexual Orientation: Understanding Prejudice against Lesbians, Gay Men and Bisexuals* (London: Sage).

Herman, D. (1994) *Rights of Passage: Struggles for Lesbian and Gay Legal Equality* (London: University of Toronto Press).

Herman, D. and Stychin, C. (eds) (1995) *Legal Inversions: Lesbians, Gay Men, and the Politics of Law* (Philadelphia: Temple University Press).

Higgins, P. (1996) *Heterosexual Dictatorship: Male Homosexuality in Post-War Britain* (London: Fourth Estate).

Hindley, J.C. (1986) 'The Age of Consent for Male Homosexuals', *Criminal Law Review*, September, pp. 595–603.

Hirst, J. (2004) 'Researching Young People's Sexuality and Learning About Sex: Experience, Need and Sex and Relationship Education', *Culture, Health and Sexuality*, Vol. 6, no. 2, pp. 115–129.

Hocquenghem, G. (1972/1978) *Homosexual Desire* (London: Allison & Busby Ltd).

Hodgkin, R. (1998) 'Crime and Disorder Bill', *Children and Society*, Vol. 12, pp. 66–68.

Holland, J. and Thomson, R. (1999) *Respect – Youth Values: Identity, Diversity and Social Change*, Economic and Social Research Council Children 5–16 Research Briefing no. 3, October (Swindon: Economic and Social Research Council).

Holland, J., Ramazanoglu, C., Sharpe, S. and Thomson, R. (1998) *The Male in the Head: Young People, Heterosexuality and Power* (London: Tufnell Press).

Home Office. (2000a) *Setting the Boundaries: Reforming the Law on Sex Offences*, Vol. 1 (London: Home Office Communication Directorate).

——(2000b) *Setting the Boundaries: Reforming the Law on Sex Offences*, Vol. 2: Supporting Evidence (London: Home Office Communication Directorate).

——(2000c) *Setting the Boundaries: Reforming the Law on Sex Offences – Summary Report and Conclusions* (London: Home Office Communications Directorate).

——(2002) *Protecting the Public*, Cm. 5668 (London: TSO).

Honig, B. (1992) 'Towards an Agonistic Feminism: Hannah Arendt and the Politics of Identity', in J. Butler and J.W. Scott (eds) *Feminists Theorize the Political* (London: Routledge), pp. 215–235.

Honoré, T. (1978) *Sex Law* (London: Duckworth).

Hooper, C.A. (1992) 'Child Sexual Abuse and the Regulation of Women: Variations on a Theme', in C. Smart (ed.) *Regulating Womanhood: Historical Essays on Marriage, Motherhood and Sexuality* (London: Routledge), pp. 53–77.

Horstkotte, H. (1984) 'Ages and Conditions of Consent in Sexual Matters', in European Committee on Crime Problems (ed.) *Sexual Behaviour and Attitudes and Their Implications for Criminal Law: Reports Presented to the Fifteenth Criminological Research Conference (1982), Collected Studies in Criminological Research*, Vol. XXI (Strasbourg: Council of Europe), pp. 165–207.

House of Lords Papers (1920) Vols III and VII.

ILGA/International Lesbian and Gay Association (2004) *World Legal Survey – Sexual Behaviour* (Age of Consent Laws), http://www.ilga.org/Information/(19 August 2003).

ILGA-Europe (1998) *Equality for Lesbians and Gay Men: A Relevant Issue in the Civil and Social Dialogue* (Brussels: ILGA-Europe).

——(1999) *After Amsterdam: Sexual Orientation and the European Union* (Brussels: ILGA-Europe).

Inaba, M. (1998) 'Some Comments on the Legal Position in Japan – 6 August 1998', http://www.ilga.org/Information/legal_survey/asia_pacific/supporting%20files/some_comments_on_the_legal_posit.htm#Prostitution (20/08/2003).

Independant Advisory Group on Teenage Pregnancy (2002) Response to *Setting the Boundaries*, unpublished paper.

Jackson, S. (1982) *Childhood and Sexuality* (Oxford: Basil Blackwell).

——(1995) 'Gender and Heterosexuality: A Materialist Feminist Analysis', in M. Maynard and J. Purvis (eds) *(Hetero)sexual Politics* (London: Taylor & Francis), Chapter 1, pp. 11–26.

——(1996a) 'Heterosexuality and Feminist Theory', in D. Richardson (ed.) *Theorising Heterosexuality: Telling it Straight* (Buckingham: Open University Press), Chapter 2, pp. 21–38.

——(1996b) 'Heterosexuality as a Problem for Feminist Theory', in L. Adkins and V. Merchant (eds) *Sexualizing the Social: Power and the Organization of Sexuality* (London: Macmillan), Chapter 1, pp. 15–34.

——(1998) 'Sexual Politics: Feminist Politics, Gay Politics and the Problem of Heterosexuality', in T. Carver and V. Mottier (eds) *Politics of Sexuality: Identity, Gender, Citizenship* (London: Routledge), pp. 68–78.

——(1999) *Heterosexuality in Question* (London: Sage).

Jackson, S. and Scott, S. (eds) (1996) *Feminism and Sexuality: A Reader* (Edinburgh: Edinburgh University Press).

——(eds) (2002) *Gender: A Sociological Reader* (London: Routledge).

James, A., Jenks, C. and Prout, A. (1998) *Theorizing Childhood* (Cambridge: Polity Press).

Jamieson, L. (1996) 'The Social Construction of Consent Revisited', in L. Adkins and V. Merchant (eds) *Sexualizing the Social: Power and the Organization of Sexuality* (London: Macmillan), pp. 55–73.

Jeffery-Poulter, S. (1991) *Peers, Queers and Commons: The Struggle for Gay Law Reform from 1950 to the Present* (London: Routledge).

Jeffreys, S. (1985) *The Spinster and Her Enemies: Feminism and Sexuality 1880–1930* (London: Pandora Press).

——(1996) 'Heterosexuality and the Desire for Gender', in D. Richardson (ed.) *Theorising Heterosexuality: Telling It Straight* (Buckingham: Open University Press).

Jenkins, R. (ed.) (1998) *Questions of Competence: Culture, Classification and Intellectual Disability* (Cambridge: Cambridge University Press).

Jenks, C. (1996) *Childhood* (London: Routledge).

Johnson, A.M., Wadsworth, J., Wellings, K. and Field, J. with Bradshaw, S. (1994) *Sexual Attitudes and Lifestyles* (Oxford: Blackwell Scientific Publications).

Johnson, A.M., Mercer, C.H., Erens, B., Copas, A.J., McManus, S., Wellings, K., Fenton, K.A. *et al.* (2001) 'Sexual Behaviour in Britain: Partnerships, Practices, and HIV Risk Behaviours', *The Lancet*, Vol. 358, no. 9296, 1 December, pp. 1835–1842.

Joint Select Committee (1920) 'Report of the Joint Select Committee of the House of Lords and the House of Commons on the Criminal Law Amendment Bill [H.L.], the Criminal Law Amendment (No. 2) Bill [H.L.], and the Sexual Offences Bill [H.L.]', in *Reports from Committees* 1920, Vol. VI, no. 1, report no. 222.

Joint Working Party on Pregnant Schoolgirls and Schoolgirl Mothers (1979) *Pregnant at School*, September (London: National Council for One-Parent Families).

Jones, G.P. (1990) 'The Study of Intergenerational Intimacy in North America: Beyond Politics and Pedophilia', *Journal of Homosexuality*, Vol. 20, nos 1/2, pp. 275–295.

Kaplan, M. (1999) 'Who's Afraid of John Saul? Urban Culture and the Politics of Desire in Late Victorian London', *GLQ: A Journal of Lesbian and Gay Studies*, Vol. 5, no. 3, pp. 367–414.

Katz, J.N. (1995) *The Invention of Heterosexuality* (New York: Penguin).

Kelly, L. (1988) 'What's in a Name? Defining Child Sexual Abuse', *Feminist Review*, no. 28, pp. 65–73.

Kinsey, A., Pomeroy, W. and Martin, C. (1948) *Sexual Behaviour in the Human Male* (London: W.B. Saunders Company).

Krickler, K. and Wien, H. (1998) 'United Nations Human Rights Committee Requests Austria To Repeal Article 209', *ILGA Euroletter*, no. 66, December, p. 5.

Kymlicka, W. (1990) *Contemporary Political Philosophy: An Introduction* (Oxford: Oxford University Press).

Labour Party (1997) *New Labour: Because Britain Deserves Better, Labour Party Manifesto* (London: Labour Party).

——(2001) *Ambitions for Britain: Labour's Manifesto 2001* (London: Labour Party).

Lacey, N. (1997) 'Unspeakable Subjects, Impossible Rights: Sexuality, Integrity and Criminal Law', *Women: A Cultural Review*, Vol. 8, pp. 143–157.

——(2001) 'Beset by Boundaries: The Home Office Review of Sex Offences', *Criminal Law Review*, pp. 3–14.

Lacey, N. and Wells, C. (1998) *Reconstructing Criminal Law: Text and Materials*, second edition (London: Butterworths).

Laclau, E. and Mouffe, C. (1985) *Hegemony and Socialist Strategy* (London: Verso).

Lane, C. (1997) 'Psychoanalysis and Sexual Identity', in A. Medhurst and S. Munt (eds) *Lesbian and Gay Studies: A Critical Introduction* (London: Cassell), pp. 160–175.

Lansdown, G. (1994) 'Children's Rights', in B. Mayall (ed.) *Children's Childhoods: Observed and Experienced* (London: Falmer Press), pp. 33–44.

——(1995) *Taking Part: Children's Participation in Decision Making* (London: Institute for Public Policy Research).

Lavender, R. and Neustatter, A. (1997) *Childrenfirst*, Winter 1997/1998, special issue on children's rights.

Law, C. (1997) *Suffrage and Power: The Women's Movement 1918–1928* (London: IB Tauris).

Law Commission (1995) *Consent in the Criminal Law*, Consultation Paper no. 139 (London: HMSO).

Leahy, T. (1996) 'Sex and the Age of Consent: The Ethical Issues', *Social Analysis: Journal of Cultural and Social Practice*, no. 39, April, pp. 27–55.

Lestòn, C. (1998) 'Spain', in ILGA-Europe (ed.) *Equality for Lesbians and Gay Men: A Relevant Issue in the Civil and Social Dialogue* (Brussels: ILGA-Europe).

Levine, J. (2002) *Harmful to Minors: The Perils of Protecting Children from Sex* (London: University of Minnesota Press).

Lewis, J. (1984) *Women in England 1870–1950: Sexual Divisions and Social Change* (Sussex: Wheatsheaf Books).

Liberty (1994) *Sexuality and the State: Human Rights Violations Against Lesbians, Gays, Bisexuals and Transgendered People*, report 6 (London: National Council for Civil Liberties).

Lind, C. (1998) 'Law, Childhood Innocence and Sexuality', in L.J. Moran, D. Monk and S. Beresford (eds) *Legal Queeries: Lesbian, Gay and Transgender Legal Studies* (London: Cassell), pp. 81–95.

Lister, R. (1997a) *Citizenship: Feminist Perspectives* (London: Macmillan).

——(1997b) 'Citizenship: Towards a Feminist Synthesis', *Feminist Review*, no. 57 (Autumn), pp. 28–48.

Llamas, R. and Vila, F. (1997) 'Passion for Life: A History of the Lesbian and Gay Movement in Spain', trans. S. Brown, in B.A. Adam, J.W. Duyvendak and A. Krouwel (eds) (1999) *The Global Emergence of Gay and Lesbian Politics: National Imprints of a Worldwide Movement* (Philadelphia: Temple University Press), pp. 214–241.

Lucas, I. (1998) *Outrage! An Oral History* (London: Continuum).

Lukes, S. (1974) *Power: A Radical View* (London: Macmillan).

Lyotard, J. (1984) *The Postmodern Condition* (Manchester: Manchester University Press).

Mackinnon, C. (1989) *Towards a Feminist Theory of the State* (Harvard: Harvard University Press).

Mann, O.L. and Sawyer, M. (2003) ' "The Heterosexual Age of Consent", Global Map of Ages of Consent Accompanying M. Sawyer "Sex is not just for grown-ups" ', *The Observer*, Review, 2 November 2003, pp. 1–2.

Marcuse, H. (1955) *Eros and Civilisation* (Boston: Beacon Press).

Marshall, T.H. (1950) *Citizenship and Social Class, and Other Essays* (Cambridge: Cambridge University Press).

Mason, M. (1994) *The Making of Victorian Sexual Attitudes* (Oxford: Oxford University Press).

Matthews Lovering, K. (1995) 'The Bleeding Body: Adolescents Talk about Menstruation', in S. Wilkinson and C. Kitzinger (eds) *Feminism and Discourse: Psychological Perspectives* (London: Sage), pp. 10–31.

Mayall, B. (ed.) (1994) *Children's Childhoods: Observed and Experienced* (London: Falmer Press).

McCarthy, M. and Thompson, D. (2004) 'People with Learning Disabilities: Sex, The Law and Consent', in M. Cowling and P. Reynolds (eds) *Making Sense of Sexual Consent* (Aldershot: Ashgate), Chapter 13.

McGhee, D. (2000) 'Wolfenden and the Fear of "Homosexual Spread": Permeable Boundaries and Legal Defences', *Studies in Law, Politics and Society*, Vol. 21, pp. 65–97.

——(2001) *Homosexuality, Law and Resistance* (London: Routledge).

McGrellis, S., Henderson, S., Holland, J., Sharpe, S. and Thomson, R. (2000) *Through the Moral Maze: A Quantitative Study of Young People's Values* (London: Tufnell Press).

McIntosh, M. (1968) 'The Homosexual Role', *Social Problems*, Vol. 16, no. 2 Fall, pp. 182–192; reprinted in K. Plummer (ed.) (1981) *The Making of the Modern Homosexual* (London: Hutchinson), pp. 30–44.

——(1997) 'Seeing the World from a Lesbian and Gay Standpoint', in L. Segal (ed.) *New Sexual Agendas* (London: Macmillan), pp. 205–213.

McNair, B. (2002) *Striptease Culture: Sex, Media and the Democratisation of Desire* (London: Routledge).

Meehan, E. (1995) 'Citizenship and the European Union', *Contemporary Politics*, Vol. 1, no. 2, Summer.

Mill, J.S. (1962) *Utilitarianism, On Liberty, Essay on Bentham* (London: Collins).

——(1974) *On Liberty*, ed. G. Himmelfarb (Harmondsworth: Penguin).

Millett, K. (1971) *Sexual Politics* (London: Hart-Davis).

——(1984) 'Beyond Politics? Children and Sexuality', in C.S. Vance (ed.) (1992) *Pleasure and Danger: Exploring Female Sexuality*, second edition (London: Routledge & Kegan Paul), pp. 217–224.

Mills, C.W. (1959) *The Sociological Imagination* (New York: Oxford University Press).

Moerings, M. (1997) 'The Netherlands', in D.J. West and R. Green (eds) *Sociolegal Control of Homosexuality: A Multi-Nation Comparison* (New York: Plenum Press), pp. 299–312.

Molan, M. (1996) *Criminal Law*, tenth edition (London: HLT Publications).

Monaghan, G. (2000) 'The Courts and the New Youth Justice', in B. Goldson (ed.) *The New Youth Justice* (Dorset: Russell House Publishing), Chapter 9, pp. 144–159.

Monk, D. (1998a) 'Beyond Section 28: Law, Governance and Sex Education', in L.J. Moran, D. Monk and S. Beresford (eds) *Legal Queeries: Lesbian, Gay and Transgender Legal Studies* (London: Cassell), pp. 96–112.

——(1998b) 'Sex Education and the Problematization of Teenage Pregnancy: A Genealogy of Law and Governance', *Social and Legal Studies*, Vol. 7, no. 2, pp. 239–259.

——(2004) 'Childhood and the Law: In Whose 'Best Interests'?', in M.J. Kehily (ed.) *An Introduction to Childhood Studies* (Maidenhead: Open University Press), Chapter 10, pp. 160–177.

Moore, A. and Reynolds, P. (2004) 'Feminist Approaches to Sexual Consent: A Critical Assessment', in M. Cowling and P. Reynolds (eds) *Making Sense of Sexual Consent* (Aldershot: Ashgate), Chapter 2, pp. 29–44.

Moore, S. (2000) 'Child Incarceration and the New Youth Justice', in B. Goldson (ed.) *The New Youth Justice* (Dorset: Russell House Publishing), Chapter 7, pp. 115–128.

Moran, J. (2001) 'Childhood Sexuality and Education: The Case of Section 28', *Sexualities*, Vol. 4, no. 1, pp. 73–89.

Moran, L.J. (1995) 'The Homosexualization of English Law', in D. Herman and C. Stychin (eds) *Legal Inversions: Lesbians, Gay Men and the Politics of Law* (Philadelphia: Temple University Press), pp. 3–28.

——(1996) *The Homosexual(ity) of Law* (London: Routledge).

——(1997) 'Enacting Intimacy', *Studies in Law, Politics and Society*, Vol. 16, pp. 255–274.

——(1998) ' "Oscar Wilde": Law, Memory and the Proper Name', in L.J. Moran, D. Monk and S. Beresford (eds) *Legal Queeries: Lesbian, Gay, and Transgender Legal Studies* (London: Cassell), pp. 10–25.

Moran, L.J., Monk, D. and Beresford, S. (eds) (1998) *Legal Queeries: Lesbian, Gay, and Transgender Legal Studies* (London: Cassell).

Moran, R. (1998) *New Direction? Or Tested, Tried and Backward Distortion? Current Legal Proposals on 'Intentional' HIV Transmission*, unpublished paper, presented at Gender, Sexuality and Law Conference, 19–21 June 1998, University of Keele.

Morgan, W. (2000) 'Queering International Human Rights Law', in C. Stychin and D. Herman (eds) *Sexuality in the Legal Arena* (London: Athlone Press).

Mort, F. (1980) 'Sexuality: Regulation and Contestation', in Gay Left Collective (ed.) *Homosexuality, Power and Politics* (London: Allison & Busby), pp. 38–51.

——(1987) *Dangerous Sexualities: Medico-Moral Politics in England since 1830* (London: Routledge & Kegan Paul).

——(1994) 'Essentialism Revisited? Identity Politics and Late Twentieth-Century Discourses of Homosexuality', in J. Weeks (ed.) *The Lesser Evil and The Greater Good* (London: Rivers Oram Press), pp. 201–221.

Mouffe, C. (1993) *The Return of the Political* (London: Verso).

Mouzelis, N. (1995) *Sociological Theory: What Went Wrong?* (London: Routledge).

Mrazek, D.A. (1990) 'Response to the Bauserman Critique', *Journal of Homosexuality*, Vol. 20, nos 1/2, pp. 317–318.

Muncie, J. (2000) 'Pragmatic Realism? Searching for Criminology in the New Youth Justice', in B. Goldson (ed.) *The New Youth Justice* (Dorset: Russell House Publishing), Chapter 2, pp. 14–34.

Myers, B. (2004) 'State Age of Sexual Consent Laws', http://www.actwin.com/eatonohio/gay/consent.htm (5 July 2004).

Nardi, P.M. and Schneider, B.E. (eds) (1997) *Social Perspectives in Lesbian and Gay Studies: A Reader* (London: Routledge).

National Council for Civil Liberties (1971) *Children Have Rights*, pamphlet (London: National Council for Civil Liberties).

——(1976) *Sexual Offences: Evidence to the Criminal Law Revision Committee*, NCCL report no. 13, February (London: National Council for Civil Liberties).

National Society for the Protection of Cruelty to Children (1999) *Response to "A Review of Sex Offences"*, unpublished paper.

Nelson, A. and Oliver, P. (1998) 'Gender and the Construction of Consent in Child-Adult Sexual Contact: Beyond Gender Neutrality and Male Monopoly', *Gender and Society*, Vol. 12, no. 5, October, pp. 554–577.

New Law Journal (1994) 'Tarnished Legislation', editorial, *New Law Journal*, Vol. 144, no. 6637, p. 257.

Newburn, T. (1992) *Permission and Regulation: Law and Morals in Post-War Britain* (London: Routledge).

North American Man-Boy Love Association (NAMBLA) (1980) 'The Case for Abolishing the Age of Consent Laws – Editorial', *NAMBLA News*; reprinted in M. Blasius and S. Phelan (eds) (1997) *We are Everywhere: A Historical Sourcebook of Gay and Lesbian Politics* (London: Routledge).

NOP Solutions (1999) *Age of Consent: Research Carried Out for Stonewall on Age of Consent*, February, NOP/420022 (London: NOP Research Group Limited).

NSW Gay and Lesbian Rights Lobby (2003) 'About Time, NSW!', press release 6 May 2003, accessed at http://wwwglrl.org.au/publications/press_releases/2003/ (28 June 2004).

O'Connell Davidson, J. (1998) *Prostitution, Power and Freedom* (Cambridge: Polity Press).

Okin, S.M. (1989) *Justice, Gender and the Family* (New York: Basic Books).

Oosterhuis, H. (1999) 'The Netherlands: Neither Prudish Nor Hedonistic', in F.X. Eder, L.A. Hall and G. Hekma (eds) *Sexual Cultures in Europe: National Histories* (Manchester: Manchester University Press).

Oram, A. and Turnbull, A. (2001) *The Lesbian History Sourcebook: Love and Sex between Women in Britain from 1780 to 1970* (London: Routledge).

Osgerby, B. (1998) *Youth in Britain since 1945* (London: Blackwell).

Palmer, S. (1997) 'Rape in Marriage and the European Convention on Human Rights', *Feminist Legal Studies*, Vol. V, no. 1, pp. 91–97.

Parker, J. (1988) 'No Going Back', in B. Cant and S. Hemmings (eds) *Radical Records: Thirty Years of Lesbian and Gay History* (London: Routledge), pp. 259–266.

Parton, N. (1991) *Governing the Family: Child Care, Child Protection and the State* (London: Macmillan).

Pascall, G. (1986) *Social Policy: A Feminist Analysis* (London: Routledge).

Pateman, C. (1988) *The Sexual Contract* (Cambridge: Polity Press).

Petchesky, R. and Judd, K. (eds) (1998) *Negotiating Reproductive Rights: Women's Perspectives Across Countries and Cultures* (London: Zed Books).

Petchesky, R.P. (2000) 'Sexual Rights: Inventing a Concept, Mapping an International Practice', in R. Parker, R.M. Barbosa and P. Aggleton (eds) *Framing the Sexual Subject* (London: University of California Press), pp. 81–103.

Phillips, J. (1988) 'Coming to Terms', in B. Cant and S. Hemmings (eds) *Radical Records: Thirty Years of Lesbian and Gay History* (London: Routledge), pp. 60–68.

Phillips, O. (1997a) 'Zimbabwean Law and the Production of a White Man's Disease', *Social and Legal Studies*, Vol. 6, no. 4, pp. 471–491.

——(1997b) 'Zimbabwe', in D.J. West and R. Green (eds) *Sociolegal Control of Homosexuality: A Multi-Nation Comparison* (London: Plenum Press), pp. 43–56.

Pilkington, B. and Kremer, J. (1995) 'A Review of the Epidemiological Research on Child Sexual Abuse: Community and College Student Samples', *Child Abuse Review*, Vol. 4, pp. 84–98.

Pitts, J. (2000) 'The New Youth Justice and the Politics of Electoral Anxiety', in B. Goldson (ed.) *The New Youth Justice* (Dorset: Russell House Publishing), Chapter 1, pp. 1–13.

Platform Against Article 209 (2003) 'European Court of Human Rights Condemns Austria for Persecution of Gay Men', *ILGA EuroLetter*, no. 104, January, pp. 2–3.

Plummer, K. (1975) *Sexual Stigma: An Interactionist Account* (London: Routledge & Kegan Paul).

——(1981) 'Homosexual Categories: Some Research Problems in the Labelling Perspective of Homosexuality', in K. Plummer (ed.) *The Making of the Modern Homosexual* (London: Hutchinson).

——(1990) 'Understanding Childhood Sexualities', *Journal of Homosexuality*, Vol. 20, nos 1/2, pp. 231–249.

——(1995) *Telling Sexual Stories: Power, Change and Social Worlds* (London: Routledge).

Plummer, K. and Stein, A. (1994/1996) ' "I Can't Even Think Straight": "Queer" Theory and the Missing Sexual Revolution in Sociology', *Sociological Theory*, Vol. 12, July; reprinted in S. Seidman (ed.) (1996) *Queer Theory/Sociology* (Oxford: Blackwell), pp. 129–144.

Policy Advisory Committee on Sexual Offences (PAC) (1979) *Working Party on the Age of Consent in Relation to Sexual Offences* (London: HMSO), June.

——(1981) *Report on the Age of Consent in Relation to Sexual Offences*, Cmnd. 8216 (London: HMSO), April.

Pollard, N. (1993) 'The Small Matter of Children', in A. Assiter and A. Carol (eds) *Bad Girls and Dirty Pictures: The Challenge to Reclaim Feminism* (London: Pluto Press).

Povinelli, E.A. and Chauncey, G. (1999) 'Thinking Sexuality Transnationally: An Introduction', *GLQ*, Vol. 5, no. 4 (special issue on Transnational Sexualities), pp. 439–449.

Power, L. (1995) *No Bath but Plenty of Bubbles: An Oral History of the Gay Liberation Front 1970–1973* (London: Cassell).

Prendergast, S. (1995) 'With Gender on My Mind: Menstruation and Embodiment at Adolescence', in J. Holland and M. Blair with S. Sheldon (eds) *Debates and Issues in Feminist Research and Pedagogy* (Clevedon: Open University Press), pp. 196–213.

Radicalesbians (1970) 'The Woman-Identified Woman', reprinted in M. Blasius and S. Phelan (eds) (1997) *We are Everywhere: A Historical Sourcebook of Gay and Lesbian Politics* (London: Routledge), pp. 396–399.

Rahman, M. (2000) *Sexuality and Democracy* (Edinburgh: Edinburgh University Press).

Rawls, J. (1971) *A Theory of Justice* (London: Oxford University Press).

Rayside, D. (1998) *On the Fringe: Gays and Lesbians in Politics* (London: Cornell University Press).

Read, M., Marsh, D. and Richards, D. (1994) 'Why did They Do It? Voting on Homosexuality and Capital Punishment in the House of Commons', *Parliamentary Affairs*, Vol. 47, no. 3, pp. 374–386.

Reavey, P. and Warner, S. (eds) (2002) *New Feminist Stories of Child Sexual Abuse: Sexual Scripts and Dangerous Dialogue* (London: Routledge).

Reekie, A. (1997a) 'European International Control', in D.J. West and R. Green (eds) *Sociolegal Control of Homosexuality: A Multi-Nation Comparison* (London: Plenum Press), pp. 179–195.

Reinhold, S. (1994) 'Through the Parliamentary Looking Glass: "Real" and "Pretend" Families in Contemporary British Politics', *Feminist Review*, no. 48, Autumn, pp. 61–79.

Rengger, N.J. (1995) *Political Theory, Modernity and Postmodernity* (London: Blackwell).

Reynolds, P. (ed.) (2002/2003) *Rape, Law and Sexual Consent*, special issue of *Contemporary Issues in Law*, Vol. 6, no. 1.

Rich, A. (1980) 'Compulsory Heterosexuality and Lesbian Existence', *Signs*, Vol. 4, no. 4, pp. 631–660.

Richardson, D. (ed.) (1996) *Theorising Heterosexuality: Telling It Straight* (Buckingham: Open University Press).

——(1998) 'Sexuality and Citizenship', *Sociology*, Vol. 32, no. 1, pp. 83–100.

——(2000a) *Rethinking Sexuality* (London: Sage).

——(2000b). 'Claiming Citizenship? Sexuality, Citizenship and Lesbian/Feminist Theory', *Sexualities*, Vol. 3, no. 2, pp. 255–272.

Rind, B. and Tromovitch, P. (1997) 'A Meta-Analytic Review of Findings from National Samples on Psychological Correlates of Child Sexual Abuse', *The Journal of Sex Research*, Vol. 34, no. 3, pp. 237–255.

Rind, B., Bauserman, R. and Tromovitch, P. (1998) *An Examination of Assumed Properties of Child Sexual Abuse Based on Nonclinical Samples*, unpublished paper presented at 'Der Andere kant van de Medaille' study day at the Pauluskerk, Rotterdam, The Netherlands, 18 December 1998.

Rind, B., Tromovitch, P. and Bauserman, R. (1998) 'A Meta-Analytic Examination of Assumed Properties of Child Sexual Abuse Using College Samples', *Psychological Bulletin*, Vol. 124, no. 1, pp. 22–53.

Roberts, R. and Maplestone, P. (2001) *The Age of Consent and Gay Men in New South Wales* (New South Wales: New South Wales Gay and Lesbian Rights Lobby).

Rose, H. (1996) 'Gay Brains, Gay Genes and Feminist Science Theory', in J. Weeks and J. Holland (eds) *Sexual Cultures: Communities, Values and Intimacy* (London: Macmillan), pp. 53–72.

Rose, N. (1999) *Governing the Soul: The Shaping of the Private Self*, second edition (London: Free Association Books).

Royal College of Psychiatrists (RCP) (1976) *Submission to Criminal Law Revision Committee* (London: Royal College of Psychiatrists).

Rubin, G. (1984) 'Thinking Sex: Notes for a Radical Theory of the Politics of Sexuality', in C.S. Vance (ed.) *Pleasure and Danger: Exploring Female Sexuality* (London: Routledge & Kegan Paul), pp. 267–319.

Sandel, M. (1984/1992) 'The Procedural Republic and the Unencumbered Self', in S. Avineri and A. de-Shalit (eds) *Communitarianism and Individualism* (Oxford: Oxford University Press), pp. 12–28.

Sandfort, T. (1982a) *The Sexual Aspect of Paedophile Relations: The Experience of Twenty-five Boys*, English edition (Amsterdam: Pan/Spartacus).

——(1982b) *The Experience of Boys in Paedophile Relationships* (Amsterdam: Pan/Spartacus).

Sandfort, T., Brongersma, E. and van Naerssen, A. (eds) (1990) *Journal of Homosexuality, special issue: Male Intergenerational Intimacy: Historical, Socio-Psychological and Legal Perspectives*, Vol. 20, nos 1/2.

Sawyer, M. (2003) 'Sex is not Just for Grown-ups', *The Observer*, Review section, 2 November, pp. 1–2.

Schalet, A. (2000) 'Raging Hormones, Regulated Love: Adolescent Sexuality and the Constitution of the Modern Individual in the United States and the Netherlands', *Body and Society*, Vol. 6, no. 1, pp. 75–105.

Schofield, G. and Thoburn, J. (1996) *The Voice of the Child in Decision Making* (London: Institute for Public Policy Research).

Schofield, M. (1965) *The Sexual Behaviour of Young People* (London: Longmans, Green & Co. Ltd).

Schuijer, J. (1990) 'Tolerance at Arm's Length: The Dutch Experience', *Journal of Homosexuality*, Vol. 20, nos 1/2, pp. 199–229.

——(1993) 'The Netherlands Changes its Age of Consent Law', *Paedika: The Journal of Paedophilia*, Vol. 3, no. 1, Winter; reprinted in J. Geraci (ed.) (1997) *Dares to Speak: Historical and Contemporary Perspectives on Boy-Love* (Swaffham, Norfolk: Gay Men's Press), pp. 207–212.

——(1999) 'In Memorium: Edward Brongersma', *Journal of Homosexuality*, Vol. 37, no. 4, pp. xxi–xxv.

Scott, S. (2001) *The Politics and Experience of Ritual Abuse: Beyond Disbelief* (Buckingham: Open University Press).

Scott, S., Jackson, S. and Backett-Milburn, K. (1998) 'Swings and Roundabouts: Risk Anxiety and the Everyday World of Children', *Sociology*, Vol. 32, no. 4, pp. 689–705.

Scraton, P. (ed.) (1997) *'Childhood' in 'Crisis'?* (London: UCL Press).

Sedgwick, E.K. (1990) *Epistemology of the Closet* (Berkeley: University of California Press).

Segal, L. (1994) *Straight Sex: The Politics of Pleasure* (London: Virago).

——(1999) *Why Feminism?* (Cambridge: Polity).

Seidman, S. (1993) 'Identity and Politics in a "Postmodern" Gay Culture: Some Historical and Conceptual Notes', in M. Warner (ed.) *Fear of a Queer Planet: Queer Politics and Social Theory* (London: University of Minnesota Press), pp. 105–142.

——(1994) *Contested Knowledge* (Oxford: Blackwell).

——(ed.) (1996) *Queer Theory/Sociology* (Oxford: Blackwell).

——(1997) *Difference Troubles: Queering Social Theory and Sexual Politics* (Cambridge: Cambridge University Press).

——(1998) 'Are We All in the Closet? Notes Towards a Sociological and Cultural Turn in Queer Theory', *European Journal of Cultural Studies*, Vol. 1, no. 2, pp. 177–192.

Seidman, S., Meeks, C. and Traschen, F. (1999) 'Beyond the Closet? The Changing Social Meaning of Homosexuality in the United States', *Sexualities*, Vol. 2, no. 1, pp. 9–34.

Sexual Law Reform Society (1974) 'Report of the Working Party on the Law in Relation to Sexual Behaviour'; copy held in Antony Grey papers, file 2/1, at Hall Carpenter Archive, British Library of Political and Economic Sciences, London.

Shelley, M. (1970) 'Gay is Good'; reprinted in M. Blasius and S. Phelan (eds) (1997) *We are Everywhere: A Historical Sourcebook of Gay and Lesbian Politics* (London: Routledge), pp. 391–393.

Shildrick, M. (1997) *Leaky Bodies and Boundaries: Feminism, Postmodernism and (Bio)Ethics* (London: Routledge).

Showalter, E. (1992) *Sexual Anarchy: Gender and Culture at the Fin de Siècle* (London: Virago).

Sinfield, A. (1994) *The Wilde Century: Effeminacy, Oscar Wilde and the Queer Moment* (London: Cassell).

Smart, C. (1989) *Feminism and the Power of Law* (London: Routledge).

——(1992a) 'The Woman of Legal Discourse', *Social and Legal Issues: An International Journal*, Vol. 1, no. 1, pp. 29–44; reprinted in C. Smart (1995) *Law, Crime and Sexuality: Essays in Feminism* (London: Sage), Chapter 11, pp. 186–202.

——(ed.) (1992b) 'Disruptive Bodies and Unruly Sex: The Regulation of Reproduction and Sexuality in the Nineteenth Century', *Regulating Womanhood: Historical Essays on Marriage, Motherhood and Sexuality* (London: Routledge), pp. 7–32.

——(1995) *Law, Crime and Sexuality: Essays in Feminism* (London: Sage).

——(1996) 'Desperately Seeking Post-heterosexual Woman', in J. Holland and L. Adkins (eds) *Sex, Sensibility and the Gendered Body* (London: Macmillan), pp. 222–241.

——(1999) 'A History of Ambivalence and Conflict in the Discursive Construction of the "Child Victim" of Sexual Abuse', *Social and Legal Studies*, Vol. 8, no. 3, pp. 391–409.

——(2000) 'Reconsidering the Recent History of Child Sexual Abuse, 1910–1960', *Journal of Social Policy*, Vol. 29, no. 1, pp. 55–71.

Smith, A.M. (1994) *New Right Discourse on Race and Sexuality* (Cambridge: Cambridge University Press).

Smith, D. (1995) 'Anatomy of a Campaign', in A.R. Wilson (ed.) *A Simple Matter of Justice?* (London: Cassell), pp. 10–31.

Smith, J.H. (1996) 'Foreward', in M. Bulmer and A.M. Rees (eds) *Citizenship Today: The Contemporary Relevance of T.H. Marshall* (London: UCL Press), pp. ix–xiii.

Smith-Rosenberg, C. (1989) 'Discourses of Sexuality and Subjectivity: The New Woman, 1870–1936', in M. Duberman, M. Vicinus and G. Chauncey (eds) *Hidden from History: Reclaiming the Lesbian and Gay Past* (London: Penguin), pp. 264–280.

Smyth, C. (1992) *Lesbians Talk Queer Notions* (London: Scarlet Press).

Social Exclusion Unit (1999) *Teenage Pregnancy*, Cm. 4342, June (London: HMSO).

Solomos, J. (1996) 'Splitting the Difference', review article, *Times Higher Educational Supplement*, 10 May, p. 23.

Spencer, J.R. (2003) 'The Shameful Sex Crimes of Adrian Mole, Aged 13 3/4', *The Times*, 7 October 2003, p. 12.

——(2004) 'Retrial for Reckless Infection', *New Law Journal*, Vol. 154, no. 7130, 21 May, p. 762.

Squires, J. (1999) *Gender in Political Theory* (Cambridge: Polity Press).

Stacey, J. (1991) 'Promoting Normality: Section 28 and the Regulation of Sexuality', in S. Franklin, C. Lury and J. Stacey (eds) *Off-Centre: Feminism and Cultural Studies* (London: HarperCollins), pp. 284–304.

Stainton Rogers, W. and Stainton Rogers, R. (1999) 'What is Good and Bad Sex for Children?', in M. King (ed.) *Moral Agendas for Children's Welfare* (London: Routledge), pp. 179–197.

Stanley, L. (1995) *Sex Surveyed, 1949–1994: From Mass-Observation's 'Little Kinsey' to the National Survey and the Hite Reports* (London: Taylor & Francis).

Stein, E. (ed.) (1992) *Forms of Desire: Sexual Orientation and the Social Constructionist Controversy* (London: Routledge).

Steinberg, D.L., Epstein, D. and Johnson, R. (eds) (1997) *Border Patrols: Policing the Boundaries of Heterosexuality* (London: Cassell).

Stevenson, K., Davies, A. and Gunn, M. (2003) *Blackstone's Guide to the Sexual Offences Act 2003* (Oxford: Oxford University Press).

——(2004) *Blackstone's Guide to the Sexual Offences Act 2003* (Oxford: Oxford University Press).

Stone, R. (1999) *Offences Against the Person* (London: Cavendish).

Stonewall (1993) *The Case for Change: Arguments for an Equal Age of Consent* (London: Stonewall Lobby Group).

——(1994) *Stonewall Briefing: Sexual Offences Seminar*, unpublished paper, 12 November 1994 (London: Stonewall Lobby Group).

——(1996) *Vote for Equality! A Gay Guide to the General Election* (London: Stonewall Lobby Group).

——(1997a) *Equality 2000* (London: Stonewall Lobby Group).

——(1997b) 'Legislation Round-up', *Stonewall Newsletter*, Vol. 5, no. 2, April, p. 6.

——(1998) *The Case for Equality: Arguments for an Equal Age of Consent* (London: Stonewall Lobby Group).

Sturgess, B. (1975) *No Offence – The Case for Homosexual Equality at Law* (London: Campaign for Homosexual Equality, Scottish Minorities Group and Union for Sexual Freedom in Ireland).

Stychin, C. (1995) *Law's Desire: Sexuality and the Limits of Justice* (London: Routledge).

Stychin, C. (1998) *A Nation by Rights: National Cultures, Sexual Identity Politics and the Discourse of Rights* (Philadelphia: Temple University Press).

——(2003) *Governing Sexuality: The Changing Politics of Citizenship and Law Reform* (Oxford: Hart Publishing).

Stychin, C. and Herman, D. (2000) *Sexuality in the Legal Arena* (London: Athlone Press).

Sullivan, B. (2004) 'Prostitution and Consent: Beyond the Liberal Dichotomy of "Free or Forced" ', in M. Cowling and P. Reynolds (eds) *Making Sense of Sexual Consent* (Aldershot: Ashgate), Chapter 8, pp. 127–140.

Sutherland, K. (2001) *Sluts, Sissies and Born-again Virgins: Law and the Construction of Teenage Sexualities*, PhD thesis, Harvard Law School.

Tanner, J.M. (1989) *Foetus into Man: Physical Growth from Conception into Maturity* (Ware: Castlemead).

Tatchell, P. (1992) *Europe in the Pink: Lesbian and Gay Equality in the New Europe* (London: Gay Men's Press).

——(1996a) 'Is Fourteen Too Young for Sex?', *Gay Times*, June, pp. 36–38.

——(1996b) 'It's Just a Phase: Why Homosexuality is Doomed', in M. Simpson (ed.) *Anti-Gay* (London: Cassell), pp. 35–54.

——(2002) 'Why the Age of Consent in Britain Should be Lowered to Fourteen', *Legal Notes 38* (London: Libertarian Alliance).

Taylor, C. (1985/1992) 'Atomism', in S. Avineri and A. de-Shalit (eds) (1992) *Communitarianism and Individualism* (Oxford: Oxford University Press), pp. 29–50.

Temkin, J. (2002) *Rape and the Legal Process*, second edition (Oxford: Oxford University Press).

Terrence Higgins Trust (1997) *Response to Law Commission Consultation Paper No. 139: Consent in the Criminal Law* (London: Terrence Higgins Trust).

——(1998) *Review of the 'Offences Against the Person Act' 1861: Issues Concerning HIV Transmission* (London: Terrence Higgins Trust).

——(2002) *Criminalisation of HIV Transmission Policy*, August, policy paper (London: Terrence Higgins Trust).

Thompson, B. (1994) *Sadomasochism* (London: Cassell).

Thomson, R. (1993) 'Unholy Alliances: The Recent Politics of Sex Education', in J. Bristow and A.R. Wilson (eds) *Activating Theory: Lesbian, Gay, Bisexual Politics* (London: Lawrence & Wishart), pp. 219–245.

——(1994) 'Moral Rhetoric and Public Health Pragmatism: The Recent Politics of Sex Education', *Feminist Review*, no. 48, Autumn, pp. 40–60.

——(2000) 'Legal, Protected and Timely: Young People's Perspectives on the Heterosexual Age of Consent', in J. Bridgeman and D. Monk (eds) *Feminist Perspectives on Child Law* (London: Cavendish), pp. 169–186.

——(2004) ' "An Adult Thing" '? Young People's Perspectives on the Heterosexual Age of Consent', *Sexualities*, Vol. 7, no. 2, pp. 133–149.

Thomson, R. and Blake, S. (eds) (2002) *Sex Education in England and Scotland*, Special issue of *Sex Education*, Vol. 2, no. 3, November.

Thorstad, D. (1990) 'Man/Boy Love and the American Gay Movement', *Journal of Homosexuality*, Vol. 20, nos 1/2, pp. 251–274.

Trenchard, L. and Warren, H. (1984) *Something to Tell You: The Experiences and Needs of Young Lesbians and Gay Men in London* (London: London Gay Teenage Group).

Trumbach, R. (1997) 'Are Modern Western Lesbian Women and Gay Men a Third Gender?', in M. Duberman (ed.) *A Queer World: The Center for Lesbian and Gay Studies Reader* (London: New York University Press), pp. 87–99.

Tsang, D. (ed.) (1981) *The Age Taboo: Gay Male Sexuality, Power and Consent* (London: Gay Men's Press).

Turner, B.S. (1990) 'Outline of a Theory of Citizenship', *Sociology*, Vol. 24, no. 2, May, pp. 189–217.

——(ed.) (1993) *Citizenship and Social Theory* (London: Sage).

——(1995) *Medical Power and Social Knowledge* (London: Sage).

——(1996) 'R. Beiner (ed.) (1995) Theorising Citizenship (New York: State University of New York Press)', book review, *Sociological Review*, Vol. 44, no. 1, pp. 131–133.

——(1997a) 'Citizenship Studies: A General Theory', *Citizenship Studies*, Vol. 1, no. 1, February (Oxfordshire: Carfax), pp. 5–18.

——(1997b) 'M. Bulmer and A.M. Rees (eds) (1996) Citizenship Today: The Contemporary Relevance of T.H. Marshall (London: UCL Press)', book review, *Sociological Review*, Vol. 45, no. 1, February, pp. 176–179.

Turner, B.S. and Hamilton, P. (eds) (1994) *Citizenship: Critical Concepts*, Vols I–II (London: Routledge).

Turner, G. (1996) *British Cultural Studies: An Introduction*, second edition (London: Routledge).

United Nations (1989) *Convention on the Rights of the Child* (London: UK Committee for UNICEF).

Vance, C.S. (ed.) (1984) 'Pleasure and Danger: Towards a Politics of Sexuality', *Pleasure and Danger: Exploring Female Sexuality* (London: Routledge & Kegan Paul), pp. 1–27.

——(1989) 'Social Constructionist Theory: Problems in the History of Sexuality', in D. Altman *et al.* (eds) *Homosexuality, Which Homosexuality? Essays from the International Scientific Conference on Lesbian and Gay Studies* (London: Gay Men's Press), pp. 13–34.

——(ed.) (1992) 'More Danger, More Pleasure: A Decade After the Barnard Sexuality Conference', *Pleasure and Danger: Exploring Female Sexuality*, second edition (London: Routledge & Kegan Paul), pp. xvi–xxxix.

Vereniging MARTIJN (2001, updated 2002) *Vereniging MARTIJN's Commentary on the Dutch Cabinet's Intention to Abandon the Requirement of Complaint in Moral Law*, paper available from Vereniging MARTIJN, Postbus 93548, 1090 EA Amsterdam, The Netherlands.

Vicinus, M. (1989a) ' "They Wonder to Which Sex I Belong": The Historical Roots of the Modern Lesbian Identity', in D. Altman *et al.* (eds) *Homosexuality, Which Homosexuality?: Essays form the International Scientific Conference on Lesbian and Gay Studies* (London: Gay Men's Press), pp. 171–198.

——(1989b) 'Distance and Desire: English Boarding School Friendships, 1870–1920', in M. Duberman, M. Vicinus and G. Chauncey (eds) *Hidden from History: Reclaiming the Lesbian and Gay Past* (London: Penguin), pp. 212–229.

von Rosen, W. (1994) 'A Short History of Gay Denmark 1613–1989: The Rise and Possibly Happy End of the Danish Homosexual', *Nordisk Sexologi*, Vol. 12, pp. 125–136.

Waaldijk, K. (1993) 'The Legal Situation in the Member States', in K. Waaldijk and A. Clapham (eds) *Homosexuality: A European Community Issue* (London: Martinus Nijhoff Publishers), Chapter 3.

Waaldijk, K. and Clapham, A. (eds) (1993) *Homosexuality: A European Community Issue* (London: Martinus Nijhoff Publishers).

Waites, M. (1995) *The Age of Consent Debate: A Critical Analysis*, MA Culture and Society dissertation, Department of Sociology, University of Essex.

——(1996) 'Lesbian and Gay Theory, Sexuality and Citizenship', review article, *Contemporary Politics*, Vol. 2, no. 3, Autumn, pp. 139–149.

——(1998) 'Sexual Citizens: Legislating the Age of Consent in Britain', in T. Carver and V. Mottier (eds) *Politics of Sexuality: Identity, Gender, Citizenship* (London: Routledge), pp. 25–35.

——(1999a) *The Age of Consent, Homosexuality and Citizenship in the United Kingdom (1885–1999)*, PhD thesis (London: South Bank University).

——(1999b) 'The Age of Consent and Sexual Citizenship in the United Kingdom: A History', in J. Seymour and P. Bagguley (eds) *Relating Intimacies: Power and Resistance* (London: Macmillan).

——(2000) 'Homosexuality and the New Right: The Legacy of the 1980s for New Delineations of Homophobia', *Sociological Research Online*, Vol. 5, no. 1, May (themed issue on 'The New Right'), <http://www.socresonline.org.uk/>.

——(2001) 'Regulation of Sexuality: Age of Consent, Section 28 and Sex Education', *Parliamentary Affairs*, Vol. 54, no. 3, July, pp. 495–508 (special issue on family and sexuality, edited by Martin Durham).

——(2002a) 'Inventing a "Lesbian Age of Consent"? The History of the Minimum Age for Sex between Women in the UK', *Social and Legal Studies*, Vol. 11, no. 3, pp. 323–342.

——(2002b) 'Adult Sexual Abuse of a Child?', *New Law Journal*, Vol. 152, no. 7047, 13 September, p. 1342.

——(2003) 'Equality at Last? Homosexuality, Heterosexuality and the Age of Consent in the United Kingdom', *Sociology*, Vol. 37, no. 4, November 2004, pp. 637–655.

——(2004) 'The Age of Consent and Sexual Consent', in M. Cowling and P. Reynolds (eds) *Making Sense of Sexual Consent* (Aldershot: Ashgate).

——(2005) forthcoming 'The Fixity of Sexual Identities in the Public Sphere: Biomedical Knowledge, Liberalism and the Heterosexual/Homosexual Binary in Late Modernity', *Sexualities*, Vol. 8, no. 5.

Walby, S. (1990) *Theorizing Patriarchy* (Oxford: Basil Blackwell).

——(1994) 'Is Citizenship Gendered?', *Sociology*, Vol. 24, no. 2, May, pp. 379–395.

Walkowitz, J.R. (1980) *Prostitution and Victorian Society: Women, Class and the State* (New York: Cambridge University Press).

——(1992) *City of Dreadful Delight: Narratives of Sexual Danger in Late-Victorian London* (London: Virago).

Walmsley, R. and White, K. (1979) *Sexual Offences, Consent and Sentencing*, Home Office Research Unit Study no. 54, May (London: HMSO).

——(1980) *Supplementary Information on Sexual Offences and Sentencing*, Home Office Research Unit Study No. 54, Paper 2 (London: HMSO).

Warner, M. (1993) 'Introduction', in M. Warner (ed.) *Fear of a Queer Planet: Queer Politics and Social Theory* (London: University of Minnesota Press), pp. vii–xxxi.

Warner, N. (1983) 'Parliament and the Law', in B. Galloway (ed.) *Prejudice and Pride: Discrimination Against Gay People in Modern Britain* (London: Routledge & Kegan Paul), pp. 78–101.

Warren, H. (1984) *School* (London: London Gay Teenage Group).

Watney, S. (1980) 'The Ideology of GLF', in Gay Left Collective (ed.) *Homosexuality: Power and Politics* (London: Allison & Busby), pp. 64–76.

——(ed.) (1992) 'Gay Teenagers and Gay Politics', *Practices of Freedom: Selected Writings on HIV/AIDS* (London: Rivers Oram Press), pp. 266–268.

Weait, M. (1996) 'Fleshing it Out', in L. Bentley and L. Flynn (eds) *Law and the Senses* (London: Pluto Press).

——(2001) 'Taking the Blame: Criminal Law, Social Responsibility and the Sexual Transmission of HIV', *Journal of Social Welfare and Family Law*, Vol. 23, no. 4, pp. 441–457.

——(2004) '*Dica*: Knowledge, Consent and the Transmission of HIV', *New Law Journal*, Vol. 154, no. 7130, 28 May, pp. 826–827.

Weeks, J. (1977) *Coming Out: Homosexual Politics in Britain from the Nineteenth Century to the Present* (London: Quartet Books).

——(1980) 'Inverts, Perverts and Mary-Annes: Male Prostitution and the Regulation of Homosexuality in England in the Nineteenth and Early Twentieth Centuries', in M. Duberman, M. Vicinus and G. Chauncey (eds) (1989) *Hidden from History: Reclaiming the Lesbian and Gay Past* (London: Penguin), pp. 195–211; reprinted from *Journal of Homosexuality*, Vol. 6, nos 1/2 (Fall/Winter 1980/1981).

——(1981) *Sex, Politics and Society: The Regulation of Sexuality since 1800* (London: Longman).

——(1985) *Sexuality and Its Discontents* (London: Routledge & Kegan Paul).

——(1989) *Sex, Politics and Society: The Regulation of Sexuality since 1800*, second edition (London: Longman).

——(1990) *Coming Out: Homosexual Politics in Britain from the Nineteenth Century to the Present*, second edition (London: Quartet Books).

——(1993) 'An Interview with Jeffrey Weeks – Interviewed by Ken Plummer', *Journal of Homosexuality*, Vol. 25, no. 4, pp. 121–131.

——(1995) *Invented Moralities: Sexual Values in an Age of Uncertainty* (Cambridge: Polity Press).

——(1998a) 'The "Homosexual Role" After 30 Years: An Appreciation of the Work of Mary McIntosh', *Sexualities*, Vol. 1, no. 2, pp. 131–152.

——(1998b) 'The Sexual Citizen', *Theory, Culture and Society: Special Issue on Love and Eroticism*, Vol. 15, nos 3–4, pp. 35–52.

——(1999) 'Supporting Families', *The Political Quarterly*, Vol. 70, no. 2, April, pp. 225–230.

——(2000) *Making Sexual History* (Cambridge: Polity Press).

Weeks, J., Donovan, C. and Heaphy, B. (1999) 'Everyday Experiments: Narratives of Non-Heterosexual Relationships', in E. Silva and C. Smart (eds) *The New Family?* (London: Sage), pp. 83–99.

Weeks, J., Heaphy, B. and Donovan, C. (1999) 'Partnership Rites: Commitment and Ritual in Non-Heterosexual Relationships', in J. Seymour and P. Bagguley (eds) *Relating Intimacies: Power and Resistance* (London: Macmillan), pp. 43–63.

——(2001) *Same-Sex Intimacies: Families of Choice and Other Life Experiments* (London: Routledge).

Weeks, J., Holland, J. and Waites, M. (eds) (2003) *Sexualities and Society: A Reader* (Oxford: Polity Press).

Weeks, J., Plummer, K. and McIntosh, M. (1981) 'Postscript: "The Homosexual Role" Revisited', in K. Plummer (ed.) *The Making of the Modern Homosexual* (London: Hutchinson), pp. 44–49.

Wellings, K., Nanchahal, K., Macdowall, W., McManus, S., Erens, B., Mercer, C.H., Johnson, A.M. *etal.* (2001) 'Sexual Behaviour in Britain: Early Heterosexual Experience', *The Lancet*, Vol. 358, no. 9296, 1 December, pp. 1843–1850.

Werbner, P., Yuval-Davis, N., Crowley, H. and Lewis, G. (1997) *Feminist Review, 'Citizenship: Pushing the Boundaries'*, no. 57, Autumn.

Wertheimer, A. and Macrae, S. (1999) *Family and Household Change in Britain: A Summary of Findings from Projects in the Economic and Social Research Council Population and Household Change Programme* (Oxford: Centre for Family and Household Research, Oxford Brookes University).

West, D.J. (1984) 'Homosexuality and Social Control', in European Committee on Crime Problems (ed.) *Sexual Behaviour and Attitudes and Their Implications for Criminal Law: Reports Presented to the Fifteenth Criminological Research Conference (1982), Collected Studies in Criminological Research*, Vol. XXI (Strasbourg: Council of Europe), pp. 125–164.

West, D.J. and Green, R. (eds) (1997) *Sociolegal Control of Homosexuality: A Multi-Nation Comparison* (New York: Plenum Press).

West, D.J. and Wöelke, A. (1997) 'England', in D.J. West and R. Green (eds) *Sociolegal Control of Homosexuality: A Multi-Nation Comparison* (New York: Plenum Press), pp. 197–220.

West, J. (1999) '(Not) Talking About Sex: Youth, Identity and Sexuality', *Sociological Review*, Vol. 47, no. 3, August, pp. 525–547.

Whisman, V. (1996) *Queer by Choice: Lesbians, Gay Men and the Politics of Identity* (London: Routledge).

White, S. (1998) 'Interdiscursivity and Child-welfare: The Ascent and Durability of Psycho-legalism', *Sociological Review*, Vol. 46, no. 2, pp. 264–292.

Whitehead, J. (1996) 'Bodies of Evidence, Bodies of Rule: The Ilbert Bill, Revivalism, and the Age of Consent in Colonial India', *Sociological Bulletin: Journal of the Indian Sociological Society*, Vol. 45, no. 1, March, pp. 29–54.

Wilkinson, S. and Kitzinger, C. (eds) (1993) *Heterosexuality: A Feminism and Psychology Reader* (London: Sage).

——(eds) (1995) *Feminism and Discourse: Psychological Perspectives* (London: Sage).

Wilson, A.R. (1993) 'Which Equality? Toleration, Difference or Respect', in J. Bristow and A.R. Wilson (eds) *Activating Theory: Lesbian, Gay, Bisexual Politics* (London: Lawrence & Wishart), pp. 171–189.

——(ed.) (1995) 'Their Justice: Heterosexism in a Theory of Justice', *A Simple Matter of Justice?* (London: Cassell), pp. 146–175.

Wilton, T. (ed.) (1998) 'Subject to Control: Lesbians and the State', *Lesbian Studies: Setting an Agenda* (London: Routledge), pp. 181–204.

Wintemute, R. (1995) *Sexual Orientation and Human Rights* (Oxford: Clarendon Press).

Wise, S. (2000) ' "New Right" or "Backlash"? Section 28, Moral Panic and "Promoting Homosexuality" ', *Sociological Research Online*, Vol. 5, no. 1, <http://www.socresonline.org.uk/5/1/wise.html>.

Wittman, C. (1970) *A Gay Manifesto* (London: Agitprop); reprinted in M. Blasius and S. Phelan (eds) (1997) *We are Everywhere: A Historical Sourcebook of Gay and Lesbian Politics* (London: Routledge), pp. 380–388.

Young, I.M. (1990) *Justice and the Politics of Difference* (Princeton: Princeton University Press).

Yuill, R. (2004a) *Constructing a Radical Framework for Navigating the Contested Narratives on Male Age-Discrepant/Intergenerational Sexualities and Relationships (MADIS)*, unpublished conference paper delivered to Irish Postgraduate Sociology Conference, Belfast, April.

——(2004b) *Male Age-Discrepant Intergenerational Sexualities and Relationships*, unpublished PhD thesis, Department of Sociology, University of Glasgow.

Yuval-Davis, N. (1997) 'Women, Citizenship and Difference', *Feminist Review*, no. 57, Autumn, pp. 4–27.

Index

United States of America (US), 7, 26, 46–8,
  52, 54, 84, 97, 214–15, 221, 239
  diversity among US states, 7
  psychology, 26
Universal Declaration of Human Rights
  (1948), 55, 171
utilitarianism, 31, 67, 105, 112, 116,
  121, 151, 172, 208, 225–6
  legal, 105, 208, 225

vaginal intercourse, 42, 43, 48, 64
  see also sexual intercourse
Vereniging MARTIJN, 25, 52
victim(s), 47, 77, 79, 82, 93, 186,
  196, 198, 219
Victorian, 24, 67, 71, 73, 129
violence, 21, 55, 57, 62, 164, 165, 196
  sexual, 19, 128
virginity, 14, 47, 62, 69, 71, 72, 79, 218
vulnerability, 10, 232, 233

Waites, Matthew
  facilitation of focus groups, 215–16
  intervention in policy debates, 194
  observation of parliamentary
    debates, 158
  perspective and proposals, 208–41
  see also methods, research
Wales, *see* England and Wales
Walkowitz, Judith, 2, 7, 77–8, 80, 82
Walmsley, Baroness, 201–3, 226
Warner, Michael, 126
Watney, Simon, 123, 124, 125
websites, 6, 42, 44
Weeks, Jeffrey, 2, 36, 81, 82, 83,
  107, 108, 122, 123, 124, 125,
  152, 171, 182
welfare state, 109, 111
white, 19, 53, 69
Whitehead, Judith, 45
Wilde, Oscar, 83, 85–6
Wilde, Ralph, 160
will, *see* free will
Wilson, Prime Minister Harold, 133, 269
Wolfenden Committee, *see* Committee
  on Homosexual Offences and
  Prostitution (1954–1957)

Wolfenden Report (1957), 8, 88, 96–118,
  148–55, 171, 209, 225, 268
Wolfenden, Sir John, 97, 101, 115
woman, 13, 14, 62
  of legal discourse, 65
Woman, New, 68
women, 15, 19, 62, 70–3, 90, 92,
  94, 122, 130
  consent, absence of entitlement, 5, 19
  Fourth World Women's Conference,
    Beijing (1995), 55
  human rights, 55
  sex between, *see* homosexuality,
    female; lesbianism
  sexual contact with male children,
    27, 142
Women, Risk and AIDS Project
  (WRAP), 188
women's liberation movement, 15, 120,
  122, 124, 128, 134, 222
World Women's Conference, Fourth,
  Beijing (1995), 55

Young, Jock, 107, 108
young man's defence, 189
young people, 1, 11–14, 92, 122,
  124, 129–30, 187, 190, 193–4,
  196, 206, 222, 225, 236
  competence, 29
  consent to sex, 28–32
  objectification of, 129
  participation, 22, 193, 194
  sexual behaviour, 9, 24–8, 92,
    187, 213, 236
  see also citizenship, young people
young person(s), 14, 131
  indecent assault on a, 64
  legal definition, 61
young sexual abusers, 229
youth, 1, 2, 6, 11–14, 121, 122, 124,
  128, 129, 167, 193–4, 213, 215
  justice, 172, 196, 206, 208, 227–9
  organisations, 134, 167, 193, 197
  policy, 13, 187, 194, 197, 205, 206
  protection, 44
  transitions, 13
Yuill, Richard, 27